Guerrilla Warfare

GUERRILLA WARFARE:

Analysis and Projections

N. I. KLONIS

Robert Speller & Sons, Publishers, Inc.
New York, New York 10010

© 1972 by Robert Speller & Sons, Publishers, Inc.

Library of Congress CIP Card No. 72-8372
ISBN 0-8315-0134-0

First Edition

Dedicated to the people of the Captive Nations
and all other dominated people.

Contents

List of Illustrations

Guerrilla Warfare

I

Introduction

Introduction

This is a comprehensive study on the subject of guerrilla warfare. It is intended to provide an analysis of the forces which are acting in any conflict where guerrilla warfare is employed. It also provides the reader with a single source of historical, tactical, and technical information on the subject.

Discussions and studies on guerrilla warfare have become quite fashionable since the early 1960's. The interest on the subject has been generated by a number of conflicts at the wake of World War II where guerrilla tactics were employed as the principal method of warfare by one of the parties in each conflict. In many, but not all, of these conflicts the guerrillas have achieved, at least in part, their objectives.

Because our national interests have coincided in many of the above conflicts with those of the parties against whom the guerrilla tactics were being applied, we have developed specific interest in counterguerrilla warfare. Most of the literature published in the U.S. in recent years deals, therefore, principally with the subject of counterguerrilla warfare and counterinsurgency.

It is apparent that both among the people who have a casual interest in the subject and among those who have acquired some expertise, a certain trend of ideas has developed. They include the following.

That guerrilla warfare assures ultimate victory to the militarily weaker of the parties in conflict, if the guerrillas can only hold on long enough.

That conventional forces are ineffective against well led and determined guerrillas.

That guerrilla warfare can be a shortcut to military victory in all conflicts short of all-out nuclear war.

That guerrilla warfare has been principally employed by dominated people in insurrection against their colonial. masters or dictatorial governments.

And that guerrilla warfare is the principal method of warfare used by the communist High Command in its efforts to expand its control over the rest of the world.

The above ideas disclose a passive or defensive approach to guerrilla warfare. This passive approach falls in line with the ideas of Mao Tse-Tung who dogmatically states that guerrilla war must continue as long as the Red Army is the weaker contestant. When the situation is reversed, he claims, the enemy will not use guerrilla warfare.[1]

One of the reasons we have attempted this study is our conviction that the tables can be turned. We, with our allies, can utilize guerrilla warfare in order to take the initiative of expansion away from the communists and use it to overthrow a number of communist regimes. Some communist regimes are more vulnerable than others. They can be brought down through internal insurrection with little outside intervention. Others are more firmly established and in the present circumstances cannot be overthrown without a general war. However, conditions do change. It is possible that some day even the Soviet Union itself could be subjected to insurgency in which guerrilla warfare is used.

At this point it is appropriate to define guerrilla warfare. The word guerrilla itself is of Latin origin and it literally means small or lesser war. It is rather unfortunate that the English language got stuck with this term which is neither descriptively nor functionally accurate.

In recognition, perhaps, of this inadequacy, several authors have attempted to substitute other terms. Thus, we find the term low-intensity-warfare being used lately to denote less than full scale warfare between two adversaries where at least one of them is committed to only limited objectives.

Another term which has been used is insurgency. This leads to yet another term being used recently: revolutionary warfare. But revolutionary warfare could be a conventional conflict where both adversaries employ conventional armies and conventional tactics. This presents us with the necessity of having to define conventional warfare before we can proceed with the definition of guerrilla warfare. For our purposes an appropriate definition of conventional warfare is the following: Warfare waged by opposing military forces with the objective of obtaining decisive victory against each other, but without the use of either thermonuclear weapons or guerrilla methods of warfare.

What is then, guerrilla warfare?

Guerrilla warfare is a variation of what B. H. Liddell Hart[2] describes as the "indirect approach". It is a method of warfare by which one of the adversaries avoids direct confrontation with the enemy main forces. It is a method of warfare where operations are conducted in enemy controlled territory by relatively small forces which strike the enemy where he may be relatively weak or where the guerrillas can obtain a temporary superiority over a localized enemy force.

These operations have any or all of the following objectives:

To harass the enemy sufficiently so that he may be forced to divert forces away from his main effort.

To harass the enemy to the point where he concludes that territorial control is militarily too expensive and therefore undesirable. Consequently, the enemy may decide to evacuate the territory in question and leave it to the control of the guerrillas or to conventional forces friendly to the guerrillas.

To make territorial control politically embarrassing to the enemy, thus forcing him to negotiate a political compromise favorable to the guerrillas.

To deny the enemy complete control of occupied territory, thus interfering with his administration and uninterrupted exploitation of human and material resources.

Guerrilla warfare has certain unique characteristics. The most important one is the absolute absence of a "front" as far as guerrilla operations are concerned. When guerrilla forces appear in a frontal order of battle, one of two events has taken place. Either the guerrillas have been absorbed by a conventional unit, or the guerrilla force has grown in size and mission and has assumed the characteristics of a conventional force.

Another characteristic of guerrilla warfare is that the guerrillas are usually indigenous to the general region of operations. However, many exceptions to this will be found particularly in the cases where the guerrillas are being supported or controlled by external sources.

Guerrilla warfare is never an end in itself. When this appears to be happening, it is an indication that the guerrillas have degenerated to banditry or other forms of ordinary criminal activity. Guerrilla warfare is but one of the methods available in waging war. Therefore, it is usually related to broader political and/or military objectives. Consequently, guerrilla operations are most often interdependent with conventional military operations, resistance movements against enemy occupation, resistance movements against hostile governments, subversion, political and psychological warfare, and intelligence collection operations.

Our intention is to provide an analysis of the subject of guerrilla warfare. Such an analysis has to include an examination of History. History provides a guide for present and future action. Some people study History from the cultural point of view, but our objective is to obtain the experience of the past so that we can profit from it and do things better in the future.

Conflicts in which guerrilla warfare has been employed must be studied in order to identify any trends which may exist and to obtain the benefits from the lessons which History makes available. A detailed historical account of past guerrilla wars is obviously not practical within a book of this size. We chose, therefore, to present to the reader only the highlights of several guerrilla conflicts together with an assessment of the effectiveness of the guerrilla operations in each case. In order to assist the reader who may wish to obtain more detailed information about any particular guerrilla war, we have included comprehensive bibliographical notes with appropriate comments.

The guerrilla conflicts which have been presented in this study were chosen for presentation on the basis of two criteria. The first one is the importance of guerrilla operations in relation to the overall conflict in each case. The second criterion is the availability to us of reliable information about the guerrilla operations in each particular case. Unfortunately, the lack of detailed and unbiased information has prevented the inclusion of several extremely interesting recent guerrilla operations.

The casual student of History may be surprised to find out that guerrilla warfare is not a discovery of the 20th century. If we follow our definition of guerrilla warfare, we will find that its utilization dates back to classical times. We chose, however, not to go that far back in History to present information for this study. At the same time we felt that limiting the Historical presentation to contemporary conflicts would not be an adequate treament of the subject. Rather arbitrarily, we chose to start our Historical presentation with the Napoleonic Wars.

The study of History requires more than a dry recount of events. Equally important is the analysis of events. We have tried to present such an analysis in Chapters II, III, and IV.

The rest of the book comprises a discussion of military and political problems which can be expected in any future conflict involving guerrilla operations. Basically, the line of reasoning which we try to present is as follows: Where and under what conditions is guerrilla warfare possible in the future? Once this is established, the next question depends upon which side one belongs. Those who are interested in the utilization of guerrilla warfare are interested in developing a methodology for its application. Those on the other side are, of course, interested in preventing guerrilla warfare and in the methodology of defeating guerrillas. Needless to say one's ideological and political orientation is irrelevant to which side of a guerrilla conflict he is interested. Western Nations should be interested in guerrilla methods for counterguerrilla warfare and counterinsurgency, which are defensive in nature, but they should also study potential offensive applications of guerrilla warfare so that they may be utilized when necessity should dictate use of this part of our arsenal as the best weapon in the global struggle for freedom. This also holds true for the military High Commands of the "Eastern Bloc" Nations or any individual or group of individuals charged with military responsibilities, anywhere.

II

Historical Background
Napoleonic Wars to World War II

1. Guerrillas During the Napoleonic Wars

NAPOLEON'S ARMIES encountered guerrillas at the Eastern and Western extremes of the European continent. In both cases the guerrillas were being supported by conventional armies and in both cases the guerrillas and the forces allied to them were victorious. The two cases under review are the Peninsular War and Napoleon's Russian Campaign.

The Peninsular War of 1808 to 1814 was fought between Napoleon's army on one side and a British army on the other, assisted by the armies of Portugal and Spain. The significant part of this war is that the Spanish and Portuguese armies involved were mostly armies of irregulars. This was caused by the fact that the national governments of Portugal and particularly that of Spain had for the most part disintegrated or ceased to function. The popular feeling in those countries, though, favored armed resistance to the French invaders and the individuals who answered the call to arms had no choice but to join the spontaneously organized guerrilla bands or the provincial armies. Even the provincial armies, however, were compelled to operate as guerrillas on most occasions because they were inferior professionally to Napoleon's regulars.

9

Napoleon had entertained the thought of establishing French authority in Spain for a long time and was only waiting for an excuse to step in. The excuse was provided by the degenerate Spanish Court which was preoccupied with the intrigues of Charles IV, his Queen, and minister Godoy (who also was the Queen's lover) against Charles' heir Ferdinand. Their ineptitude as conspirators was such that they all ended up as Napoleon's prisoners within 1808.

With the Bourbon Royal Family out of the way, the French army, which had by then infested Spain, coerced the "Junta of Regency" to offer the Spanish crown to Napoleon's brother Joseph. Within a short time after Joseph had been proclaimed King, the whole country flared up into rebellion.

While the various provincial or local Spanish armies were fighting and losing battles with French garrisons throughout the Peninsula, the British landed an expeditionary force under Wellington at Mondego Bay in Portugal. This force was destined to eventually chase all French forces out of Portugal and Spain.

Initially, the British commanders on the Peninsula had hopes of conducting a joint campaign with the local forces. It took very little time for the British to decide that the effectiveness of Spanish and Portuguese troops was nil. However, their contributions as irregulars operating on the French rear were substantial. Thus, when a French army under Marshal Soult arrived at Oporto and hoped to proceed further down the coast to recapture Lisbon, it found that it was cut off from all communications with other French armies by insurgents in its rear. The remnants of Portuguese forces that had been beaten before Oporto were hanging on the French left flank. Soult could not garrison Oporto against the guerrillas and have a sufficient force to advance against Lisbon. He stayed at Oporto, therefore, and expended his energies hunting down insurgents in Northwestern Portugal until, worn down, he was recalled to Central Spain where events had taken a turn for the worse.

Wellington, apparently realizing the value of popular support, sought and obtained permission from the Portuguese Regency to order all people in the invaded districts to abandon the towns and take to the hills. This situation created for the

French the problem of securing provisions. A few years later, the French were faced with an almost identical situation during the campaign in Russia.

Napoleon, realizing that the situation in the Iberian Peninsula was not going to be the pushover he had expected, committed progressively more forces. In spite of his superior generalship, he was unable to ever master the military situation there. Had it not been for the guerrillas, the French armies could probably have exerted a concerted effort and decisively defeated the British army. It was impossible, however, for the French forces to concentrate on a single stroke against the British because as many as three-fourths of their troops were diverted to chasing insurgents, guarding crossroads, and garrisoning towns. It is ironic that History's greatest general was defeated in a war because of the activity of guerrilla troops who had turned into guerrillas only because they had failed as regulars.

One may speculate that Napoleon could have eventually been victorious in Spain had he not undertaken the Russian campaign simultaneously. But in Russia, too, he faced guerrillas and was unable to cope with them.

Why? Perhaps, because overconfident with his previous successes he did not understand or did not try to understand guerrilla warfare.

Almost simultaneously with the actions taking place on the Iberian Peninsula on the other side of the European Continent, guerrillas were being instrumental in the defeat of the greatest army that ever took the field under Napoleon's personal command.

Napoleon's Grand Army invaded Russia and after the Battle of Borodino entered Moscow early in the fall of 1812. However, the stubborn Russians were not yet ready to call it quits. Their armies were not destroyed and although they themselves believed that their forces were inferior to Napoleon's, they also realized that the Grand Army was not capable of surviving a winter in the heart of Russia. The French could only do one of two things after the fall of Moscow.

They could retreat to winter quarters.

They could remain in Moscow and the surrounding area, sustaining the losses that would be inflicted upon them by the lack of food and the severe climatic conditions. In this case, the French would be weakened sufficiently so that the Russian Army would have a chance of success in battle.

Napoleon decided to retreat and in the course of this retreat his army was practically destroyed. Instrumental in the destruction of the French army were the irregular and semi-irregular forces that the Russians recruited and sent to operate on Napoleon's rear and flanks.

The Russian land mass was ideal for guerrilla operations. In addition to its vastness and the scarcity of roads, the winter snows made matters worse for Napoleon's army. Another factor to the advantage of the Russians was the lack of French mobile troops which could effectively pursue and destroy the guerrillas. Mobile troops in 1812 meant cavalry. Napoleon had plenty of cavalry on paper, but the cold weather and lack of fodder progressively decimated his animals and the ones that were left were no match for the well-cared for Russian mounts.

There were two types of guerrillas with the Russians. One type was the armed peasants of the invaded areas. These peasants operated in small bands of ten to twenty men, usually from the same village, and were not under the command of Prince Kutuzov, the Russian Commander-in-Chief. They operated independently, motivated by feelings of patriotism, desire for revenge, or desire for plunder. They operated in conjunction with the Russian army on local operations, but were never shown on the Russian tables of organization or order of battle.

The other type was the Kozaks. These troops, known to the West mostly through fiction, require further examination.

The word Kozak was used to designate certain semi-nomadic people in Southern and Southwestern Russia. As could be expected, such people were in perpetual state of war with the settlers of the adjacent regions. In the case of the Kozaks, the forces of the Russian state were never able to completely subdue them. Instead, the Tsars came to terms wth the Kozaks and coerced them into taking semi-permanent residence on designated lands. The Kozaks retained their identity and a kind of autonomy, but were considered subjects of the Tsars. Their chiefs, known as atamans, usually elected by the Kozak elders, were recognized by the Tsars and given military rank corresponding to the local population's size. This peculiar practice was retained through the collapse of tsarism in World War I. It is indeed a peculiar practice because it combines elements of feudalism with those of a democratic society.

The Kozaks were required to furnish conscripts for the tsarist armies. Unlike the other Russian army conscripts, the Kozaks entered the service furnishing their own mounts and in older days their own uniforms and arms. Most important, they served in units composed exclusively of their own people under their own officers. The Kozak units were initially all cavalry units, but later they included artillery and some infantry.

The importance of the Kozak units in the campaign of 1812 is not the fact of their existence, but rather, the method of their employment.

Although several Kozak regiments were assigned to operate with the regular Russian forces, particularly those of General Mihail Andreyevich Miloradovich who commanded the advance guard, the majority of the Kozak units were sent to operate independently along the French flanks and rear. Thus, we know that after the evacuation of Moscow by the French, the following Kozak units were grouped.[1]

One of thirteen regiments under the ataman of the Don Kozaks General Count Matvei Ivanovich Platov was to shadow the retreating French. This force was reporting directly to Kutuzov's headquarters.

Five independent detachments were directed to infest the Smolensk-Moscow road. Those detachments were placed under Colonel Kaisarov (three regiments), Colonel Prince Kudachev (two regiments), Lieutenant Colonel Davidov (two regiments), Captain Seslavin (less than one regiment), and Captain Figner (less than one regiment). These detachments were for the most part out of touch with Kutuzov's headquarters.

In the 1812 Russian military establishment, a cavalry regiment was composed of six troops. Each troop had about 100 men, sixteen of whom were equipped with carbines and the rest with sabres or lances. We have no information on the exact composition of the Kozak regiments. Probably, they were inferior to the regular cavalry numerically and were issued fewer carbines, but they acquired numerous French firearms.

Davidov was immortalized in Leo Tolstoy's novel "War and Peace" as "Colonel Vassili Orlov-Denisov". He was the most imaginative of the guerrilla leaders and exerted great energy in organizing the peasants to actively resist the French troops. He admits that he developed some of his ideas on guerrilla warfare by studying the news dispatches from Spain.

According to Klauswitz, Kutuzov firmly believed that his army was inferior to Napoleon's. The correct policy, according to him, therefore, was to wear the invader down. The Russian winter and Napoleon's own imprudence would see that the French army was worn down. But Kutuzov wished to expedite this process by sending the Kozaks to the enemy's rear where, without risking a pitched battle with a superior force, they would continuously harass the enemy by attacking his foraging parties, sniping at his trains, shooting stragglers, etc. Shooting stragglers was also a favored operation of the armed peasants. If any one of the Kozak detachments was maneuvered by the French into giving battle and destroyed, Kutuzov figured that the loss still would not be too great. The important point was that his main army would remain intact and able to give battle whenever he chose to. Having his mind made up, Kutuzov proceeded to carry out this policy in spite of the opposition of his subordinate generals who wished to attack the French as soon as possible. The Tsar, apparently, had confidence in Kutuzov's decision because he retained him as Commander-in-Chief.

The Battle of Vinkovo (see Figure 1), in which the irregular Kozaks stampeded the bivouacked French cavalry, constitutes the turning point of the campaign. Napoleon, had probably decided to abandon Moscow before this action took place. That day, however, the French suffered a decisive defeat and commenced their retreat from Moscow. The conservative Kutuzov, though, failed to exploit the French defeat fully.

On the morning of 18 October, the French forces South-Southwest of Moscow were deployed on a line from West to East facing South. Positioned there were the III Cavalry Corps, commanded by St. Germain, followed by the V Corps, composed entirely of Poles under Prince Poniatowski, and finally on the extreme left (East) of the French line was the 2nd Light Cavalry Division commanded by the Corsican General Sebastiani.

The Russians sent their II, III, and IV Corps to attack the main French positions. On the extreme Russian right, Kozak units under Davidov were to attack Sebastiani's Cavalry in the early morning hours, while still dark. This the Kozaks were able to do, catching the French dismounted and following through to the village of Spas-Kuplia at the rear of the French line. Through Spas-Kuplia led the only road towards Voronovo and Moscow. However, the attack on the main French position faltered after some initial success. Murat[2] with a small force of carabiniers counterattacked on the front of the Poles and during this counterattack the Russian Commander of the II Corps fell. This seemed to slow down the Russian advance. Davidov, seeing the retreating French infantry coming up to Spas-Kuplia, abandoned this position. This decision was apparently prompted by the general conviction among the Russians that the Kozaks were no match for regular troops. Murat was, therefore, allowed to retreat to Voronovo pursued, but not hardpressed by Miloradovich and the regular Russian cavalry.

The above action at Vinkovo is a typical example of proper use of guerrillas by a conventional command, but of failure to follow through and exploit the favorable situation created by the guerrillas' action. The supposition that the guerrillas could not hold their own against the regulars was, in this case, probably true. Had the Kozaks dismounted and attempted to form a line at Spas-Kuplia, they would have probably been overrun by a determined attack of the French infantry since the Kozaks did not have any experience in static warfare. If, however, the Russian Army Command had the prudence to support the Kozaks with a substantial infantry force, it could have cut off the retreat of the French and gained a great victory.

A total of 30,000 Kozaks were used against Napoleon in 1812. No accurate estimate of the armed Russian peasants participating in the harassing operations can be made. These men engaged units of the French army every day from the evacuation of Moscow until the Battle of Berezina.

The contribution of guerrillas in defeating Napoleon's armies in Spain and Portugal and in Russia was decisive. On the

Iberian Peninsula, the French army could have been victorious over the British if it did not have to cope with the indigenous guerrillas. In Russia, the situation was somewhat different. Napoleon would have to retreat regardless of the guerrilla activities because the French resources were not sufficient to cope with a protracted war. But without the guerrillas it is doubtful that the French retreat would have developed into the complete rout which resulted in the defeat of the French army in detail. From the point of view of Napoleon's enemies, however, the conclusion has to be that guerrilla potential was not exploited to its fullest. Guerrilla operations were haphazard and mostly uncoordinated. It is rather obvious that neither side had a proper appreciation of guerrilla operations as an instrument of total warfare.

However, the successes of guerrilla operations against the French greatly influenced military operations in the subsequent years, because guerrilla warfare played a significant part in the nationalistic revolutions of the 19th century. The Principle of Nationalism was first concretely expressed by the German philosopher J. G. Fichte. In essence, this principle defines the right of any nationality which constitutes the undisputed majority of the population in any given geographic area to establish an independent and sovereign state incorporating all the people and area in question. The morality of this principle is axiomatic and has been repeatedly reasserted in international relations by many outstanding statesmen, including President Wilson in his fourteen points. It is obvious that the impetus of nationalism is still a strong factor in international affairs today, as the revolutions in Algeria, Cyprus, etc. indicate.

In practical terms, the initial driving force of these nationalistic revolutions was furnished by the Napoleonic Wars. A few years after Napoleon's defeat in Russia the Greek War of Independence broke out; this was primarily a guerrilla war. The victory of the Greeks further illustrated to several other subjugated nations that success in such ventures was possible. The enthusiastic support which the Greek War of Independence received from the American and European intelligentsia planted the idea of revolution in the minds of many future rebels.

Between 1800 and 1900 A.D. the Spaniards and Portuguese were forced to abandon their American possessions, Garibaldi integrated the Italian States into one Kingdom, Karageorgi established the Independence of the Serbs, etc. In all of these cases the insurrectionists initially operated as guerrillas. Many nationalist movements, however, were not as successful. The Polish movement presents such an example and also the attempts of the South Slavs to leave Austria and join Serbia, which eventually sparked World War I.

2. American Experiences in Guerrilla Warfare Through the Civil War

In the 19th century, the Army which accumulated the most extensive and diversified experience in guerrilla and counter-guerrilla operations was the U. S. Army. In a sense, this experience started during the Revolutionary War with the Minutemen. Although the Minutemen probably never thought of themselves as guerrillas, their operating methods were guerrilla-type in the sense that the Minutemen would assemble for the execution of an attack and they would disperse as soon as their objective had been gained or when they were confronted by a superior British force. The origin of the popular American saying of the Revolutionary War, "He who fights and runs away, lives to fight another day" reflects this method of operations.

George Washington did manage to defeat the British army in conventional battles, yet it is doubtful that such victories would have been possible without the contribution to the Revolutionary effort that was made by the Minutemen in New England and by the forces of men like Francis Marion in the South.

Marion, nicknamed the "Swamp Fox" was responsible for salvaging the Revolution in South Carolina when it was only one step away from collapse.

When the Revolution commenced, Marion was a member of the South Carolina Provincial Congress. He was commissioned Captain in one of the two militia regiments that were organized in the State. By 1780 he was a Lieutenant Colonel in the same regiment. The success of the Revolution in South Carolina had been very limited up to that year. The sympathies of the population were divided between the Revolution and loyalty to the British Crown. British forces were in control of Georgetown and all the coastal cities. Reinforcements were sent from the North under General Horatio Gates, but in August of that year this force suffered a resounding defeat by General Cornwallis at Camden, South Carolina.

It appeared then that the Revolutionary forces in the south had been decisively defeated and that the country was about to revert to uncontested British control. Marion, however, assumed command of what was left of the South Carolina Militia and commenced guerrilla operations along the Peedee and Santee Rivers. Marion had probably learned the rudiments of guerrilla warfare during the Indian Wars against the Cherokees when he had served in the South Carolina Company of Light-Horse Militia. He began by raiding the Tory encampments at Black Mingo, Blue Savannah, and Tearcoat Swamp. When the strength of his force increased somewhat, he attempted raids aginst the British regulars, including a rather daring operation against Georgetown. After each raid he would return to the swamps and morasses around Show's Island where his pursuers were unable to follow.

Eventually the continentals returned to South Carolina. Marion was promoted to Brigadier General and took part in several conventional battles, finally driving the British to Charleston in September 1781.

In the years between the War of Independence and the Civil War, the U. S. Army was almost continuously involved in counter-guerrilla operations against Indians in the Western Frontiers and in the Florida swamps and against Mexican irregulars during the Mexican War.

Although the outcome of the American Civil War was decided by the performance of huge conventional armies which took the field, maneuvered, and fought bloody pitched battles, guerrilla operations did play an important part in the outcome of operations in some theaters.

The best known and most effective guerrilla organization of

the Civil War was the one led by Confederate Colonel John Singleton Mosby.

The Confederate General J. E. B. Stuart, after his unsuccessful cavalry raid around Middleburg, Virginia, in December 1862, authorized the then Captain Mosby to remain behind the Union lines with nine men in order to harass the enemy with raids on his communications and supply trains and to collect intelligence for the benefit of Stuart's force. Mosby had been serving in Stuart's command for almost a year at that time; he had on several occasions requested permission to organize a guerrilla force and operate in the enemy's rear, but such permission had been denied till then.

Mosby's force eventually grew to eight companies totalling about 700 men. They were officially designated the "Partisan Ranger Battalion". Their activities were centered around Fauquier County, but extended through Northern Virginia and occasionally into part of Maryland.

The most famous of Mosby's raids is the one that took place one night in March of 1863 at Fairfax Court House and resulted in the capture of Brigadier General Stoughton of the Union Army. Mosby, with about twenty-five men, infiltrated through the Union lines and remained in the center of the village undetected by the numerous Federal troops for an hour and a half. It is said that Stoughton was asleep in his quarters and awakened by a guerrilla who lifted the bed covers and whacked the General on his bare posterior with the flat of a sword. This story, however, is not substantiated by the testimony of anyone who took part in the raid.[3] In any case, Mosby's raiders left Fairfax undetected, as they came in, taking with them in addition to Stoughton thirty-two other prisoners and fifty-eight horses.

Several other successful raids were made by Mosby's guerrillas, who became very troublesome for the Union forces operating in the area, especially after the guerrillas acquired a mountain howitzer which they used to attack railroad trains. The direct result of this activity was that the Federal troops in Northern Virginia were obliged to divert substantial units to escort their supply columns and guard their installations in addition to detailing several cavalry units to actively search for and pursue the guerrillas. On at least one occasion they almost succeeded. On 2 May 1863 the 1st Vermont Cavalry and 8th New York Cavalry were able to cut off Mosby's force at Warrenton Junction. But Mosby and most of his men were able to escape by swift flight and dispersal.

Mosby's operations were systematic and methodical. Before each raid all pertinent intelligence was collected, utilizing for this purpose the noncombatants in the area who were in sympathy with the Confederates. A reconnaissance would follow, usually conducted by Mosby himself with two or three other men. If the projected target appeared to be too strong for the guerrillas to negotiate successfully or if the possibilities of surprising the enemy did not seem to be too good, Mosby had no inhibitions about scrapping his plans for that particular raid and trying some other time, maybe at some other place. He made exceptions to this rule only when a specific operation had been requested by Generals Stuart or Lee, in which case every effort was made by Mosby personally to see such request satisfied. Requests from Stuart and Lee, though, were fairly rare because the intention of these Generals was to let Mosby plan his operations independently. After the decision had been made to go through with a given raid, the individuals or units to participate in the operation were selected. The whole command was never committed to a single operation. In fact, on several occasions, while Mosby with one or two companies was operating in one place, another company of his organization was conducting another raid several miles away. The advantages of this were that in this manner Mosby gave the impression of being omnipresent and thus the pursuers were greatly confused. After the raid was over, the participants would disperse immediately and go into hiding among the farms or villages of rural Virginia. Needless to state here that the civilians in the area were completely cooperating with the guerrillas and voluntarily provided for them shelter, food, medical care, etc. A few days later the guerrillas would rendezvous at a prearranged place to receive instructions for their future moves.

Mosby's force was self-sustained. The Southern government did not have to furnish weapons, animals, or any other equipment, with the exception of the one mountain howitzer previously mentioned. The guerrillas lived entirely off the land and obtained most of their equipment from captured Union stores. In fact, all items captured from the Union forces, including cash, were distributed to the participants after each operation. For this reason Mosby remarked once that his command resembled the Democratic Party at least in one respect, it was held together by the cohesive power of desire for public plunder. [4] Except for this form of modified plunder, Mosby insisted that his men conduct themselves within the customs of war. His treatment of prisoners was, in general, humane if not chivalrous.

On one occasion he did order that seven Union soldiers out of twenty-seven captured from General Custer's command be selected by lot and hung in retaliation for the hanging of seven of his men by General Custer and Colonel Powell at Fort Royal in September 1863. This retaliatory incident took place on November 6th of the same year. Three of the selected men were actually hung and two shot while the remaining two escaped. Following the executions, Mosby sent a letter to the Union commander explaining that he would not, in the future, kill any more prisoners unless any of his own men were similarly treated. No captured guerrillas were hung after that. It must be remembered that all of this took place long before the signing of the Geneva and Hague Conventions.

After Lee surrendered the Army of Northern Virginia at Appomattox, the purpose for the existence of Mosby's organization disappeared. On April 21, 1865, Colonel Mosby held a last review of his command at Salem, Virginia. Six hundred mounted men, in eight companies, passed in review for the last time. After the conclusion of the ceremony, Mosby read his last order to the men, disbanding the command in preference to surrender. Later, in June, after being assured of amnesty, Mosby gave himself up.

Mosby's personality was remarkable indeed. The man appears to have been a mixture of old-fashioned sentimentalism and hard realism. He was a scholar in his own right, having entered the University of Virginia at the age of sixteen and became an expert on the Greek language. While at the University, he had to shoot a man once in self-defense. He was tried by a local

jury and found guilty unjustly. Although an Appeals Court
nullified this decision, Mosby spent a few months in prison.
This experience had a profound affect on his character, without
making him bitter or misanthropic. He objectively remarked
that this prejudice of the local inhabitants toward the students
is a feeling which always springs up where a community, peculiar in its characteristics, resides in the bosom of another community.[5]

After the conclusion of the War, Mosby turned Republican
and accepted Federal appointments in the Grant and Hayes
administrations, including one as Consul in Hong Kong. His
political views were motivated by a sincere desire to let bygones be bygones and to help in the reconstruction of his country. But this attitude was not appreciated in the South and his
popularity among his former comrades diminished.

In addition to Mosby's organization, several other guerrilla
units were active throughout the country in support of the
Southern cause and, on several occasions, many regular Confederate formations operated as guerrillas. In fact, as the war
progressed and Southern fortunes waned, the Richmond government placed progressively greater reliance on the activities of
such irregular formations, many of which were hardly anything
better than an assemblance of bandits and highwaymen. After
Lee's surrender of the Army of Northern Virginia, the hope
was entertained among some Southerners that resistance could
continue in the Trans-Mississippi areas through the use of guerrillas, but with the exception of few bands, most of which
eventually degenerated into out-and-out banditry, very little
guerrilla activity took place after 1865. The Southern people
had accepted defeat.

Among the regular Confederate formations occasionally operating as guerrillas were those commanded by Generals Morgan
and Forrest.

Morgan's raid into Kentucky, Indiana, and Ohio, was not
intended to be a pure guerrilla raid, but in its execution it
obtained certain guerrilla characteristics, so we feel that it is
worth reviewing here.

John Hunt Morgan was a Kentuckian with no military experience prior to the Civil War. He had a reputation among

his home-town folks as a ladies' man and a gambler. With the war's outbreak he joined the Confederate Army and rose rapidly in rank.

In late June of 1863 Morgan, with a force of 2,500 cavalry, was directed to raid into a Union-controlled area of Kentucky in order to divert General A. E. Burnside's force from East Tennessee. The Southern High Command hoped that Morgan's presence in his native Kentucky would be interpreted by the Washington government as a serious effort to lead that State firmly into the Confederacy. The force of 2,500 cavalry, was actually too small a force for such an undertaking and Morgan's instructions were to withdraw after the Union forces were diverted.

Morgan's force crossed into Kentucky on July 2, 1863. He went through Columbia, Lebanon, Springfield, and Bardstown in Eastern-central Kentucky without any serious encounters with Union forces. He avoided Louisville which had a strong Federal garrison. Then, contrary to his instructions, Morgan crossed the Ohio River near Bradenburg, Indiana, and continued his raid north of the river.

It is not clear why Morgan decided to extend his raid beyond Kentucky. It is possible that he was dissatisfied with the effectiveness of his diversion, since the Federal campaign in Tennessee did not appear to lose momentum, and wished to intensify the efforts of his command by such a bold venture. It is also possible that he saw an opportunity for his force to act in a punitive manner in the Northern States. Finally, the possibility must not be discounted that Morgan saw in such a risky undertaking the opportunity to establish his reputation as a great commander of an independent calvary force.

In any case, the news of his presence in Indiana spread fear and apprehension in that State. Particularly, since this news was accompanied with stories of indignities and cruelties to which the noncombatants of the invaded areas were subjected at the hands of Morgan's men. Although some of those stories were exaggerations, it is true that the behavior of Morgan's men was anything but exemplary and this fact had a lot to do with the eventual destruction of Morgan's command.

For a while Morgan toyed with the idea of storming Indianapolis where a substantial arsenal was located and several thousands of Confederate prisoners were interned in camps outside the city. Intelligence was received, however, that Norton, the very energetic governor of the State, was diligently assembling troops for the capital's defense and Morgan abandoned the idea. Instead, he turned eastward and crossed into Ohio State through Cincinnati's suburbs.

In the meantime, several Federal forces were attempting to intercept Morgan. Realizing that he could not successfully cope with the Union forces pursuing him, he evaded them as long as possible and on July 18 attempted to cross back into Kentucky near Pomeroy, Ohio. Unfortunately for him, the rivei was swollen and he was forced to fight a much superior force with the result that he had 800 casualties. The Union commanders pursuing Morgan were able to receive exact intelligence of his whereabouts from civilians in the area. Although Morgan himself escaped capture during the encounter, his force practically disintegrated and on July 26 he was forced to surrender near East Liverpool, Ohio. He was interned in the State Penitentiary in Columbus, but managed to escape on November 27th.

Morgan's raid was indeed a daring undertaking, but its practical effectiveness is very much in doubt. Its most outstanding feature is the speed with which Morgan's force moved. This was accomplished by constantly exchanging the tired animals of his troopers with fresh mounts appropriated from local farms. However, this practice angered and alienated the local farmers, many of whom had been sympathetic to the Southern cause since they were actually Kentuckians who had migrated into Indiana or Ohio. Had Morgan been able to capitalize on the sympathies of this segment of the population in Indiana and Ohio, he could have created a most serious diversion and effectively challenged the established authority of the Federal Government in the area.

Nathan Bedford Forrest has presented an interesting personality in American history. The man was perhaps the second best[6] cavalry commander, the Southern armies had, yet lacked formal military schooling; in fact he could barely read and write. When the war began, he enlisted as a private in one of the cavalry units recruited in Tennessee; before the war was over, he had been made a Lieutenant General. Forrest had a rare ability to comprehend military matters and an amazing correctness in second-guessing his adversaries' moves.

The first operation in which Forrest employed guerrilla tactics was his raid on Murfreesboro on July 13, 1862. Forrest was given a cavalry brigade for this operation. He started out of Chattanooga; he cut off all liaison with the Confederate armies, crossed the Tennessee River and reached the suburbs of Murfreesboro inside the Union lines without being detected. At daylight on the 13th, he stormed the city, captured several hundred prisoners and material, and withdrew as swiftly as he had attacked. Several Union detachments were sent after him trying to intercept and destroy him, but he avoided them all by changing direction of march several times and hiding in the heavily wooded Tennessee hills. Eventually he returned to the Confederate lines of General Bragg.

On another occasion, Forrest with 270 men and four pieces of artillery infiltrated through the Union forces in Northern Mississippi and established a base of operations at Okolona in Western Tennessee. Strong Federal forces moved against him, but he escaped, taking with him approximately 3,000 men whom he recruited among the civilians in the area who were loyal to the South.

In an effort to divert the Federal forces operating in Mississippi, Forrest conducted another raid against Memphis in September 1864. Although he obtained a limited surprise during this raid, the Union forces in that city were too strong and he was forced to withdraw without any substantial gains. Forrest suffered one of his many wounds in this operation.

After Sherman's march towards Atlanta was well under way, the Southern government attempted to turn Forrrest loose against Sherman's rear. In this operation, however, Forrest was not successful.

Sherman's operation was novel for those days. Sherman had liberated his army from dependence on the railway lines for resupply. His army lived off the land and for all practical purposes did not have to maintain a line of communications. With no line of communications to attack, Forrest had no other target except Sherman's army itself; this army was too strong for a light cavalry force to attack successfully. It appears, too, that during this phase of the war, Forrest completely lost his head and ordered the execution of any recaptured liberated slaves. He was lucky to escape court-martial and hanging for this act after the Federal victory.

After the war was over, Forrest expressed bitterness against his former commanders, particularly General Bragg. He felt that his abilities were never fully recognized and that his advice was generally ignored. There is probably a certain amount of truth in this. Forrest was disliked by his fellow Generals because he did not fit their idea of a gentleman. Not only was he not a professional military man like the rest of them, but his origin was humble and he had been a slave trader before the war, which was considered a dishonorable occupation, even among the upholders of slavery.

"Bushwhackers" was a term used by the Northern forces to designate the Confederate bands operating West of the Mississippi River, particularly in the Missouri-Kansas border. Notwithstanding all testimony to the contrary, the fact still remains that these bands were saturated with individuals of questionable motives who used the war as an excuse to rob and murder with impunity. Guerrilla bands are vulnerable to infiltration by such elements; this is the reason why extreme caution must be exercised in selecting prospective guerrillas in the future, if the High Command wishes to confine the activities of the guerrilla organization to the strictly military field.[7]

A typical band of bushwhackers was the one led by Charles W. Quantrell. This man was a native of Maryland. Orphaned at an early age, he moved to Missouri when a teenager, where an older brother had settled. It appears that Quantrell got involved in the prewar squabbles between Kansas abolutionists and Missouri slaveholders and possibly he had already committed a murder or two before the commencement of hostilities.

In the fall of 1861, Quantrell and another man from Missouri named Blunt travelled to Richmond, Virginia, where they persuaded Jefferson Davis to give them commissions as Captains in the Confederate Army and authority to organize bands of guerrillas to operate in the Trans-Mississippi States.

Quantrell's band initially consisted of nine men only, but eventually grew to about three hundred,[8] including the brothers Frank and Jesse James who joined this band in 1863. In spite of their preoccupation with bank robbing and horse-thieving, they conducted several purely military operations and contributed to the military effort of the South by diverting several Union formations from other campaigns to garrison duties in the frontier towns.

Quantrell developed a method of operations which consisted of fast strikes followed by quick withdrawals and dispersions. This is, of course, typical guerrilla method, but Quantrell was not taught this in any school. He learned it the hard way. He observed after his second attempt to storm Independence, Missouri, that the majority of Federal casualties were inflicted during the first few minutes of each attack, whereas most of his losses were suffered during the latter part of each prolonged raid.[9] He changed his tactics after that raid and placed appropriate emphasis on timely withdrawals.

The band lived entirely off the land and utilized to a great extent the isolated ranches of Southern sympathizers for hiding places. The topography of the land and the low density of the settlements were factors favoring the guerrillas. During the winter, they moved South to Mississippi and Texas, thus avoiding what they considered needless exposure to severe weather.

After Lee's surrender, Quantrell, fearing reprisals from his former victims, decided to leave Missouri and return to his native Maryland. He started eastward accompanied by forty-eight of his men. At Nelson County, Kentucky, they got into a fight with Federal troops and during the fight Quantrell was severely wounded. He died a few days later in a military hospital in Louisville. The James brothers and some other members of Quantrell's band lived on as outlaws in the West for several years and eventually most of them got killed in gunfights or were hung after being tried and found guilty for crimes of the common penal code.

On the Union side, guerrilla activity was limited to the hilly country of East Tennessee where the population was loyal to the Union. One may also consider Sherman's campaign through Georgia as having several guerrilla characteristics. These were:

The independent operation of Sherman's command.

The fact that they were operating deep into the enemy's rear.

His lack of contact with other Union forces.

Their nondependence on Union supplies for subsistence.

On the other side, it can be argued that a force of three army corps can hardly be considered a guerrilla force and also that Sherman's campaign did not have the character of a raid, but that of a protracted sustained attack. The main reason, however, that Sherman's campaign cannot be classed with guerrilla operations is that Sherman held the territory he captured.

In retrospect, one has to conclude that guerrilla operations in the Revolutionary War were significant, but not decisive. During the Civil War, Union guerrilla operations were practically nonexistent. Confederate guerrilla operations were considerably more extensive, but they had mostly nuisance value and never presented a serious threat to the Union forces. The most successful guerrilla force was that of Mosby, but it never seriously challenged the security of communications lines of the Army of the Potomac. In order to accomplish this, Confederate guerrillas would have had to operate deep into South Central Pennsylvania where the population was loyal to the Union; therefore, success of Confederate guerrillas would have been extremely difficult. In the Western states, however, the situation was different. In the Southern regions of Ohio, Indiana, and Illinois, and in Missouri there was a substantial number of people with Southern sympathies, particularly in Missouri where the Union forces effectively controlled only St. Louis and the immediate area. Here there was potential for guerrilla warfare which the Southern High Command exploited only superficially. If the Southern High Command had been able to exploit this potential fully, the successes of the Union armies in the West could have been delayed or, perhaps, might never taken place.

3. Campaigns Against the Western Indians

After the conclusion of the Civil War, the Federal Government could again devote its attention to the Western Territories and the numerous small conflicts between the various Indian tribes on one side, and the white settlers or American authorities on the other.

The opinion has been advanced that the Indian Wars of the last century were inevitably caused by the clash of the two civilizations: The modern civilization of the white Americans expanding westward, and the nomadic civilization of the Indians, struggling to maintain the status quo.

Another opinion has been that the wars with the American Indians have been caused by the greed of the white man, who aimed to take away from the Indians every means of existence and completely destroy them or reduce them to a status of virtual confinement in reservations. One thing must be said, however, to the credit of the American whites: they, at least, did not wish to reduce the Indians into a status of servitude as the Spaniards did in the parts of the New World which they colonized, although the reason, perhaps, is that they found the Plains Indians unsuitable for servitude.

A certain amount of truth exists in both assertions. The nomadic economy of the western tribes required such vast amounts of land, completely out of proportion with the number of individuals per acreage, that coexistence with the agricultural and industrial economy of the whites was impossible. Impossible, at least, without the good will and toleration of the whites. And the whites lacked good will and toleration. This is where greed enters as a factor and compounds the problem.

The Indians were forced into reservations and compelled, one way or another, to farm or pursue other vocations. This was, perhaps, a good policy, but poorly executed, because habits of generations do not change within a few years. But the Indians would not be left in peace, even in the reservations. They were moved from reservation to reservation. The reservation location becoming progressively less desirable because the greed of the white settlers always desired the better land. In addition, crooked or incompetent officials would always manage

to offend or aggravate the tribes and cause outbreaks. Irrespon-
sible civilians would also sell them bad whiskey, or guns, or
trespass on the reservations, etc. Finally, a factor not to be
ignored, was the predjuce of certain whites toward all members
of the human race whose skin is less white than theirs. So much
for the nonmilitary aspects of the Indian Wars.

The kind of warfare waged by the Indians in most, but not
all, cases was guerrilla warfare. There are several reasons for
this. The terrain was so vast and sparsely populated that it
afforded every opportunity for maneuver, concealment, evasion,
escape, and dispersal. Technological advances did not yet offer
the regular army the advantages of aerial surveillance or mobility through motor transport. Finally, raiding was part of
the Indian's elementary education among several tribes. The
Apaches, for instance, earned at least part of their livelihood
by raiding other tribes and Mexican or American settlements.
When Geronimo went on the warpath the first time, he did
not have to teach any member of his band the principles of
guerrilla tactics because they knew them already. The Apache
knew how to raid and run. He did not fight a pitched battle
ever, unless he was either cornered or overwhelmingly outnumbered his adversary.[10]

Consequently, the United States Army's mission of controlling or fighting the Indians was not an easy one. Neither was
the Army in the field always in line with the policy of "annihilation or concentration," as many of its commanders have testi-
fied.

The Indian Wars produced several outstanding guerrilla
leaders among the Indians and several outstanding anti-guerrilla commanders among the Americans. Osceola, Cochise, Geronimo, Chief Joseph the Younger, Crazy Horse, Rain-in-the-
Face, and Sitting Bull are only a few of the first group. General
Crook is the outstanding member of the other.

We must not neglect to mention here that the above Indian
leaders did not have the advantage of any formal military
schooling; in fact, they did not have any formal schooling at
all.

All operations by the Indians were not always made on guerrilla lines. Several times, the Indians fought pitched battles

against the Army and, on occasion, were victorious. The most famous such battle was the "Battle of Little Big Horn" in which Lieutenant Colonel George A. Custer with about 215 troopers of the 7th Cavalry moved against the main force of the Sioux and allied tribes on 25 June 1876. The result was that he and every member of his command (less one horse) were killed. The Battle of Little Big Horn is a classic example of how not to fight a battle. Custer hastily moved against the enemy, contrary to the advice of his staff and his scouts, without bothering to reconnoiter and obtain some idea as to the size of the enemy force. In addition, he split his command into three columns and deployed them to move in such a way that the two other columns on his left could not speedily come to his assistance, even if the enemy had not intervened to stop them.

During most of his life and for many years afterwards, Custer was regarded as a national hero of a sort. In recent years though, objective studies of his life have led military historians to recognize him as the poor tactician and fool that he really was. Custer's career in the Army is worth reviewing briefly here because of the lessons that it can teach us on the subjects of war preparedness and officer career development.

Custer graduated 38th in a class of 38 cadets from West Point after the Civil War had just begun. He immediately joined the Federal Armies in the field. The Federal forces, a year prior to the beginning of the War, consisted of only about 7,000 regulars; now they were confronted with the problem of augmentation to over a million, with no substantial reserve organization to provide for trained officers and noncoms. The field was, therefore, wide open for a young, ambitious, slightly vain, but brave officer such as Custer to obtain speedy promotions. And Custer, despite his other faults, was indeed a brave officer. Within a year he was promoted from 2nd Lieutenant to Captain. Within four years after his graduation from West Point, he was Brevet Brigadier General and then Major General. A Major General less than thirty years old! Is this normal progress in an officer's career? Of course, those ranks were only temporary; "brevet" meaning just that. The practice of giving temporary ranks is applied today in several military establishments, but the difference in ranks does not extend to such extremes.

After the conclusion of the war, Custer was reverted to the permanent rank of Captain, and by 1876 he was up to Lt. Colonel. In the postwar years, the vain part of his personality asserted itself, and he apparently found it disturbing to be a lesser officer again and not an important general and brave war hero. That is why we always find him in the middle of controversies, doing deeds of questionable merit, in an apparent attempt to get back in the limelight. This is why newspapermen were always present in his headquarters; and this is why he maintained a voluminous correspondence with various important personages of the time; kept a diary; and even wrote poetry. There was one person in this world of whom Custer thought a lot: That person was George A. Custer.

One of his many deeds that give him and the U. S. Army everlasting shame is his cowardly attack on the camp of Chief Black Kettle of the Southern Cheyennes at dawn on 28 November 1868, while the Indians were peacefully camped on the banks of the Washita. This was pure murder, the victims being mostly squaws and pappooses. Yet, this man professed to be a Christian.

It has been reported that prior to his final battle he was out of favor with the powers-to-be in the War Department. For this reason he wished to move fast, before the main Army under Generals Terry, Gibbon, and Crook joined him, so that he could defeat the hostile Indians alone and get back in the good graces of headquarters. It has also been said that Custer had political ambitions and that he hoped to obtain the presidential nomination from the Democratic Party. He was seeking, perhaps, a spectacular military victory as the means through which he could obtain this nomination.

If the ratio of guerrillas to the regular forces engaged in their pursuit is an indication of the ability of the guerrilla leader, then the Apache Geronimo is the most able guerrilla leader of record, especially since Geronimo always frustrated the efforts of his pursuers, and his band was never captured nor suffered a decisive defeat.

Geronimo's band during most of his raids consisted of only

a couple of dozen men. Most of them were related to him; a few were renegades of a sort; and two were Navajos. General Miles' force engaged in his pursuit in 1886 included 5,000 U. S. Army regulars, 500 Indians engaged as scouts, and an unrecorded number of armed settlers.[11] There were also Mexican troops under their own commanders simultaneously engaged in Geronimo's pursuit. Geronimo's band, at the same time, consisted of thirty-five men, eight boys, and 101 women and children, since the Apaches always took their families with them. The ratio of guerrillas to their pursuers is about 1 to 200 or more, which is an impressive ratio in anyone's book.

Goyahkla, which was Geronimo's Indian name, was a Chiricahua Apache. The Apaches, in the last century, were spread over the Southern half of Arizona and New Mexico and the northern parts of the Mexican States of Sonora and Chihuahua. Ethnologically, the Apaches can be described as a nation because they possessed the following characteristics of nationhood: Common language, common religion, common origin (as accurately as we can establish), and common traditions and habits. Politically, though, they were divided into several tribes or bands. The more important of the tribes were the Tato, White Mountain, San Carlos, Coyotero, Jicarila, Papago, Ojo Calliente, Mescalero, and Chiricahua. The Majave, Maricopa, and Yuma were related to the Apache to a degree, but were not Apache proper. Each tribe constituted a political unit around a hereditary chief. There were also smaller groups within each tribe, composed mostly of members of two or three family groups under one subchief, or chief of lesser rank, also hereditary. When they were first contacted by American frontiersmen, their society was characterized by strong family ties, and their economy was entirely nomadic.

Among the Apache chiefs of record we have Mangus Colorado, Delgadito, and Cochise. Mangus Colorado was killed by Americans and Delgadito by the Mexicans. Cochise lived for awhile in the Warm Springs (Ojo Calliente) reservation in peace, but was frightened away by an inept young Army officer who was going to arrest him for no good reason at all. Cochise hid in the Dragoon Mountains west of Ft. Bowie and it is assumed that he eventually died in his mountain hideout.

After Cochise died, Victorio took over actual leadership of the tribe because Cochise's son, Nachite, was considered too flighty to be a reliable chief.[12] Nachite later joined Geronimo's band. Cochise had another son who died during a visit to Washington. Visits to Washington and other Eastern cities for influential Indians were conducted purposely in the hope that on their return they would recount their experiences and impress the other Indians with the number and strength of the whites. This experiment was a failure because the visiting Indians could not comprehend what they saw and, besides, their stories were called lies by the Indians who had remained in the reservations.

Victorio did not care for reservation life, and eventually organized a band and went on a raid in Mexico. He left a trail of blood and destruction, killing all Mexicans he encountered and stealing cattle and horses. The Mexicans sent several expeditions after him, but Victorio, after each strike, would retreat into parts of the country that were apparently waterless, and the Mexican troops would not follow him there. The Indians, however, knew how to find water in that part of the desert. Finally, Victorio was caught in a trap in a small canyon west of El Paso, and was killed.

After Victorio's death, leadership of the Chiricahuas was taken over by Juh. Actually, after Cochise's death, there was no strong central leader of the tribe; the several subchiefs were more or less left on their own. Among those subchiefs were Chato, Nanay, Zele, Benito, Chihuahua, and others. It is interesting to note that Geronimo's rank in the Apache language is lesser than that of the above-listed subchiefs. This is because Geronimo's status as leader was not hereditary nor was he accepted as such by every member of the tribe. Juh drowned one night when he fell off his horse in a creek as he was returning drunk to his camp after a visit to the nearby Mexican town. His position as military chief of the Chiricahuas was then claimed by Geronimo. Geronimo was not recognized as such by all of the Chiricahuas nor was he followed by the tribe as a whole when he left the San Carlos reservation and went on the warpath. As a matter of fact, several of the Chiricahuas were enlisted as scouts and participated in the operation against him.

In the ten years following the Civil War, most of the Apaches were concentrated in the Warm Springs reservation in New Mexico. This reservation was located on a high plateau where game was plentiful and the climate agreeable; but, unfortunately for the Apaches, reports of the existence of gold on the reservation were circulating among the settlers and prospectors in New Mexico and the Federal government was under pressure from their respective lobbies to move the Indians some place else so that the whites could lay their hands on the gold. No substantial strikes of gold were made later, but this is of no consequence because all the Warm Springs Apaches were forcibly moved to a new reservation in San Carlos, Arizona, where the land was arid, the temperature rose to 100° daily, and the game was scanty.

Over 4,000 Apaches were concentrated at San Carlos before the outbreak of 1878. Most of them were idle, waiting for the weekly distribution of rations by the Government agents. All of this idle time gave them plenty of opportunity for discontent and mischief. So, in 1878, an outbreak took place, and the majority of the Chiricahuas fled the reservation. The instigator and organizer of the outbreak was Victorio with his followers. Geronimo participated in this outbreak, but apparently not in a leadership capacity.

The insurgents struck out for the Sierra Madre range and then returned to Warm Springs where they killed a few prospectors and ranchers. In 1879 an expedition was sent to convince them to return to San Carlos. The majority of them, including the old chief Loco, agreed to return, but Victorio and Nanay with a band of about forty warriors refused. They hid in the Black Mountains of Warm Springs and later went on the raid in Mexico that we previously mentioned in which Victorio was killed.

Geronimo also did not return to San Carlos until 1883 when he was persuaded to do so after meeting with General Crook himself. In the intervening years, he remained at large, raiding on both sides of the border. Since Victorio's band was also at large during part of the same period, Geronimo has been credited (or blamed, depending on one's point of view) for some of Victorio's raids. During all this time, Geronimo's band did not seem to have been under any particularly strong pressure by either the Mexican or U.S. forces. To the contrary, their losses appear slight, and they were well supplied with modern weapons, ammunition, horses, and cattle that they took from their victims. In fact, when the band did return to the reservation in 1883, they brought with them a herd of stolen cattle which they hoped to sell in order to provide themselves with some gambling money. The herd was confiscated by the reservation authorities and this greatly angered Geronimo.

Conditions at San Carlos did not improve any. Some of the Indians did make a not-too-enthusiastic effort at farming, but the land was not suitable for farming. Their favored pastime was drinking a crude alcoholic beverage made out of mescal, and sitting around the campfires reminiscing and swapping lies about their old raids and discussing the latest rumors. One such rumor was that Geronimo was about to be arrested and sent to Alcatraz in irons. This rumor apparently started when Lt. Britton Davis, in command of the small garrison, forbade brewing the mescal and also made a rule against wife-beating. Geronimo was apparently guilty of this latter offense because it is reported that on one occasion he told Lt. Davis through the interpreter, Mickey Free,[13] that his agreement with General Crook covered only the matter of his returning to San Carlos and that nothing had been said between him and the General about him, Geronimo, taking lessons in domestic relations from officers of Lt. Davis' age.

In such an atmosphere the outbreak of 1884 took place. Geronimo was followed by a small band only, having failed to convince the rest of the tribe that they should jump the reservation. He also arranged for the assassination of Lt. Davis by one of the scouts, but the assassination attempt did not succeed.

Later, Geronimo expressed regrets for not being able to convince all Chiricahuas that they should follow him on the warpath. He was convinced that those who remained at San Carlos would be imprisoned. Four years later, this was indeed done. He did take with him his family and the families of his followers.

Geronimo's band headed for the Guadalupe Mountains and then into Mexico. Geronimo this time again struck to the old proven tactics which can be described as follows:

1. Hit and run, never fought unless he had to.

2. Chose targets carefully. He seldom attacked garrison towns because he did not consider them worth the risk. Ordinarily he could get what his band needed, i.e., ammunition, horses, and food, by attacking isolated ranches which were defended by a few men only, yet were well supplied with the above commodities. Caravans and packtrains with merchandise were another favored target. Occasionally, too, he attacked sizeable towns such as Galena in Sonora, but we doubt the prudence of that raid; it was rather an act of defiance when he was getting too bold and contemptuous of the Mexicans.

3. After each strike, he would move out speedily, dispensing with victory celebrations which were traditional with the Indians. He would withdraw over the most difficult terrain for troops to follow — mountains, preferably, or desert. During his withdrawal, he would use all kinds of ruses to throw off the pursuers. One such ruse was to set fake camps near water holes. He also maintained a system of predesignating assembly points where the band would assemble after each dispersal, etc. This was made possible by the fact that each member of the band was well familiar with the territory over which they were operating. He usually moved at night, and remained under cover during the daylight hours.

The speed with which Geronimo's band could move over extremely difficult terrain is phenomenal. They could cover on foot 50 to 75 miles in one march, without rest. One of their members reports that on foot the Apaches could move faster than mounted; and that they used the animals primarily for the women and to carry their belongings.[14] Another point worth mentioning is that the presence of so many women and children within the band did not seem to hinder their movements any.

Geronimo's raids after 1884 spread terror and frustration on both sides of the Mexican border. The United States government was employing a great proportion of its available field forces in the operations against Geronimo, and an agreement was reached with the Mexicans according to which either Army could operate under certain conditions on the other side of the border. Yet, a lot of the stories circulating about Geronimo were exaggerations. For instance, it was not true that he had a coat made of human scalps, because scalping was not practiced by the Apaches. It is true, however, that Geronimo and his band were responsible for a lot of senseless killings. Among their victims were hundreds of unarmed Mexican peasants whose financial status was only one step better than destitute. The practical result of Geronimo's guerrilla raids, from the Apache point of view, was that the American authorities were convinced that this group of "savages" was perfectly capable of creating an awful lot of trouble; therefore, in subsequent years did treat them somewhat more considerably.

General Crook's force was never able to force Geronimo's band into a fight, although it did succeed in harrying them to the extent that they considered surrender. General Crook's success, in our opinion, can be attributed to the following two factors:

1. His extensive use of Chiricahua and other Apache scouts. This can be a lesson to those directing future anti-guerrilla operations. It is always prudent and inexpensive to use the guerrillas' compatriots to contribute to the fight against the guerrillas, as long as these people are willing to do so, and assuming that their reliability can be established. In General Crook's case, only three out of 500 scouts deserted.

2. He increased the mobility of his force by abandoning its horse-drawn wagons and transporting all his supplies by pack trains; the pack trains could go where the wheeled wagons could not.[15] The organic composition of the pack trains was forty packs in each train. With one chief packer and ten packers.[16]

Despite all these innovations, his main force was still somewhat slow and his troops of scouts were always one or two days' march ahead of the main force.

On 27 March 1886, after a parley that lasted two days, Geronimo and his band agreed to surrender to General Crook. The same night, however, Geronimo, Nachite, and twelve other men escaped after getting drunk on mescal sold to them by a renegade American named Tribolet. This caused a lot of embarrassment to General Crook. General Sheridan now wanted

Crook to abandon pursuit of Geronimo and concentrate on the static defense of the settlements. Crook did not agree with this method of warfare, and asked to be relieved on April 1, 1886. He was replaced by General Miles. Geronimo surrendered to Miles the following August, primarily because he was concerned about the fate of his family, which had remained in custody.

Following Geronimo's last surrender, all Apaches, including the ones who never left San Carlos and those who served the Army as scouts, were imprisoned in Ft. Pickens, Florida, while their families were detained at Ft. Marion, near St. Augustine.[17] This was another gross injustice. However, after two years they were sent to a new reservation at Ft. Sill, Oklahoma. There Geronimo died on February 17, 1909. While at Ft. Sill, he was enlisted as a scout and assigned to be in charge of a village. In his last years he was somewhat of a celebrity, receiving many newspapermen and other visitors, and was asked to appear in several public meetings throughout the country. He also attended President Theodore Roosevelt's inauguration in Washington.

After a few years, those Apaches who wanted to were allowed to return to Warm Springs by the ex-Confederate General Fitzhugh Lee, who had returned to Federal service and was in charge of the Southwestern Military Department.

In retrospect, it appears that the warfare waged by the Indians during the reviewed period was unsuccessful. Their objectives were to retain the status quo and stop the advance of the whites. They were not able to achieve this, but their military resistance was responsible for their obtaining slightly more favorable terms of settlement from the U.S. Government. These terms, incidentally, were not always adhered to by the Americans. Given the imbalance of resources that existed, the Indians could only use guerrilla warfare against their enemies. They were able to utilize this method of warfare expertly. From the point of view of the Americans, the Indian Wars gave the U.S. Army very extensive experience in this type of warfare. This experience served the U.S. forces well in later years in the Philippines and in the Mexican expedition of 1916.

4. Guerrilla Activities in Mexico

The Mexican nation obtained its independence from Spain after a series of bloody revolts that took place between 1810 and 1821.

The occupation of Spain by Napoleon in 1808 and the example of the French and United States revolutions were some of the many factors contributing to the causes of the separatist movement in Mexico. Initially, however, the revolt had a purely racial character as the Indians under the leadership of Fr. Miguel Hidalgo slaughtered indiscriminately all persons of Spanish descent they could lay hands on. Hidalgo was proven an inept leader and was soon captured, defrocked, and executed. Leadership of the revolution fell eventually on Agustin Iturbide, a man of more moderate views.

When the Mexican Republic was finally established, it retained several of its colonial characteristics; i.e.; the privileged position of the Catholic Church and the predominantly agricultural economy with land holdings concentrated in the hands of a few landlords. After a few years the war with the United States ensued, as a result of which Mexico lost almost half of its territory. The war and the ineptitude of the governments resulted in heavy indebtedness to foreign investors and economic crises.

The Liberal Party, with Benito Juarez as its leader, came to power in the 1860's and a program of social reforms was initiated. Unfortunately for the Mexicans, this program was interrupted by the French intervention and the establishment of the puppet empire with the Habsburg Archduke Maximilian as emperor.

Maximilian was supported by the conservative elements in the country but his primary source of support came from the expeditionary force that the French had landed in Mexico under Marshal Bazaine. The Republican government, unable to cope militarily with the French troops, took to the hills. There Juarez, an Indian himself, is reputed to have had a conversation with an Indian shepherd boy who described to him how his dogs killed a wolf by working together and attacking the wolf with quick thrusts from the sides. This, is said, gave

Juarez the idea to utilize bands of irregulars to harass the French garrisons. For a time thereafter, the only Republican troops opposing the French and Imperial Mexican forces were guerrillas.

The situation changed with the conclusion of the American Civil War. The Washington Government sent troops to the Mexican border and arms and supplies to Juarez. Simultaneously, it exerted pressure on Napoleon to withdraw his forces from the American continent. Napoleon complied and this spelled Maxmilian's doom. His native forces were defeated by the Republicans who now abandoned the guerrilla tactics and organized standard formations equipped with U.S. material. Maximilian, chivalrous to the end among people who could not understand chivalry, refused to leave the country, so he was captured and executed in 1866, together with Generals Miramon and Mejia, who had remained loyal to him.

After the defeat of Maximilian, a new liberal constitution was proclaimed in 1873, which abolished the privileges of the religious orders and the landed gentry. A few short years of reform followed until Porfirio Diaz was elected President in 1877. Diaz had served with Juarez against the French. He was reputed to have been an able commander and daring guerrilla, but in checking the History of that period, we have failed to find any outstanding operations of record that were conducted under his leadership. His best claim to personal courage is a rather adventurous escape from a French prison where he was being held. Diaz ruled Mexico until 1911, with a short interruption between 1881 and 1884. His regime was, in essence, a dictatorship, benevolent in some respects, but oppressive. He failed to cope with Mexico's two fundamental problems, which were the low educational level of the masses and land reform. The violence of the following decade could have been avoided if any progress had been made towards land reform. In addition, there were the lesser evils that are inevitably associated with one-man regimes of such duration, such as corrupt public officials, etc.

Instrumental in the overthrow of Diaz were the following four people of widely divergent personalities and objectives.

Francisco Madero was a politician. His later murder by

Huerta made him a martyr and his memory was almost wor-
shipped by the rank and file of the revolutionary armies. In
reality, he was a very moderate liberal. He did nothing to promote land reform during his tenure and it appears that he was
more interested in securing the government for himself and
associates than in the welfare of his followers. In fact, one of his
first acts as president was to pay out of the almost bankrupt
treasury the equivalent of a quarter of a million American dol-
lars to members of his family as war indemnities.

Francisco Villa, according to John Reed, one of his few non-
Mexican admirers, was an ex-bandit. He was an illiterate, but
clever man. The complexities of the civilized world around him
left him perplexed; this is perhaps the reason why he attempted
the raid against Columbus, New Mexico. Yet, it appears that
he had qualities as a military leader and was able to make
good estimates of military situations. One of his shortcomings
was that he liked to think of himself as a great war captain and a
leader of a great revolutionary army on the Napoleonic style.
He could have done much better if he had stuck to guerrilla
tactics throughout. This has been a shortcoming of many otherwise successful leaders throughout History. In Villa's case this
condition was accentuated by his complex about his humble
origin, his past as a bandit, and his contacts with snobbish
military professionals.

Emiliano Zapata was the best guerrilla leader who ever came
out of Mexico. Unfortunately for Mexico, he was incapable of
capitalizing politically on his military successes. A full-blooded
Indian from the State of Morelos, illiterate until his adulthood,
he could not grasp Mexico's overall problems. When his forces
entered Mexico City he was so modest that he refused to live
in the presidential palace. The revolution was over for him
when the enemy was chased out of Morelos. He instituted his
own program of land reform for the peasants of Morelos and he
was ready to call the show finished if the outsiders would only
leave him alone. They would not, so Zapata kept on fighting
for his people and their land until his last day. In doing so, he
conducted many a brilliant guerrilla raid.

Alvaro Obregon is the fourth member of the group we mentioned above. He distinguished himself as a fence-jumper. He

changed sides more than once in the struggle and it appears that he had no principles at all.

Madero's faltering regime ended with his murder by Huerta's troops. Huerta, a general suposedly loyal to Madero, sided with a group of insurgents under Felix Diaz, the former dictator's nephew. Huerta declared himself president and the elements of the old regime sided immediately with him; so did Obregon. Villa and Zapata continued the struggle against him. Venuciano Carranza, one of the State governors, sided with the revolutionaries and formed a provisional government.

On the military side, Huerta's forces were entrenched in Central Mexico garrisoning all towns along the rail lines. Villa, after securing Ciudad Juarez on the American border, started South towards Mexico City. On the way he had to storm every city along the railroad, with great losses on both sides. Just south of Mexico City, Zapata managed to keep his own state of Morelos free of government troops, but he did not coordinate any offensive actions with Villa's forces of the North.

The Huerta government finally fell under the blows of Villa, Zapata, and President Wilson, who obstinately refused to give it diplomatic recognition on the grounds that it was an immoral government founded on murder. On 15 July 1914, Huerta resigned and left for Jamaica. A year later he was arrested at Newman, New Mexico where he had gone in an effort to cross over into Mexico. He was imprisoned at Ft. Bliss, Texas until his death on January 13, 1916.

After Huerta's flight, Carranza established himself as the President of Mexico. It did not take very long before he and Villa were at odds. Those two had little liking for each other from the days of their reluctant cooperation in 1913.[18] Villa's following, however, was diminishing. Many of his better lieutenants were dead; others had been coerced by Carranza; a great many more had tired of the continuous fighting and had gone home. A few die-hards remained, and with them Villa was able to control part of the Northern States of Chihuahua and Coahuila.

Although the United States Government was not exactly against Villa, friction developed between Villa on one side and the United States consular officers and border authorities on the other. Villa was particularly offended whenever he thought that the United States officials did not treat him with due respect. In this background the Columbus raid took place.

During the night of 8 to 9 March 1916, a force of armed Mexicans crossed the border near Columbus, New Mexico, and attacked the town and the barracks of the garrison. The raiders withdrew before daylight. Two United States Cavalry troops gave chase and penetrated twelve miles south of the border; they returned when their ammunition and animals were exhausted. Seven enlisted men and eight civilians were killed and two officers, five enlisted men and two civilians wounded among the Americans. Mexican casualties were reported as sixty-seven killed and seven captured wounded.

On the 10th of March, Major General Funston, commanding the Southern Department, received orders to prepare a force under Brigadier General John J. Pershing for the purpose of pursuing Villa's band into Mexican territory and capturing or destroying Villa and his followers.

This force was organized into two columns as follows.

The first column assembled at Columbus and proceeded to Casas Grandes by way of Palomes, Ascension, and Corralitos. This column was composed of the following combat elements:

> Seven troops of the 13th Cavalry
> The 6th Infantry Regiment
> The 16th Infantry Regiment
> Battery C of the 6th Field Artillery

The second column assembled at Culberson's Ranch and proceeded by way of Ojitos to Colonia Dublan, four miles North of Casas Grandes. This column was composed of the following combat elements:

> The 7th Cavalry Regiment
> Ten troops of the 19th Cavalry
> Battery B of 6th Field Artillery

The above forces were ready on March 15. Their march South was slow, hindered with transport difficulties because of the inadequacy of railroads and the unfavorable terrain. When the two columns reached their destination around Casas Grandes they were ordered to halt and establish a base. From this base, daily scouts and reconnaissance-in-force were conducted in an effort to find Villa. Obviously, the United States government did not wish an energetic pursuit of Villa for political reasons.

Although the expedition had orders to respect Mexican Sovereignty[19] and attempt to befriend the Mexican civilians, the attitude of the Mexicans in general, including the Carranza government officials, was extremely unfriendly. Carranza's position was precarious anyway, and he could become more unpopular if it was thought that he was inviting in the "gringos".

In addition to the political considerations, the military difficulties were considerable. The terrain was favorable to the guerrillas and the population was definitely on their side.

Several engagements with regular and irregular Mexican forces took place, but Villa was neither captured nor found. Some of the engagements are described briefly below.

On 12 April, Major Frank Tompkins with K and M Troops of the 13th Cavalry was located outside the town of Parral. The Major with a small detachment went into the town for the purpose of purchasing supplies. In town they were received by the civil authorities and by General Lozano who accompanied them back to their camp. On their way back, however, they were jeered, stoned, and fired upon by civilians and soldiers. The two troops withdrew to Santa Cruz, eight miles north of Parral. They lost two enlisted men killed, two officers and four enlisted men wounded and one enlisted man missing.

On the 21st of June, Captain Charles T. Boyd with C and K Troops of the 19th Cavalry was scouting around Carrizal and sought permission of General Gomez to pass through the town. Gomez refused permission. While the conference was in progress, Mexicans in uniform and armed civilians were seen trying to flank the American troops. Defensive positions were immediately taken and engagement followed. Captain Boyd, one other officer, and seven enlisted men were killed; one officer and nine enlisted men were wounded, and twenty-three enlisted men and a civilian interpreter were captured, but later released. Among the Mexican casualties was General Gomez who was killed.

Villa also attempted several diversionary raids into American territory. On May 5 he sent a band to raid Glenn Springs, Texas. The Americans lost three enlisted men and one civilian killed and three enlisted men wounded. Two Mexicans were found dead in the vicinity of the fighting.

Another raid was made against San Ygnacio, Texas, on June 15th. American casualties were four enlisted men killed and five wounded, while Mexican confirmed casualties were six killed.

Another Villa band raided Ft. Hancock, Texas, on July 31, killing one customs inspector and one enlisted man. Three Villistas were killed during this raid and another three were captured by Mexican Government gendarmes.

The United States Government called to active duty the National Guard of Arizona, New Mexico, and Texas on May 9, and of the remaining States and the District of Columbia on June 18. This step was taken because the size of the peacetime regular establishment was so small that it precluded effective guard or even surveillance of a border line as extensive as the US-Mexican frontier. A total of 110,000 National Guardsmen were deployed on the border in 1916. The National Guard remained on the border until Pershing's expedition was withdrawn on February 5, 1917. Most of the guard units were then demobilized, with the exception of the cavalry.

A number of valuable observations about the Mexican guerrillas must not escape our attention. The first one concerns the overall contribution of guerrillas to Maxmilian's defeat. Maximilian's regime collapsed because of a number of reasons, seemingly unrelated to the military activities of the guerrillas. These reasons were the regime's inherent weakness, the hostility of the Mexicans, its dependence on foreign troops, and the pressure exerted against it by the United States. The guerrillas, however, provided the instrument through which political authority of the Juarez government, though diminished, could manifest itself during the days of the French and Imperial Supremacy. In this manner a continuation of legitimacy was provided, and when the U.S. government was ready to intervene politically it did not have to operate in a military and political vacuum. The situation would have been entirely different if by 1865 Juarez and his government had left Mexico and the guerrillas loyal to them had ceased operations. Then the U.S. Government would have been confronted with the following dilemma: either accept Maximilian's regime or undertake a military expedition to overthrow Maximilian by force. If this was to take place, the possibility of war with France would have to be considered. Under this circumstance, it is not at all certain that the Mexicans would not have rallied under Maximilian and considered the Americans as the aggressors.

The next observation has to do with the inability of guerrillas to capitalize politically on their military successes during the period of Zapata-Villa cooperation. The guerrillas were parochial in outlook, fragmented under the leadership of mutually suspicious military leaders, who in turn were fragmented in loyalties to opportunistic politicians. Consequently, none of the guerrilla political objectives were realized. Those objectives were the reestablishment of representative government and institution of land reform. If a similar situation existed some place else today, it would present a good opportunity to a small, well-organized communist cadre to take over the guerrilla movement.

A number of observations can be made about Pershing's expedition in 1916. To this day, the real objectives of this undertaking are not clear. Was it supposed to be a simple show of force? A punitive expedition against the Mexican people? Or was it supposed to find Villa's bands and defeat them in detail? If the last supposition was really the objective, then we must conclude that the restrictions imposed on the military commander by the political leadership were too severe and made success next to impossible. To begin with, Pershing's force was not numerically strong enough to penetrate deep into Mexico and secure its daily stretching communications lines. Then, operations in a hostile environment were further complicated by the requirements to respect local authorities. With the benefit of hindsight, we can suggest that Pershing's force should have been followed by eight or ten infantry regiments and another three regiments of cavalry. Such forces became available through the mobilization of the National Guard — the much maligned force of American citizen-soldiers who have borne the burden of much fighting and have paid for the stinginess with which Congress has periodically treated the military establishment. Such a force would have been strong enough to induce the local authorities to cooperation and to control the lines of communications and the outlaying areas, thus cutting off Villa's sources of animals and food. Under such circumstances, Villa would have been forced to either fight or retreat in the Southern Mexican States where he had no following. Another, radical for those days, approach would have been to reduce Pershing's force to the equivalent of about two cavalry regiments. They should have included the Indian Scouts who were available at Ft. Huachuca. This force, without wheeled transport, could have left the frontier behind, ignored Mexican sovereignty, disregarded communications, and lived off local resources through foraging. It is probable that it could have been successful in finding Villa or his principal bands and defeated him in an ambush or a raid.

Mention should be made of the fact that during the 1916 Mexican Expedition, for the first time in History, the American Army used airplanes in combat and motor vehicles in large numbers for the transportation of men and materiel.

In general, the Americans gained considerable experience by both observation and involvement in the Mexican guerrilla operations. However, this experience was not further developed in the subsequent years. The U.S. military establishment, like most other military establishments, was influenced by the experience of positional warfare of World War I. Therefore, the study of guerrilla and counterguerrilla operations as a method of warfare was neglected.

5. The Boers

The Boers are the descendants of the Dutch colonists who established the first white settlements in South Africa. British immigration followed several years later, but by 1835, it was sufficiently strong to have the British firmly established in the

Cape Colony. The Boer's general dislike of the British, and particularly the British law abolishing slavery, caused a mass migration of Boer families inland. This migration became known as the "Great Trek" and resulted in the establishment of the two independent Boer Republics, the Transvaal Republic in 1852 and the Orange Free State in 1854.

Wars with native tribes and financial bankruptcy resulted in the annexation of the Transvaal Republic by the British in 1877. However, in 1881 an insurrection took place in Transvaal, which became known as the First Boer War. The British Government, controlled by Gladstone's Liberal Party, agreed to restore the Transvaal's independence, but retained control of the Republic's foreign affairs.

Things remained quiet for a few years until the discovery of gold in the Transvaal in 1886. The gold strikes brought a mass immigration of British and other foreigners (*uitlanders,* in the Boer language) into Transvaal. This immigration threatened the social and economic order of the Boers who were mainly agricultural and pastoral people, deeply religious and freedom loving in their own way, although they denied to the black natives this same freedom they were so willing to fight for.

Friction developed between Boers and British and mounted every day. Numerous provocations took place, instigated by both sides. The most notorious such provocation was a rather childish raid attempted under the leadership of Cecil Rhodes' friend, Dr. Leander S. Jameson in 1896. Jameson, with a party of would-be empire builders, crossed into Transvaal to attempt a rising in Johannesburg, but was defeated by Boer forces under Piet Cronje.

The president of the Transvaal Republic was Paul Kruger, a man of extreme views. He arranged a formal military alliance with Martinus Steyn, president of the Orange Free State and then sent an ultimatum to the British, knowing that the terms of the ultimatum were totally unacceptable. The war, thus, commenced.

The Boer strategic plan was fairly simple. It called for a simultaneous invasion of the Cape Colony by separate Boer forces and an insurrection by the Boers still residing in the Cape.

Before we proceed, let us examine the composition of the Boer Army, which was unique in many respects. The Boer military system resembled the Swiss militia system to the extent that it was based on the wartime mobilization of all male citizens. Every Boer was expected to be transformed overnight into a soldier. For this purpose, he possessed all the necessities of soldiering from civilian life. These consisted of rifle, horse, and training provided through years of semimilitary existence as a farmer or rancher in a land full of hostile natives and wild animals. No uniforms or other auxiliary equipment were necessary although on several occasions the Boer was accompanied in the field by native servants, his family, and wagons loaded with food and provisions.

Military organization was centered around the district commandos. Each ward, which was the lowest subdivision of civil administration, mobilized a commando. Thus, the commandos varied in strength from a handful to several hundred men, depending on the population density of the ward and the success of mobilization. This system violated all principles of military organization, but it provided an unparalleled flexibility of great advantage in guerrilla-type operations. If the district commando yielded too numerous a force, it was subdivided into smaller units placed under the command of corporals.

The corporals and all other officers, i.e., a commander and a so-called field cornet for each commando, were elected by the members of the unit. Election of officers resembled a political election. Personal friendships and family ties weighed more than considerations of the candidate's military abilities. However, this was not too important anyway, because discipline was rather loose since each Boer, through conviction and religious belief, considered himself as able a military leader as any man. So, the Boer performed the necessary routines of camp life not by direction, but through his own free will. Consequently, control of such troops in battle became an extremely complex task. Each man attacked when he thought it was time to attack, and he retreated when he thought it was time for him to retreat. It is a wonder that under such circumstances the Boer Army had any successes at all. But let us not forget that in spite of all the above shortcomings, the Boer had certain undisputed military qualities. He was an expert rifleman and horseman. He probably learned the use of firearms in his early teens and was taught horsemanship as soon as he was old enough to sit on a horse. His equipment was of high quality. His rifles, mostly Mausers, were far better than the British Enfelds and his horses had been bred for endurance. Then, the Boer being familiar with the land and used to living outdoors, had all the qualifications of an expert scout. On top of all this was his conviction of the divine right of his cause and his love of freedom, which spurred him into great efforts and personal sacrifices.

In addition to the commandos, there were the artillery units and the police. The governments of the Boer Republics, recognizing the fact that the above described military system was not suitable to a technical arm such as the artillery, prudently organized an artillery arm along conventional lines with the assistance of French and German officers. The Boer artillery was of high quality and of substantial quantity in the early stages of the war. The majority of the field pieces were German Krupps and French Canets. The police forces of the two Republics participated in the military operations as standard military formations.

During the first few weeks of hostilities, Boer forces crossed into the Cape territory, overwhelmed initial British resistance and besieged the garrisons of Kimberley, Mafeking and Ladysmith. In spite of their successes in field operations, the Boers were not able to speedily subdue the besieged garrisons.

The British forces were under the supreme command of Sir Redvers Buller. He had a force of about 50,000 assembled. This force was very weak in cavalry, a fact which placed it at a decisive disadvantage to the Boers, who were completely mounted. Buller sent a small holding force under Generals J. D. P. French and Sir William Gatacre to the West Cape with the mission to repulse any invasions from that direction. Another part of his force of about 13,000 under Lord Methuen advanced to relieve Kimberley and Mafeking. The main British force of 18,000, under Buller himself, advanced towards Ladysmith.

All three British counterstrokes failed. Gatacre was stopped at Stromberg. Methuen met disaster at Magersfontein. And

Buller was defeated at Colenso by Boer forces under Louis Botha. Parenthetically, we should mention that Botha, prior to the Colenso battle, had left the siege lines of Ladysmith and conducted a raid on the British rail lines. During this raid he intercepted a train bringing up replacements. In the train several British correspondents, including one young man named Winston Churchill, who was taken prisoner.[20] All three British disasters took place during the week of December 10, 1899; this week became known as the "black week" to the British.

The London government reacted to the defeats of black week by sending substantial reinforcements to the Cape and assigning Lord Roberts to command all South African forces, with Kitchener as his chief of staff.

The initial military failures of the British had taught them several lessons. Roberts, taking advantage of these lessons, reinforced his cavalry and utilized ox carts and wagons to transport his supplies, thus freeing his army from dependence on the railroads. In February 1900 Roberts moved to flank the Boer forces at Magersfontein and open the road for the relief of Ladysmith. The Boers retreated, but were cut off at Paaderberg and 4,000 of them under General Cronje surrendered. This defeat demoralized the Boers and their forces began a general withdrawal from the Cape Colony. Roberts' forces continued their advance towards Johannesburg and Pretoria. After their capture, Roberts proclaimed the annexation of Transvaal and the Orange Free State to the British Crown.

The Boer forces were not ready to give up the struggle yet, however. Botha's commandos concentrated in Northeast Transvaal to cover the withdrawal of Kruger into Portuguese territory, from where he departed for Europe. This task having been accomplished, the Boer commandos reversed direction of march, infiltrated through the British lines, and embarked into a full-scale guerrilla war. In the meantime, the British had begun a partial demobilization and Roberts had returned to London, leaving Kitchener in command.

This guerrilla war lasted for almost two years, and it turned out to be far more costly to the British in terms of casualties and expeditures of the treasury than the operation had been until the fall of Johannesburg and Pretoria. The Boers, under

Botha, Christian DeWet, Jan Smuts, and others, were in virtual control of the countryside and limited British occupation to the urban centers and a precarious hold on some of the communications lines.

Kitchener reacted with energy and boldness. He pursued the Boers, instead of tying his forces down into purely static defensive missions. In order to match the mobility of the Boers in such operations, he mounted as much of his infantry as possible. And in order to match the Boers cunning and expert knowledge of the country, he enlisted black native troops. This measure antagonized the Boers and increased their bitterness towards the British, but it was very effective. Finally, Kitchener attempted the concentration of as many of the Boers and Boer families as possible in camps. For this the British were criticized severely in the international press because sanitary conditions in the camps were primitive and disease took a heavy toll of the inmates. In fact, the Boers suffered about 80% of their total casualties through deaths in the concentration camps and only 20% in action. The concentration policy was initiated in the hope that by evacuating from the rural countryside civilians friendly to the guerrillas, the commandos would lose the indispensable-for-such-operation services of the noncombatants. In practical terms, this was a feasible undertaking in South Africa where the Boers actually constituted only a minority of the inhabitants.

The Boers were finally persuaded to lay down their arms. "Persuaded" is the correct word here because in May 1902, when the Vereeniging Agreement which ended the war was signed, the Boer forces had not been completely defeated. They still possessed substantial capabilities of continuing resistance although they had no realistic hopes of completely defeating the British and reoccupying their land. In essence, the guerrilla war in South Africa had not been decisive at all, and a military stalemate had been reached. A political solution was, therefore, needed in order to end the war.

The agreement reached made substantial concessions to the Boers. There was going to be no war tax, no franchise for the natives, Dutch would be allowed as a second official language, and the Boers were permitted to retain their personal weapons.

In exchange, the Boers had to acknowledge the English King and his heirs as their sovereign. The most important condition of the agreement was the one postponing the decision on native franchise. This gave the opportunity to the descendants of the Boers, half a century later, to disassociate themselves from the British Crown and assume absolute control, not only of the former Republics, but also of the Cape, Natal, and the former German Colony of Southwest Africa as well. Had the British had the fortitude to insist on conditions for native franchise, this could not have happened.

During World War I, DeWet and some other of the Boer leaders took up arms against the British again. Botha was then Prime Minister of the Dominion and he appointed Smuts as field commander of the forces sent against them. This was distasteful to Smuts, but he concluded that campaign successfully. Then he turned against the Germans in East Africa where General Paul Emil von Lettow-Vorbeck with a small force of 3,000 Germans and 12,000 native askaris was giving the Allies a fit.

In 1916 Smuts cleared a substantial area of German East Africa, but was unable to completely neutralize von Lettow-Vorbeck, who retreated in the interior with most of his army intact. Lettow-Vorbeck, realizing that the war would not be decided in Africa, limited his activities to fighting rear guard actions and occasional raids into Portuguese East Africa and Northern Rhodesia. He was able in this manner to force the Allies to retain considerable forces in Africa which could have been used in other theaters. Finally, on November 14, 1918, three days after the Armistice on the Western Front, he surrendered with about 150 German officers and 3,500 native troops and porters.

The fact that von Lettow-Vorbeck managed to sustain his army in continuous warfare for over four years without any kind of support from outside sources illustrates how much a determined and resourceful guerrilla commander can accomplish. It must be mentioned here that the first attempt to resupply guerrillas by air was made during World War I by the Germans who on one occasion sent airships to East Africa, but the airships returned without making contact with the German forces there.

From the purely military point of view, the Boer War was inconclusive. When the Vereeniging Agreement was signed, neither the British nor the Boer forces had suffered defeat to the point where they were unable to continue military operations. Thus, we find the first case among the conflicts which we are reviewing where guerrilla warfare produces a military stalemate. The stalemate induced both parties of the conflict to reach an agreement. In this case, the agreement was more advantageous in the long run to the Boers than to the British.

In terms of effectiveness of the guerrilla forces, one can hardly find anything unfavorable to say about the conduct of operations by the Boers. Particularly after the middle of 1900, the Boer forces displayed an unequal expertise in this type of warfare. It is reasonable then to ask why did they agree to lay down their arms under such circumstances. The answer is simple. The proposed terms of settlement were attractive. After all, in exchange for the rather abstract allegiance to the British Crown they were offered the opportunity to resume their former pastoral or commercial enterprises.

From the point of view of the British, this turned out to be a very costly venture. A face-saving political settlement was, therefore, highly desirable. The British military commanders at first were totally unsuited by disposition and background for warfare of this type. This fact, combined with the inadequacy of military resources available in the Cape Colony, was responsible for the initial British military defeats. However, all this was changed when reinforcements from England and India began to arrive and Kitchener was elevated to overall command. Kitchener had many disagreeable personal traits, but he was without a doubt an outstanding military leader. He had the ability to correctly assess a military situation. In addition, he possessed the prestige and conviction to act in accordance with his best judgement, disregarding convention and political expediencies. He was, therefore, responsible for the fact that the British forces were able to achieve a military stalemate against the Boer guerrillas. Less resourceful commanders would have been forced to occupation of urban centers and communications lines, leaving the countryside to guerrilla control. But Kitchener was able to meet the Boers on their own ground. He achieved this principally by increasing the mobility of his own forces and by employing the natives who could match the Boers' cunning and knowledge of the country. It is interesting to speculate how different World War I might have been if Kitchener had lived through it.

6.   Lawrence and the Arab Revolt

The guerrilla warfare waged by the Arabs during World War I against the Turks has been irrevocably associated with the name of T. E. Lawrence and his book "Seven Pillars of Wisdom".

Lawrence, a scholar who had travelled through Arabia prior to the war and who spoke Arabic fluently, was serving in the office of the British High Commissioner in Cairo. The idea of Arab revolt was not his, nor does he claim it as his in the "Seven Pillars of Wisdom". The idea of revolt had already matured in the minds of some of the Arab chieftains and Lawrence's superiors in Cairo, knowing about it, sought to exploit it in the war against Turkey and Germany.

Before we proceed with the story of the Arab revolt, we must say a few words about the Arabs. Lawrence defines the Arabs as the people who lived from Aleppo East to the Persian Gulf and South to the tip of the Arabia Peninsula, and who spoke Arabic. By this definition he obviously attempts to emphasize, through omission, the absence of racial integrity and national consciousness. This definition was probably accurate enough in World War I, prior to the era of pan-Arab Nationalism.

The Arabs were subjects of the Ottoman Empire. As such, they were subordinate to the Turks. However, their alleged descent from the Prophet placed them in a position of privilege and their leaders enjoyed a kind limited autonomy and independence from the central government, not uncommon in feudal states. The Ottoman Empire was such a feudal state prior to World War I[21] when the Yeni Turan (Young Turk) movement attempted to change all this and transform the Empire into a modern state after dethroning the reactionary Sultan Abdul Hamid. This attempt of modernization, however, can best be described as "too little and too late". One of the major difficulties confronting the reformers was the lack of ethnic homogeneity among the Empire's subjects. The Young Turks, recognizing this fact, attempted to coerce the non-Turkish elements into accepting a Turkish national consciousness. This they were unable to do successfully. Instead, they managed to antagonize the other ethnic elements, including the Arabs, and thus hastened the dissolution of the Empire.

Turkey entered World War I as an ally of Germany. The Turkish Army had suffered, only two years before, decisive defeats in the Balkan Wars; therefore, it was anything but a formidable force. However, the Anglo-French capabilities for offensive operations against the Turks in Palestine and Mesopotamia were also very limited because of the magnitude of effort demanded on the Western Front and because of the imprudent conduct of the Dardanelles campaign.

The advocates of peripheral warfare in the Allied camp were able to convince the High Command that it was feasible to maintain active fronts in Palestine and Mesopotamia with limited allied forces, if the Arabs were persuaded to revolt. This plan had merits. The Turkish front in Palestine would be located 400 miles deep into the Arab land. This land was sparsely populated; few towns existed and between them roamed bands of nomads. Local food production was hardly sufficient to support the local inhabitants; supplies for the Turkish troops had to be brought on the vulnerable Hejaz railway which had only two spurs of line extending South of Jerusalem, one terminating at Beersheba and one just north of Gaza.

At this point Lawrence entered the course of events. He was sent on an underground mission to establish contact with the Arab leaders. On his return he gave a favorable report on the basis of which further plans were formulated and Lawrence went again to Arabia to act as advisor to the Arabs. In this capacity, Lawrence had to cope with both political and military problems.

The political problems were focused on the necessity to per-
suade the numerous Arab tribes or tribal groups to actively
participate in military operations against the Turks. Although
there were always individual tribesmen willing to take part in
raids, hoping to share in the plunder of the enemy camp that
usually followed, the more politically conscious tribal chiefs
were willing to support the British cause only after assurances
of postwar political independence or satisfaction of dynastic
ambitions. Lawrence apparently made such promises in good
faith, but these promises were not fulfilled later. This demonstration of bad faith is responsible for the anti-British and anti-
French attitude which has prevailed in Arab political thinking
ever since. Of course, the Jewish immigration into Palestine
and the eventual creation of the State of Israel have compounded the problem.

On the military side, Lawrence had to overcome such difficulties as leading undisciplined troops to combat, lack of supplies, and problems of coordinating the efforts of his Arab
bands with each other and with the regular forces of General
Allenby and the French Commissioner Colonel Bremond. The
supply difficulties are, of course, omnipresent in guerrilla warfare. Lawrence was particularly irritated with his shortage of
machine guns and complete lack of mountain artillery, which
he considered necessary for his attacks on trains. The British
had no mountain guns except for the 10-pounders of the Indian
Army. This piece was not satisfactory. In contrast, Bremond
had several excellent Schneider-Danglee guns which he kept at
Suez and refused to employ with the guerrillas.[22] The use of
land mines was eventually substituted for artillery for the
attacks on trains. Also several detachments of machine gunners
from the Indian Army were employed with the Arabs in the
later stages of the conflict.

In spite of all the above difficulties, Lawrence waged guerrilla warfare successfully against the Turks. In 1917, there
were more Turks fighting Arabs than British on the Palestine
Front; so, it can be said with certainty that the guerrilla effort
contributed greatly to the eventual Turkish collapse. The majority of the guerrilla operations were directed against the rail
lines. Occasionally, garrisoned towns and even dug-in positions

and strong points of the Turkish line were attacked (see Figure 2).

The military successes of the Arab guerrillas could have been limited, if the Turks had employed more aggressive methods. Usually, a Turkish garrison would stay entrenched in its camp in full view of the guerrillas hanging around it in the surrounding hills. After the guerrilla attack was in progress, the Turkish troops would attempt to break it up through the use of superior firepower. Occasionally, particularly when calvary was available, attempts to flank or pursue and disperse the bands were made, either before or after the guerrilla attack developed. However, this was not done often enough. The reason, perhaps, was not the lack of aggressive spirit by the Turkish commanders, but the experiences on the Western Front which had influenced tactical thinking in favor of statically defending prepared positions with massive firepower.

Lawrence was unique among the world's guerrilla leaders, in that he possessed literary talents and had the opportunity to record his thoughts and experiences in the "Seven Pillars of Wisdom". This book constitutes, in our opinion, his greatest contributions to the science of war, even greater than his field operations. In it he attempts to explain war on a philosophical, if not moral basis. The book is highly recommended reading for the student of guerrilla warfare, particularly his discussion on the topics of elements of revolt, tactical deductions, and motives of the insurgents. We must make it clear, however, that we do not subscribe one hundred percent to certain of his theses. For instance, his discussion on ἐπιστήμη, δόξα and νόησις,[23] with its statements and conclusions about the value of the commander's intuition, we find incorrect.

In any case, Lawrence had a remarkable, although extremely complex personality, and he has definitely left his mark on History. Unfortunately, too many people have attempted to copy him unsuccessfully. In World War II the British sent too many would-be guerrilla leaders in the Balkans to operate against the Germans. These people obviously attempted to draw heavily from Lawrence's teachings and duplicate his methods, not recognizing the fact that they were operating under entirely different conditions. Most of them turned out to be miserable failures as guerrilla leaders. But this story belongs to another chapter which will be discussed later.

In general, it can be said that guerrilla warfare in Arabia during World War I was prudently waged by the Allies. The guerrilla potential of the Arabs was exploited almost to its fullest. The materiel support, however, given to the guerrillas by the Allied High Command was considerably less than what it could have been. The immediate results of this guerrilla effort were very significant. The threat to the Suez Canal was removed. The Arab guerrillas absorbed the greatest portion of the Turkish forces, which otherwise could have been used against the Allies in the Balkans and Caucasus. Further, the guerrilla operations necessitated an infusion of German troops and materiel to strengthen the wavering Turks. If one makes a comparison of the human and materiel resources expended on the Western Front against those in the Arab peninsula, he has to conclude that the results were very much out of proportion in favor of guerrilla warfare.

III

Historical Background — World War II

1. The Chinese Communists

THE GUERRILLA activities of the Chinese communists may have influenced the course of History more than the activities of any similar group of combatants. It is unfortunate that there is so very little documentation by reliable sources of the events which took place in China between 1920 and 1937. It appears to us that a precise and objective study of this period of Chinese History could furnish Westerners a basis for the objective analysis of events which have followed since, and of the many more which will undoubtedly take place in the near future.

The pro-Russian, if not pro-Communist, orientation of China dates from the first years of the Chinese Republic under Sun Yat-Sen. The Republic which followed the Manchu Empire constituted at best a very limited government. Most of China was under the control of regional military chiefs whose rule and attitude towards the unfortunate peasantry was anything but benevolent. The western powers and Japan were constantly taking advantage of this instability and weakness of the Chinese government in order to further their colonial ambitions on China's soil. For these reasons Sun Yat-Sen opposed China's entry into World War I, knowing that whatever its outcome China could not benefit. Therefore, it is no wonder that after

61

the Versailles Treaty relations between Sun Yat-Sen's government and the government of Soviet Russia, the then outcast
of Europe, took a decisive turn for the better.

During this period of Sino-Russian cooperation, the infant
Chinese communist party was instructed to join the Kuo-Min-
Tang. The Kuo-Min-Tang leaders accepted the Chinese communists with the thought that the communists were being
integrated into the Kuo-Min-Tang. The communist objective,
however, was not the same. Their purpose was to take advantage
of this apparent unification in order to infiltrate the Kuo-Min-
Tang organization and utilize the already established Kuo-
Min-Tang party apparatus to pursue their own aims. This they
were able to accomplish successfully.

In the meantime, Chiang Kai-Shek, the superintendant of
Whampoa Military Academy, was emerging as the strong man
among the Kuo-Min-Tang ranks. Shortly after Sun Yat-Sen's
death, he took over control of the central Chinese government.
Probably, in order to achieve this, Chiang made several under-
the-table deals with certain of the provincial warlords. It is
possible that during the years of communist cooperation,
Chiang visited Soviet Russia. It is certain that one of his sons
studied in Moscow. In any case, a number of Russians arrived
in China in order to advise the Chinese Government and/or
the Chinese communists; the most prominent among them was
a man named Michael Borodin, who had served in a similar
capacity in Mustafa Kemal's headquarters during Kemal's war
against the Greeks.

The break between the Kuo-Min-Tang and the communists
took place in 1927 with the Canton uprising. The communist
organization in Canton attempted to establish a Soviet government in that city. Chiang, who was committed to establishing
a strong central Chinese government, could not tolerate this;
therefore, he sent his troops against the communists. This event
is significant in view of the ideological estrangement which has
taken place between the Russian and Chinese communist parties in recent years. It has been reported that the Canton uprising was instigated under orders from Zinoviev in Moscow.
Zinoviev, later purged by Stalin, was a leader of the left wing
within the Russian communist party which advocated the im-

possibility of coexistence with capitalism and the necessity of "permanent revolution". It appears that some of the present Chinese communist leadership has retained the influence exerted on them by their first Russian advisors such as Zinoviev.

With Chiang determined to exterminate all Chinese communists, the Chinese communist High Command had no choice but to organize an army of its own. Chu Teh, an ex-warlord, was put in command, with Mao Tse-Tung as political commissar. Mao Tse-Tung was a man with no formal military schooling. Yet, he appears to be gifted with the rare quality of understanding military situations without the benefit of formal military schooling. Mao realized that, for the time being at least, the communists were not capable of matching Chiang's military strength. He proposed, therefore, that the Red Chinese Army be organized on guerrilla lines and that it should be prepared to apply guerrilla tactics. His opinion prevailed, although other prominent communists such as Li Li-San opposed it. It is reported that during this early period of the Red Chinese Army, Mao developed the tactical principles of operation of Chinese partisan warfare, the summation of which were published as his famous four slogans. Those were:

1. When the enemy advances, we retreat!
2. When the enemy halts and encamps, we trouble them!
3. When the enemy seeks to avoid battle, we attack!
4. When the enemy retreats, we pursue!

These four slogans do not constitute any new principles of guerrilla warfare "discovered" by Mao. In fact, they have been applied for centuries. However, Mao, with typical communist ability to coin slogans, expressed them so completely and in such concise form that they can be understood and applied by the lowest echelons of guerrilla leadership.

It cannot be said that all communist military units were organized as guerrillas. In Hunan and some other areas, concentration of communist forces was sufficient to organize them into standard formations. With one of those formations Li Li-San attempted to storm the town of Changsha. He was repulsed with heavy casualties and after this failure his influence waned and he was eventually sent to Moscow, leaving Mao as the undisputed political and military leader of the Chinese communists.

Now Chiang Kai-Shek decided that he had better do some serious campaigning in order to rid himself of the communists. Between 1930 and 1931, he conducted three major campaigns which, however, brought very limited results. The communists forces would allow the advancing enemy armies to penetrate deep into their territory and then hit them in the flanks. The Kuo-Min-Tang commanders, with no exceptions, were unable to sustain any of their drives and force the communists to give battle under favorable for the Kuo-Min-Tang forces conditions. Then in 1932, the Japanese invasion of Manchuria took place which forced Chiang to divert his attention to the foreign enemy. This gave the communists the opportunity to regroup their forces and reestablish themselves as the government in Hunan, Fukien and adjoining territories.

In April 1933, Chiang launched his fourth campaign against the communists, but again he met with no success, and he called this operation off. In October of the same year, he launched his fifth campaign, but this time he managed such concentration of forces that the Red Army was facing possible extermination. In addition, his army had the benefit of advice from a German military mission under the former Chief of the Reichswehr, General von Seecht, who was without doubt one of the outstanding military organizers of all times.

The Red Chinese High Command now decided to extricate all its forces from South China and transfer them to Northern Shensi, near the Mongolian border, where the conditions were favorable for establishing a base for future operations. This operation, known as the "Long March" has been heralded throughout the communist world as an epic of guerrilla warfare. In all fairness, it has to be acknowledged as an outstanding operation, unique in the History of warfare and unprecedented since Xenofon's descent to the sea in the 5th Century B.C.

The red forces had to cover a distance of almost 6,000 miles over enemy territory, pursued by the much superior forces of their enemy. True, the Kuo-Min-Tang control over part of the territory in question was very loose and the momentum of the pursuing force at times seemed to come to a standstill. Yet, the

Kuo-Min-Tang forces were much superior and, most important, possessed an air force which, no matter how inefficient, offered them the great advantage of aerial surveillance. In spite of this, the communist forces never presented themselves as a target within range of the enemy artillery. They melted away in the countryside, constantly moving, frequently changing direction of march, assembling only in order to strike in concentration against enemy points obstructing their retreat. Needless to state, they lived off the land, requisitioning or bartering provisions from the local inhabitants. Prudently, they avoided antagonizing the local population on whose good will and toleration they depended for the supply of food, intelligence about enemy moves, etc. Of the approximately 80,000 men and women who started the march, less than half made it to the final destination. Among those who arrived, only a fraction were among the initial force, the rest were among those who had been recruited later during the course of the march. All their heavy equipment and wheeled transport was also lost. But in the long run, those losses were unimportant. The important point was that a nucleus of the Red Army was salvaged, and this army, with assistance from Soviet Russia, was later able to reappear on the political scene and effectively challenge Chiang Kai-Shek's rule of China.

The United States became actively involved in Chinese matters with Japan's invasion of the Chinese mainland. The U.S. Government was alarmed at the prospects of Japanese aggression and so were the private American commercial interests who were threatened with financial losses because 'of the Japanese occupation. They both came to the assistance of Chiang's government. Generally speaking, Chiang enjoyed, between 1937 and 1943, uiniversal prestige in America and the Chinese communists were ignored or discounted by all except the outright communists and communist sympathizers. Certain private American citizens found employment in Chiang's service. The most famous of which was the ex-Air Corps officer Claire Chennault, who in true condottiere fashion commanded an air unit composed entirely of American expartriates in Chiang's Army.

After Pearl Harbor the complexion of the Chinese problem radically changed. Chiang's Army, in spite of its relative impotence, was holding down several Japanese divisions. In addition, the land mass of China constituted the only place from where bomber aircraft could be eventually based within striking distance of the Japanese home Islands. The thought was thus entertained in the Allied camp that Chiang should be assisted and sustained in the war at all costs. And Chiang, capitalizing on this advantage, bargained with typical oriental shrewdness and received from the Americans substantial amounts of war material and financial assistance. At least ten Chinese divisions were completely equipped with U.S. lend-lease material. These divisions had an organic strength of about 12,000 men with infantry support weapons, twelve pack artillery pieces, and 1,000 animals each; this composition was slightly weaker than the composition of the light divisions which were formed in the U.S. Army. In addition, several corps artillery and support units were equipped with American material. The difficulties in delivering all this equipment to the China Theater were tremendous since most of it had to be airlifted over the Hump.[1]

The performance of the Chinese Army, however, was below the expectations of the Americans. This was caused primarily by the reluctance of Chinese commanders to engage the enemy. Stilwell, the senior U.S. officer in China, attributed this to the fact that the prestige of each Chinese commander was directly proportional to the size and strength of his unit. If his unit was engaged in combat and suffered casualties, the commander suffered a proportional loss of prestige; therefore, the prudent thing to do was to avoid combat.[2] In one case, Stilwell complained that twelve Chinese divisions were reluctant to engage one weakened Japanese division (the 56th). Generally, the cooperation of Chinese and American headquarters left a lot to be desired. Stilwell, also known as "Vinegar Joe", was not a man with a personality suited for such a sensitive job. Neither did the command structure help the situation any. Stilwell held the positions of commander of U.S. forces in the China-Burma-India Theater, combined Chief of Staff for the same theater, Corps commander under Mountbaten, and Chief of Staff to Chiang. Some of these positions he held simultaneously. It is peculiar, to say the least, that he was Chief of Staff to

Chiang when Chiang obviously had no confidence in him. The presence of Mme Chiang in the Chinese headquarters and her intervention in command functions is also inexplicable.[3] It is probable that Chiang was reserving his forces for possible future use against the communists. If this thought was in the back of his mind, he was partially justified because the Chinese communists were doing the same thing. In a message to President Roosevelt on 17 March 1944, Chiang complained that his troops in Sinkiang were attacked by communist forces supported by aircraft which had red stars painted on the fuselages and which came from the direction of Outer Mongolia.[4] Probably the civil war was continuing in China in the face of the Japanese invasion and in spite of pledges to the contrary by both sides. In fact, sufficient evidence exists today to ascertain that the Chinese communists continued a limited trade with the Japanese throughout the war and that many informal accommodations and local truces had been agreed between Japanese commanders on one side and Chinese Communist or Nationalist area commanders on the other.

We also have no evidence of any substantial guerrilla activity taking place behind the Japanese lines by forces loyal to Chiang, though some limited communist guerrilla activity behind the Japanese lines seems to have taken place.[5]

The American confidence in Chiang began to wane. After the Cairo Conference, President Roosevelt indicated that if the Chiang government collapsed, the Allies should search for another man or group of men to carry on. He did not indicate who the others might be. The alternatives could be the communists or some of the dissident warlords like Marshal Li Chi-Shen.[6] John P. Davis, Jr., attached to Stilwell's headquarters as political advisor, proposed and actively pursued a policy of establishing liaison with the communists. Several Americans in positions of responsibility attempted to support the communists or undermine Chiang, while many others, including Chennault, insisted that China's salvation could only be accomplished through Chiang Kai-Shek. Official U.S. policy vacillated between the two points of view until the collapse of Chiang's forces on the mainland in 1948.

In essence, the U.S. was facing for the first time, the dilemma which was to plague her repeatedly in the 50's and 60's. The question of what to do in the case where the anti-communist forces in a given country are led by a government which is oppressive, undemocratic, corrupt, or inefficient? Should such a government be supported, or should the U.S. deny assistance to this government and let the communists take over the country in question? This precisely has been the issue in recent years in Portugal, Spain, Turkey, Laos, South Vietnam, and many other places, including several in the Western Hemisphere.

The military collapse of the Kuo-Min-Tang regime was caused by a multitude of factors, but we must not overlook the fact that when the Russian army invaded Manchuria in August 1944 it captured over 300,000 Japanese troops and subsequently turned their equipment over to Mao Tse-Tung's army. This gave the Chinese communists the material means to challenge Chiang on an equal basis. The Red Chinese Army of 1948 was no longer an army of guerrillas, but a conventional force. It might be of interest to note that part of this equipment which was turned over to the Chinese by the Russians was used against the South Korean and U.S. forces in 1950, and later against the French in Indochina in 1954.

It is clear in this review of events in China that guerrilla activities can be divided into two periods. The first period extends through 1941, when the United States entered the War. The second covers the time between late 1941 and the collapse of the Nationalist regime on the mainland. During the second period, guerrilla activities were insignificant in relation to the overall military situation. During the first period, guerrilla activities are dominated by the "Long March" to Shensi.

The prime reason for the success of the communist guerrillas during this period was the relative impotency of their adversaries. This fact, however, does not diminish the credit due the Chinese Communist High Command for having decided to engage in guerrilla operations. If they had attempted to hold on in some urban centers in South or Central China, their forces probably would have been annihilated by the forces of Chiang. By engaging in guerrilla warfare and retreating to the remote plains of Shensi, they were able to salvage a nucleus of a military force which remained available for reemployment later. This force, when opportunity presented, was transformed into a conventional army which was able to challenge the Chinese Nationalist forces successfully.

2. The Battle of Suomussalmi

Suomussalmi is a small village in North Central Finland, about 30 miles West of the Russo-Finnish frontier. The battle that bears its name was fought during the 1939 Russo-Finnish War between an overwhelming Soviet force and small Finnish units. It is significant because in this battle the Finns employed guerrilla tactics to infiltrate the Soviet lines and totally defeat the invaders. An analysis of this battle, however, discloses that in addition to the unquestionable skill of the Finns in this type of warfare, the Russian defeat is also attributable to the ineptitude and indecision of the Soviet field commanders.

The Soviet Union in 1939, after the conclusion of the Russo-German treaty, was following an extremely expansionist policy. By late 1939 it had absorbed Eastern Poland and the Baltic States. Assured of German nonintervention and the inability of the Anglo-French Allies to oppose its policies, it invaded Finland.

The Soviet military plans called for simultaneous invasion of Finland by strong forces through all available invasion routes. Apparently, the Soviet leaders also entertained the hope that the approach of the Soviet forces would result in an uprising among the Finnish workers. The uprising never took place.

The main Soviet effort was made against the Mannerheim Line, a fortified position along the Karelian Isthmus between Lake Ladoga and The Gulf of Finland. Two Soviet armies,[7] including 13 infantry divisions and five tank brigades took part in this attack. Immediately North of Lake Ladoga, another Soviet Army of nine divisions and one tank brigade operated as far north as Ilomantsi. The 9th Soviet Army with five divisions, including the 163rd and 44th which took part in the operation against Suomussalmi, was to force its way through

Central Finland to the Gulf of Bothnia. Another Soviet Army of three divisions attacked the Finnish Arctic port of Petsamo. Finally, amphibious forces were to land on the Southern Finnish ports of Turku, Hango, and near Helsinki. Thus, the Soviets were employing over 30 divisions and six brigades against the Finns, who could mobilize only about nine divisions. The Soviet divisions had a composition of three infantry and two artillery regiments. The tank brigades had two tank regiments each, with a nominal strength of 180 tanks.

The Southern third of Finland includes over one-half of the country's total population and almost all of its industry. Consequently, the bulk of the Finnish forces were mobilized in the South. The Finns were able to mobilize nine divisions, plus approximately 100,000 men in the Civic Guard.

An explanation of what the Civic Guard was becomes necessary. The term Civic Guard is an attempt to literally translate the Finnish term *Suojelus Kunta* which more accurately means "citizens' guards". The citizens' guards originated in the 1917-1918 period when the non-communist Finns, following the example of the other ethnic minorities in the disintegrating Tsarist Empire, formed a provisional government and declared their independence. In order to realize this independence, however, they first had to rid the country of the marauding bands of armed laborers from the factories, who called themselves the "Red Guards," and the garrisons of Russian troops who had fallen under the control of the Petrograd Soviet. The armed strength at the disposal of the Nationalist Finnish government was at first very limited. The Finns were exempt from Russian conscription; therefore, there were few Finns with military training. There were some, however, who had voluntarily served in the Russian Army. Among them, was Lieutenant General Baron Carl G. E. von Mannerhein, a Finno-Swede who had commanded a cavalry corps on the Polish Front. Mannerheim was appointed commander-in-chief and he created a national Finnish Army from scratch. He had about 1,200 Finns who had obtained some training with the Germans as volunteers in the Jägerbataillon Nr 27.[8] And he had the two and one-half million peasant Finns who, although they lacked formal military schooling, possessed fundamental military qualities. These peasants, as weapons became available, were organized into the Civic Guards. Their organization was regional. Their units were not standardized. Primarily they were interested in protecting their farms and villages from the Red Guards. Under Mannerheim's leadship, however, and with limited assistance from Sweden and Germany, they were able to defeat the Reds and establish the independent state of Finland. After that war, the Civic Guards were retained as a separate branch of the Finnish Armed Forces with its own commander. Their organization remained regional, but the composition of the units was standardized. Units of regimental strength were formed, but in Northern Finland regimental headquarters was usually over a hundred miles from company headquarters. It was not unusual to have platoons of Civic Guards in remote villages separated by many hundred square miles of forest from their nearest friendly unit. They were equipped with small arms, including automatic rifles and machineguns, but no mortars or other heavy weapons. Their mission was, in case of invasion, to operate in the flanks and rear of invading columns in order to harass and delay the enemy. This is exactly what they did, and in the Battle of Suomussalmi they were instrumental in literally cutting two Soviet divisions to shreds.

The area around Suomussalmi, like most of Finland, consists of dense forests interrupted by swamps and lakes which freeze in the winter. There are roads, but most of them are poor unsurfaced roads used for logging. Suomussalmi is a small village which straddles the center of Lake Kianta (see Figure 3). This is a long lake with three narrow fingers extending North, Northeast, and Southeast. However, the village was in the center of a road hub. There was a paved road running from the village ESE for 40 miles to the Russian frontier; this was called the Rattee Road. Another road came from the North, between the N and NE fingers of the Lake Kianta. Two additional roads extended from the village Westwards and connected with Oulu on the Gulf of Bothnia.

The Soviet plan required two divisions of the 9th Army to capture the Suomussalmi junction and from there to proceed to Oulu on the Gulf of Bothnia, thus cutting Finland in half.

The 163d Division advanced along the Northern road and the 44th along the Rattee Road.

On December 9, 1939, the 163d Soviet Division and the 305th Regiment of the 44th reached Suomussalmi, which had been evacuated and burnt by the Finns. At first, the Finnish forces in the area consisted of a battalion of frontier forces covering the Rattee Road and 60 Civic Guards covering the road from the North. Then the Soviet forces committed their first error. Instead of pursuing the Finns, they established themselves along the roads and began to dig in. The Soviet forces were not properly equipped for fighting on this type of terrain. Their transport was mechanized or horse-drawn. They had some sleighs and ski equipment, but they were unfamiliar with fighting in the forest. They remained on the roads and seldom sent out patrols. The few patrols they did send out never ventured deep into the forest. Finnish reports say that no Soviet patrol was ever seen more than four miles from the road. The Russians could not effectively patrol the forests because of their lack of skill with skis and because their small unit leaders lacked familiarity with the forests, initiative, and determination. This story was repeated constantly in the following days and this is one cause of the defeat of the Soviet forces.

Early in December of 1939, in spite of the relative Russian passivity, the situation could hardly have looked too encouraging to the Finnish High Command. Mannerheim, therefore, decided to reinforce the North Central sector with his only available major formation, 9th Division. All the other Finnish divisions had by then been committed to. battle, six on the Karelian Isthmus Front and two in the area immediately North of Lake Ladoga. The 9th Division, however, was mobilized in South Finland, and its transfer to the Suomussalmi sector had to be made by rail through Tampere and Oulu. The distance to be covered was over 500 miles. The division began to arrive on December 15th. Its arrival was by stages and was not complete until about the first of the year. In addition to the 9th Division, Civic Guard units from the region surrounding Suomussalmi were assembled and sent as reinforcements, but they amounted to the equivalent of only two weak battalions.

General Tuompo was the Finnish Commander of the Suomussalmi sector. He had established his headquarters near Ylinaljanka, 30 miles west of Lake Kianta. Most Finnish troops engaged at Suomussalmi were under the direct command of Colonel Siilasvou.

Tuompo decided not to wait for the arrival of all expected reinforcements. He sent a reduced battalion on the tenth to attack the Russian forces in the village before they could establish themselves defensively. Simultaneously, small ski patrols kept harassing the Russian forces on the roads. The harassment was effective. The Finns moved through the forest to positions within a few hundred yards from the road, preferably at night. Then, covered by the forest and darkness, they would throw automatic weapons fire on the exposed Russians. The Russians would react with small arms and artillery fire. But small arms fire at unseen targets was ineffective and artillery fire against targets in the forest also brought minimum results. The Russians would not venture into the forests to chase the troublesome Finns. On 13 December, the Soviet 305th Regiment, which had its advance elements into the village, withdrew. The 163rd Division also withdrew its advance elements further North along the road. Thus the junction of the two Soviet columns was lost.

Tuompo now decided to concentrate on the stronger of the enemy columns first. On the 15th he had nearly a regiment of the 9th Division. He sent that force against the 163d. Small Finnish units were able to infiltrate between the Russian strongpoints along the road to the road's east side. In this manner the Russians were attacked from both their East and the West flanks. On the 20th, the Finns were able to establish themselves on the road, thus cutting the 163d in two. For the next few days the Finns did not attempt any major attacks, but they continued their incessant harassment from the flanks. Russian casualties mounted. Ammunition and other supplies were being exhausted. Fuel for the vehicles was unavailable. The Soviet animals were dying from lack of nourishment. During the night of the 25/26 December the Finns launched their major attack on the 163d from six points along the road.

On the 27th the Soviet 9th Army gave permission to the 163d Division to retreat. At this point, the division commander made the prudent decision to leave the road and move his remaining forces on the frozen Lake. The remnants of the division moved northwards on the Lake. Since the width of the Lake was longer than the effective range of the Finnish small arms, this retreat was relatively successful. The Finns did not have the strength to leave the cover of the forest and attack the Soviet troops on the Lake surface. Neither did they have heavy artillery with which to break the surface ice. They did send three Bristol-Blenheim bombers, but those aircraft were chased away by Soviet fighters and did not reach the Lake. So, the 163d Division retreated beyond the frontier, but it left behind most of its heavy equipment in addition to suffering heavy casualties in personnel.

While the Soviet 163d Division was being destroyed piecemeal, the command of the Soviet 9th Army was unable to coordinate operations of its 44th Division and provide effective relief.

The 305th Soviet Regiment could have moved against the Finns in Suomussalmi to relieve the pressure on the 163d. This move, however, was not attempted until the 23d of December when the 163d was already in jeopardy. Two weak Finnish companies stopped the leading elements of the 305th outside the village and the 305th, instead of pressing the attack, stopped and began to dig in. All this time, the balance of the 44th Soviet Division, for some unknown reason, remained East of the frontier without making any attempts to join the battle. The commander of the 305th Regiment sent a radio message to his division reporting that he was stopped and being attacked from the sides. This message was intercepted by the Finns. In fact the Finns were managing to intercept most Russian messages. Since the Russians were not encoding their messages and since a large number of Finns understand Russian, the Finnish field commanders were being immediately informed about the condition of the Soviet forces by the Russians themselves.

The balance of the 44th Division did not cross the frontier to advance towards Suomussalmi until the 27th. Exactly the same day that the 9th Soviet Army was giving permission to its 163rd Division to retreat along the Northern Road, it was sending the 44th Division Westwards on the Rattee Road. The balance of the 44th consisted of the 146 and 25 Infantry Regiments, two artillery regiments, a unit of about 45 tanks, and various other smaller formations. This was still a stronger force than all of the forces available to General Tuompo on that day. But again the Soviet commanders displayed an inexplicable passivity. The 305th Regiment did not attack the two weak Finnish companies East of the village. The fresh Russian column advanced on the Rattee Road until its lead elements (146th Regiment) joined the Easternmost elements of the 305th. Then this column stopped and began to dig in right on the road. The 44th Soviet Division, including 305th Regiment, was spread like a giant serpent over 15 miles on the narrow road. It stayed in this position for the next three crucial days. During those three days the only coherent Finnish force in contact with the 44th Soviet Division were the two rifle companies east of Suomussalmi. The rest of the Finnish forces available in the area were preoccupied with the destruction of the 163d Division further North. A determined push by the 305th Regiment during the 28, 29, or 30th of December could have thrown completely off balance the Finnish forces in Central Finland and altered the outcome of that war.

Early on the 31st of December, Colonel Siilasvou began the transfer of those elements of the 9th Finnish Division engaged in the North Sector to the South. Again the Finns moved their infantry through the woods unseen and unobstructed by the enemy. This, of course, had the disadvantage that heavy equipment depending on vehicular transport had to be left behind. On New Years Day, January 1, 1940, Siilasvou had just enough forces south of Suomussalmi to do the following: Send one company to cut the Rattee Road on the frontier, send two platoons of Civic Guards to capture a bridge on the Rattee Road about nine miles West of the frontier, and attack the advance element of the Soviet Column (305th Regiment) with three companies from the West.

The next day, the Soviet commander of the 44th Division, Colonel Vinogradov, alarmed by what was happening, sent a battalion of the 25th Regiment to attack the Finnish company which had cut the road on the frontier. This attack failed. In the meantime, the balance of the Finnish 9th Division was arriving and assembling at points running parallel to and south of the Rattee Road. As each unit reached its assembly area, it was allowed to rest for a few hours, given a meal, and then moved on to attack the Russians on the road. The method of attack was the same. The Finns would move to the edge of the woods, set up firing positions and for a few minutes throw as large a volume of fire as possible on the Russians, then move parallel to the road a short distance away and repeat the same thing. When Russian resistance from the road appeared to be subsiding, the Finns would move onto the road to capture and destroy equipment, particularly rations, fodder, and fuel. It is true that the Russians, at times, fought hard; anyone will fight hard when his back is against a wall. But the Russian fighting was ineffective. For the first few hours Vinogradov tried to use his tanks to reinforce each point on the road which seemed to be under particularly heavy pressure. This maneuver required that the tanks move along the narrow pavement which was already crowded with other vehicles and equipment. They accomplished nothing and only created traffic jams. It is reported that the Finns at Suomussalmi had only four 37mm antitank guns. Since this is a light gun, easily handled by its crew in that type of terrain, it is reasonable to assume that all of the 44th Division's armor could have been destroyed if the Finns had had a few more of those guns.

January 4th was the day of hardest fighting. The Russians tried to resupply the division from the air. The drops missed the drop zones and were recovered by the Finns. This was, perhaps, the deciding factor which prompted the Army headquarters to send Vinogradov a radio signal at 5 p.m. allowing him to retreat. This signal, too, was intercepted by the Finns.

The 44th Soviet Division fared a lot worse than the 163d during its retreat. Between 4 and 9 January the Finns literally mopped up the Rattee Road and only small groups of Russians managed to reach the frontier. For all practical purposes the division did not retreat, but was destroyed in place. The reason was that it faced a much stronger Finnish force than the 163d. Whereas the 163d faced composite units of advance elements of the 9th Finnish Division and Civic Guards, the 44th faced the bulk of the 9th Finnish Division.

The Finns reported that they lost 900 men killed and 1,770 wounded in the Battle of Suomussalmi. The Russian losses were estimated at 27,000 men killed, wounded, and missing, 90 tanks, and all the artillery of two divisions. The estimate is probably accurate enough. Correspondents who visited the Rattee Road while the mopping up was still going on have reported that they counted over 80 artillery pieces on a stretch of ten miles.

Why did the Soviet troops perform so badly? The explanation accepted by most observers has been that the Russians were unprepared for fighting at subarctic latitudes in midwinter. This is only part of the reason. For purposes of analysis, a very significant fact in this story is the rank of the commander of the Soviet 44th Division, Colonel Vinogradov. The fact that the commander of a combat division was a colonel, two grades lower than what normally is authorized, may signify that a serious shortage of commanders existed within the Soviet forces two years after the Tuhhachevsky purge. The conduct of Soviet regimental and division commanders during the battle was marked by indecision and continuous referral to higher headquarters. This is very significant; it probably means that the psychological impact of the purges had reduced the Soviet commanders to dummies unable to think for themselves who had to have all decisions made for them by big daddy in Moscow. Since we are discussing the performance of the Soviet commanders, another observation is in order. The command structure was unsatisfactory. The Army headquarters in this case controlled five divisions extending over 200 miles in an area of poor communications. It would have been better for the Soviets if they had established under the 9th Army a corps headquarters to direct operations of the two divisions engaged at Suomussalmi.

The fact that the Soviets had serious deficiencies in equipment and training for warfare under the conditions encountered in Suomussalmi is also a probable reason for the defeat, but these obstacles could have been overcome by resourceful commanders. For instance, an awful lot has been said about the Russian motor vehicles jamming the roads. Yet, both Russian divisions had enough horses and sleighs that they could have been relatively free from dependence on motor vehicles if they had the prudence to move the sleighs off the pavement. It has also been said that the Russians suffered from the lack of skis. Yet, ski equipment was captured by the Finns during the last stages of the operation in large quantities; also publications (the equivalent of our Field Manuals), on the subject of technical and military use of skis. The Finns were convinced that these publications had been written by people who were familiar with skiing as a sport, but with no experience in the military utility of skiing. In practical terms, what the Russians needed for operations in Central Finland was specialized troops. By this we mean troops with special equipment and with specialized training for operations in the subarctic regions.

The analysis of the planning and operations of the Finns has to come to the conclusion that the Finnish performance was outstandingly good. In the first place, the Finnish High Command was able to make optimum use of its limited resources. Realizing the impossibility of matching the Soviet strength and defeating the Soviets in conventional warfare, it made the necessary planning to engage the invaders by unconventional means, thus taking advantage of those factors which were in the Finns favor; i.e.: terrain, climate, and personnel proficiencies. This is what guerrilla warfare is. The imagination and forsight of the Finnish High Command is doubly commendable when one considers that conventional military establishments in the pre-World War II period were not at all inclined to plan along these lines. Also when one considers that Finnish politicians of that period were considering the possibility of a war with Russia only in reference to a world war in which the Western powers would be providing the major effort to overthrow the Soviet regime.

The Finns were fortunate to have during that period the guidance and leadership of Marshal Mannerheim who is, undoubtedly, one of the outstanding military personalities of History. It is somewhat ironic that Mannerheim in all probability did not consider himself a Finn until he had reached middle age. His family had settled in Finland when Finland was a Swedish province. As a child he probably thought of himself as a Swede. In his late teens he joined the Russian Army as a cadet in the Nicholaievshky Cavalry School and subsequently he faithfully served Russia until the revolution of 1917. He had accepted Russian culture and had been married in the Russian Church. The circumstances of the revolution made him a Finn. Had he been in the South when the revolution broke out, he probably would have joined the White Army in the Don. He spoke Finnish with an accent. Among his many qualities, he had an unusual insight into the Russian character and accute appreciation of military intelligence. He was responsible for the very effective intelligence organization which the Finns possessed between the two World Wars.

However, no military establishment is ever the work of a single man. The officers corps, in fact the Finnish Nation as a whole, displayed outstanding military qualities during the Winter War of 1939-40 and later. These qualities did not enable them to preserve Finland's territorial integrity, but they did manage to retain their national existence outside the Soviet orbit, a fact which under the circumstances has to be considered a success.

3.   The Guerrillas in Yugoslavia

In the European theater, the earliest organized large scale guerrilla activity recorded commenced in Yugoslavia on May 10, 1941. On that day, only three weeks after the Yugoslav Army had capitulated, a Colonel named Drahgha Mihailovich organized his first guerrilla band in the village of Ravna Gora.

In recounting the World War II guerrilla activities in Yugoslavia, it is impossible to separate the purely military operations from the paramount political issues of that period. So, instead of trying to de-emphasize politics, let us attempt to place them in their proper perspective.

Looking at events in retrospect, one has to conclude that the creation of Yugoslavia was an error of the post-World War I treaties. The Yugoslav state not only lacked homogeneity, but included mutually antagonistic elements within it. The reason of the antagonisms are many and we shall not discuss them. We shall only mention that the Croat underground organization, the Ustasha, was active for almost 20 years prior to 1941. Its leaders, Pavelich and Kvaternich, had planned the assassination of King Alexander in Marsailles in 1934, although the triggerman was not a Croat, but a Macedonian member of the IMRO named Valdimir Georgiev-Chernozemski.[9]

On March 25, 1941, the Yugoslav Government of Regent Prince Paul signed the Tripartrate Pact, thus joining Axis. Less than 48 hours later, the Yugoslav Army revolted, deposed the government and repudiated the pact. In that revolution, the Army had the wholehearted support of the Serbian people; however, it did not have the support of the Croats. When the German army attacked Yugoslavia, the Croat units mutinied and thus became the prime factor in the Yugoslav Army's collapse. The local communists also participated actively in the numerous acts of treason that doomed the Yugoslav Army.[10]

Following the conclusion of the campaign, the Germans allowed the Italians and Bulgarians to occupy most of Yugoslavia and created the independent state of Croatia under the Ustasha Leader AntePavelich. The new state included within its borders a substantial minority of Serbs. The Croat government proceeded to ruthlessly exterminate the Serb minorities, using methods similar to those used by the Germans for the extermination of the Jews. It appears also that there was no significant dissenting opinion to this policy of extermination and that the majority of the Croats, including the intelligensia and the Catholic clergy, approved or tolerated it. The reaction among the Serbs was one of bitterness and violence. Mihailovich and the Chetnits concentrated their efforts on attacking the Ustashi and rescuing the Serbs in the disputed areas rather than harassing the Germans. Probably, although he did not go on record as advocating this, Mihailovich felt that it was time to dissolve the unhappy union of the Yugoslav state. Nor was he alone in this thought. President Roosevelt is reputed to have favored a homogeneous united Serbia to a heterogeneous disunited Yugoslavia.[11]

In spite of the heavy odds against him, the Mihailovich organization grew substantially. It was known as the Chetnits,
the word " четниц ," meaning irregular fighter, or guerrilla
in Serbo-Croat. The same term had been used for the Serb
guerrillas that participated in the revolutions against the Turks
in the previous century and the underground wars against the
Macedonian Komitadjis between 1903 and 1914. Mihailovich
was promoted to general and made Minister of War in the
Yugoslav-Government-in-Exile in London. The Allied radio
and press, including the Russian, heralded his successes daily
to the free world. During those days (1941 and 1942) allied
military successes were few and far between; the existence of
an active guerrilla movement in occupied Europe was, therefore, a psychological warfare item of paramount importance.

Then, all of a sudden, Radio Moscow in July 1942 for the
first time, announced that there was a guerrilla movement in
Yugoslavia under someone called Tito. Why was Tito and his
movement — the Partizans, ignored by Moscow until 1942?
One theory has been that Tito, or Iosip Broz, which is his real
name, having been one of the organizers of the International
Brigades during the Spanish Civil War, was on Stalin's black
list as were all of the communists involved in that affair. This
could well be true; it has been established that the majority of
the communist leaders who returned to Russia from Spain
were executed during the purges of 1937 and 1938. However,
we do not have sufficient authentic information on these intra-
party struggles to verify this theory. It is more likely that Tito
had been ignored by radio Moscow until July 1942 because:

1. The Partizan movement was late in getting organized.

2. It did not have any substantial following.

Tito's apologists, of course, deny both of these counts. However, it has been established that none of the communist underground movements in Europe got underway until after Germany's attack on Russia.[12] By virtue of this fact alone, it is a
simple matter of arithmetic to establish that Mihailovich preceded Tito in the field by at least 48 days; this assuming that
Tito got started the day of the German attack on Russia, which
is from the practical point very unlikely.

As for Tito's following, it developed en masse later, in 1944, when it became apparent that the Allies were favoring his organization over the Chetnits. In the beginning, the Partizans could not possibly have any substantial following outside the proletariat. Since the labor force in prewar Yugoslavia was very small, this following could not have been anything but negligible.

The Partizan movement could not have any appeal to the middle class or the peasants among any of Yugoslavia's ethnic groups. In any case, what issue could attract the peasantry to Tito? The Croat peasantry had already committed itself to cooperation with the Axis while the Serb peasants, naturally, had espoused the Chetnits movement.

The slogan "land for the peasants" could not have the appeal in Yugoslavia it did have in Russia in 1917.[13] Yugoslavia, like the remaining Balkan Countries, in spite of their backwardness in other fields, had few landless peasants or farm laborers; the vast majority of the peasants were proprietors of their own small plots. If anything, the communists would take "land from the peasants" and force them into collectives. For this reason, the communist movement's following among the Balkan peasants has always been infinitesimal; as a matter of fact, opposition to communism from among the peasants has been fierce and effective. This peasant opposition is one of the reasons why the communists failed in Greece and they would have also failed in Yugoslavia but for the British intervention in favor of Tito.

Land reform is, therefore, one of the first steps that must be taken by a country wishing to avoid revolution. And the countries who still retain substantial numbers of landless peasants, such as Iran, Portugal, and several South American Republics, will most likely see substantial communist gains in the next few years.

The military activity of the Partizans was concentrated towards attacking the Chetnits rather than harassing the Germans. The Chetnits, naturally, defended themselves and the result was civil war. The Partizan tactics against the Germans, whenever they did operate against the Germans, consisted of a hit-and-run tactics; this is an acceptable guerrilla method, except that the attacks were carried against relatively unimportant targets. After the withdrawal of the Partizans, the local inhabitants were left alone to face the German reprisals. This method of guerrilla warfare is catastrophic to the noncombatants. A conservative estimate of the Yugoslav losses among noncombatants in World War II is the staggering number of 800,000 out of a population of 16 million. The losses inflicted to the Germans are estimated at 16,000. This ratio of 50:1 is entirely unjustifiable.[14] Yet, the British, from their Middle East Headquarters in Cairo, encouraged this.[15]

A note must be made to the fact that after 1942 a lot of the operations conducted by the Chetnits were credited to the Partizans by the BBC radio. We have, for instance, the case of the three railroad bridges over the river Lim on the Uzice-Vishegrad line which were blown up in September 1943 by Chetnits under the command of a Colonel Ostoyich. That operation was conducted after a request by the British Middle East Headquarters. BBC radio reported that the bridges were blown by Partizans and in spite of protests by Brigadier Armstrong (British) and Colonel Seitz (American), the two allied liaison officers present at the operation, BBC did not correct the error. Very little mention was also made of the fact that the Chetnits, at considerable loss, rescued 552 downed American and British airmen who had bailed out over Yugoslav territory.

In contrast with the Partizans, the Chetnits were organized along territorial lines. Their units, although not being entirely static, were operating within territorial regions and composed of inhabitants of these regions. The members of the units would usually stay in the villages and pursue their normal activities until they were alerted for a specific operation. This way, they were on hand to defend the villages against attacks by the Germans, Bulgarians, Italians, Ustashi, or Partizans.

It can generally be said that during 1942 the Chetnits were much the stronger of the two guerrilla groups, but their activities were largely confined to Serbia with few peripheral units operating in Montenegro, Bosnia and Herzegovina. The last two were in part under Croat administration. Tito, in 1942, was unable to establish himself militarily in Serbia al-

though in the summer the Partizan organization made a concerted effort to do so. Towards the end of the year, Tito gave
up and retreated with his few followers into Bosnia where he
tried to establish a new guerrilla base.

While the two guerrilla groups were competing with each
other, the Germans took the attitude that this is a case of
"dog eats dog" and left them alone. However, with the coming
of 1943, undisputed control of communications, particularly
of the rail line running South from the Austrian border to
Salonica through Zagreb and Belgrade, became for the Axis
forces a matter of vital importance. In November of 1942 the
Allies had landed in North Africa, and the German High
Command was desperately trying to maintain a bridgehead in
Tunisia and Tripolitania. A large volume of supplies for the
Axis forces in Africa was passing through this line. So between
January and March of 1943 the Germans conducted a series
of operations intended to clear the areas adjacent to the line between Zagreb and Belgrade. The Germans used a total of seven
divisions in this operation, but they were never simultaneously
engaged. Some of the units employed were Italian, Croat, and
Bulgarian of relatively low proficiency. This combined Axis
operation was generally successful. Tito's followers suffered the
brunt of this offensive because they happened to be in this
area, whereas the Chetnits were operating mostly South and
West-Southwest of Belgrade. The Germans, however, have reported that they met more stubborn resistance from the Chetnits than the Partizans. This may indicate that Mihailovich
was becoming preoccupied with retaining territorial control,
a fatal error in guerrilla warfare, whereas the Partizans were
prudently withdrawing so they could come back some other day.

In the summer of 1943 the Germans sent a reinforced mountain division against the Partizans. These special troops moved
away from the communications lines and attacked the Partizans
in their hideouts. For a while it looked like the guerrilla movements in Yugoslavia could well be on their last lap. The Partizans could be finished in a few weeks and then the Germans
could, if they so decided, turn their strength against Mihailovich
and the Chetnits. But in the meantime, radical changes were
taking place at the fronts. The Axis forces were thrown out of

Africa in April and following that the invasion of Italy took place. In September, Italy capitulated. The Italian capitulation not only saved the Partizans from probable annihilation, but provided them with the material means to overwhelm their adversaries; i.e. the Chetnits. The Partizans had made up their minds that the Chetnits would be their long range enemies after the Allied victory.

The equipment of ten Italian divisions, including some of the artillery, was turned over to the Partizans. The Italian equipment which the Chetnits were able to acquire was of insignificant quantities. The reason for this imbalance can be found in the intervention of the British Middle East Headquarters. The terms of the Armistice provided for the Italians to surrender their weapons to the nearest Allied forces. The Italians were only too happy to do just that and get out of it all. But where were the nearest Allied forces? The Italian commanders wanted to know. This is when the British Headquarters intervened and through its mission in Yugoslavia indicated the Partizans as the intended recipients.

The acquisition of artillery gave the Partizans a decisive advantage over the Chetnits from then on. In the areas evacuated by the Axis forces, conventional engagements were bound to develop between the Partizans and the Chetnits for control of the territory and artillery would be the decisive factor. Tito wasted no time in capitalizing on this new advantage. In October his forces attacked the Chetnits in Montenegro. The Chetnits were commanded by General Djukanovich and Colonel Stanishich. They retreated to the Ostrog Monastery where after a few days seige, they capitulated. At about the same time, the Bulgarian occupational forces in South Serbia began to openly favor the Partizans[16] and succeeded in expelling the Chetnits from that area also. The territory under the influence of Mihailovich was rapidly shrinking.

In 1944 the German reactions to guerrilla activities in Yugoslavia became progressively more passive. The German troop shortages were becoming severe. They were unable to launch offensive operations against the guerrillas. In January they sent the 1st Brigade of the Kozak Calvary Division to clear the area near Karlovach SW of Zagreb.[17] The Brigade consisted of the

1st Kozak Regiment (Don) and the 3d (Kuban). It was engaged by superior forces and went on the defensive in the forest near Vojnits. Later the Germans sent the 2d Kozak Regiment (Sibirsk) with one artillery battery as reinforcements and the whole force managed to extricate itself and retreat towards Zagreb.

The last major operation against Tito took place on 24 May. The Germans dropped a battalion of paratroopers on Tito's Headquarters at Dvar after their intelligence was able to locate where the Headquarters were. Tito took to the hills and was later rescued by a British aircraft which flew him to Bari, Italy. After a few days in Italy, Tito set up a new headquarters on the Dalmation island of Vis protected by British troops. This operation is important because it is the first one on record where airborne troops were used against guerrillas.

Why did the Allies finally abandon Mihailovich, thus turning 16 million people over to the communists?

Well, why did the Allies give away the rest of Eastern Europe, Manchuria and half of Korea?

For these blunders the Allies are suffering now and may suffer for generations to come.

It is known today that the Western leaders sincerely hoped for a postwar cooperation with the Soviet government. They also feared the possibility of a separate treaty between the Nazis and the Soviets who, after all, has consummated such a rapprochement once before in 1939, with the Ribbentrop-Molotov agreement. To avoid such a calamity the Western leaders were prepared to make all kinds of concessions and give what was not theirs to give. In making these concessions, they were helped greatly by the numerous members of the "lost generation" of the 30's who, out of misguided idealism or lack of political acuity, believed that the world would be better off with increased Soviet influence. Literally thousands of these people were located in positions of responsibility (usually away from the fronts) and were able to influence major decisions.

In Yugoslavia's case in particular, the decisions made were greatly influenced by the reports of the British Military Mission with Tito which was headed by the then Brigadier Fitzroy MacLean and which included Major Randolph Churchill.[18]

Also instrumental in these decisions was the head of the intelligence section in the British Headquarters, Middle East, Major Kluggman[19] who, after the war, became "Director of Education" for the Communist party of England.

A factor, no doubt, also was the opportunistic attitude of British foreign policy with its belief that concessions to the Russians in Yugoslavia would induce them to relieve the pressure on other parts of the Empire, such as India (still a Crown Colony then) and the Middle East.

On the American side, a concerted effort to sway American public opinion on Tito's side was made by the avowed Croat Communist Louis Adamic, but we doubt that he had any substantial influence among official circles.

It must be acknowledged, to the credit of the U.S. Government, that it abandoned Mihailovich with reluctance. But Churchill at the Quebec conference in September 1944 insisted that the U.S. withdraw its mission from Mihailovich and Roosevelt complied.

Tito's apologists have advanced the theory that Mihailovich had turned quisling and was cooperating with the Italian occupation forces. They cite certain "accommodations" that were allegedly made between the Chetnits and the local Italian Commanders. This is pure nonsense. Such "accommodations" are always taking place in guerrilla warfare;[20] besides, the alleged "accommodations" have never been investigated by anyone who is impartially reliable. To the contrary, the Partizan cooperation with the Nazis is a matter of record. One need to only mention the fact that Franya Pritz, who became commander of Tito's Air Force, fought with a Croat air unit at the Eastern Front and was decorated by the Germans[21] with the Knight's Cross of the Iron Cross. And how about the traitorous conduct of the communists when the German attack on Yugoslavia commenced in April 1941?

The only real reason that the communist Partizans had for wishing the extermination of Mihailovich and the Chetnits is that they presented a formidable obstacle to the communist plans of sovietizing Yugoslavia. Thanks to British intervention and American indecision they realized their plans.

The attempt to assess the effectiveness of guerrilla warfare in

Yugoslavia presents us with the interesting feature that it has to be a comparative assessment of two different groups of guerrillas. However, a fair assessment has to take in consideration the political and military objectives of the two groups and of the Allied High Command.

The Allied objective was to inflict as much material damage as possible to the Axis forces regardless of what casualties the guerrillas and civilians may suffer. There were no immediate political objectives manifested by the Allied High Command; the tendency was to subordinate or defer political problems.

The Partizans' objectives were principally political. Like good communists, they were concerned with controlling the Yugoslav government after the war. To this objective they subordinated military operations.

The Chetnits' objectives, at first, coincided with those of the Allies. But as they realized that they were being caught in the middle between the Axis forces and the Partizans, their objectives gradually changed and became preoccupied with establishing their control over Serbia, Bosnia, and Herezgovina.

Militarily, from the Allied point of view, the guerrilla operations in Yugoslavia should be considered only a partial success. The material damage inflicted on the Axis forces was small. But the potential threat of the guerrillas to the Axis communications lines compelled the German High Command to deploy in Yugoslavia a large number of combat formations at the expense of other theaters; this, in spite of the fact that very substantial forces from the German satellites were also available for occupation and security missions in Yugoslavia.

The military and political objectives of the Partizans were attained 100% whereas those of the Chetnits were a complete failure. The reasons, in our opinion, can be found in the Allied, particularly British, intervention which favored the Partizans over the Chetnits for the reasons explained in this chapter.

4. Eastern Front

In terms of territory covered and personnel involved, the Russian guerrilla movement behind the German lines in World War II was the biggest one. Its effectiveness was also of considerable magnitude, although not in the strictly military sense. As we shall see, the Soviet guerrillas did not appreciably interfere with German operations, but their presence in the German-occupied lands served as an extension of the Soviet political authority during the duration of the occupation.

The war plans of the Soviet High Command prior to 1941 had made provisions for a guerrilla momevent through the organization of "destruction battalions". These were units with a core of fanatic party members with the mission to allow the advancing enemy columns to bypass them and then to engage in demolitions and attacks against communications works. However, in the first few months of the war, the surprise of the German attack and the speed of the advance completely disorganized this preplanned guerrilla apparatus.

After the Soviet High Command recovered from the surprise, it established a position of Chief of Staff for Guerrillas. This assignment went to Lieutenant General Ponomarenko who maintained his headquarters throughout the war in Moscow.[22] Ponomorenko's organization assumed the responsibility of organizing and directing guerrilla operations behind the German lines. In this manner, the Russian guerrilla movement was dictated from above, in contrast to guerrilla movements in other occupied countries which were initiated more or less spontaneously from among relatively junior officers of the defeated armies and civilians of the occupied countries. With this method the Soviet government was able to maintain control of the guerrillas and was not confronted with the problems of other governments[23] which had to cope with several bands of guerrillas without centralized command and which eventually lost all military effectiveness enmeshed in political controversies.

Ponomarenko's organization, during the first few months after its establishment, succeeded in infiltrating behind the German lines a substantial number of key personnel who were the "organizers" of the Soviet guerrilla bands. These key personnel had party backgrounds and were considered loyal communists. A few of them were former members of the unsuccessful destruction battalions, some were Red Army officers, some were KGB members.

The organizers were working in groups of two to ten. Some groups were airdropped and others were infiltrated by land. Once behind the German lines, the organizers would contact potential guerrillas and form cohesive military formations. Ironically, the depth of the German penetrations and the rapidity of the German advances were responsible for the availability of large numbers of potential guerrillas behind the German front. The Soviet large scale withdrawals resulted in numerous Soviet units of varied size being cut off, bypassed, and overlooked during the mopping-up operations. Personnel of these units composed the largest percentage of the rank and file of Soviet guerrilla units. Their motives for joining the guerrillas were seldom ideological. For most of them, joining a guerrilla unit was a matter of survival. Membership in a guerrilla band meant that the individual would be, at least temporarily, fed and sheltered whereas surrender to the Germans in many instances meant death. This was particularly true for Red Army men found deep in the German rear. In spite of these conditions however, all Red Army men did not voluntarily join the guerrilla movement. Many took to hiding in the forests in small groups or individually, out-and-out banditary, or were sheltered in the villages where they set up housekeeping with single women. Coercion and threats had to be used to induce these individuals to join the guerrillas.

Another group of potential guerrillas came from the urban residents of the industrial cities. The urban population appears to have been more loyal to the communist regime than the rural. In addition, German occupation policies were much harsher in the cities than in the country, therefore, a number of urban residents were driven to the guerrillas; particularly those who had been government functionaries, teachers, minor intellectuals, etc.

Very few of the rural residents joined the Soviet guerrillas. To the contrary, the rural areas provided a substantial number of collaborator troops and volunteers for the Ostruppen.[24] In fact, the rural population in the occupied areas welcomed the German forces. But the stupidity of the German occupation policy soon changed this attitude of collaboration to one of indifference and in some cases resistance. Particularly after the Germans forced the farmers back into the collective farms which the Russian peasants, on their own initiative, had dissolved distributing the land among themselves. The German policy was to continue the collective farm system because it facilitated their requisitioning.

It is difficult to state with certainty what the total number of Soviet citizens who engaged in guerrilla activities really was. It is probable, however, that their number was lesser than the number of Soviet citizens who fought with the Germans.[25] According to the surrender document signed by Generaloberst Jodl in 1945, on the day of surrender there were 655,000 former Soviet citizens in German uniforms. If one considers that by then these troops had suffered considerable losses through combat casualties, capture, desertion, etc., one must conclude that over 1,000,000 Soviet citizens fought with the Germans. The total number of Soviet guerrillas can safely be estimated to have been less than half of that. Since about 55 million people from the Soviet Union had been subjected to German occupation, the conclusion has to be that the Soviet guerrilla movement had no mass appeal.

The organization of the Soviet guerrilla units followed conventional lines with many modifications. The largest guerrilla unit was the brigade. The regimental echelon was not always used. More often, battalions were grouped into brigades; the battalions in each brigade sometimes numbered as many as seven or eight. The battalion strength varied from 200 men to as many as 1,000. Battalions were usually equipped with heavy machineguns and 82mm mortars, but there was no standardization of equipment quantities. Companies were two to four per battalion. Company, platoon, section, and squad echelons were also utilized. Quite often Soviet guerrilla units were completely mounted, using Red Army animals or animals requisitioned from the farms. Light artillery, including pack pieces, heavy mortars, and anti-tank guns were sometimes found in the brigade order of battle. A considerable number of guerrillas were used at each echelon for supporting and medical services. Some of the headquarters had disproportionately large staffs. As a rule, political commissars and political instructors[26] were attached to each headquarters even though in the Red Army commissars were done away with during World War II.

In general, the Soviet guerrilla unit organization appears to have been flexible enough to cope with the varied conditions and situations.

Conditions on the Eastern Front were almost ideally suited for guerrilla warfare. The country is vast, punctuated with forests and swamps which offer good possibilities for concealment. There was a substantial railroad network, but few roads suited to truck traffic and even fewer that could be regarded as all-weather roads; this state of development and the condition of the roads made the German communications quite vulnerable. Another advantage for the guerrillas was the fact that their adversaries did not have troops in sufficient quantity to control the vast area under occupation. There were many occasions where German formations such as security regiments, which had specific anti-guerrilla missions, were diverted from anti-guerrilla operations to the front in order to react to particular crises which had developed. The occupying army, in fact, did not attempt to control the occupied area in toto, but concentrated on safeguarding its lines of communications and key industrial cities. Punitive expeditions against the guerrillas were launched only when the guerrillas became too aggressive. But, in spite of their relative passivity, the guerrillas, contribution to the eventual Soviet victory in the Eastern Front was significant because of the guerrillas' potential in disrupting rear area traffic at a crucial point of any given battle.

Because of the above reasons, the guerrillas' principal activity was to defend the area under their control. In order to accomplish this, in many instances they constructed field fortifications deep in the forests. These fortifications consisted mainly of pillboxes made of tree trunks and earth. The guerrillas were inclined to defend these positions against German expeditions and they would abandon them only if the German pressure became too heavy, in which case they would withdraw and infiltrate another area. Such withdrawals were generally successful because the Germans did not deploy sufficient troops.

The following areas had a relatively high concentration of guerrilla units: Yelnya-Dorogobuzh, Bryansk, Polotsk-Vitebsk, Voronezh, Vyazma, the area West of Krivoy Rog, and for a brief period the Northern Caucasus.

The guerrillas in the Polotsk-Vitebsk area figured significantly in the plans of the Soviet High Command because during the winter of 1943-1944 the Red Army attempted to drive the 3rd German Panzer Army against the guerrillas operating West of Vitebsk, thus effecting the Panzer Army's annihilation. This attempt failed, although the failure cannot be attributed to the guerrillas, but to the conventional Red Army units employed in this operation.

A joint operation of guerrillas and conventional forces conducted by the Red Army from Janary through March 1942 is of particular interest because of the large-scale use of airborne forces. The operation was conducted in order to relieve German pressure on Moscow by interdicting rail and truck traffic in the vicinity of Vyazma. The Soviet plan called for a parachute assault South of Vyazma where two airfields could be captured with the assistance of guerrillas. After capture of the airfields, additional forces would be landed. These, forces, which should have amounted to 24 battalions, would then try to establish themselves astride the Smolensk-Moscow rail line and the two roads running roughly parallel to it. The 1st Guards Calvary Corps would then try to reach the paratroops by a thrust from the South, while the 10th and 33d Soviet Armies would put pressure on the Germans by frontal attacks from the East and Southeast (see Figure 4).

This operation was only a limited success. The Russians were unable to make simultaneous drops of more than two battalions at each time. The reason was that although they had plenty of airborne infantry available, they lacked a sufficient number of transport aircraft. In addition, the crews were inexperienced and the drop zones usually missed, thus spreading the troops over very wide areas. Another reason was that the weather was too adverse and the operation of the airfields was extremely difficult. Finally, there was the reason of German air superiority which restricted the air assault operations to the hours of poor visibility only. Rather disappointing also were the frontal thrusts of the conventional Soviet forces. Only the Calvary Corps under General Belov managed to reach the airheads. It was soon cut off, but for a while it operated behind the German lines. After the airfields were recaptured by the Germans, it was soon eliminated as an effective force. Characteristically, the nonavailability of supplies from Soviet sources, combined with the lack of fodder for the animals from local sources in mid-winter effected its near destruction.

Another guerrilla force which figured prominently in the operations on the Eastern Front was the one commanded by Sidor Kovpak. In October of 1942, this force, consisting of two or three guerrilla brigades, left its base South of Novgorod and penetrated over 400 miles into German-held territory. Some authors[27] have asserted that the prime mission of this raid was not to harrass the Germans, but to punish the Ukrainian nationalists, about whom more will be said later. Kovpak was a very able commander who had distinguished himself in the Russian Civil War when he conducted calvary raids against the Whites in traditional Kozak style.

The presence of this relatively large force at their rear alarmed the Germans enough to withdraw from the front their only available calvary division, the 8th SS "Floryan Geyer" and send it against Kovpak.[28] In addition, they assembled a multitude of minor antipartizan formations, some of which were composed of native volunteers. Under pressure from the Germans and their collaborators, Kovpak withdrew to the Pripyet marshes where he spent the winter. He constructed a small airfield on a frozen lake, but the Luftwaffe spotted it and destroyed it by bombing the ice. Finally, Kovpak with his force escaped to the Russian lines after a march eastward in May, 1943. His operation greatly upset German military plans in that region, but on the negative side it precipitated the military collaboration with the Germans of several thousand Ukrainian Nationalists.

Full details about the military activities in World War II of the Ukrainian Nationalists are not available in the West. However their movement was of sufficient magnitude to create concern within the Soviet High Command.

An undercurrent of nationalist feeling has always existed

among the Ukrainians. On June, 30, 1941, a provisional government was established in Lvov by the Nationalists, but later its
members were arrested by the same Germans whom they were
hoping to befriend. Consequently, the Ukrainian Nationalist
movement went underground and bands of Ukrainian guerrillas operated against both the Germans and the Russian communists. The bands seem to have included people with various
motives. In addition to the Nationalists, there were former Red
guerrillas who had become disaffected with the Soviet regime,
Red Army deserters, and even ordinary bandits. The Ukrainian
guerrillas were not under a single direction militarily or politically. There were two competing groups under the leader-
ships of Stepan Bandera and Andrey Mel'nyk. In addition, a
third group of followers and associates of Skoropadsky, the
Tsarist general who had run a separatist government after
World War I, was active in the cities.

It is probable that some of the Ukrainian Nationalist guerrillas remained active long after the re-occupation of Ukraine
by the Red Army, perhaps as late as 1950. In fact, on May 12,
1947, they ambushed a motorcade and killed the Polish Vice-
Commissar for War, General Swierczewski, who was none other
than "General Walter" the commander of one of the international brigades in the Spanish Civil War. After this incident,
Russian, Polish, and Czech units conducted joint operations in
order to exterminate the Ukrainian guerrillas.

Bandera was assassinated by communist agents on October
15, 1959, in Munich where he was living as a refugee. Mel'nyk
is reported to be still living in Luxemburg.[29]

As far as the Soviet High Command was concerned, the military activities of the Soviet guerrillas were only one part of
their mission. Equally important to the Soviet High Command
was the political significance of maintaining Soviet guerrillas
in the occupied territory, because the guerrillas, as long as
they remained firmly under Societ control, constituted an extension of the Soviet authority in the occupied land. Because
of the separatist and anti-communist feelings which were being
manifested to an alarming degree among the peasants in practically all regions occupied by the Germans, it became necessary
to remind these people that Soviet authority had not vanished

yet. The guerrillas became the instrument of this policy. Therefore, they were entrusted with the appropriate missions for
this task, including assassination of known collaborators, collection of taxes, dissemination of political propaganda, etc. Tax
collection became particularly important because the proceeds
of tax collection were used to maintain the guerrillas themselves. Tax collection among the peasants was made through
contributions in kind. These contributions, in addition to the
infrequent but severe German requisitions, kept the Russian
peasants in a state of near destitution. But this too fell within
the objectives of the Russian High Command which could not
afford to have its former subjects enjoy any kind of relative
prosperity during an occupation by an enemy.

In spite of the efforts by the Soviet guerrillas, collaboration
with the enemy did take place. This collaboration varied in
degree from place to place. In some areas wholesale collaboration took place; in some others it was very limited. Collaboration was not always prompted by ideological reasons. In many
cases it was a matter of necessity in order to avoid German pressures. But it can be said that generally, the presence of Soviet
guerrillas behind the German lines served to impede collaboration.

It is interesting to analyze the attitudes and reactions of the
Germans toward the guerrillas. Obviously, it was to the Germans' advantage to prevent the development of a guerrilla
movement, and if this could not be prevented, it was necessary
to bring about its destruction. But the Germans were unable
to accomplish either of these objectives. Prevention would have
required an entirely different occupation policy than that which
the Germans were prepared to follow. Destruction required
forces which were not available. Therefore, the German established policy towards the Soviet guerrillas amounted to passive
protection of communications and industrial centers and conducting offensive operations against the guerrillas only if the
guerrillas threatened the security of communications or industrial centers. The remote areas of the countryside where the
guerrillas could hide were left to the guerrillas' control. Under
the existing circumstances, this policy was militarily prudent,
although not politically desirable. But any attempt by the

Germans to permanently occupy the vast countryside would have further weakened their limited forces and would have risked their defeat in detail.

Responsibility for the counterguerrilla operations did not always rest with the Wehrmacht. In the areas immediately behind the front, the Wehrmacht retained this responsibility. But the balance of the occupied territory was administered by the SS or by other agencies which were also charged with guerrilla control.

Offensive operations by the Germans against the Soviet guerrillas consisted usually of area sweeps or attempts of encirclement. The forces used were invariably inadequate and usually second rate, although sometimes units of special composition and training for anti-guerrilla missions were used. But such units were not available in sufficient quantities. Most effective against the Soviet guerrillas were units composed of native defectors. Occasionally, members of such units would counterdefect to the guerrillas, but this did not occur frequently enough to present much of a problem until late in the war. The effectiveness of the units of native defectors was particularly high when these units were composed of inhabitants of the region where they were employed. Their effectiveness diminished as these units were employed in areas far away from their homes.

In some areas, the total responsibility for the anti-guerrilla mission was left to the native units. Thus, in Byelorussia a unit of nearly 10,000 men organized under a man named Kaminsky, who had been a minor government functionary at Minsk before the war, was quite successful in keeping Byelorussia free of guerrillas. When the Red Army reoccupied Byelorussia, the Kaminsky Brigade, as it was identified. was evacuated and used against guerrillas in other regions. When the Warsaw uprising took place in the summer of 1944, the Kaminsky brigade was used against the Poles and acquired dubious fame for its ruthlessness. Finally, the Germans decided that Kaminsky was too much of a rascal and exterminated him and his principal collaborators.

Another unit with good anti-guerrilla capabilities was the Kozak Calvary Division which was later expanded to the XV

Calvary Corps. This unit was composed of Kozaks some of whom were natives of Siberia, but was led by able German officers. It was commanded by General Von Panwitz. However, this unit was not utilized against the Soviet guerrillas much, but saw extensive service in the Balkans against Tito. Hitler, who was suspicious of Russian collaborator troops, on at least one occasion had decided to disband this unit, but was prevented from doing so through the intervention of some of his staff. This is typical of the imprudent use which the Germans made of this kind of troops. If they had played their cards right they could have changed the character of the war by having Russians fighting Russians.

The overall assessment of the effectivity of the Soviet guerrillas comes to the conclusion that their contribution to the war against Germany was significant, but considerably less than what it could have been. The guerrillas' relative passivity did not materially damage German capabilities on the Eastern Front. But the presence of guerrillas and their potential had an affect on German tactical decisions. The guerrillas' biggest contribution was mostly on the negative side through the prevention of wholesale collaboration with the enemy.

5.   Guerrillas in the Philippines

After the surrender of the U.S. and Filipino forces to the Japanese in 1942, numerous guerrilla bands sprang into existence throughout the Archipelago. Many of these developed into well-organized, well-disciplined military units. The Filipino guerrilla bands included the more or less usual number of opportunitists and even common criminals, but they also included a high proportion of former American and Filipino Army men who had managed to escape capture.

The more important, in respect to numerical strength, of the above units were the following:

The 92nd Philippine Army Division in Leyte, with a
peak strength of 209 officers and 2,981 enlisted men;
Volckmann's Division of Northern Luzon; The Buena
Vista Regiment in East Central Luzon; Colonel Wen-

dell Fertig's force in Mindanao; Colonel Macario Peralto's force in Panay; Magsaysay's Battalion; and several others.

The creation of these bands had to be attributed to the spirit of resistance that prevailed among the American escapees and the patriotism of the Filipino ex-servicemen whose fanatic devotion to duty surpassed in many instances even the fanaticism of the Japanese. These men organized the guerrilla units on their own initiative without direction or initial assistance from General MacArthur's headquarters. Unfortunately, this lack of direction from a higher headquarters was also responsible for a certain amount of antagonism among some of the groups or leaders, such as the prolonged strife between Lt. Colonel Ruperto Kangleon and General Miranda in Leyte.[30]

General MacArthur's headquarters established initial contact with Fertig's group in Mindanao in February of 1943 by landing a liaison group from a submarine. Gradually, contact was established with all the groups operating in the Islands and was maintained until the return of the American forces in 1944.

Throughout the Japanese occupation, the guerrillas did not engage the Japanese forces in any significant action. No widespread campaign of sabotage or harassment of the Japanese rear was attempted. This was because General MacArthur did not wish to expose the Filipino people to the inevitable cruel reprisals of the Japanese. This is indeed a contrast with the policy pursued by the Allied headquarters in the European and Middle Eastern theaters where the local guerrillas were constantly being encouraged to engage German formations in actions of limited military value, thus frequently exposing the noncombatants of the countryside to German "countermeasures". The countermeasures resulted in the murder of countless civilians for every German casualty and the wholesale destruction of villages. General MacArthur's idea of guerrilla resistance was to organize the bands and ascertain their continuous existence. The fact of their mere existence was sufficient to maintain the morale and spirit of resistance among the occupied Filipinos. In addition, MacArthur's headquarters expected and received from the guerrillas intelligence pertinent to the strength and dispositions of the enemy forces. In carrying out their intelligence mission, the Filipino guerrillas were outstandingly successful and in this manner MacArthur had the advantage of detailed knowledge of the enemy capabilities prior to the Allied invasion of the Philippines; an advantage not possessed in many of the other landings undertaken in the Pacific Theater.

Eventually, however, after the landings of the US forces took place, in the face of stiff Japanese resistance and inadequate US personnel replacements, the guerrilla units were called to participate in the fighting as scouts and reconnaissance units. Gradually, they were all incorporated into the reestablished Filipino Army.

An evaluation of the Filipino guerrilla activities in World War II has to recognize two outstanding facts. The first of these is the spontaneity of the organization of the guerrilla units. The second is the limited employment of guerrillas by General MacArthur's headquarters.

The spontaneous character of the guerrilla movement was attributed to the spirit of resistance that prevailed among the Islanders and Americans. This is particularly noteworthy because it took place in a period when military adversity prevailed in the Allied camp. It is also interesting to observe that the Filipinos remained loyal to the Allied cause in spite of the Japanese psychological efforts to convince the Filipinos that they were being liberated from American colonial domination.

The limited employment of the Filipino guerrillas after their emergence is attributed entirely to the decisions made by General MacArthur's headquarters. These decisions appear now to have been correct. Intensified military activity by the guerrillas could not have significantly weakened the Japanese. The damage that the guerrillas could inflict on the Japanese would not have been commensurate with the losses and hardships which the noncombatant natives would have suffered. In general, therefore, it can be said that guerrilla warfare in that Theater was prudently waged.

The experience gained by the Filipinos during World War II contributed greatly to the success which the Filipino Army enjoyed after the war when it conducted a counterguerrilla campaign against the Communist-led Huks.

6. The Long Range Penetration Groups in Burma

In the fall of 1943, the US High Command sent to the China-Burma-India Theater the first contingent of American combat troops. Until that time there were no U.S. forces organized as a combat unit in this Theater; the only American troops were the service units in India and the 2,500 Americans serving with the Chinese. This is indicative of a fairly low priority assigned to the CBI Theater.

General Marshall, the American Chief of Staff, perhaps considering the small number of troops available, decided that quality could be substituted for quantity to some extent. For this reason, the group was composed entirely of volunteers from units stationed in tropical areas (Canal Zone, Florida, South Pacific). In addition, these 3,000 men were not to be formed into a standard infantry formation. Instead, they were to be organized as three commando-type long range penetration battalions to operate behind the Japanese lines. The British, who were heavily engaged in this Theater, already had such units in operation under the guidance of Major General Orde Charles Wingate. He was invited to assume responsibility for training the American unit.

A few words must be said about Wingate and his experience in unconventional warfare.

The man was obviously influenced by Lawrence's book on guerrilla operations against the Turks in World War I. However, Wingate did not share Lawrence's sympathy towards the Arabs. To the contrary, during an assignment in Palestine in the 30's he became friendly with the Jewish underground. It has been reported that he taught the Jewish leaders the fundamentals of guerrilla operations which they applied in 1947 in their war which resulted in the establishment of the Jewish State.

In late 1940, Wingate, a brigadier, was given 70 British officers and noncoms and approximately 1,000 Sudanese and Ethiopians with whom he was supposed to invade Ethiopia from Sundan and harass the rear of the Italian Army. His success in Ethiopia was spectacular. The Italian hold on Ethiopia had never been too firm. Guerrilla and bandit groups had remained at large since 1935 in spite of the Italian conquest. In 1940, the Italian forces in East Africa, although numerically superior to the invading British, were completely isolated from metropolitan Italy, with no prospects for relief. In addition, their morale was completely shaken after the Italian defeats in Albania by the Greeks and in Libya by the British Western Desert Force. These events, of course, do not minimize the accomplishments of Wingate's group which after months of daring operations in one of the world's most difficult terrains, entered the Ethiopian capital on April 6, 1941, triumphantly escorting the Emperor Haile Selassie.

Field Marshal Wavell was favorably impressed by Wingate. Therefore, when he was transferred to India from the Middle Eastern Command, he asked the War Office in London to give him Wingate, whom he hoped to utilize on a similar mission against the Japanese in Burma. In Burma, Wingate eventually assembled and trained a formidable force which was given the cover designation name 3rd Indian Division, although it included relatively few Indians. This division was composed of six brigades, the 14th, 16th, 23rd, 77th, 111th, and 3rd West African, each of four battalions of special composition — a total of 24 battalions with some artillery. In addition, Wingate organized and armed bands of natives among the warlike Kachin tribe, who were friendly to the Allied cause. These units operated at the rear of the Japanese lines semi-independently, but in conjunction with and in support of operations conducted by the regular Allied forces of this Theater. Resupply of these units, when operating behind the enemy lines, was accomplished almost entirely by air drops. Special training had been given in order to facilitate aerial delivery of supplies.

The American unit was given the code name "Galahad." It was also known as the 5307 Composite Provisional Regiment, and later the 475 Infantry Regiment (Long Range Penetration). No provisions were made for a normal flow of replacements to this unit. It was expected that after 90 days of operations behind the Japanese lines, attrition would be so great that the unit would have to be evacuated. This expectation of evacuation after 90 days caused serious morale problems later on. Brigadier General Frank D. Merrill was placed in command of this unit. From him the group derived its popular name "Merrill's Marauders". Initially, the regiment was composed of three battalions. Each battalion included two combat teams of sixteen officers and 456 enlisted men. Each combat team had a rifle company of three rifle platoons and a heavy weapons section. In addition, the combat team had a heavy weapons platoon, a reconnaissance platoon, a pioneer and demolitions platoon, and a medical platoon (see Figure 7 for the organizational chart of 5307 Regiment). The combat team was issued the following weapons:[31]

M1 rifles	306
Carbines	86
Submachineguns	52
60 mm Mortars	4
81mm Mortars	4
Light machineguns	2
Heavy machineguns	2
2.36" rocket launchers	3

The three battalions had a combined animal strength of 700 mules and horses which provided capability of pack transportation of ammunition and supplies in the jungle. Resupply was to be accomplished through air drops. Evacuation of casualties was to be made by L-4 aircraft whenever possible.

The "Galahad" force was under the operational control of General Stilwell. Stilwell opposed the idea of turning the long range penetration groups loose behind the Japanese lines to roam in the jungle aimlessly, striking occasionally at targets of opportunity. He insisted that they be used in conjunction with conventional operations.

The first operation in which the "Galahad" force participated was the attack on Walawbum, in the Hukawng Valley. This town was located at the northernmost terminus of a trail coming from Kamaing. To the north and west of the town was deployed the Japanese 18th Division, commanded by General Tanaka. This division was much weakened. Against this Japanese division, Stilwell was driving with a force consisting of

the American-equipped Chinese 22nd and 38th Divisions and
a Chinese provisional armored group, commanded by Colonel
R. H. Brown.

The mission assigned to the long range penetration groups
was to flank the Japanese by a wide march from their assembly
point near Ningbyen, eastward to Tawang Hka stream which
was to be forded, then turning south to Tonai Hkna stream
which also was to be forded, and then Southwestward to Walawbum (see Figure 6). This meant that the Americans would
have to march over 75 miles through the jungle before they
could come in contact with the enemy. This march was accomplished between February 23 and March 4, 1944. On March
4th the II battalion established a road block about two miles
west of Walawbum. The Japanese were momentarily surprised.
However, General Tanaka, taking advantage of the relatively
slow southward progress of the Chinese 22nd and 38th divisions, decided to concentrate as much of his force as possible
on an attack against the Americans, hoping to wipe them out.
The long range penetration force was, therefore, compelled to
dig in and fight a static battle for two days. They held their
ground, however, until the Japanese extricated themselves and
withdrew southward toward Kamaing because Colonel Brown's
tanks and the Chinese 64th and 66th regiments were approaching.

Later during the same month, between the 12th and the
23rd, the 5307 was engaged in a similar operation further down
on the road to Kamaing. In addition to the Chinese and Americans, the British long range penetration groups of the 3rd
Indian Division participated. The commander of this Division,
General Wingate, was killed after the conclusion of this operation in an air crash on the 24th of March.

The II and III battalions of the 5307 this time made a wide
march of about 120 miles around the Japanese right flank
before they established a road block at the rear of the Japanese
18th Division near Inkangathwang. The I battalion conducted
a much shorter march and established a road block about
30 miles northeast of Inkangathwang. (see Figure 5). The
American penetration, however, this time did not remain undetected and their march was interrupted by frequent skir-

mishes with Japanese patrols and two major engagements of the I battalion. Japanese reaction during this operation was much more formidable. Artillery reenforcements arrived consisting of several 75 mm mountain guns and two 150 mm guns which have a much longer range than the American 75 mm pack pieces. The 150 mm guns were finally destroyed through the cooperation of observation aircraft which expertly directed the fire of Galahad's pack pieces, placed at their extreme range.

By May 1944, the Galahad force had only about 1,400 men fit for duty of the original 3,000. Battle casualties had taken their toll, but primarily, malaria and dysentery were responsible for this great proportion of losses. The majority of the men listed as present for duty were in a deteriorated state of health also. The men expected to be evacuated from the combat zone in accordance with the original plan. But by this time, the Allied High Command decided that a drive should be made to capture the town of Myitkyina and the nearby airfield which they considered essential for reopening the road to China. In view of the fact that no other American combat troops were available in the Burma Theater at that time, the decision was made to retain Galahad in the combat zone and use it in the drive against Myitkyina. This decision was not well received by the men of Galahad and morale was very adversely affected. Eventually, however, morale was reestablished and the unit's performance left nothing to be desired. The regiment was reorganized into two battalions and was reinforced by Chinese and Kachin rangers. It was utilized during the drive to Myitkyina in a more conventional manner and was not required to make deep penetrations of the magnitude of the operation at Inkangathwang.

By June 4, 1944, the total number of casualties in the Galahad force had reached 2,394, approximately 80% of the original number.[32] Of the above casualties 93 were killed in action, 293 wounded in action and 8 missing. The remaining casualties, including 30 deaths, were caused by tropical disease of various kinds.

In August, the survivors of the original Galahad force were used to form the nucleus of the 475 Infantry Regiment. Replacements, sent from the United States, brought the regiment up to authorized strength. The 475th was intended to become part of a composite Chinese-American light division. Other elements of the division were supposed to be the American-equipped 1st Chinese Separate Regiment, and the 124th U.S. Cavalry Regiment, plus artillery and supporting formations. The Chinese regiment was never made available, so this unit was designated 5332 Provisional Brigade, composed entirely of American formations. These were the 475th Infantry; the 124th Cavalry, dismounted;[33] the 612th Field Artillery Battalion (pack) ; the 613rd Field Artillery Battalion (pack); Six Quartermaster Pack Troops; the 44th Portable Surgical Hospital; and the 18th Veterinary Evacuation Hospital.

This force participated in the operations against the Burma Road. It infiltrated through the Japanese lines on several points at the Nam Maw Valley and reached the Burma Road proper in January 1945. A patrol of the 124th Cavalry blew a crater in the road on January 19th. The Japanese withdrawal terminated this operation before it was fully completed.

The activities of the long range penetration forces in Burma in World War II are significant because this was the first occasion in contemporary times where the U.S. Army organized and utilized formations of this kind.

The decision to attempt a substitution of quality for quantity by organizing units of special composition and training, which would have the mission to operate in the enemy's rear was, under the prevailing circumstances, correct. Those circumstances were dominated by the inability of the U.S. High Command to deploy a sizable force in a remote Theater in which, nevertheless, it maintained considerable interest for reasons of overall strategy.

In application, the employment of this special force had a number of shortcomings. The most obvious shortcoming is the fact that tactical missions assigned to the long range penetration forces were not always commensurate with their special organization and training. One example of this is the static deployment at Walabum.

Other shortcomings appear to have existed in the training and conditioning of the employed troops. This is indicated by the high ratio of casualties which were not attributed directly to combat.

Finally, the cooperation and utilization of the Kachins and other natives was not exploited to its fullest potential. There were, perhaps, reasons of security which prevented full exploitation of this resource.

There were other problems also which mitigate the above shortcomings. The most irritating problem was the inter-allied command structure, particularly as it affected the coordination of operations with the Chinese forces.

Another problem was the less-than-perfect understanding of guerrilla warfare by those directly responsible for its application in this Theater.

Last, but not least, there was the big problem of inexperience in operations under the prevailing climatic conditions.

It is evident, however, that as time passed, commanders and men were accumulating the necessary experience. As shortcomings were being eliminated and the problems solved, the performance of the force increased proportionately. It is reasonable to assume, therefore that if hostilities had continued, the 5332 Brigade could have contributed even more significantly in defeating the Japanese in Burma.

IV

Historical Background
Guerrilla Conflicts Since World War II

1. The Bandit War in Greece

What is commonly referred to as the Greek Bandit War, covers the communist effort to take over the government in Greece through the application of guerrilla warfare between 1945 and 1949. It is an extremely interesting conflict, particularly in view of subsequent communist efforts elsewhere, because it provides us with the first case since World War II where communist expansionist efforts through guerrilla warfare have failed.

Although in the strict sense this conflict chronologically falls in the post-World War II period, its origins go back to the events in Greece during World War II proper. A recount of those events, therefore, becomes necessary.

Greece was invaded by Italy on 28 October 1940. Much to the amazement of everyone, except the inner group of the Greek High Command, this invasion resulted in a disaster for the Italian Army. During the first few days the Italian forces seemed to be making progress. An Alpini division penetrated deeply into the Pindos mountain range while the main Italian force advanced towards Ioannina. But the Greeks were able to outmaneuver the Alpini in the rough terrain of Pindos and defeat it in detail, capturing in the process a large number of combat troops and most of the division's artillery and animals. On the other sector, the Italian advance lost momentum and was finally broken by resistance at the main Greek defensive position. The Greeks followed through with well coordinated counterattacks and the Italians were forced to retreat deep into Albania,[1] suffering substantial casualties.

The defeat of the Italians constituted the first victory by any Allied ground force in World War II, a feat for which the Greek Army is justifiably proud. This success of the Greeks can be attributed to the quality of their military leadership, their ability to maximize the utility of their limited war material, the quality and expert use of their mountain artillery,[2] and the spirit of the individual Greek soldier.

Yet, this spectacular Greek victory was destined to be of short duration because Italy's senior partner came to her rescue. Hitler had already made the decision to attack Russia and this operation was scheduled for the summer of 1941. An active front in the Balkan Peninsula would constitute a threat for the rear and right flank of the German armies operating in Russia. It was necessary, therefore, for the Germans to intervene in Greece and obtain a speedy and complete decision over the Greek Army before the beginning of the Russian campaign. German troops, with the consent of the Rumanian and Bulgarian governments, had already moved through Rumania to Bulgaria from where they could launch the attack on Greece. The Yugoslav government of Regent Prince Paul was also coerced into joining the Axis, but a coup by the Yugoslav Army on March 27, 1941 deposed this government and repudiated the agreement with Germany. This event further complicated the problem for the German Army, which now had to campaign against Yugoslavia in addition to Greece. It is a credit to the German Staff planners that within about ten days they changed plans and dispositions accordingly.

In the meantime, in the Allied Camp, it was becoming evident that Greece could not resist Italy and Germany combined without substantial assistance. But assistance from where? Turkey insisted on remaining neutral in spite of treaty obligations to Greece and British efforts to bring her into the war on the side of the Allies. The British themselves were extremely short of troops and material. Greek demands for deliveries of supplies such as aircraft, anti-aircraft and anti-tank artillery, and motor transport could not be met. Understandably, the Greek High Command became disillusioned with this state of affairs and the obvious lack of preparation for war by a major power. The position of the British government was not at all envious either. If it failed to assist Greece, she would face criticism at home and perhaps, a vote of non-confidence in parliament. In seeking a solution to this problem, the British government chose the worst possible one. It decided to withdraw from General Wavell's force in Cyrenaica three infantry divisions and one armored brigade and send them to Greece. This force was too small to save Greece, but it could have sustained the British advance in North Africa had it stayed there. As it turned out, both Greece and Cyrenaica were lost. It is to the credit of the Greek Government and the Greek General Staff that they recognized this decision as a fundamental error of strategy and, initially, rejected the offer of this limited force. But Metaxas, the Greek Premier, died on January 30, 1941 and was succeeded by Koryzis, a man who did not possess Metaxas' military background nor strength of conviction. Koryzis submitted to British pressure and accepted their inadequate force.

The German campaign against Greece and Yugoslavia commenced on the morning of April 6, 1941. By the end of the month the Germans were in complete control of Yugoslavia and continental Greece. In the process, they annihilated the pathetically weak British expeditionary force. Characteristic of the weakness and poor preparedness of this force is the fact that the armored brigade was not provided with any spare tracts nor tract pins for its vehicles. This provides us with a perfect example of how not to do things in the future. In May the Germans launched an airborne invasion of Crete, the last Greco-British stronghold. Here again the British and Greek forces were defeated in detail.[3]

Just prior to the capitulation of Crete, the Greek government, headed by King George II, left Crete and established itself in Cairo, Egypt. The government was accompanied by the remnants of the Greek armed forces and a few civil servants. Of the armed forces, only the Navy was a significant force. It had managed to salvage about a dozen destroyers and submarines and a few additional auxiliaries. The Army and Air Force did not include any combat formations, but only about 2000 individual servicemen without organization and without weapons. By escaping from the occupied country, the government managed to maintain the image and ideas of national sovereignty and continuing resistance, but in reality it became a ward of the British.

In the meantime, in occupied Greece, within a month after the fall of Crete at least a dozen resistance organizations sprang up in Athens alone. They were truly indigenous resistance groups without contacts with outside Allied intelligence or military organizations. They were composed mainly of idealistic young men and conscientious junior officers of the disbanded Greek armed forces. Incidentally, these officers were at large because the Germans released all captured Greek prisoners of war in accordance with the terms of capitulation; later, in 1943, they reneged and rearrested some of them. The effectiveness of these resistance groups in military terms was near zero. Not only they lacked contacts with their own government and allies, but they also lacked the fundamental resources with which to engage in any kind of overt or covert military activity. Their positive contribution was that their existence did have a good psychological effect on the population.

It is significant to note that among the initial resistance groups there were none sponsored by the communists. Their later propaganda efforts had everyone outside Greece believing that they were the pioneers of resistance. The facts, however, are different. The communist-sponsored resistance organization, EAM,[4] did not make its appearance until late in 1941 after the German campaign against the Soviet Union had commenced and after the local communist hierarchy had received its appropriate directions from Moscow. As far as the rest of the resistance groups are concerned, the lack of communist sponsorship does not mean that they also lacked political orientation or political objectives. They ranged from loyal followers of the exiled government to radical republicans and people of various other party loyalties. In fact, the absence of resources with which to conduct clandstine military operations resulted in correspondingly increased political activity among the resistance groups. The end result was that eventually they lost all military value because of their preoccupation with politics.

Once the Greek communists committed themselves to organizing a resistance movement, they proceded to do so with great intensity and achieved relative success. The communist objective was simple: To prepare for eventual takeover of the Greek government after the war. At first, however, they took pains to conceal their real objective. Later in 1943 and 1944 they became considerably more open about it and this caused a relative reduction in their following. In general, though, the communist underground organization was considerably successful in attracting a mass following. The communist had several advantages which they exploited fully. Those advantages included the destitute state of the population, the inability of the noncommunist underground to provide the desired leadership, and the already existing underground apparatus of the communist party which had been outlawed before the war.

Early in 1942, both the Greek government in exile and the British Middle East Headquarters established contacts with the underground. The Greeks landed by submarine a small liaison group under Major Tsigantes. This group was fairly well supplied with money which they distributed to the underground organizations in proportion to the effectiveness of each, using Tsigantes' judgment as sole yardstick of this effectiveness. Tsigantes cooperated with EAM and gave them the lion's share of material help. After a few months, however, he became aware of EAM's duplicity and real objectives and cut them off. In retaliation, the communists disclosed to the Italians Tsigantes' hideout in Athens. The carabinieri raided the hideout and Tsigantes was killed in a shootout.

Until the summer of 1942, the military activities of all underground groups were confined to collection of intelligence and acts of industrial sabotage. In the summer of 1942, the first guerrilla groups appeared in the remote rural areas. From the beginning the guerrillas were distinguished between those of the communist-controlled EAM and the others, commonly referred to as nationalists. The nationalist guerrillas were mostly uncoordinated small groups under relatively junior officers of the disbanded Greek Army. In general, however, the army officers found guerrilla warfare unattractive. Most of them were attracted to Egypt where the exiled Government was attempting to reestablish a military force to fight with the allies in the North African fronts. The most adventurous of them tried, therefore, to escape to Egypt. Both communist and noncommunist guerrillas initially were extremely short of materiel. They used primarily the few caches of small arms which the army had managed to conceal for such eventuality prior to its capitulation. Allied supplies through submarine deliveries and airdrops were at first very limited.

The communist High Command forsaw that guerrillas not under its control would be a serious obstacle to its postwar takeover, so they immediately attempted to ruthlessly exterminate all such groups. In Central Greece, they surrounded a group of guerrillas under Colonel Sarafis and gave them the alternative of extermination or joining up with them. Sarafis chose to join the communists and became the military chief of the communist guerrillas. In other regions, however, bloody encounters took place. In Rumeli, near the small town of Lamia, a small group of guerrillas under Colonel Psaros was annihilated. In Southern Greece another group under two calvary officers, Captain Vretakos and Captain Skalkos had the same fate. Captain Skalkos himself escaped and the communists in retaliation killed his two brothers and teenage nephew. The fate of another group in the same region under Major Marinakos was similar. This established the pattern of communist treatment of those who were unwilling to work with them, and this is in part responsible for the communists' eventual failure.

Among the nationalist guerrillas there were two groups which managed to evade communist extermination. They were Colonel Zervas' organization in Northwestern Greece and another group under Fosterides, an ex-sergent, in Eastern Macedonia.

The purely military activities of the Greek guerrillas against the Axis forces were of relatively little importance. The only significant one is the operation which destroyed the Gorgopotamos rail bridge in November of 1942. This operation took place at the insistence of the British who were interested in interrupting the rail trafic from the North to Athens. It was important at that time to stop the flow of supplies to the German Army in North Africa because of the Allied operations in that theater after the Battle of El Alamein and the landings in Northwest Africa. The British dispatched to Greece a mission under Brigadier E. C. W. Myers. He was able to obtain the temporary cooperation of Zerras' guerrillas and the communists. The communists allocated to this operation a substantial force under their acting political commissar Aris Klaras.[5] Under the overall command of Myers a guerrilla force was assembled which was far superior to the two Italian platoons guarding the bridge. The Italian garrison was overpowered and the bridge was blown up. Then, the guerrilla force withdrew before reinforcements arrived. This operation was well conceived and well executed. However Myers afterwards allowed himself to be charmed by the communists. His reports to the British Middle East Headquarters were biased in favor of the communists and he went out of his way to supply them with materiel while to Zervas' group he gave only token assistance. He was an engineer officer well-suited for the task of blowing up a bridge, but in every other respect he was inept, if not outright foolish.

With the exception of this operation, communist guerrilla activities amounted to isolated attacks against single German vehicles or small conveys. Militarily these attacks accomplished nothing. But they did bring about criminal reprisals by the Germans who, in many instances, practiced wholesale destruction of villages in retaliation. In all probability, this practice by the communist guerrillas was premeditated and was prompted by a desire to retaliate against villages where the population was not quick enough to espouse the communist cause. The Germans capitalized on the psychological effects of this communist policy and offered the Greeks an opportunity to organize a number of lightly armed "Security battalions" which were used to garrison rural centers against the guerrillas.

The biggest boost to communist military strength came about with the Italian capitulation in the fall of 1943. The Italians surrendered to the communists the weapons of their Pinerolo

Infantry Division, including all its artillery and mortars. Another source of heavy weapons was the Bulgarian Army in Western Macedonia. The Bulgarians, when they switched sides and established a pro-communist government in Sofia, delivered heavy equipment to their Greek comrades.

When the German forces were evacuating Greece in the fall of 1944, the military-political situation was as follows:

There were two nationalist guerrilla groups. One in Northwest Greece with about 4000 armed guerrillas and one in Eastern Macedonia with about 300 armed guerrillas. The group in Northwest Greece was under attack by the communists who had conducted a truce with the Germans for this purpose.

The remaining part of rural Greece was under the control of ELAS, the communist guerrilla organization. The Allied insistence that the "Security battalions" be disbanded and their members interned as collaborators was of significant help to the communists in sercuring control of rural Greece. The weapons of the security battalions in most cases were turned over to the communists. ELAS had about 40,000 men in its major formations and about 45 artillery pieces.

In Athens and the surrounding area there were about 9,000 policemen and gendarmerie. There were also about 500 armed members of the underground who were actively opposing the communists. The communists had an unknown number of armed members in the Athens area and were speedily converging towards Athens all of their better-equipped guerrilla bands.

The Greek Army of Middle East, most of which had recently been engaged in the Italian Campaign, amounted to seven commando and infantry battalions, a calvary regiment on bren gun carriers, and an artillery regiment. These forces landed around Athens without their heavy weapons at the insistance of the communist members of the cabinet. Communists had been accepted in the emigre government in an effort to achieve a semblance of unity on the eve of liberation.

The British landed a small force including mostly auxiliary and service troops. The only combat strength of the British force was provided by three battalions of a paratroop brigade.

Under the prevailing conditions, in December of 1944, complete communist takeover in Greece appeared to be only a matter of time. As long as the ELAS guerrillas could make their presence felt in the countryside, their coercive methods would have resulted in an electoral victory of the communist or communist-approved candidates if an election was held. The communist leadership, however, chose not to wait for an election, but to attempt a forcible takeover immediately. An incident was therefore fabricated during a communist demonstration in Athens when some of the demonstrators fired at the police and the police fired back at the mob. This gave the communists an excuse to launch an attack against all police stations and all forces loyal to the government in and around Athens. The few British forces present were ordered to resist the communists. Within less than 24 hours the fighting in Athens became general and the scene reminded some of the events of the Russian Civil War.

The communists were almost successful. The isolated police stations were overcome and all captured policemen were slaughtered, usually after they witnessed the execution of their relatives. At the peak of communist military success the area under the control of the British and loyal Greek forces amounted to just a few square blocks in the center of Athens. But the communists were not able to overcome the resistance of the Gendarmerie Barracks which was located at the key point controlling the main artery between Athens and its port city of Piraeus. The resistance at this point prevented a complete sweep of all British and loyal Greek positions in the center of Athens and gave the British the opportunity to bring in reenforcements. The 4th Indian Division was brought over from Italy. The communist guerrillas could not hold their own against this experienced division of regulars, particularly in positional battles. Within a few days the tide was turned. The communist forces were severely beaten and commenced a precipitate withdrawal from Athens, heading back to the mountains or across the frontiers into the sanctuary of Greece's northern neighbors who were emerging as communist satellites. When the communists realized that the game was up, they completely lost their heads and committed wholesale atrocities against the local inhabitants.

A pursuit of the disengaging guerrillas at that time would have finished them off and saved the Greek people the hardships of the following five years. Yet, although such pursuit was militarily feasible and politically prudent, it did not take place. The British government made the mistake of offering the communists an armistice. In addition, it prevailed on the non-communist Greek parties to accept a political compromise which made it possible for the communists to stage the "third round", i.e. their next attempt at takeover. Under the terms of this compromise the return of King George was deferred and the Archbishop of Athens, Damaskinos, assumed the functions of regent. The Archbishop was technically a collaborator since he had been enthroned by the occupying forces after his predecessor had refused to swear-in a quisling government in 1941. This was indeed a very peculiar solution to be advocated by the British who appeared at that time to be very sensitive about collaborators. In fairness to them, however, it has to be mentioned that some of the shortsighted Greek politicians also supported this solution out of pure opportunism.

Immediately after its military defeat of December 1944, the Greek communist High Command began its preparation for its next effort. A former political commissar of ELAS, Markos Vafiades, was appointed commander-in-chief and he established his headquarters at Bulkes in Yugoslavia. In Yugoslavia the principal guerrilla base was situated, with secondary bases in Albania and Bulgaria. Markos turned out to be an energetic commander. Colonel Sarafis was not utilized. Aris Klaras probably would have been chosen instead of Markos, but he had been killed in an encounter with gendarmes in 1945. The material means for guerrilla warfare were provided by Yugoslavia, Bulgaria, and Albania. Personnel were provided by volunteer Greek communists and their sympathizers, at first, but later the guerrillas had to forcibly induct villagers. The guerrilla units were organized to a large extent on conventional lines, particularly in the later stages of the War. The principal guerrilla combat unit was the battalion. Guerrilla battalions had a strength of about 500 men and were well supplied with small arms and support weapons. In fact, during 1946 and 1947 the guerrilla battalion was superior in firepower to the National Army battalion, principally because of the number of mortars and machineguns available to the former. Battalions were sometimes controlled by regional headquarters, but more often they were grouped into brigades which were in turn placed under division headquarters. Eight guerrilla divisions were reported at various times, and one horse calvary bridgade. Artillery was also available to the guerrillas, including 105 mm and 75 mm Skoda mountain howitzers, 37 mm anti-tank guns, and light anti-aircraft pieces.

Reinfiltration of communist guerrillas into Greece began in late 1945. True guerrilla tactics were utilized at first, consisting of attacks on undefended or lightly defended villages such as the attack on the small village Skra, near the Yugoslav frontier, in November 1946. The guerrillas would hold each captured village long enough to recruit new members, destroy the crops and publically put to death their opponents. Priests, teachers, and municipal officers were usually the victims. Then, the guerrillas would withdraw before army or gendarmerie units appeared. During 1946 and 1947 they expanded such raids to cover all of Greece. They were considerably successful in these raids because their opposition was exceedingly weak. The Greek National Army was in the process of complete reorganization and was numerically small and very short of heavy weapons and transport. In fact, it was absolutely incapable of sealing off Greece's frontiers from infiltration. There is a possibility that if the communists had continued their purely guerrilla operations, they could have been successful in effecting a collapse of the Greek State. This assumption is made based on the degree of success which the guerrillas achieved in demoralizing their opponents through the raids.

However, the communists were utilizing guerrilla warfare only as a substitute for conventional revolutionary warfare after their failure in the venture of December 1944. The Greek Communist Party was impatient to establish a provisional government which would obtain recognition from the other communist governments. In order to accomplish this, they felt that they must permanently hold some small portion of Greek territory. Consequently, they changed their tactics from purely guerrilla raids to frontal attacks on towns. The change in tactics was gradual. For a long period, both tactics were used. However, the conventional operations gradually absorbed considerably more of the resources available to the communists and eventually were one of the prime factors of their failure.

The first indication of the communist change in tactics was experienced on December 25, 1947 when the guerrillas attempted to capture the small town of Konitsa near the Albanian frontier. Two communist brigades with eight pieces of artillery were utilized for the attack. The defenders at first had only two infantry battalions and one battalion of gendarmerie. The operation was well planned, and initially well-executed. The guerrillas achieved complete surprise, captured a bridge to the West of the town and a number of the surrounding heights, thus effecting an almost complete isolation of the town (see Figure 8). However, the Greek Army reacted energetically. Reinforcements were speedily dispatched and the Air Force intervened quite effectively in spite of adverse weather conditions. After nine days of battle the communists withdrew into Albania. They suffered about 340 casualties against 500 casualties of the defenders, but the damage to communist morale was far greater. The value of across-the-border sanctuary was very dramatically demonstrated in this operation.

In Konitsa the guerrillas achieved a tactical surprise and some strong outposts of the defenders were completely isolated prior to or shortly after the commencing of the operation. However, the main battle was conventional requiring frontal assaults on prepared positions. The guerrillas, to insure success, should have infiltrated the inner defenses, i.e.: the town itself, before the battle. This they could not do though, because in a small town like Konitsa where the inhabitants were hostile to the guerrilla cause their presence would have been detected. We have here one more case illustrating how important it is for the guerrillas to obtain the cooperation of the local people.

Following the unsuccessful attempt to take Konitsa, three additional major operations were made by the communists with the objective of taking and holding some town of significance in order to make it the seat of their provisional government. They were the operations of Kastoria in September 1948, Karditsa in December 1948 and Florina in February 1949. These operations have to be differentiated from other attacks on

towns or cities made for harassing purposes, such as the shelling
of Salonica with one 75 mm gun in February 1948; or attacks
made to divert counterguerrilla operations of the National
Army, such as the operation against Karpenisi in January
1949.

The guerrilla frontal attacks on towns had a number of common characteristics. They were the following:

1. The guerrillas were always able to move their forces to
the assembly areas undetected. They were usually able to initially surprise their adversaries.

2. They conducted the attack with a numerical superiority
of 2:1 or 3:1 over the defenders. This is translated in an even
greater superiority of firepower because the guerrilla units
were allocated a proportionately higher ratio of heavy weapons. The firepower superiority, however, was not maintained
as the National Army brought in reinforcements.

3. The guerrillas were unable to prevent the National Army
from sending strong relief columns to the threatened towns.

4. The guerrillas achieved their successes during the first
two or three days of each operation. Afterwards, guerrilla
attacks seemed to lose momentum. In addition, they seemed
to be unable to maintain a flow of ammunition and replacements to the battle area.

5. Usually, after each failure the guerrillas were able to stage
a more-or-less successful withdrawal and avoid entrapment.

Parallel with their military effort, the communists waged an
intense political and psychological warfare. The objective of
political and psychological warfare was to hold or obtain the
support of the population in general. However in this field they
were considerably handicapped because in reality they had very
little to offer the Greeks. In a country where 95% of the people
were either farmers with small holdings or artisans and professional men, communism is not attractive. The Greeks were
convinced that they could achieve relative material prosperity
only if they remained outside the iron curtain. In addition,
Greek national sensitivities were affected by the obvious collaboration of the guerrillas with Greece's Northern neighbors
who had territorial claims on the province of Macedonia. This

is an emotional subject with all Greeks. The Athens government exploited this subject fully and it affected the communists adversely.

In general, the Greek people rallied and opposed the communist guerrilla efforts successfully. The political parties set aside their differences and cooperated in a coalition government. Republican Greeks withdrew their ideological opposition to the Monarchy and affirmed their loyalty to the constitution and the King. King Paul[6] proved to be a very popular and effective Monarch. His compassion for the victims of the war and his efforts towards their rehabilitation are almost without precedence in the long History of the Greek Nation.

It is probable that the communist guerrilla effort would have been of much shorter duration if the Greek National Army was not so understrength in 1946 and 1947. In reality, it had serious shortcomings in personnel, materiel, and organization throughout the Bandit War. In 1946, the army was limited to 100,000 men by a previous agreement with the British government. The World War II equipment of the Greek Army was lost in the war. According to the above agreement, the British had undertaken to reequip the Greek Army. But they wished to limit its size and strength because they feared that if the Greeks were too strong militarily, they might have attempted to forcibly integrate into their state the Greek-inhabited provinces of Southern Albania. The British wished to avoid this kind of development which would have antagonized the Soviets and would have worsened the already tense relations between East and West. Incidentally, similar thinking by the Americans was responsible for the weak condition of the South Korean armed forces in 1950. The Greek government in 1946 had no choice but to comply with British wishes because the magnitude of devastation which the country had suffered during World War II allowed its government very few material means with which to pursue an independent military policy.

In 1946 the Greek Army was organized into three corps with a total of three mechanized and four mountain divisions. These units were weak in artillery and unsuited for operations in mountainous terrain such as that which prevails in Greece. The infantry battalions had 36 Bren automatic rifles each, twelve 2 inch mortars and four 3 inch mortars. There were no machineguns in the battalion, but there was a company of 16 Vickers organic to each division. The infantry was handicapped by an almost total lack of animals for transport in the mountains. This fact made them practically static units except for the infantry of the mechanized divisions which had a sufficient number of trucks.

There were three regiments of mechanized cavalry for the mechanized divisions. They were equipped with Bren gun carriers and Humber armored cars. Both of these vehicles proved unsatisfactory in Greece. There was also an armored regiment with 36 light tanks. There were plans to equip each mountain division with a reconnaissance troop of horse cavalry, but this was accomplished only later.

In 1946 there were plans to organize six field artillery regiments of sixteen 25-lb guns each. The artillery regiments would be allocated two to each mechanized division. There were also eight 5.5-inch guns as general artillery reserve. There were no immediate plans to equip the mountain division with artillery.

There were 3000 trucks of all kinds. The condition of the roads, however, during the immediate postwar years was so poor that the utility of motor transport was seriously handicapped and the problems of vehicular maintenance compounded.

This composition of the army was absurd. The advantages which a conventional army may have in a war against guerrillas are its better and more numerous equipment. These advantages the Greek Army did not have.

Conditions improved significantly when the U. S. Government, pursuing the policy of President Truman, undertook to supply the Greeks with war materiel. Gradually the strength of the Army was increased to 265,000 men. The number of divisions was increased to eight and the distinction between mountain and mechanized was dropped. Several separate brigades and lesser units were also created. In order to relieve the army from the burden of static defense of rural centers and communications works, 96 light infantry (or National Guard) battalions were formed.

Very substantial changes were made in the infantry. Machineguns (Brownings A6 and A4 were reintroduced in the battalion, the unit of normal employment for this weapon. The British mortars were gradually replaced with US-made 60 mm and 81 mm mortars. Rocket launchers and 75 mm recoilless rifles were introduced in 1948. They proved particularly effective against the communist machinegun nests in the Grammos and Vitsi battles.

The equipment of the armored cavalry was changed to half-tracked personnel carriers, M8 armored cars, and M24 tanks. The regiments were removed from the divisions and allocated to the corps. Each division was given a horse cavalry troop for reconnaissance, but later the troops were grouped into two regiments for better general use. There is no evidence, however, that they were employed much at regimental strength.

Most important were the changes in the artillery. Each division was given a battalion of mountain artillery. They were U.S. 75 mm pack howitzers. An attempt to use the British 3.7 inch pack piece proved unsatisfactory. This piece disassembles into loads weighing about 375 lbs each, which is too heavy for mules. Maybe this weapon was designed for camels or, perhaps, elephants. The existing field regiments were reallocated to the corps. American made 105 mm and 155 mm howitzers were also introduced, but too late to have a decisive effect on the operations. In fact the rate of introduction of the new equipment was extremely slow and even in 1949 the average division possessed only six 75 mm pieces. In order to compensate for this shortage of artillery at division level, the available artillery was "pooled" at corps or battle area level and batteries were withdrawn and reallocated from division to division in order to satisfy operational needs as they developed.

To a degree, the shortage of artillery was compensated for by aircraft which became available in relatively high numbers in 1949. In fact, dependence on air support by ground units became a little too prominent.

Other changes included the introduction of special counter-guerrilla units, the seven battalions of mountain commandos, and the increased availability of mules. Some infantry battalions had over 100 animals. In the days prior to the refinement of helicopter, mules were indispensible for operations on mountainous terrain.

Besides the materiel improvements, changes were also instituted in the High Command. The role of the British Advisory Mission was diminished. This was supposed to be an advisory mission but in practice it interfered with the command functions. This fact resulted in providing frustrations and easy excuses for the various Greek command echelons. General James Van Fleet was placed in command of a similar American mission. He was an exceptional officer with a keen mind who was able to obtain the complete confidence of the Greeks. The Greeks themselves made a very significant command change when they appointed General Alexander Papagos as Generalissimo. Papagos was their Chief of Staff during World War II and the years preceding it; he was, therefore, credited with the Greek victories in World War II. He was a great organizer and the most outstanding military leader in modern Greek History. Most important for the occasion was the prestige of his name and his no-nonsense attitude which made subbordinates hold him in awe.

With the improvements in the Greek National Army, the guerrillas found themselves progressively on the defensive. They were also being undermined by ideological difficulties in the communist camp. Tito broke with the Cominform and a similar struggle developed within the Greek communist leadership. Vafiades appeared to have had pro-Tito leanings but the Stalinist faction prevailed and Vafiades was deposed as commander-in-chief. His successors committed the error of practically abandoning guerrilla tactics and concentrating on holding the strongholds of Grammos and Vitsi. These two mountains are anchored on the Greek-Albanian border and extend into Greece. They are rough and unpopulated. The objective of holding them was that their permanent control by the guerrillas would provide tangible evidence that the guerrillas were firmly established on Greek soil.

The guerrilla strength was therefore concentrated on those two mountains. Field fortifications were constructed consisting mainly of machinegun nests made out of multiple tree trunks reinforced with mortar. Heavy weapons including artillery were brought from Albania. Later the Greek Army captured over 60 Skoda guns on these locations. A flanking attack on these two positions was impossible without violating Albanian territory. The Greek Army was, therefore, obliged to assault them frontally. This they did. The communists were beaten and with these two battles the communist guerrilla war in Greece ended.

Why did the communist guerrillas fail in Greece?

They failed for a combination of reasons. We list them here in what we consider order of importance.

The most important reason of their failure is that the communists did not manage to capture and hold the sympathies of the Greek people. In 1944 the guerrilla bands were in control of most of Greece. That was their golden opportunity to win over the minds and loyalties of the people. But loyalty is not won through terrorism and other abuses. This is precisely what the Greek communists practiced in 1944 and later. Consequently, the Greeks, particularly the peasants and small town dwellers, turned very decisively against them.

The next reason is the military inadequacies of the guerrillas. These inadequacies were manifested in many ways. In the conduct of operations and in staff planning it was obvious that the quality of leadership at battalion and company level was mediocre. Above battalion level the quality was more often than not, poor. Platoon and squad leaders were usually good, but the rank and file were reluctant fighters. This was caused by two facts. First, the guerrillas did not attract, with few exceptions, any career officers or people with lengthy military experience. Second, they filled their ranks with individuals who were forced to serve with the guerrillas. This became more prominent during the later years when the source of dedicated communists was more-or-less exhausted. The communists who had not become casualties were elevated to officer grades, but again the time available and training they received was not sufficient to qualify them for senior command positions. The guerrillas did not lack material resources. But the technical use of their weapons was inferior to that of their adversaries. A good example of this was the poor results of their artillery. They were well supplied with artillery in some of the later battles, but the effectiveness of their fire was extremely poor.

The third reason is related to the previous one. It has to

do with the decision to deemphasize guerrilla tactics and face the Greek Army in pitched battles. This mistake is often made by guerrilla leaders. It is the result of bad assessment of a military situation and imperfect understanding of guerrilla warfare.

The fourth reason is the military assistance which was furnished to the Greek National Army by the United States and the moral and political support furnished to the Greek government. Without it, the communist guerrillas could have been victorious notwithstanding their other shortcomings.

The final reason is the Tito-Cominform split. When the Greek Communist Party decided to remain loyal to Moscow, it lost Tito's support. If, however, it had sided with Tito, chances are that he would have gone out of his way to furnish them continuing large-scale assistance because he was hard-pressed for allies then and the friendship of another communist party would have prevented his ideological isolation within the communist camp. Their reward for remaining loyal to Moscow was half-hearted support from that source because Stalin had a very low opinion of Greek communists and because he wished to utilize his resources for expansionist efforts elsewhere.

2. Indochina

During World War II, the French administration in Indochina remained loyal to the Vichy government. Complying with Vichy's policy of compromise with the Axis, the French High Commissioner allowed Japanese troops to establish themselves in Indochina. The Vietminh movement developed during this period under the leadership of Ho Chi Minh as a resistance movement against the Japanese. Although Ho and the other leaders of the Vietminh were communists, the movement itself had a nationalist base and it advocated the eventual establishment of an independent Indochina. Small guerrilla groups were formed, but their activities against the Japanese were limited because of their lack of equipment.

In March 1945, the Japanese interned the French troops who had remained until that time at liberty.[7] This action caused a substantial loss of prestige to the French because the Japanese were obviously losing the war by then. As a result, the thought prevailed among the Vietnamese that French rule could not be resumed after the war and Bao Dai, the Emperor of Annam, proclaimed himself Head of the Independent Indochinese State. He was not recognized as such by the Vietminh, who successfully seized control of the provincial areas immediately after the Japanese collapse in August 1945. Bao Dai resigned and left for Europe. Shortly afterwards, the British occupied the Southern half of Indochina and the Chinese Nationalists the Northern half. Neither attempted to disarm or otherwise restrict the Vietminh.

Early in 1946 French troops returned to Indochina and the Chinese and British left. The French simultaneously announced that they were recognizing Vietnam as a "free state" without precisely defining the term. In the years that followed, the French repeatedly made vague promises of independence or autonomy for the Vietnamese, but were always careful not to define them in detail. They even recruited Bao Dai to head a semipuppet native administration. However, even the moderates and noncommunists among the Vietnamese viewed the French promises with skepticism and failed to rally to the French cause since the political issue of this war continued to be independence. Thus, the French High Command failed to establish a political basis for victory in this conflict. It had to be, therefore, strictly a military solution for the French.

In 1946 through the following four or five years, the French were not in a position to exert a strong military effort in Indochina. French law prohibited the use of conscripts outside France; therefore, the burden of fighting had to be born by the regular establishment and the Foreign Legion. Besides Indochina, there were commitments in Germany and North Africa. Finally, a sizable segment of the electorate and parliament were cool towards further colonial adventures.

On the Vietminh side, leadership of the military effort was entrusted to Vo Nguyen Giap, a communist who had served for a short time with the Chinese red forces. Giap published a book in 1950 in which he explains how Mao's ideas on guerrilla warfare were to be applied in Indochina. Capitalizing on the numerical insufficiency of French troops in relation to the size of the country, the low density of communications network, and the terrain which was favorable to the guerrillas, the Vietminh established "guerrilla bases" in the backwoods areas. From these bases they sent out small raiding parties to harass the French garrisons. Until 1949, however, when the Chinese Communists appeared on the border, their military successes were limited. They accomplished little more than the preservation of their organization. During all this time though, they exerted considerable effort towards the indoctrination of the population to the Vietminh cause.

Giap considers that the third phase (according to Mao's theory) of the insurrection was entered in 1950. Reinforced with Chinese equipment, Giap attacked and wiped out the French outposts on the Chinese border along Route Coloniale 4. During this operation the French lost about 10,000 troops, including three parachute battalions which were dropped to reinforce the outposts after the battle began. The Vietminh, however, were not yet quite strong enough to follow-up this success with a decisive assault on the French. In fact, the following year, the French under Marshal de Lattre de Tasigny, who replaced General Murice Carpentier as commander, inflicted defeats on the Vietminh at Vinh Yen (January 1951), Mao Khe (March 1951), and in the South. For all practical purposes the Vietminh abandoned the South and concentrated their military effort in Tonkin, in the North. Later events, i.e.; the eventual partition of Viet Nam and the renewal of the communist push in the South ten years later, prove that this was a wise decision at the time and also that the communists are not easily distracted from their ultimate objectives.

Marshal de Lattre established in the Tonkin Delta a series of mutually-supported strong points. In addition, mobile troops operating within the perimeter of these forts could speedily bear pressure to relieve any point under attack. Probably, he was hoping to create a strong base from which to strike the Vietminh after they were sufficiently weakened through attrition caused by their own offensives. But de Lattre died in 1952 from illness. He also suffered the personnel tragedy of having his only son, a lieutenant, killed in action against the Vietminh. He was succeeded by General Henri Navarre. Navarre continued the method of establishing mutually-supported strong points but, beset by manpower shortages, he neglected the mobile groups and his forces became progressively tied down to purely defensive missions.

Vietminh losses in the semi-pitched battle of 1951 and 1952 were considerable. Giap, therefore changed strategy. He abandoned the attacks on the prepared positions on the Delta and attempted to draw the French out of their base by striking at areas which were lightly held, but had a certain political or psychological significance and thus required at least a token defense by the French. This strategy of Giap was called by the French the strategy of "zones excentriques" and led to the French defeat at Dien Bien Phu and the abandonment of North Indochina to the Vietminh.

The French decided to fortify Dien Bien Phu in order to present an obstacle to the Vietminh raids on the mountain country of Northeast Laos. This decision was probably a correct one. The Vietminh operations in Laos would be in jeopardy with a strong base established at Dien Bien Phu. On the other hand, if the Vietminh decided to attack it, there was an excellent chance that they would suffer a severe defeat in view of the fact that they did not fare well in similar operations against the French positions around the Delta. But the execution of this plan by the French left a lot to be desired. The forces allocated to Dien Bien Phu were not sufficient. Artillery was particularly weak in relation to the artillery available to the Vietminh. The Chinese reds, relieved from the requirements of the Korean front after the armistice there, supplied the Vietminh with progressively more artillery pieces. But the greatest disadvantage of the Dien Bien Phu position was that of geography. The village itself is located in a valley of about ten by five miles, surrounded by hills. An airstrip was constructed on the valley, since resupply was to be furnished strictly by air. Loss of the hills surrounding the valley, meant that the airstrip would come under fire by enemy artillery on the hills. In addition, the air bases of Hanoi and Vietiane, from where resupply was to be furnished, were over 200 miles away. For these and other reasons, the selection of the Dien Bien Phu location has been severely criticized since, particularly by French air officers, and by General Cogny who commanded the French forces in North Vietnam. Navarre has claimed that this location, although not perfect, was the best available.

The seige of Dien Bien Phu lasted from about November 1953 through 8 May 1954. The most decisive factor contributing to the French defeat was the quantity of Vietminh artillery and its method of employment. The Vietminh moved their pieces at night very close to the French artillery positions and camouflaged them carefully. Come daylight, they used them in direct fire against the French artillery which was then put out of action before it could engage in successful counterbattery. In this manner, supremacy in heavy weapons was gained and Giap followed up with a series of massive frontal attacks which captured one by one of all French positions.

The quantity of Vietminh artillery was no small surprise to the French. Giap deployed around Dien Bien Phu forty-eight 105s, forty-eight 75s (mountain howitzers) and an unverified number of 120 mm heavy mortars and 75 mm recoiless rifles. The French made available at Dien Bien Phu only twenty-four 105s and four 155s. In addition, ammunition resupply became problematic for the French after the first few days whereas the Vietminh aparently managed to overcome all of their ammunition supply problems. Ammunition (as well as other supplies) had to be landed or dropped to the French from aircraft. This is no easy way to resupply a garrison during a prolonged engagement, particularly since Giap was able to assemble eithty 37 mm antiaircraft guns and about one hundred 20 mm guns and .50 cal machine guns with antiaircraft mounts which extracted a heavy toll from the French. On the other side, the Vietminh supply line continued uninterrupted in spite of the very energetic efforts of the French Air Force to interdict it. This line ran from the Chinese border to Phong-Tho, to Tsinh-Hom, to Lai-Chau. The Vietminh used trucks, animals, and human porters to transport supplies over this route. The maintenance of this uninterrupted supply route is perhaps the most important singular factor contributing to Vietminh's success.

Strictly speaking, the fall of Dien Bien Phu was not much of a loss. The French lost 12,000 men including prisoners. This was only about 5% of the French forces available in Indochina then. Conservative estimates bring the Vietminh losses to over 25,000. The impact on French morale though was so great that the French decided on armistice.

Some additional comments on the battle of Dien Bien Phu are appropriate.

In confrontation beween guerrilla and a conventional forces each side tries to take maximum advantage of conditions and factors favorable to it. The one factor which the conventional forces always have on their favor is their superiority in fire-power over the guerrillas. In guerrilla warfare, therefore, the conventional forces are always striving to find themselves in a situation where they can use this superiority in firepower and destroy the enemy. When the guerrillas themselves accept a pitched battle it can only mean one of two things: Either the guerrilla commander has been cornered or fooled, or he has managed to reverse the tables and has assembled sufficient re-sources which make him superior to the conventional force in the forthcoming battle. In the latter case, the conventional forces have to use their superior mobility (providing they have such mobility) to reestablish fire superiority over the guerrillas.

Our analysis of the battle of Dien Bien Phu concludes that the French High Command found itself in a situation where it could take advantage of neither superior firepower nor mo-bility. The inferiority in numbers of artillery available to the French was an error caused by miscalculation. Somehow, French (and American) intelligence failed to detect the trans-fer of equipment from the Chinese to the Vietminh. This situa-tion was compounded by the inability of the French Air Force to interdict the Vietminh supply line and cause an acute ammunition shortage at the battlefield. The magnitude of surprise to the French is amply illustrated by the fact that the artillery commander in the fortress, Colonel Piroth, committed suicide. After the first few days of the battle, when he realized that his counterbattery was ineffective in neutralizing the enemy guns, with typical Gallic politeness he visited the com-mand posts of each strong point and apologized for what he considered his personal failure. Then, he went to his bunker. Since he had lost one arm in World War II, he was unable to pull the slide of his service pistol, so he placed a hand grenade on his chest and pulled the arming hook with his teeth.

When the French High Command in Indochina realized that the defenders of Dien Bien Phu were outgunned, it was already too late to effectively use its available mobility to reinforce the garrison with heavy weapons. The Vietminh had already penetrated the outside defenses sufficiently to be established on the hills from which they could directly fire on the landing strip. Landing of transport aircraft became, therefore, an impossibility. However, for a few more days the French tried and in the process suffered heavy losses in both aircraft and aircrews. Resupply was dependent henceforth strictly on airdrops and helicopters. The number of helicopters available to the French in those days was limited. In addition, the H-19 (the principal helicopter then available) was too limited in range and payload and the airlifting of artillery pieces was definitely beyond its capability. The French Air Force[8] managed to sustain a steady stream of reinforcements of supplies and personnel replacements through this method, but delivering whole artillery battalions on Dien Bien Phu's shrinking drop zones was beyond its capabilities. The Dien Bien Phu garrison, therefore, was defeated in a classic siege battle for no other reason except that it engaged superior forces.

The lessons learned from this operation are self-evident.

Certain observations need to be made on the apparent ineffectiveness of airpower in Indochina. In March 1954 the French had available in this theater 163 fighters, 41 light bombers, 124 transports, 16 reconnaissance aircraft, and 230 auxiliary and utility aircraft.[9] This force was impressive in view of the fact that the Vietminh possessed no airpower whatsoever. But the development of air bases was limited and logistic support of the air fleet from France was problematic. The weather presented frequently additional difficulties. The terrain does not favor close ground support missions. Worst of all, perhaps, was the fact that the command structure was such that air officers were not being consulted in the planning of operations. In many instances airpower was misused as a substitute for, or augmentation to, artillery. The results, therefore, were not commensurate to the potential capabilities of the air arm nor to the efforts exerted by the aircrews and ground personnel.

The conflict in Indochina, in its final stages, was not a guerrilla conflict, but conventional warfare. This falls in the precise pattern for insurgency which the communist leadership has established. The success of the insurgents is attributable to the French policies. The French were unable to obtain a political basis on which they could maintain their presence in Indochina. Such political basis could have been established in 1946 or in 1947 through the creation of a native regime with affiliation to the French. Having failed to do this, the only other alternative was the employment of overwhelming military force. But the French did not make such force available and allowed the insurgents to increase their strength to the point where it equalled or even exceeded the force of the French. This became more prominent as the Chinese, freed from the burden of the Korean War, were able to devote more of their resources in support of the Vietminh. The results were a military defeat for the French and their eclipse from Southeast Asia.

3. The Algerian War

The French conquest of Algeria took place within a few years after 1830. Until that time Algeria was part of the Ottoman Empire and subjected to the usual features of Turkish misrule. When the French took over, the inhabitants of Algeria could hardly be classified as a Nation; they were an assemblance of mutually antagonistic tribes whose only common characteristics were religion (Mohamedanism) and language (Arabic). A tribal leader named Abd-El-Kader attempted to unify the tribes in opposition to the French, but was not successful.

France did not give Algeria colonial status, but annexed it to metropolitan France. Although this annexation was absurd, as we shall presently see, the French apparently took it seriously. This explains to a great extent the emotionalism with which the French have regarded the Algerian War in contrast to the War in Indochina. The absurdity of the French claim that Algeria was part of metropolitan France is caused by the fact that in over 125 years no serious effort was made to give the majority of the natives citizenship status. In view of the fact that national consciousness did not exist among the natives at the time of the French conquest, in fact did not exist at all until the present generation, it could have been a relatively easy task for the French to truly assimilate the natives and integrate them into the French Nation. This would have required a benevolent attitude toward the natives, including an effort towards public education, social reform, nondiscrimination in wages, etc. Some French governments did make such an effort. Particularly Napoleon III, in spite of his other shortcomings, followed a wise policy in Algeria. In general, however, the French policy appears to have been one of colonization through the settlement of large numbers of whites. These whites were not all Frnchmen. Thousands of Spaniards, Italians, and Maltese settled in Algeria and obtained French citizenship. Maybe the thought behind this plan was that the whites would eventually constitute the population majority. However, in 1954 only $\frac{1}{8}$ of Algeria's population was of European extraction. French claims that this minority constituted the most dynamic segment of the population do not have much substance in democratic terms. Arguments that most of the professional people come from the minority or that the minority controls the industry and commerce are rationalizations having no bearing on the principal issue. The principal issue in a democratic society always has been this: the majority rules, although the minority's rights are respected. It is unfortunate for France, and also certain other European countries, that they have found themselves with a schizophrenic personality in regards to the application of democratic principles. No logical person can seriously accept as being valid the claims of some Europeans that the same principles of majority rule which are accepted in Western Europe are not universally applicable and that they can be waived in Algeria, Sudan, or Timbuktu for this or that reason.

In spite of the French attitude towards the nonwhite native Algerians, those of them who managed to become educated did not wish to be considered as being anything but French. Ferhat Abbas, the man who eventually became the political head of the FLN, was among them. In fact, between 1927 and 1954 he led a political party whose declared objective was the acquisition of French citizenship by all native Moslems. In other words, he espoused the same objectives of assimilation and integration with France which the French governments tried to implement after 1956, when the revolt had already engulfed Algeria.

The strong winds of Nationalism were bound to affect the Algerians sooner or later. Agitation for independence was growing in neighboring Tunisia and Morocco; Libya had been made a sovereign state by the Allies after World War II; Egypt had compelled the British to evacuate Suez, Syria, and Lebanon had also been given independence. In Algeria too, the underground FLN (Front for National Liberation) made its appearance. In 1954, the first guerrilla raids against isolated French garrisons took place.

The FLN was led by a group of young men who had no previous experience in politics. Most of them, however, had some military background after serving as noncoms in the French Army during and immediately after World War II. In fact, some of them had fought on the French side in Indochina. The FLN leadership had made no serious effort to negotiate a settlement with the French government. It is certain, however, that no French government was willing to negotiate any change in Algeria's status. It was becoming obvious that colonial administrations are terminated only under the pressure of revolt.

The revolt's outbreak had been carefully planned.

Algeria was divided into six military districts (willayas). Each district had a group of armed bands reporting to the district headquarters which was responsible for planning all operations and supplying the bands with weapons. In addition, the district military commanders were given additional responsibilities as political administrators and tax collectors. Cooperation among the district commands was not always good. A general headquarters was established and operated in Tunisia. Tunisia offered shelter to the guerrillas from the beginning. In the later years of the Algerian War, substantial FLN units were formed and trained on Tunisian soil from where they returned to Algeria for raids. The French Army was aware of all this and was clamoring for an invasion of Tunisia. It was restrained by the French Goverment which figured that nothing would be gained from such a complication. On certain occasions, however, French commanders bombarded Tunisian border villages with artillery and aircraft, causing casualties among Tunisian civilians.

In spite of their claims to the contrary, the Algerian guerrillas were relatively well supplied with weapons. The whole North African coast was sprinkled with abandoned weapons from World War II and these constituted an excellent initial source for the FLN. In addition, the neighboring Arab countries, particularly Egypt, were willing suppliers.

The Algerian War was a guerrilla war throughout. Most offensive operations of the Algerians were conducted by units of company strength or less. Only once did the rebels attempt to fight what can be considered a pitched battle. In late summer of 1957 a series of engagements took place in the city of Algiers and its suburbs. Several thousand Algerians fought it out with French paratroopers in the streets and from houses and public buildings of the Arab quarter. The outcome of this series of engagements was almost disastrous for the FLN. The majority of the participating rebels were either killed or captured. In addition, the civilians, both Arab and French, suffered a great number of casualties. But this affected the two groups of civilizians in different ways. The native Moslem inhabitants of Algiers were demoralized and cowed, whereas the French, even the few who might have held moderate views until that event, were left with a strong determination to take further revenge. The FLN leadership admitted later that this operation was not a prudent one.

The French reactions to the Algerian rebellion have been analyzed in detail by certain scholars and by the international press. A lot has been written in particular about the reaction of the French Army to the Algerian War and the effect which the war's outcome may have in the future relations between the Army and the Republic. The subject is too complex to be discussed in the space available here. It is worth noticing, however, that the attitude of the French Army towards the Algerian War was responsible for the collapse of the Fourth Republic and General DeGaule's ascent to power.

The overwhelming consensus among non-French observers has been that those of the French officers who have any political convictions are conservative to the extreme, reactionary, and perhaps only too willing to try some other form of government. A dictatorship of some sort, perhaps, or even a restoration of the Bourbon monarchy. A multitude of reasons are given for this attitude of the professionals in the French Army. The capitulation of 1940, the snobbery of the British during the war, the intellectual reaction to the leftist trends of the 30's and 40's, etc. One may easily assume, after reading an account of all these reasons for frustration that the French officer corps is entirely composed of psychopaths and lunatics. The fact still remains that the majority of the French officers have remained loyal to the civil government through two major crises, i.e.: the Lagaillard putch on the barricades in January 1961 and the revolt of Generals Jouhaud, Salan, Challe, and Zeller, later in the same year. Undoubtedly, deGaulle's presence at the head of the civil government had a lot to do with the retention of the officers' loyalty.

The French Army committed 400,000 men to the war effort in Algeria. This caused a serious reduction of the French garrisons in Germany and of the French contribution to the NATO effort. The French High Command developed and employed special tactics in combating guerrillas, particularly suited to the conditions existing in Algeria. For instance, helicopters were utilized for the first time in large numbers to transport the chase units in their maneuvers to intercept the guerrillas. The French also developed the armed helicopters by mounting machineguns and other weapons on the U.S.-made H-21 and the French-made Alouette II. In spite of the French military effort, however, the FLN guerrillas were not defeated. In essence, a military stalemate was reached in Algeria; therefore, the solution of the war had to be a political one.

The military stalemate in Algeria brought about the political crises in metropolitan France which resulted in General de-Gaulle's assumption of power. Those who brought deGaulle into power in 1958 never seriously considered that he would follow a policy of extrication from Algeria. However, it appears that deGaulle concluded, and was able to prevail upon his colleagues, that this was the best solution available. He was right.

What other possibilities existed?

There was, of course, the possibility of continuing the war with appropriate changes of strategy. By then, it was becoming obvious to all rational military analysts that even a substantial increase of the French forces committed could not decisively defeat the insurgents as long as the insurgents stuck to guerrilla tactics. Under the then existing conditions, the only military action which could result in a complete defeat of the guerrillas would have been the invasion of Tunisia and Morocco and the destruction of the guerrilla bases in those countries. From the purely military point of view, this was feasible. But the long range prospects of such a solution were not too promising. It would have required the continuous maintenance of a large French force in North Africa, absorbing national energies and resources which deGaulle wanted to divert elsewhere. It would also result in an increase of communist influence among the insurgents. Situations such as this are tailormade for communist infiltration and the communists seldom miss these opportunities. Communist influence among the FLN was already substantial in 1958, although it cannot be said that the communists had taken over the movement. Finally such an invasion would have completely alienated all Arab countries from France. This too, would have been undesirable to deGaulle who was determined to seek a long-range policy of increased French influence among the Arabs.

Then, there were the political possibilities. Unfortunately for the French, lesser compromises were not acceptable to their adversaries. What would have been welcomed by the Algerian political leadership in the 30's and 40's was totally unacceptable in the late 50's and early 60's. So the terms of the political solution had to be complete independence for Algeria.

The case under study presents us with the first example since World War II where the national independence was obtained strictly through the use of guerrilla warfare by the insurgents.

An interesting side issue of the Algerian War has been the

activity of the Secret Army Organization (the OAS). This group engaged in guerrilla warfare against the French authorities and the FLN, after it became obvious that deGaulle was about to abandon Algeria to the Arabs. Its activities were limited primarily to Oran and Algiers Temporarily the OAS appeared to gain the upperhand and in effect controlled the two cities. However, in the long run it failed to achieve even a relative compromise on its objective, which was the retention of a French Algeria. There are two reasons for this failure. The first is that, although some of the French military defected to the OAS, the mass of the French Army remained loyal to deGaulle, as we have explained. The second reason is that without the support of the French military, the OAS had to rely exclusively on the support of the European colonists in Algeria. These people made good revolutionaries, but indifferent guerrillas. They suffered from the "positional" mentality, which is fatal to guerrillas. The vast majority of them were urban residents, therefore preoccupied with controlling and defending the urban areas. Their capabilities for operations outside the cities were limited because of the hostile environment in the rural areas where the population was overwhlemingly Moslem.

Without support from metropolitan France or anywhere else they were unable to sustain their effort against the Moslem Algerians and eventually they abandoned Africa and came to France, Spain and South America as refugees.

4.   EOKA and the Revolt of the Cypriots

Cyprus is a relatively large Mediterranean island which was until 1960 a British Crown Colony. Britain "purchased" Cyprus from Turkey in the last century. The Island's population consists of an overwhelming (over 80%) majority of ethnic Greeks and minorities of Turks (about 18%) and a few other nationalities.

The Island's colonial administration was one of the most authoritarian. The government was exclusively in the hands of civil servants imported from England; the Islanders were not at all represented in the government above the municipal level. Yet, with the exception of a short period of trouble in 1932, the native population remained docile and cooperative. This did not mean, however, that the Greek majority did not maintain the hope of ἕνωσις, i.e. of eventual political union with the Greek State. To the islanders this deemed a reasonable aspiration and the only ethically correct one in consonance with the democratic principles which require rule by the majority with respect for the minority's rights. Yet, the traditional friendship and alliance between Greece and England, intensified during the days of World War II, prevented the formation of any active movement advocating the overthrow of the colonial regime.

The feeling for union with Greece could not remain dormant indefinitely, however. The conclusion of World War II brought an upsurge to the ideals of Nationalism throughout the world. England had given independence to India and some of her colonies. Besides, there were people in Cyprus, as well as elsewhere, who were taking seriously the proclamations of the Atlantic Charter and assumed that the signatory countries, England included, had made the direct and implied statements of the Charter in good faith. The British government was, consequently, approached on the subject of a possible referendum which would settle the political future of Cyprus. It has been reported that Eden's remark to one such discussion was "never". The shortsightedness of such an attitude can be pointed out by the fact that today Cyprus is no longer a Crown Colony and that Eden has become a self-acknowledged political failure.

To the Cypriots, though, the unbending attitude of the British government meant that there was no hope for a negotiated political settlement. Therefore, the only road to freedom open to them was the one which led through armed insurrection. Outright rebellion was not practical because of the overwhelming difference of the forces involved — a people of about half a million against the declining, yet still formidable resources of England and her remaining possessions. The political leaders of the Cypriots chose, therefore, to use a combination of moral pressure through the United Nations and guerrilla warfare which would embarrass the British and make their maintenance on the Island very costly.

The conduct of guerrilla warfare was entrusted to the EOKA (National Organization of Cypriot Fighters), the underground organization which was led by the retired Lt. Colonel of the Greek Army, George Grivas. He was better known as Digenes, which is the pseudonym he was using to conceal his identity. But Nikos Zahariades, the Secretary General of the Greek Communist Party, revealed his true identity during a broadcast from the Moscow radio station; but more about that later. Grivas is a Cypriot by birth. He entered the Greek Military Academy when he was a young man and eventually was commissioned a 2nd Lieutenant in the Infantry. Before World War II his career was not spectacular, but promising. As a Major he attended the equivalent of the Greek Army War College and he graduated high enough in his class to be selected for further studies in the French Ecole Superiere De Guerre; this in itself was a professional distinction.[10] After his return from France he served a tour in the General Staff and during the war he was Chief of Staff of the 2nd Greek Infantry Division. During the occupation of Greece by the Axis forces, Grivas became well-known because of his leadership of the underground resistance organization known as "Organosis X". This organization was relatively small, but its membership consisted almost exclusively of cadets and junior officers of the disbanded Greek Army. The organization was known to have nationalistic views, a fact which brought it soon into conflict with the communist underground. What the "Xites" lacked in numbers, they made up in discipline and fighting ability. They were universally despised by the communists who had gotten the worst in many encounters with "Xites" in remote Athens neighborhoods.

After the war was over, Grivas resigned from the Army and ventured into politics. He failed to be elected in the parliament, and for several years afterwards he lived an obscure life as a retired officer. When he assumed the leadership of EOKA he was already in his fifties, but there could hardly be found a man better qualified for the job on hand. Grivas is austere, self-disciplined, and has an analytical mind. All this, plus his military and underground experience made him a likely prospect for guerrilla leader. In addition, it appears that he did not spend the years of his postwar retirement loafing. Apparently, the man made a study of the guerrilla movements of Word War II and drew conclusions for future reference. He utilized this accumulated knowledge in organizing EOKA and directing the guerrilla operations in Cyprus.

The foundation of the EOKA organization was the universal support which it received from the Greek Cypriots. The spearhead of the organization was a small group of about 200 guerrillas reinforced by the underground units of the towns and villages. Initially, the guerrilla force consisted of five units as follows:

Three units of about 10 men each on the Olympus Mountain area.

One unit of 23 men on the Pentadactylos Mountain area.

One reserve unit of 22 men, having no specific area of responsibility.

The weapons with which this venture was undertaken consisted of two machineguns, six automatic rifles, 21 submachineguns, 47 rifles, and seven revolvers.[11] Later, the guerrillas were supplied with additional weapons from Greece and Egypt. They also captured quantities of arms from the British and even used shotguns with rifled slugs. Since Cyprus has a relatively large number of small mines, the guerrillas were able to acquire quantities of explosives by raiding the mines, killing or capturing the guards, and walking off with the explosives. They were thus able to commit over 400 acts of sabotage[12] on military installations and police stations.

The most serious act of sabotage was committed on the night of 26 November 1957 in the Akroteri RAF base, when three Canberra bombers and a Venom fighter were destroyed by an electric bomb which exploded in one of the hangers. A time bomb was also placed under the bed of Field Marshal Harding, the British governor, on the night of 21 March 1956. Harding did not sleep in his residence that night, but when the bomb was discovered, he seems to have panicked and completely lost his head.

Besides the acts of sabotage, the EOKA guerrillas conducted several raids against isolated police stations and military patrols.

A typical raid is the one carried out on 5 December 1955. A group of eight guerrillas ambushed a patrol of about 15 men with one officer. The patrol was in two light trucks. The lead vehicle was fired at with submachineguns when it approached a curve, the driver was hit and the vehicle stopped; simultaneously, the second vehicle was fired at. The attack lasted only three minutes and the British lost five men killed. The guerrillas sustained no casualties in that raid and no trace of them could be found when reinforcements arrived from a nearby camp.[13]

Another time, on 16 December 1955, 12 guerrillas attacked a rural police station which had been reinforced by a platoon of Infantry. This engagement lasted about 15 minutes during which the Lieutenant commanding the Infantry platoon was killed. The guerrillas withdrew and no effort was made by the station garrison to give chase, although they outnumbered the guerrillas 2 to 1.

In general, the military countermeasures of the British against the guerrillas were unsuccessful. Supreme command of the British forces in Cyprus was given to Field Marshal Harding, who simultaneously headed the civil government. Harding had been Chief of the Imperial General Staff. In World War II he had competently commanded the 7th Armored Division in North Africa. In Cyprus, however, Harding turned out to be a complete military and political failure. It is inexplicable why the man accepted the post in the first place, when it was obiavously an assignment for which he was not qualified by background or experience.

The British progressively committed more forces to Cyprus. In the spring of 1958, there were 18 battalions of Infantry, Paratroops, and Commandos, and two mechanized cavalry regiments reported on Cyprus engaged in garrison and antiguerrilla duties. In addition, the police had been increased from about 1500 to over 5000. All these forces were by far greater than what the British had in Berlin during the same period, although one of the frequent Berlin crises was in process. In spite of the overwhelming odds in their favor, the British were unable to decisively defeat the guerrillas or capture Grivas, although Harding had foolishly announced on several occasions that his forces had surrounded Grivas' band and were about to capture him. The total EOKA losses were 204 dead, including 88 killed in action. The rest were executed by the British as suspected rebels. The British losses were 417 dead and over 800 wounded. Among the dead were 19 who were burned to death on 17 June 1956 during a very amateurish operation. A battalion was conducting a search for guerrillas in a wooded area near Pafos. In order to smoke-out the guerrillas they set fire to the woods; but the wind direction shifted and several British troops and vehicles were trapped by the fire.

In general, the counterguerrilla operations in Cyprus were characterized by ineptitude. There was more of an effort made by the security forces to terrorize the civilian inhabitants into submission rather than to actively pursue the guerrillas. The result was that the opposition to British rule by the civilians was intensified. Another flaw in the method of operation of the British seems to be their preoccupation with the security of their rear which hindered their purely offensive movements. For instance, on 12 December 1955, a battalion was searching an area near the village of Spelia in Central Cyprus. After about three hours of search, only one platoon with one scout dog continued the active search; the rest of the battalion had taken static positions guarding passes and hills. As a result, a 10 man guerrilla unit which was in the vicinity withdrew without being pursued.[14]

In view of the above, it has to be concluded that the EOKA guerrilla campaign was successfully conducted and the EOKA leadership must be commended for the prudent and effective use of the limited means at its disposal. Particularly, since the topography of Cyprus is not favorable to guerrilla operations because of the relatively small size of the island and the absence of enough areas of dense vegetation which could offer sufficient opportunities for maneuver and concealment.

Although the British were unable to wipe out the guerrillas, neither could the guerrillas hope to decisively defeat the

British. A military stalemate was, therefore, reached in Cyprus. In order to break the stalemate, the British tried political solutions. They enlisted the support of the Turkish minority and the Greek communists.

The Cypriot Turks had been quite impassive politically until they were prompted by the British to advance the demand that if British domination of Cyprus was to be terminated, the island should be partitioned between Greece and Turkey. This solution is, of course, absurd since there is no solid geographic area on the island where the Turks constitute the majority. Partition, therefore, would require mass relocation of population. However, the presentation of such a demand facilitated the British position because it made the whole affair look like a territorial dispute among Greece, Turkey and England instead of a purely colonial dispute between England and the majority of the island's inhabitants. The government of Turkey, which for almost a century had shown no interest in the fate of the Cypriot Turks, gladly entered the dispute, encouraging the demand for partition. Perhaps, another Turkish government would not have involved itself in such a shaky cause.[15] But in those days, Menderes was the Prime Minister of Turkey and his government was troubled with a deteriorating political and economic situation at home. The Cyprus adventure, however, did not save the Menderes regime because in 1960 a revolution overthrew his government and Menderes with Zorlou, his foreign minister, were eventually hung after having been convicted of treason and misappropriation of public funds.

The Greek communists were caught by surprise with the EOKA movement. The communists claim to be the champions of all oppressed and colonial peoples. Yet, here was a case where an anti-colonial revolt was taking place led and directed by individuals who were ardent nationalists and with whom the communists had old scores to settle. In addition, the possibility existed that in view of the fact that the Communist Party of Greece had been outlawed since the days of the Greek Guerrilla War, the Communist Organization of Cyprus would also be outlawed and its leaders forced to expatriation. To avoid such a calamity, the Cypriot communists turned traitor and tried their best to undermine the EOKA efforts, much to the delight of the British. In fact, as stated previously, Grivas' identity was not known until the Communists revealed it in a radio broadcast.

The support of the Turks and the communists was not enough to salvage the British position on Cyprus. The British were forced to concede the impossibility of their position and to grant the Island independence on the condition that it remains independent and does not join the Greek State. To this the Greek Cypriots agreed reluctantly. It has become obvious that they consider this solution temporary and on the first opportunity they will repudiate this agreement, particularly since the Cypriots themselves were not party to the Convention of Zurich which established the Republic of Cyprus. The Zurich agreement was made by the governments of Greece, Turkey, and England and was accepted by Archbishop Makarios, the titular leader of the Greek Cypriots. This agreement was never validated by a popular referendum, therefore, the solution reached is not in accord with democratic principles and will only lead to new troubles.

There are a number of items about the guerrilla activities in Cyprus that need to be noted.

The first of these is the fact that a small force of guerrillas, under certain conditions, can stand off a much superior conventional force. This fact, of course is not unique with the Cyprus experience.

Another is the importance of popular support for the guerrillas. As stated above, geographic condition on Cyprus are not too favorable for guerrilla warfare. However, this was offset by the universal support from the Greek Cypriots which the guerrillas enjoyed. In fact, the guerrilla movement was an expression of the popular sentiment.

A third item that needs to be mentioned is the relative impotency of opposition to the guerrillas by an ethnic minority, when such a minority is not geographically segregated. This was the case of the Cypriot Turks. The manipulation of the Turks by the British proved unwise. It did not salvage the British position on Cyprus and resulted in unnecessary hardships for the Turks.

Last, but not least, it is important to note the necessity of preventing national independence movements from becoming dominated by the communists. In Cyprus it was fortunate for the West that the movement was not initiated by communists. In addition, the communists were not able to infiltrate the guerrillas nor the underground organization, notwithstanding the fact that the insurgents did not receive any support from the West. This was possible in Cyprus because communism had been discredited in the 50's among the Greeks and the Cypriot insurgents were, of course, Greeks. However, in other situations the West has not been so fortunate. In the future, similar situations will probably develop in other parts of the world, particularly in Africa where state boundaries do not coincide with tribal identities. Extreme alertness and acuity of judgment on the part of the West will be required in these situations.

5.   On the War in Viet Nam
And the U.S. Involvement

As these lines are being written,[16] the war in Viet Nam is still in process. Consequently, it would be preferable to avoid analysis and comments on this particular war, as is customary among serious students of History, in contrast to news commentators. News commentators and reporters apparently feel a very strong compulsion to comment on events which they do not fully understand. This compulsion may stem from a feeling of inadequacy among these people who realize that they are observers rather than participants of events.

Our original intention was to avoid any discussion of the War in Viet Nam. However, one cannot help but have the feeling that a contemporary study on the subject of guerrilla warfare which excludes this particular war is incomplete. We shall risk, therefore, a tentative analysis of events in Viet Nam.

Any visitor to Viet Nam who possesses elementary military education will immediately realize that geographic conditions are such that offer overwhelming advantages to guerrillas in any engagement with conventional forces. The density of vegetation in the boonies (i.e. rural areas) is unbelievable. This is brought about by the high humidity and high temperatures that prevail throughout the country, even in the so-called highland areas where elevations reach 4000 feet above sea level. Conditions are favorable to guerrillas also in some of the urban centers, Saigon in particular. Saigon is located in the middle of a huge swamp where there are literally thousands of infiltration routes. Since Saigon is the political and military center of the country, it becomes imperative to keep the city secure. Saigon's security requires conservatively 100,000 troops; and yet this number can only insure moderate, not absolute security for the capital city. This number has to be subtracted from the total available for missions of all kinds; i.e.: garrisons of other towns and offensive operations against the guerrillas.

One also must observe that if Viet Nam's neighboring states are unable or unwilling to stop the guerrillas from trespassing through their territory and the conventional forces are prevented from violating the neighboring states with ground forces, the guerrillas can easily find sanctuary in these states. Any efficient guerrilla force can strike Saigon and retreat into Cambodia after about one day's march through swampy jungle where they cannot be intercepted unless the conventional force is big enough to deploy a battalion per square mile.

Another factor very favorable to the guerrillas was, and still is, the political situation of South Viet Nam. This is, perhaps, one of the most difficult aspects of the Vietnamese enterprise to explain to an American or a European. But the fact remains that the feeling of nationhood, as it is understood by the individual citizens of American and European states, is not fully developed among the Vietnamese. Among the Vietnamese other loyalties take the place of national loyalties. Even tribal loyalties are not prevalent among the Vietnamese with the exception of the approximately 1,000,000 Montagnards, who are not ethnically Vietnamese and who are at odds with whatever government exists in Saigon. These are truly pathetic people because they are neglected by Saigon, which treats them with contempt, while the communist guerrillas practice genocide every time they capture any one of their villages.

The lack of a fully developed feeling of nationhood is responsible for the lack of political consciousness among the people. Until the fifties, the only politically conscious group in Vietnam were the few thousand communists. It was easy, therefore, for the communists to operate and expand in what amounted to a political vacuum. Since the fifties, political consciousness is being developed slowly, but unfortunately it takes some undesirable characteristics. The Catholics, many of whom are refugees from the North, are being organized as a political entity. The Catholics are forced to do this by events. In the French colonial days they enjoyed certain privileges. They are converts to Catholicism, their conversion in most cases having been brought by attendance at church schools. Their education was also responsible for the privileges they enjoyed under the French, being minor officials and administrators. The Catholics, a minority incidentally of the total population, are being organized politically in order to preserve their position of privilege and leadership in the Vietnamese society.

To conteract the political influence of the Catholics, the Buddhists are also being organized politically under the leadership of their most militant leaders, who have been coerced into doing Hanoi's bidding on many occasions.

The significance of all this is that in the absence of a feeling of nationhood (and the related lack of political consciousness) it is difficult to find a large basis of popular support against the communists. The opposite of this situation prevailed in Greece at the end of World War II. In Greece the vast majority of the population was successfully mobilized against the communist guerrillas, who were identified with the national enemies of Greece.

Another peculiarity of Vietnamese society is the fact that although its national economy has been based on agriculture and its by-products, the number of farmer-landowners is relatively small. This, again, is one of the evil legacies of colonial domination. During the colonial period most productive land was parcelled into foreign-owned plantations. The owners frequently did not reside on the land. Europeans were employed as managers and the natives were utilized as farm laborers. There are considerable arguments in favor of this type of farm management. Strictly from the point of view of economics, large farms or plantations are more efficient than small farms run by a single family. In fact, in many areas of the globe the smaller farms are becoming economically untenable. Yet, this situation creates social and political problems. The absence of a large farmer-landowning class deprives the country of another basis of popular anti-communist support. A comparison with the conditions existing in- Greece during the Greek Guerrilla War is again in order. In the 1940's about 80% of the Greek population obtained its livelihood partially or totally through farming. The farms were small and marginal. But the vast majority of the farmers owned their own farms. Even though they were unhappy about their economic conditions, they were not about to exchange them for communism. They knew enough about communist agricultural policies in Russia in the twenties and thirties to realize that if their country was communized their farms would be collectivized and they would be reduced to being collective farm laborers. The result was that an army of peasants fought and defeated the communist guerrilla army. The Vietnamese peasant does not have anything like this at stake; therefore, his support of any anti-communist government is bound to be lukewarm.

When we identify all of the above conditions which are so much in favor of the communist insurgents we may be justified in reaching the conclusion that the decision to involve the U. S. militarily in South Viet Nam was an incorrect decision. It may be said that in South Viet Nam we picked the wrong battleground on which to challenge the expansionist policies of world communism. But to reach this conclusion one assumes (erroneously) that all revelant facts bearing on the problem and affecting decision making are known to him in analytical detail. Unfortunately this is not true. And herein lies one of the greatest risks in analyzing contemporary historical events. All significant factors are not known to the general public, but are classified and their knowledge is shared by relatively few public officials. There may have been other considerations which, when reviewed in 1964 by the U.S. High Command, made the decision to commit U. S. forces in that country justifiable.

Now, let us depart from the point that the decision to confront the communist guerrillas in Viet Nam was taken and that the objective of our involvement is to defeat the guerrillas

militarily, thus eliminating the danger of having the South ⟩
Vietnamese State incorporated into the communist state run
by the Hanoi government. What can we learn from the conduct
of military operations in South Viet Nam?

One thing is obvious. That although the conventional forces
of the U. S., South Viet Nam, and other allies has exceeded
1,000,000 men, including about 550,000 U. S. troops with overwhelming firepower, they were unable to defeat the guerrillas.
Neither have the guerrillas been able to defeat the conventional
forces, although they have attempted to do so both by guerrilla
tactics and in conventional battle during the Tet Offensive of
1968. Neither side has been able to achieve victory and we have
a classic case of military stalemate.

The overwhelming deployment of allied forces, however, was
not achieved overnight. At first there were only U. S. advisors in
Viet Nam. These were the personnel assigned to the U. S. Military Advisory Group. Support troops followed, and then combat
units of gradually increased numbers. This was the policy of
"gradual escalation" and in our opinion this policy constitutes
the major strategic error committed by the U. S. High Command in Viet Nam. At the risk of oversimplifying the example,
this policy in its application amounted to the following: Our
intelligence estimates tell us that in the past month an additional 300 guerrillas have infiltrated into South Viet Nam. We
react to this by committing an additional battalion to match
the increased number of guerrillas. The basic flaw of such a
policy is that it is a policy doomed to achieving nothing more
than a military stalemate. All military stalemates since World
War II involving guerrilla conflicts have resulted in political
victories for the guerrillas. Such policy violates one of the fundamental principles of war which is the principle of "concentration of force". It is inexplicable how the U. S. High Command
committed such a fundamental error. An explanation may be
the possibility that political considerations again interfered
with sound military judgement. It is possible that the intention
was to minimize the U. S. military commitment. Yet, in spite
of any such good intentions the commitment of U. S. troops
and resources was not constrained. In 1968, in order to support
the military effort in Viet Nam, other theaters were denuded,

particularly Korea and Europe. The adverse developments in Viet Nam had adverse affects at home. Some of the better known people began to wonder whether the U. S. was really capable of maintaining a position of world leadership. One senator suggested publically that we pull our forces from Europe with the exception of one division. In the next month the Soviets invaded Czechoslovakia. Maybe the invasion of Czechoslovakia would not have taken place if the Western position in Europe was stronger. No one can say for sure, but Czechoslovakia has to be listed as a possible victim of the war in Viet Nam. Anyway, people, and perhaps governments, throughout the world will never stop wondering how come the containment of communism is Southeast Asia is more important than the fate of fourteen million Czechoslavaks, particularly when it looks like the Czechoslavaks were willing to take the risks of kicking the Communists in the butt, whereas most South Vietnamese seem to be fencesitters.

Allied operations in South Viet Nam evolved around the search and destroy missions. This means that the allied forces established base camps, or operating bases from which expeditions of varied strength were launched. These expeditions were supposed to seek, find, and engage any guerrilla forces which may be operating in the countryside, particularly if the presence of guerrillas had been reported. The allied forces, particularly the U. S. forces, possessed overwhelming mobility for this type of operations. The mobility was furnished by the vast number of helicopters made available. The advantage of helicopter mobility is twofold. Not only does it provide quick reaction time so that the conventional force can reach the position of the guerrillas quickly, but it also frees the conventional force from the necessity of surface movement, thus avoiding the possibility of a guerrilla ambush somewhere between the departure and destination points. In spite of this, most engagements have been inconclusive. The guerrillas manage to withdraw or slip away through the jungle even though they sometimes suffer substantial casualties.

Here again one must point out that the term guerrillas applies not only to the South Vietnamese insurgents, commonly referred to as Viet Cong, but also to the North Vietnamese regular units which have infiltrated from the North and are operating in the South using guerrilla tactics.

Another observation has to be made in regards to the reported guerrilla casualties. In operations of this kind in a fairly densely populated country such as Viet Nam, the noncombatant civilians invariably get caught in the middle and suffer their share of casualties. Under this circumstance, it is unrealistic for anyone to believe that many of the reported guerrilla casualties are not in reality casualties of the noncombatant civilians.

Operations of this kind degenerate into a war of attrition. Since the source of guerrilla power, which is in the North, cannot be destroyed, the only hope is to destroy the guerrilla bands piecemeal as they take the field. This, no doubt, can be accomplished. But the time required exceeds the time available. If one considers the fact that each year approximately 75,000 North Vietnamese reach military age and that all of them can be infiltrated into South Viet Nam, it will take six months out of the year to eliminate each new age group if the guerrillas suffer over 2,000 casualties each week. To this, one has to add the backlog of about 400,000 men of the standing army available to the Hanoi government and the recruits from the South. It may take another six or seven years to bleed Hanoi to death under these conditions. In the meantime, other emergencies may develop which will require redirection of the U. S. military effort.

All this discussion underlines the fact that it has not been possible to "isolate" militarily the guerrillas in Viet Nam. This isolation could be achieved in a number of ways. One is the destruction of the guerrilla base in the North. Another is the interruption of the guerrilla infiltration routes to the South. Finally, there is the isolation of the guerrillas in the South by the native population, i.e.: complete hostile attitude towards the guerrillas by the local inhabitants.

The destruction of the guerrillas base in the North we better discuss later. The interception of the guerrilla infiltration routes have not proven possible, first because of the unwillingness and inability of the governments of Cambodia and Laos, and further because of the terrain features in South Viet Nam which we already discussed. The isolation of the guerrillas by the inhabitants in the South again has not proven successful. As we discussed in the beginning, no strong anti-communist feeling exists among the peasants of South Viet Nam. Consequently, even a passive attitude towards the guerillas by the local inhabitants works to the guerrillas' favor. So far, this has been one of the major advantages of the guerrillas in Viet Nam. Utilizing the typical communist tactics of coercion, threats, terror, and reprisals they have managed to obtain from the South Vietnamese shelter, food, and intelligence. It is not that the South Vietnamese willingly provide these services to the guerrillas. Only the communist propaganda makes this claim. And among the Western peoples only naive individuals and individuals ideologically inclined to the left accept this imbecility as a fact.

What about the destruction of the guerrilla base in the North? Can it be achieved and how? There are three possible ways. One is the destruction of the guerrilla base through an invasion of North Viet Nam by allied ground forces. Another way, which is really a variation of the first, is the destruction of the guerrilla base through a revolutionary guerrilla movement in North Viet Nam. Finally, there is the possibility of remotely destroying the guerrilla base by means of aerial and naval bombardment and by naval blockade.

The invasion of North Viet Nam by allied ground forces would be the most positive way of achieving the objective. It would require fewer forces than those committed to anti-guerrilla operations in the South unless the Chinese communists came to the assistance of the Hanoi government. This probably they would do. But the magnitude and effectiveness of Chinese assistance, in view of the internal problems which the Chinese have, is very much in doubt. The Chinese army, although numerically very impressive, does not possess the firepower nor mobility to face an American army in conventional battle. Therefore, the probabilities are that the combined North Vietnamese and Chinese forces would have been defeated. But then what? Can it be expected that the Chinese would give up the struggle after a series of defeats in Viet Nam? Probably not. Then the guerrilla warfare would have been transferred from South Viet Nam to North Viet Nam and South China. There are also political considerations which make this solution undesirable from the American point of view. It would require a formal declaration of war with which Congress probably would not go along, because the United States public is not psychologically conditioned to be willing to fight a war of this kind under existing conditions. The NATO allies would also oppose this step because they rightly feel that such a deep involvement of the U. S. in Asia reduces the potential of American help in Europe. The only possibility of a successful invasion of North Viet Nam without an expansion of hostilities would have been if the South Vietnamese were strong enough in 1965 to invade the North without the help of American forces. Then the likelihood of Chinese intervention would have been reduced, but not altogether eliminated. If the Chinese did intervene, the Americans would have had to come to the assistance of the South Vietnamese and the situation would not be any different.

The second possible way of destroying the communist guerrilla base in the North is the launching of anti-communist guerrilla warfare in North Viet Nam. This, in our opinion, would have been the most effective way of fighting the communist guerrillas in the South. It offers the following advantages:

It minimizes U. S. commitments of manpower.

The guerrillas would be indigenous Vietnamese, not U. S. troops. It is always better to fight Asians with other Asians, Africans with other Africans, etc. In World War II some of the most effective troops engaged against the Japanese in Burma were the Kachin tribesmen.

It furnishes the allied side with a psychological advantage by demonstrating that the government in Hanoi is unable to exercise effective control over its own people and its own territory.

Eventually, it would force the enemy to withdraw military resources from the South in order to cope with the guerrillas in the North.

Is, or was, such a solution ever possible? With the information available to us we cannot say yes for certain. But it is doubtful that this kind of solution was ever considered. As a matter of fact, the policy of "containment" of communism which has been followed by the U. S. and its allies since the end of World War II is a defensive policy and as such it has ceded all initiative to the other side. Consequently, the concept of active guerrilla warfare against communist regimes has not been developed in our planning. There were only two occasions where this idea was ever tried.[17] The first time was in 1949 when guerrillas were infiltrated into Albania. The British, as well as the Americans, were parties to this plan, but the British Secret Intelligence Service had been infiltrated by communist agents. One of those agents, Kim Philby, betrayed the plan with disastrous consequences. The adverse outcome of this venture is perhaps responsible for the fact that no other operation of similar kind was undertaken until 1961 when the attempt to overthrow Castro was made. This operation was also a complete failure, but as it was planned it did not possess the full characteristics of a guerrilla operation. The attempt to land a force of nearly 2,000 men on a beach from large ships had more of the characteristics of World War II conventional amphibious operations than the characteristics of guerrilla warfare.

If it had been tried, an anti-communist guerrilla movement in North Viet Nam could have possibilities of success.

Finally, we must examine the third and last possibility of destroying the communist guerrilla base in North Viet Nam through aerial and naval bombardment. This has been tried. The results do not seem to commensurate with the effort. There are two reasons for this. One reason is the restriction on targets which the political leadership has imposed on the military. The other reason is the fact that North Viet Nam does not really present enough targets suitable for strategic bombardment. North Viet Nam is principally an agricultural country that can produce an abundance of food. It has, however, practically no heavy industry and no concentration of military facilities. The basic means of warfare other than people, i.e. weapons, ammunition, and related supplies are imported. Most of the imports are coming through the port of Haiphong which is not on the target list. Under the above circumstances strategic bombardment can only have limited results. It does no good to drop thousands of tons of explosives over ten square miles of jungle because there is nothing in the jungle except animals and maybe half a dozen stray natives. They have no military significance. What is more important is the fact that after the bombers have left, the jungle is still there and it can still be used as an infiltration route to the South by a company of guerrillas coming from Hanoi or one of the other cities which are on the restricted list.

If North Viet Nam was a highly industralized country and there were no, or fewer, restriction of the targets which U. S. bombers and capital ships were allowed to hit, the effect of strategic bombing would be paralyzing.

For all of the above reasons the war in Viet Nam has been inconclusive. It is very damaging to the Americans. It is also quite costly to the communists. One has to admit that the communist High Command in Hanoi has directed this war with exceptional skill. It has committed only two major errors. One error is its notorious disregard of casualties; casualties of its own troops and of the noncombatant natives. This falls within the pattern of worldwide communist guerrilla operations which has been established ever since communist guerrillas first took the field. In South Viet Nam this tactic can have adverse affect on the guerrillas if it continues. There is evidence that it is slowly turning the otherwise apathetic South Vietnamese peasants against the Hanoi government. The second major error which has been committed by the communist High Command was the Tet Offensive of 1968. The communists are very doctrinal people used to stereotyped thinking. It appears that they had estimated that early in 1968 they were ready for the "third" phase of their war of liberation as described in the works of Mao and Giap. The third phase involves the abandonment of guerrilla tactics and the introduction of conventional revolutionary warfare. In the Tet Offensive the communists committed all their available forces to an all-out attack against the population centers of South Viet Nam. This operation retained some of the characteristics of guerrilla warfare, but it was primarily a conventional operation. The communist forces approached their targets using guerrilla tactics, but their assaults were conventional with positional objectives. The Tet Offensive was militarily a failure. The objectives were not attained, captured ground was not held in the face of determined counterattacks, and the population within the cities failed to rise against the Saigon government. The casualties suffered by the communists were of such magnitude that they were incapacitated from mounting any major operations for several months. From their point of view, however, they may consider as positive results the fact that the Tet Offensive influenced American internal politics and may be partially responsible for the subsequent change which took place in the U. S. Administration.

What remains to be discussed now is the possible solution of the War in Viet Nam. We will not attempt to predict the solution. We will state, however, that an outright American withdrawal does not appear likely or prudent. If American forces are withdrawn, it is doubtful that a non-communist government can be maintained in Saigon. The result, therefore, will be the absorption of South Viet Nam into the communist state run by the Hanoi government. Immediately, the communists, with their characteristic cruelty, will proceed to exterminate conservatively 1,000,000 Vietnamese who have collaborated with the Americans. The victims will not be the generals of the Saigon government, but poor peasants who have cooperated with the Americans for one reason or another.[18] If this happens, the impact on the people of the rest of the Southeast Asian countries and the rest of the world will be disastrous. The incentive to resist communist aggression is taken away because they can reasonably deduce that the Americans are likely to leave them in a lurch after a few years. Therefore, it is best for them to come to an accommodation with the communists and spare themselves the sacrifices of resistance. Nor can we assume that Viet Nam will be the end of communist ambitions in Southeast Asia. Communist policy is expansionist. The resources now devoted by them in South Viet Nam will be used for aggression elsewhere. In fact, even now before the war in Viet Nam is over, there are communist guerrillas operating in Northeast Thailand. The news media seldom say anything about this guerrilla conflict.

6. Other Conflicts Involving Guerrillas and
General Conclusions

The conflicts reviewed in this and the previous chapters are not the only ones in which guerrilla type operations were extensively utilized. There have been several others, perhaps equally interesting. We chose the ones we have reviewed on the basis of the magnitude of guerrilla warfare in relation to the overall conflict and the availability of reliable material describing the guerrilla operations.

In addition to the conflicts which we have discussed, significant guerrilla operations took place in the following wars.

In the Franco-Prussian War of 1870. From that war the term Francs Tireurs has originated. The practical contribution made by the guerrillas in this war, was limited.

The insurrection of certain Muslim Caucasian tribes against Tsarist authority during the last century had certain guerrilla characteristics. The leader of the insurgents was a chieftan named Shamyl. He fought mostly conventional engagements against the Russian forces, but he made very prudent use of terrain and exercised good flanking movements. These two factors, plus his status as a rebel, are responsible for his classification as a guerrilla by casual observers.

The wars in India's Northwest Frontier against the Afghans also bear several guerrilla characteristics.

In the Irish Rebellion of 1916, guerrilla operations played an important part. However, the main force of the rebels was eventually trapped in positional warfare within the city of Dublin.

During the Russian Civil War guerrillas were utilized by both sides. On the White side, the Volunteer Army on the Southern Front originated as a guerrilla army, more or less. After the augmentation of the White forces in South Russia and the Allied intervention, guerrilla tactics were used by the Whites frequently. They usually took the form of raids wherein units of variable strength infiltrated into Red-held areas to interrupt rail traffic and destroy or capture supply depots. The situation was favorable for operations of this kind because the fronts were usually thinly held, the populations indifferent to the Red objectives, and the communist administration not firmly established.

General Shkuro was one of the outstanding cavalry commanders who operated both in guerrilla and conventional manner with the Caucasian Army of the Whites. Shkuro, in addition to being an able field commander, had an acute awareness of the psychological aspects of war. He exploited these aspects by spreading a reputation of ferocity and ruthlessness for his troops. He supplied them with hats made of wolfskins instead of the traditional wool; this gave his force the popular name "Shkuro's wolves". The wolfskin hats were recognizable from considerable distance. Consequently, the Red infantry was prone to run away in panic whenever they detected or saw Shkuro's force at their flanks or rear. The reputation of Shkuro's troops was not entirely artificially created either. His troops were inclined to looting and to summary shooting of captured communist officials. The British decorated Shkuro with the Victoria Cross. However, in World War II he collaborated with the Germans. In 1945 he surrendered to the British who, disregarding his Victoria Cross, turned him over to the Soviets. They, in turn, after a show trial condemned him to death and executed him by hanging together with Generals Krasnov and Von Pannwitz.

Equally effective, but not quite as colorful, were Generals Konovallov and Mamentov. Both were credited with considerable success operating behind the Red lines. Mamentov in particular, came closer to Moscow than any other of the counter-revolutionary leaders. In the summer of 1920, he infiltrated approximately 10,000 troops through the Red front, then located just North of Tsaritsyn (since then renamed Stalingrad and Volgograd). He reached a line running between Voronezh and Koslov. At Koslov he was only 225 miles from Moscow. As he moved northward he raised hell with the Soviet communications, but more significant were the mass defections he caused among the Soviet troops and the peasants. His appearance behind the front caused consternation among the Soviet High Command and when he reached Koslov they were getting ready to evacuate their Headquarters from Moscow, not realizing that Mamentov's force was no more than a protracted guerrilla raid.

He did not push any further, nor could he hold the ground he had gained. Instead, he changed direction Southwards, slipped through the Soviet 8th and 13th Armies and withdrew behind his friendly lines followed by the masses of defectors.

General Vrangel himself, the most capable of the White commanders, conducted operations which had certain basic guerrilla characteristics. But Vrangel's guerrilla potential was never fully exploited when he was commanding the Caucasian Army and was subordinate to Denikin, the Commander-in-Chief. Denikin was somewhat jealous of Vrangel. In addition, he was moody, inclined to bouts of depression during which he accused his subordinate commanders of disloyalty. He never supported Vrangel sufficiently and consequently Vrangel's force was compelled to give up the deep penetrations in order to obtain the positional objectives assigned to it by Denikin. It is possible that if the White Command had paid more attention to this type of warfare, it could have been successful in overthrowing the communist government since the communist hold on the country was loose in those days. But the White guerrillas' behavior towards the non-combatants was not exemplary and this alienated the population towards them.[19] Instead of exploiting White guerrilla capabilities, Denikin's campaign towards Moscow and dispositions of forces made himself vulnerable to Red guerrilla activities. The White forces were spread over a wide frontal area with minimum security for the rear and communication lines; also there was a complete lack of reserves. This however, was only one of the many mistakes committed by the Whites during that war. Their most important strategic error was the fact that they were unable to coordinate the efforts of the many White armies operating against the Bolsheviks into one sustained blow. Another calamity for the Whites was the wishy-washy attitude of the Allies who finally abandoned them after having initially encouraged the Counterrevolution.

On the communist side, extensive use of guerrillas was made in most areas under White control, particularly behind the lines of Kolchak's Siberian Front. The total number of separate guerrilla bands operating in Siberia and the Russian Far East has been estimated at over a thousand. Many of them were no more than bands of common criminals taking advantage of the

Civil War to commit acts of banditry against either side and particularly against the noncombatant peasants. It appears that in those days all that was required to form a guerrilla band was two men with a horse and a rifle each. The most notorious of the bandits was one named Nestor Mahhno who operated in South Ukraine with a substantial force of renegades and created a big problem for the Whites by being a constant threat to their communications. Later Mahhno, whose political orientation was towards anarchism, broke with the Reds and fled to Rumania after his forces suffered a series of defeats by the Red Army.

In World War II, guerrilla activity took place in several other Axis-occupied countries, in addition to these we have discussed. They included France and Northern Italy. This activity was, in general, encouraged by the Allied governments, but it was conducted mostly without planning or prior evaluation of the anticipated objectives. In practical terms, the contribution of guerrillas to the war effort was more on the negative side. True, substantial Axis forces were diverted from active fronts to purely anti-guerrilla missions in the rear. But the losses sustained by the guerrillas themselves and by the civilian population in the areas of guerrilla activity were of such magnitude that we must conclude that the guerrilla effort was either unjustified or inexpertly conducted. We are saying this, of course, 20 years after the war's end with the benefit of 20/20 hindsight. Nor can we condemn the idea of utilizing guerrillas in general in that War. Use of guerrillas in certain areas and for certain missions where the objectives were such that the anticipated losses were justified, has to be considered prudent. The indiscriminate arming of supposed guerrillas, many of whom were nothing but bands preparing for future armed political strife, however, has to be condemned. And one can only laugh at the Western stupidity of showing favoritism to leftist guerrilla groups which hastened to turn politically antagonistic to the Western powers even before the conclusion of World War II.

On the heels of World War II followed the Palestinian War during which the Jewish underground employed guerrilla tactics until the withdrawal of the British forces in 1948. The

Jewish guerrillas were well organized and their operations very effective although terrain conditions in Palestine are such that large-scale guerrilla operations are not favored. After the British withdrawal the War took the shape of conventional conflict between Israel and the Arab Countries.

Since World War II, the British and all other colonial powers have been plagued by small or large revolutions through most of their former possessions. In all these conflicts guerrilla warfare has been employed by the insurgents at least during the initial stages of the revolt. Success appears to be with the insurgents, generally, not necessarily because of their military prowess, but rather because of the politically impossible positions into which the colonial powers maneuver themselves. The only notable exception is the War in Malaya where the British were victorious after nine years of struggle. Partial success was also obtained by the British in Kenya, where they were able to put an end to the Mau Mau uprising.

It has been a major strategic error on the part of the United States that in each of these conflicts it has appeared to favor the colonial regimes. Particularly, in view of the fact that it has been unable to reverse the trend of insurgency by the dominated nations. In terms of overall policy in opposition to communist expansion, it would have been better to side with the insurgents because in this manner we could have established predominancy of influence among the new states. Potentially, the states which have emerged from the former colonial possessions were anti- rather than pro-communist because of their traditionalist societies. By appearing to favor the colonial regimes, we have allowed most of these insurgencies to fall under the influence of the extreme left. To add insult to injury, we have not even retained in general the cooperation of the former colonial powers, whose governments have opposed our policies on many issues during the last twenty years.

Another interesting guerrilla movement has been associated with the efforts of the Kurds to carve an independent state from sections of what is now Turkey, Iraq and Iran. The Kurds are a distinct ethnic group and inhabit parts of Eastern Turkey, Northern Iraq and Northwestern Iran. There are two aspects of the Kurdish movement which make it noteworthy. The first aspect is the fact that it has been going on since about 1922 without any spectacular success, but also without any indications that the Kurds are ready to accept the status quo.[20] The other interesting aspect is the Soviet attitude towards the Kurds since about 1960. For a while, the Kurds were receiving substantial material help from the Soviets. It appeared then that it was only a matter of time before the Kurd guerrillas would come under the complete operational control of the Soviets. Then, suddenly, the Soviets dropped their sponsorship of the Kurdish independence cause. The reason can be found in the realignments of the Soviet policy in the Middle East necessitated by their opportunistic search for allies and influence among the Arab states. The Kurds were abandoned as part of a bigger deal with the Iraqis, and in the process the Turks got a break also.

The most successful guerrilla war of recent years has been Castro's movement in Cuba. This subject, however, is so highly charged emotionally that we find it difficult to analyze objectively yet.

Recently, some guerrilla activity was registered in Nigeria by the Biafran insurgents. The Biafran leadership, however did not make extensive use of guerrilla tactics. The Biafran leadership was preoccupied with the protection of the Ibo tribesmen because it feared the possibility of genocide by the federal Nigerian troops. This policy required that the rebels exercise territorial control over an area where the Ibos could find refuge. Ordinarily, the guerrillas cannot be burdened with the protection of large numbers of noncombatants. Consequently, guerrilla warfare was bypassed in favor of conventional tactics and this strategy led to the eventual defeat of the rebels. It is possible that the Biafrans could have been victorious if they employed guerrilla tactics on a large scale. This assumption can be safely made because the Nigerian federal troops were extremely ineffective. Even in conventional engagements they were unable to get the upper hand until they began to receive massive material assistance from the communist bloc.

This brief review of guerrilla warfare, covering a time span of almost two centuries, indicates that guerrilla warfare has had widespread use. It reveals that this method of warfare has been used principally, but not exclusively, by rebels. Conventional armies have utilized guerrilla tactics. Good examples of this are the German operations in East Africa in World War I, the Finnish operations around Suomussalmi, and the American long range penetration units in Burma. It also reveals that the communists have had no monopoly in the utilization of guerrilla warfare since the end of World War II. The Cypriot guerrillas provided us with an example of this.

We find that the success of guerrilla warfare, in relation to achieving the guerrillas' stated objectives, depends on the conditions under which it is applied. Usually, we find that the more successful guerrilla operations are those conducted in coordination with conventional warfare. In these cases the contribution of guerrilla warfare to achieving the overall military objectives has varied from negative to very substantial. It becomes necessary, therefore, to question the prudence of allocating resources for this type of warfare in certain situations.

There are examples where the guerrillas obtained their objectives without assistance from conventional forces; Algeria and Cyprus, for instance. It is clear however, that in both of these cases the military success of the guerrillas was indirect. The guerrillas were not able to obtain a decisive victory over their enemies. Neither were their enemies able to destroy the guerrillas. In such cases a military stalemate results. Military stalemates of this nature have usually resulted in political settlements favorable to the guerrillas.

It is apparent that guerrilla forces have a tendency to change through evolution into conventional armies. This happens in particular after the guerrillas have had successes and if their enemies temporarily evacuate large areas. When this happens the guerrillas become vulnerable if they try to meet their enemy in positional battles without outside help. A very vivid example of this were the defeats of the Greek communists on Grammos and Vitsi. However, one must remember that communist theorists of guerrilla warfare encourage this transition. We have, therefore, in advance at least part of the master plan of any insurrection in which communist guerrillas are involved.

There are examples where the guerrillas have not been successful. Greece and Malaya are the two post World War II examples. The failure of the guerrillas in both cases is attributed to the relative degree of effectiveness of the guerrilla effort and the counterguerrilla effort exerted by those who oppose them.

It becomes obvious that the success of guerrilla warfare depends on the thorough understanding and proper exploitation of all factors bearing on each case where guerrilla warfare becomes a possibility. The rest of this study attempts to identify and analyze all such factors.

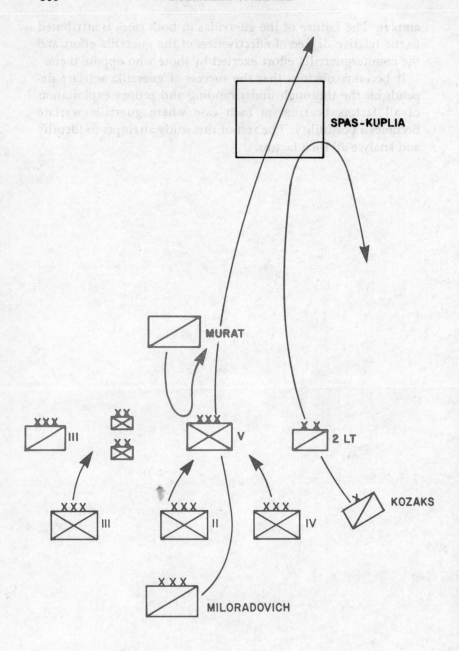

Figure 1. The Battle of Vinkovo — 1812.

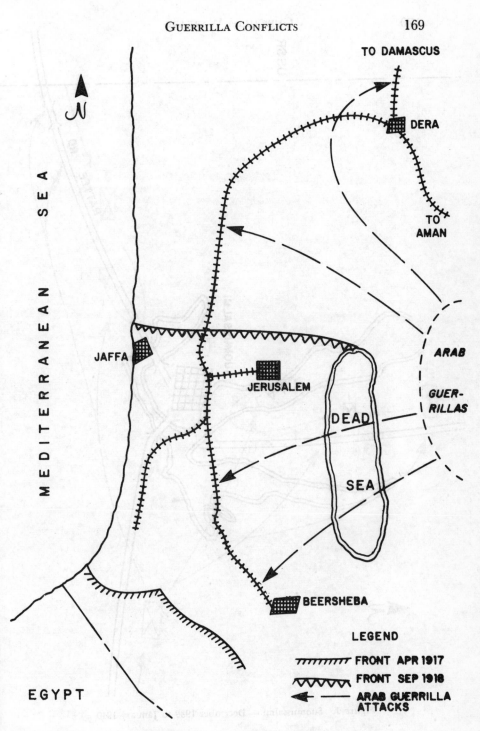

Figure 2. Operations in Palestine — World War I.

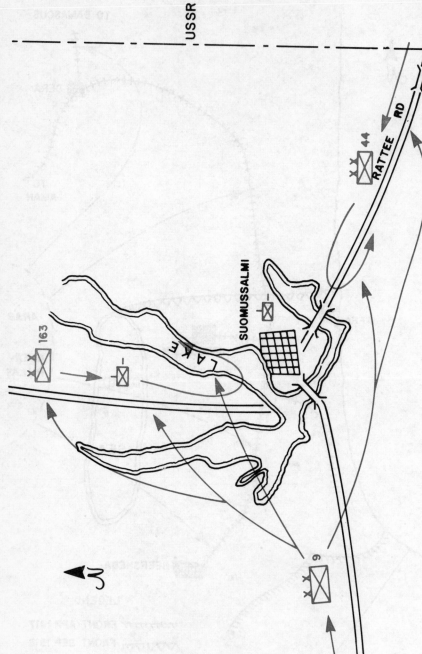

Figure 3.   Suomussalmi — December 1939 to January 1940.

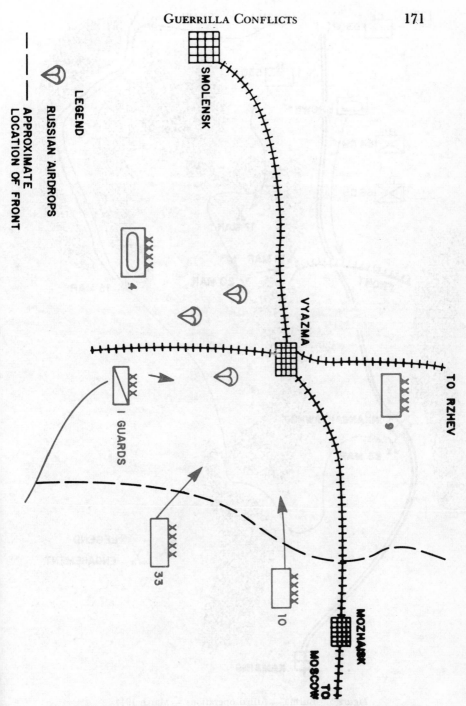

Figure 4. Vyazma 1942. Soviet attempts to interdict the Smolensk-Moscow roads.

GUERRILLA WARFARE

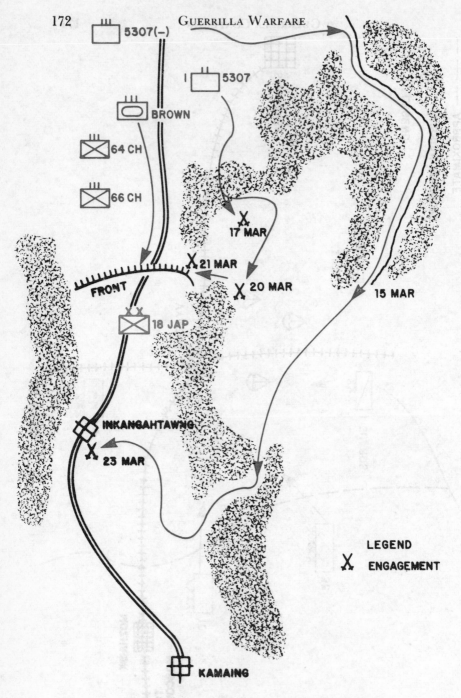

Figure 5. Burma — Allied operations — March 1944.

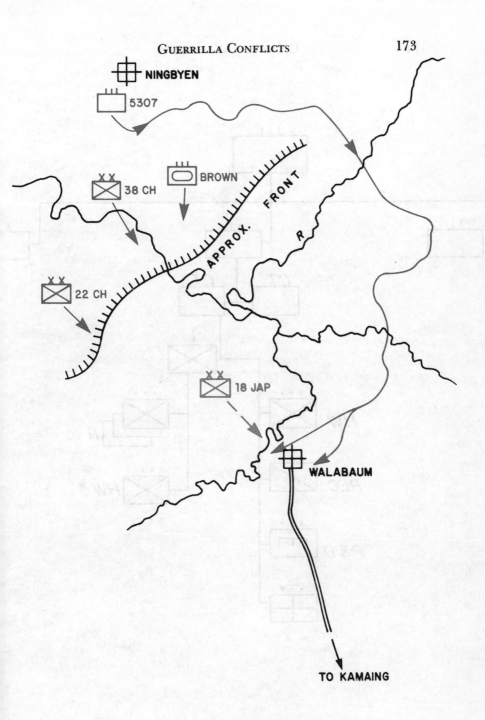

Figure 6. Burma — The advance to Walabaum.

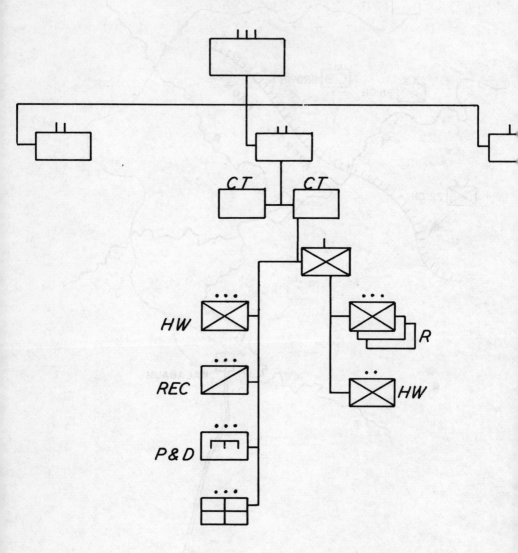

Figure 7. Organizational chart — 5307 Long Range Penetration Group.

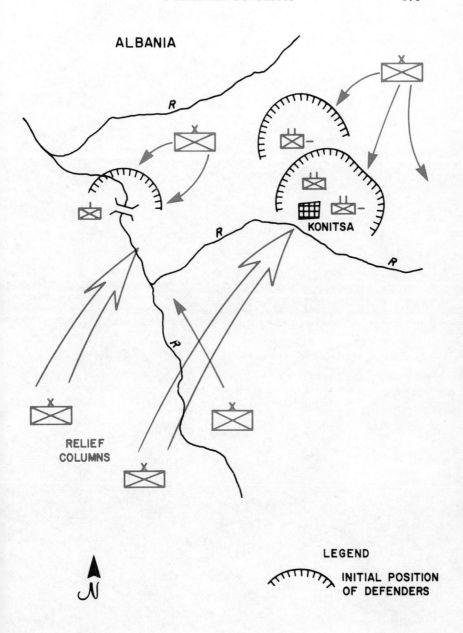

ALBANIA

R

KONITSA

RELIEF
COLUMNS

N

LEGEND

INITIAL POSITION
OF DEFENDERS

Figure 8. The attempt to take Konitsa — December 1947.

V

Legal Status of Guerrillas—
International Treaties—War Crimes Trials

IN ATTEMPTING to analyze all aspects of guerrilla warfare, one comes to an early realization that the legal status of guerrillas is a significant factor to be considered.

It is unfortunate that this topic can not be treated in depth here. The reason being that the discussion is made not by a lawyer, but by a layman. It represents, therefore, a layman's understanding of the subject. It is better, however, to give this topic an inexpert treatment than to ignore this very significant aspect of the overall subject of guerrilla warfare.

In the 20th Century, war among the so-called civilized nations is supposed to be conducted within the restrictions set forth by two International Agreements: The Hague Convention concerning the Rules and Usages of Land Warfare, and the Geneva Convention concerning the Amelioration of the Fate of Wounded and Sick in the Active Army.

Both of these International Agreements were drawn up for the specific purpose of reducing the severity of wars. Although a cynic may joke at this apparent contradiction in statement, there is little doubt that the Hague and Geneva Conventions have had some affect in reducing the horrors of armed conflicts.

If nothing else, they have provided a legal basis for the prosecution of war criminals after World War II.

The question that concerns us here in relation to these documents is whether they have any application to guerrilla warfare at all. In other words, is guerrilla warfare within the rules established by these two agreements?

The answer can be found within the agreements themselves. Article 1 of the Hague Convention provides that: "The laws, rights, and duties of war apply not only to armies, but also to militia and volunteer corps fullfilling the following conditions.

1. To be commanded by a person responsible for his subordinates.

2. To have a fixed distinctive emblem recognizable from a distance.

3. To carry arms openly.

4. To conduct their operations in accordance with the laws and customs of war.

As long as the guerrillas fulfill all of the above conditions they are lawful belligerents and their enemy is obligated to treat them as such upon capture. If he does not treat the guerrillas as lawful belligerents he acts in violation of the International Agreements, therefore, he is then the one who is conducting operations not in accordance with the laws and customs of war.

It is obvious, therefore, that the initial step to keep guerrilla warfare within the limits of International Law has to be taken by the guerrillas themselves. This means that they must comply with all four conditions of Article 1 of the Hague Convention. Conditions 1 and 4 usually present no problems. Compliance with condition 1 is necessary because no organized effort can take place without having appropriate leadership and command structure. Compliance with condition 4 is also advantageous to the guerrillas themselves. Conditions 2 and 3, however, are more difficult. Compliance with these two conditions means that the guerrillas must, to a considerable degree, give up the advantages of concealment and surprise which can be obtained through the use of inconspicuous clothing and through carrying concealed weapons. A choice, therefore, has to be made by the guerrillas between the protection of the Hague Convention and the sacrifice of these advantages.

The Hague Convention also extends its protection to armed civilians. Article 2 of the Hague Convention states that:

"The inhabitants of a territory which has not been occupied, who, on the approach of the enemy, spontaneously take up arms to resist the invading army without having had time to organize themselves in accordance with Article 1, shall be regarded as belligerents if they carry arms openly and if they respect the laws and customs of war."

In our opinion, this Article is applicable in some situations of guerrilla warfare. However, the statement about "—— a territory which has not been occupied ——" will exclude application of this Article in the majority of cases because guerrilla warfare usually takes place behind the enemy's lines, therefore on territory already occupied by the enemy.

Unfortunately, we find that the provisions of the Hague and Geneva Conventions have not always been observed in situations involving guerrilla warfare. As a matter of fact, many of the provisions and restrictions have not been observed by belligerents in conventional warfare situations.

During World War II, the principles of the Hague Convention were not observed in guerrilla warfare. As background, we must mention that one of the major belligerent powers, Soviet Russia, had not been a signatory to either agreement. The Soviet Union, initially, had repudiated all treaties and agreements made by the Tsarist Governments; by implication this meant the Geneva and Hague Conventions also. In 1925, however, by decree, the Soviet Union declared that it considers itself bound by the Geneva Convention and in August 1941, it declared that it considers itself bound by the Hague Convention also, providing that Germany observes the Convention's rules.[1] The Soviet guerrillas, though, purposely did not comply with conditions 2 and 3 of Article 1 of the Hague Convention, thus repudiating the Convention's protection for the advantages of concealment.

German reaction to this was that all Soviet guerrillas, if captured, were executed after interrogation. Legally, the Germans were within their rights in doing so; but they went a lot further than that.[2]

In the German war organization the responsibilities of the various branches of their service were frequently overlapping. It is generally thought that the SS were responsible for maintenance of order in the occupied territories and security in the rear army areas. There is also considerable confusion in regards to the SS. After the assassination of Röhm (1934), the SS developed into two branches: the Waffen SS which was a kind of special politically indoctrinated army, and the SD or security police. The Waffen SS units were usually employed in the front together with the standard army formations, whereas the SD were utilized for security missions, counter-espionage, etc. In addition, the Army had its own "Field Police" which corresponds, roughly, to the American Military Police. In regard to the responsibility for combating guerrillas, there was no central directive assigning this mission to any one branch of the Wehrmacht; circumstances, rather than policy, determined that. Usually the pattern would develop as follows: Guerrilla activity would register in the area of responsibility of an army unit and this unit would become involved initially. If it met with little success, it would be reinforced with other army units, SS units, SD units, Field Police, and even units of native defectors. It follows, therefore, that the army was as much involved in the anti-guerrilla operations as the SS or SD.

The German High Command on 25 June 1941, issued a general order, known as the Kommissarbefehl or as the "Commissar Order" in which it instructed the Germany Army on such matters as the treatment of enemy civilians, treatment of enemy soldiers who continued resistance after their parent units had surrendered, and treatment of captured commissars. Briefly, the commissars were to be shot immediately, if captured, and the same was to be done with soldiers resisting after their units surrendered, armed civilians or guerrillas. In essence, therefore, the German High Command deliberately intended to violate the International Agreements *before* Russian guerrilla activity commenced. It is true that several of the army commanders covertly refused to implement this order. Guderian, for instance, claims that he did not know that the order about shooting the commissars had been issued because his army group commander did not forward it to subordinate echelons; at least that is what Guderian supposes. Others though, such as Field Marshal Reichenau, issued supplemental directives on the detailed execution of the High Command general order. Subsequently, several other directives were issued by the High Command and local Theater Commanders dealing with the subject of treatment of captured guerrillas and treatment of civilians suspected of giving assistance and comfort to guerrillas in any way.

In general, the directives specified that:

1. Captured guerrillas would be shot after interrogation.

2. Individual civilians suspected of being guerrillas would be shot.

3. Villages in the proximity of which guerrilla bands had registered activity would be burned and the male inhabitants usually shot or arrested en masse and sent to labor camps in Germany.

This policy was followed not only in Russia, but in all the occupied territories. It is known today that as the war progressed, guerrilla activity was generally intensified and the above severe measures did not restrain it much, but to the contrary, drove a lot of civilians, in desperation, into joining the bands. The German Army leaders were not stupid; the majority of them easily identified the fundamental error of this policy. Yet, in most cases they did nothing about it.

Why?

We do not propose to answer this question here; particularly since there have been enough volumes written since the conclusion of the war on the subject of the German Army's reactions to the Nazi policies. We do wish to point out though that failure by the military to act in a matter of policy vital to the conduct of the war caused both political and military disasters.

It is also reasonable to point out that this deliberate violation of the International Agreements has become a permanent black mark on the honor of the German Army. This is indeed ironic because the excuse most frequently used by the German Generals for not acting contrary to orders such as the "Commissar Order" is that they were prevented from doing so by their oath of loyalty to the Fuhrer and their sense of military honor.

Some of the generals did take action. General Busse states that in 1943, Army Group South issued a leaflet to the troops regarding relations with the Russians:[3]

The contents of this leaflet, with appropriate modifications, could constitute a guide for the treatment of occupied civilians in the future. Unfortunately for the Germans, steps like this were taken too late. The damage was already done.

Guderian claims[4] that the "severe countermeasures" of the German authorities against the guerrillas were brought about by the guerrillas own atrocities against German personnel and the guerrillas' disregard of the Geneva and Hague Conventions.

This represents a more-or-less universal position that all Germans have taken since the end of the war, with a few exceptions.

Let's examine their argument.

First of all, morally it is not valid. Maybe it is ridiculous to mention morality here and we would have not, but for the fact that Guderian himself makes repeated references to the "Western Christian" ideas of which he and his comrades were adherents.

Secondly, in actual practice, the countermeasures were seldown applied against the actual committer of the alleged atrocities. It was always the noncombatant peasants who were summarily shot, tortured, imprisoned, or made homeless. The immediate results of such countermeasures were that they provided more recruits for the guerrillas and widened the gap between the occupying Germans and the occupied civilians.

Another point to dispute with Guderian is his definition of atrocities. Without any doubt, atrocities against German military personnel were committed. Particularly in areas where communists were active such actions were preplanned. The communists purposely would shoot one or two Germans near a village, mutilate their bodies, then withdraw and wait for the German punitive deatchment that would arrive to shoot all the male inhabitants and burn the village. This is a well established communist tactic designed to impoverish the population and facilitate the social revolution. An auxiliary objective was to force the surviving villagers to join the guerrillas.[5]

But in many instances the alleged atrocities consisted of no more than a surprise attack, raid, or ambush of an isolated patrol. This type of activity constitutes legitimate warfare and the participants of such activity should be treated as war prisoners if captured.

It also has to be recognized that the Hague Convention allows an occupying army certain latitude on the measures it can take for its own security and for the maintenance of law and order among the occupied civilians.

However, it does not allow such things as shootings of hostages or even captured guerrillas who have compiled with the conditions of Article 1.

After the conclusion of World War II and the defeat of Germany, the International Military Tribunals have adjudicated cases of war crimes including charges relating to treatment of guerrillas. A review of the decisions in some of these cases indicates that the Tribunals have:[6]

1. Acquitted the commanders charged with executing captured guerrillas who did not comply with the provisions of the Hague Convention. There is, however, a difference of opinion between British and American judges on the matter of whether a trial of the guerrilla is required. The American view has been that once the fact has been established that the captured man is a Franctireur, i.e. an armed individual not protected by the Convention, he may be punished even by the death penalty without a formal trial. The British view has been that some sort of a trial is required.

2. Convicted the commanders charged with shooting hostages, suspected guerrillas, etc.

3. Expressed the opinion that the Hague and Geneva Conventions are binding to all governments, even though they may have not been signatories of the conventions.

This last opinion is quite important, in view of the multitude of newly independent states whose governments did not exist at the time of the original drafting of the Conventions.

Undoubtedly, the precedence established by the post-World War II decisions will be a factor in deciding any future cases of possible war crimes.

Since World War II, guerrilla warfare has been waged in conjunction with several internal revolutions and national revolutions by colonial peoples. The difficulty in discussing the legal status of guerrillas who are operating against their own government or against the government of a colonial adminstration is that none of the International Agreements makes any mention of them. It would be reasonable to assume, though, that as long as the rebel guerrillas are complying with the conditions set forth by Article I of the Hague Convention the government and the government army against which they have rebelled should grant them treatment similar to that granted to captured enemy soldiers. By doing so, though, the government could be recognizing by implication the existence of a rebel army and, perhaps, a rebel government. In addition, the rebelling guerrillas have probably violated existing statutes dealing with sedition, mutiny, firearms possession, etc, which compounds the complexity of their legal status.

Any attempt to define the legal status of guerrillas who have operated against their own governments requires a research of those cases where guerrillas have been brought to trial. However, one finds that usually indigenous guerrillas have been treated according to political considerations rather than according to any preestablished legal principals.

In Greece for instance, an attempt was made to rehabilitate captured guerrillas through special indoctrination in camps. This turned out to be effective since a considerable number of the Greek guerrillas had been forced to join the bands. Diehard communists though were tried in accordance with the penal code of Greece.

The treatment of Viet Minh and Algerian guerrillas by the French was ambivalent. There are several cases where captured guerrillas were mistreated or summarily shot by the French military authorities. In other instances, however, the captured guerrillas were treated as prisoners of war.

In Cyprus, under the emergency powers assumed by the Island's governor, captured guerrillas and even suspected guerrillas were detained, tried, and in some cases hanged. In retaliation the guerrillas put to death at least two captured British servicemen. In our opinion, both parties acted in violation of the International Agreements.

In Viet Nam, the treatment of captured guerrillas received

prominent attention after the international press published during the Tet Offensive a photograph of General Nguyen Ngoc Loan shooting a captured guerrilla with a revolver. The press people are notorious for their inaccurate reporting of military events. But if the facts as reported are true, General Loan acted within the limits of International Law in shooting the captive. The man, as shown in the picture, was definitely wearing civilian attire; therefore, he was not entitled to the protection of the International Agreements. The Hague Convention does not require under the circumstances a trial for the captive. As discussed previously, the necessity of a trial has been a subject of disagreement among the judges of International Tribunals since World War II. But again, since the press reports are not very reliable, it is possible that the man was only a guerrilla suspect, in which case his summary execution was illegal. The criterion in this case would be whether he was caught armed, or participating in military operations in some other way while he was wearing civilian clothing.

From the above, it becomes obvious that International Law recognizes the legitimacy of guerrilla warfare. This recognization comes through the two International Agreements and through the decisions of International Tribunals where cases involving guerrillas or the treatment of guerrillas have been tried. However, it is also obvious that this recognition of legitimacy has not been universally accepted in the field. Policy and tactical expediency, rather than determination to adhere to legal principles, have been the dominant considerations in the conduct of guerrilla warfare.

VI

Strategic Considerations
Capabilities and Limitations of Guerrilla Warfare —
Conditions Necessary For Its Development

1. Capabilities and Limitations

THE PRECEDING review of the past conflicts in which guerrilla forces were utilized provides ample proof that with relatively limited resources, guerrilla warfare furnishes us the capability to engage a much superior enemy force. This capability is the result of the following characteristics of guerrilla warfare.

1. The guerrillas remain concealed, therefore unexposed to enemy action until the time of actual combat.

2. The guerrillas maintain operational initiative, therefore they usually achieve tactical surprise.

3. The guerrillas have the ability to assemble superior forces to attack one of the enemy's weakest units.

4. The guerrillas have the ability to evade pursuit by the enemy and find refuge in areas unaccessible to the enemy.

5. The guerrillas do not maintain a front, but operate at the enemy's rear, therefore they are in a position to strike the enemy's exposed and vulnerable positions.

187

Consequently, one of the major problems facing any High Command charged with the responsibility of preparing for a future war is the problem of guerrilla warfare. This problem has both offensive and defensive aspects. The defensive aspects deal with a situation where guerrillas are employed against one's own forces. The defensive aspects we shall examine later. First, we shall examine the application of guerrilla warfare as an offensive method of warfare.

This aspect of the problem can be stated in the following questions: Is it feasible to utilize guerrilla warfare in modern war? If so, under what conditions? And how?

The answers to these questions require comprehension of the capabilities and limitations of guerrilla warfare.

The Historical review in which we have engaged indicates quite clearly that proper utilization of guerrilla forces offers to the High Command the opportunity to influence activities in areas far remote from any active front and beyond the range of conventional weapons, with the exception of inter-continental ballistic missiles and strategic bombers. Guerrilla forces, therefore, can be considered an additional strategic weapon available to the High Command. Successful employment of guerrillas can bring about results which are practically as effective, but not quite so destructive, as the employment of ballistic missiles and strategic bombers. In addition, it is apparent that in terms of monetary investment and commitment of other resources, including personnel and material, guerrilla warfare is a relatively inexpensive way to wage war.

Since the employment of guerrilla forces takes place, by definition, behind the enemy's front, it is essential that potential guerrillas can be made available within the territory controlled by the enemy. This means that guerrillas must be recruited from among the enemy's subjects, or allied nations subjugated by the enemy, or one's own nationals who are left behind in territory temporarily occupied by the enemy army. The alternative to this is infiltration of guerrillas through the enemy's lines; a task possible with today's technological means, but infinitely more difficult in terms of protracted operations.

The specific strategic missions which the guerrillas should be capable of performing successfully are the following:

1. Interdiction missions in enemy controlled territory. Such missions include attacks on communication lines, administrative centers, and relatively weak enemy garrisons. The objective of these attacks is to effect losses to the enemy army and impede its mobility. In this manner, the enemy High Command can be forced to divert combat forces from the active fronts in order to suppress the guerrillas, thus benefiting the friendly forces facing the enemy on the respective active fronts. Or, in the case of purely revolutionary movements with no overt support from friendly conventional forces, to compel the enemy High Command to seek a nonmilitary solution in order to terminate an undesirable military solution.

2. Strategic intelligence missions. Such as determination of enemy order of battle, dispositions, target acquisition, and target damage assessments.

3. Missions related to psychological warfare, with the objective of undermining the enemy's will to continue its war effort or to strengthen the occupied population's will to resist.

4. Missions associated with the instigation of revolt or insurgency.

Experience reveals that all guerrilla military activity in the past has been related to the four types of strategic objectives listed above, or variations of these. Within the scope of strategic objectives, or independent of them, the guerrillas can be expected to carry out the following tactical missions.

1. Raids of varied kinds against enemy units which are weaker than the force which the guerrillas can assemble and employ in the specific raid.

2. Raids against selected enemy installations, particularly railroad or highway bridges, pipelines, and other works of the enemy communications network.

3. Raids against enemy supply columns and warehousing facilities with the objective of impeding or interrupting the flow of enemy resupply, or for capturing supplies from the enemy in order to use them by guerrillas.

4. Temporary seizure of key terrain to facilitate airborne, amphibious, or other operations of the friendly conventional forces.

5. Diversionary attacks for the benefit of friendly conventional forces.

6. Reconnaissance, screening, and probing missions for the benefit of the friendly conventional forces.

7. Operations of pure psychological value such as acts of sabotage, terrorism, and raids of no apparent military significance with the objective of making the presence of guerrillas known to the enemy and to the noncombatants living in the general area.

A fully developed guerrilla movement can be expected to be able to undertake any of the above tactical missions repeatedly and with good prospects of success. On the other side of the coin, however, there are certain serious limitations to the capabilities of guerrilla warfare which need to be identified and analyzed. They are the following.

1. Limitations in the guerrillas' capability to fight a protracted offensive engagement. This limitation is caused by the usual superiority in strength and mobility of the guerrillas' enemy, the conventional army. Once the guerrillas have revealed their presence through an offensive action, their enemy has the ability to dispatch reserves which can overcome the guerrillas. In a protracted offensive operation, therefore, the guerrillas risk the probability of defeat in detail.

2. Extremely limited capabilities for defensive operations. The guerrillas can assist in territorial defense by fighting delaying actions and by harassing the flanks and rear of conventional advancing columns. But their capabilities in static defense are almost nil. This is caused by almost the same reasons mentioned in the previous paragraph. The conventional army with its superior firepower and mobility can make available the necessary forces to overcome any guerrillas who are deployed to defend statically any given position.

3. Difficulties of the guerrilla intermediate and higher command echelons to timely concentrate forces. This is caused by the fact that guerrilla units are usually dispersed in order to maintain maximum security. Therefore, reaction time is seriously impeded.

4. Communications among the several guerrilla units and be-

tween guerrilla High Command and headquarters of friendly conventional forces are slow, vulnerable to enemy interception, and full of technical difficulties.

5. Limitations caused by the dependence on the local civilian population for many kinds of support.

6. Finally, perhaps the most important limitation is the fact that friendly civilians in the area of guerrilla activity are exposed to enemy reprisals.

Guerrilla warfare must be considered in its relation to the overall war plan. Identifying its capabilities and limitations constitutes one phase of the evaluation of the feasibility of utilizing guerrilla warfare in a future conflict. The next phase of this evaluation requires an assessment of the specific objectives which will be assigned to the guerrillas, the magnitude of effort which the support of the guerrilla movement will require, and the long-term effect which the guerrilla movement may have on the civilian population of the territory under consideration. The decision of whether to use guerrillas or not will depend largely on balancing the value of the attainable objectives against the required effort for supporting the guerrillas and the affect on the civilians.

Let us now discuss the objectives. The objectives may be either military or politico-military. But they must be substantial enough in relation to the other two factors. It would be pointless to engage guerrillas in an area which is of no interest to the enemy. It is likewise useless to engage the enemy with guerrillas in a territory where the enemy dispositions are such that very little damage can be inflicted on the enemy. To the contrary, possibilities of tying down substantial enemy forces,[1] serious interruption of enemy communications in an active theater, substantial damage to industrial installations, or disruption of the enemy's administration and control of the population are objectives which justify a guerrilla effort and should be exploited.

But the effort required to establish and support the guerrillas should be commensurate with the anticipated benefits to be derived from the realization of the objectives. Above all, careful consideration should be given to how much of ones resources could be devoted to planning and supporting the guerrilla effort without seriously impairing the war effort elsewhere or neglecting some other, perhaps more decisive, field of activity.

One should never lose view of the fact that guerrilla warfare *alone* will not assure a nation ultimate victory. Guerrilla warfare constitutes only one of the several instruments of strategy available to a High Command. Although in a future conflict the contribution of guerrillas could be very substantial, one must not be misled into believing that a major war can be won by guerrilla warfare alone. It would become disastrous for any government to rely too much in this method of warfare and neglect the development of its conventional forces. It is our belief that the most decisive factor in winning the next war shall be the possession and proper employment of offensive intercontinental weapons systems and missile defenses. Yet, if guerrilla operations are properly employed in coordination with the other means of warfare, they can produce results out of all proportion to the manpower and material invested.

2. Conditions Necessary for the Successful Development of Guerrilla Warfare

In view of the above discussion, it is reasonable to conclude that under certain conditions, guerrilla warfare is an advisable means with which ones military or politico-military objectives can be promoted. These conditions are the following:

1. When the ratio of forces is to the advantage of the enemy in great proportion.

2. When possibilities of offering effective resistance to the enemy through conventional means are limited.

3. If ones' territory, or part of it, is already occupied by the enemy army.

4. When, even though opposing forces are more-or-less evenly matched, one can create a diversion into the enemy's rear through the employment of guerrillas.

5. When the enemy line of communications is extended and/or his rear area is vulnerable.

6. When the enemy army operates in territory where the local population is generally hostile.

7. When revolt or insurgency provides the only means through which political objectives can be realized.

It is not necessary to have all of the above conditions bearing on a situation simultaneously before guerrilla warfare becomes feasible. But it is obvious that the advisability of launching a guerrilla movement is increased correspondingly with the increase in the number of the above conditions.

However, it is also reasonable to conclude that in order to have a guerrilla movement with reasonable possibilities of success, certain favorable prerequisites must exist. These prerequisites are:

1. Personnel; i.e.: people willing and able to support passively and to actively participate in guerrilla operations.

2. Materiel which are suitable and available for operations of this kind.

3. Favorable geographic conditions.

These prerequisites are essential in the development of guerrilla warfare. The rest of this chapter, therefore, will be utilized in their analysis.

PERSONNEL

The essential element in any conflict are the people who partake or otherwise support the hostilities. Obviously, there are two categories of people that we are discussing: the members of the armed forces and the noncombatant civilians. Victory, to a great extent depends on the efforts of the people and to a lesser extent on the material means available. Even authoritarian governments, therefore, pay great attention in times of war to the task of psychologically conditioning their people so that their war will appear as a "popular" war. The psychological conditioning of the civilians is as important as the psychological conditioning of the members of the armed forces, unless the government possesses a completely mercenary army, as often happened in the Middle Ages.

In guerrilla warfare the mental attitude of the people is the most essential factor. This is the first consideration of any High Command which contemplates guerrilla operations in any given area at any time. If, for example, guerrilla warfare is planned in a country which is occupied by an enemy army, it must be ascertained that the spirit of resistance is strong enough among the majority of the inhabitants so that they are willing to risk the reprisals of the enemy. In some circumstances guerrilla movements can develop without this positive attitude of the population around them if the guerrilla movement is furnished strong external support. But at least its toleration by the population is the absolute minimum required. The obvious reason for this is that the security of the guerrilla bands is placed in jeopardy if they are operating in an area where the inhabitants are hostile or apathetic towards them.

Which are the conditions which may influence the mental attitude of the people in favor of a guerrilla movement? They are usually associated with the following.

1. Desire to obtain National Independence.
2. Desire to eliminate foreign occupation or administration.
3. Desire to resist foreign invasion.
4. Attempt to bring about a domestic political change.
5. Attempt to bring about a social change.
6. Reaction to religious oppression or expression of religious fanaticism.

The desire to obtain National Independence is directly responsible for most of the guerrilla movements which have taken place since World War II. The desire to terminate foreign occupation was the motivation behind most of the guerrilla movements during World War II. The utilization of military means, such as guerrilla warfare, to bring about political or social changes will be encountered usually only in societies where the political structure is such that it precludes normal political and social evolution. The reaction to blocked evolution is eventual revolution. Guerrilla movements as a purely religious expression have not been common occurances in Europe during the last two centuries. They are, however, very probably in Africa and Asia. Religion can also be associated with political objectives as the case was in Ireland and Israel.

It has to be recognized that it is not enough to simply have the above conditions in existence. The people affected have to be aware of the existence of the unsatisfactory conditions, be dissatisfied with the status quo, and be mentally prepared to commit acts of violence in order to bring about the desired change. They must also have faith in the probability of an eventual victorious outcome of their struggle. You can not expect people to make sacrifices for causes which have little or no prospect of success. If the people are apathetic towards their conditions, they are not likely to support a guerrilla movement. The guerrilla movement must then be preceded by a propaganda campaign which, if successful, will change this attitude of apathy to a desire for action.

Of course, among the people there must be a sufficient number of individuals who are willing and able to join the guerrilla units as active members. Obviously, the best source for guerrillas are former servicemen and individuals with military experience in general. However, it must be recognized that obtaining this type of individuals may be problematic. If the territory in question has been occupied by the enemy, it is very likely that the enemy is holding all indigenous servicemen as prisoners of war, or he is keeping them under close surveillance. In this case, alternate sources of guerrillas have to be found. The best alternate source is students and young men in their late teens and early twenties. If such men lack military experience, adequate provisions must be made to train them in relatively secure areas, in-country or externally, and then reinfiltrate them in the territory of the prospective guerrilla activity.

To some extent a guerrilla movement can be initiated and sustained with personnel from external sources. This means regular troops of allied forces who are capable of operating as guerrillas in the enemy's rear. Again, these troops *must* have the active support or toleration of the local inhabitants. It is best, however, not to rely on external sources for the maintenance of the guerrilla movement and the guerrillas from external sources are best utilized when they provide nuclei for the development of indigenous guerrilla units and as technical specialists.

MATERIEL

One of the gross advantages of guerrilla warfare is the fact that with relatively few material means it can bring about disproportionate destruction to the enemy. This, however, does not mean that guerrilla operations can be established on a shoestring.

There must be some sources from which the guerrillas can be equipped with weapons and other essentials of warfare.

There are two general categories of equipment which are needed for guerrilla warfare. The first category includes weapons and related items; i.e.: firearms, ammunition, dynamite, and destructive devices of all kinds. The second category covers all other kinds of equipment associated with the maintenance of an armed force. It includes clothing, food, medical equipment, communications equipment, transportation equipment, etc.

Because of the nature of guerrilla warfare, such equipment need not be as numerous nor as complex as the equipment required by conventional forces. But equipment are needed, and one must investigate thoroughly their probable sources.

Generally speaking, equipment can be obtained from three sources. From civilians who are sympathetic to the guerrillas, from the enemy, and from outsiders including allies and neutrals.

Civilians who are sympathetic to the guerrillas can be expected to furnish hunting and sporting weapons, if available. Equipment which do not belong to the category of weapons should be available from friendly civilian sources with relative ease. Another possible source could be the concealed or abandoned weapons and equipment which belonged to a defeated or disbanded army. In most cases, obtaining this equipment requires the cooperation of indigenous civilians. In World War II, in Eastern and Southeastern Europe and in the Philippines guerrillas got their initial supplies through this method.

The enemy army itself could be a source of equipment through pilfering or barter. So can industrial plants under the control or administration of the enemy army. After the commencing of operations, equipment can be captured from the enemy. In fact, captured enemy supplies should be an essential source during the developing phase of a guerrilla movement.

External sources of materiel include neutrals and allies. Equipment can be purchased in neutral countries for the guerrillas if funds are available. This type of operation though is vulnerable to the activities of enemy agents who may get information about the transactions. Intercepting the shipments becomes then relatively easy for the enemy. The best source, in terms of quantity of materiel, is an allied army or a foreign government friendly to the guerrillas. Most successful guerrilla movements have had some external assistance in terms of materiel. Obtaining equipment from this type of source, of course, presents the problems of transportation and issue of the equipment to the guerrillas. In most cases this requires infiltration of equipment through enemy lines or through territory controlled by the enemy. This can be a serious technical problem, but it can be worked out by utilizing aerial deliveries and/or an efficient underground organization working with the guerrillas.

TERRAIN

The importance of terrain and topography in guerrilla operations can not be overemphasized. Terrain has been a factor bearing on military problems since prehistoric times. Even today's technology has not been able to overcome the many constraints which terrain imposes on military operations. Of the three prerequisites for guerrilla warfare which we are discussing — personnel, materiel, and terrain — the last one is the one about which practically nothing remedial can be done by the organizers of guerrilla operations. One either has favorable terrain conditions, or he does not. If favorable conditions do not exist, guerrilla warfare cannot be developed.

What, then, constitutes favorable terrain for guerrillas?

The first and most important characteristic of favorable terrain is that which provides maximum opportunities for concealment. Guerrillas spend more time hiding than fighting their enemy. What kind of terrain features offer good possibilities for concealment?

In older days, prior to the era of aerial surveillance, any part of the earth's land surface, if large enough, offered opportunities of concealment for guerrilla bands. This no longer holds true. The size of the area alone will not provide the proper opportunities for concealment, as long as the guerrillas' oppo-

nent has at his disposal even rudimental means of aerial surveillance. Since the advent of the airplane, the only kind of
terrain which offers possibilities of concealment for guerrillas
is that which has severe irregularities on its surface or dense
vegetation which conceals the earth's surface. In other words:
mountains, forests, and swamps; or any combination of these.

How about urban areas?

They too can be considered potential area for guerrilla operations because they offer excellent opportunities of concealment to indigenous guerrillas. However, the high density of
population in urban areas has certain disadvantages for the
guerrillas. One disadvantage is that of security. The urban guerrillas can be observed by too many people and it is usually
impossible to tell which of the observers are enemy agents and
which are not. Another disadvantage is the probability of extremely high casualties among the noncombatants if military
operations take place within the confines of the urban area.
Assuming that the noncombatants are friendly to the guerrillas,
this high rate of casualties will be detrimental to the guerrillas
and in extreme cases can cause a change of attitude among the
people on whom the guerrillas depend for support. A third
disadvantage is the fact that the conventional forces' usual
superiority in firepower can be most effective within an urban
area, particularly if the conventional forces disregard the damage that can be inflicted on the city. The guerrillas can easily
be trapped and annihilated by an enemy who may choose to
destroy the city block by block. This, of course, would not be
an advisable method of eliminating the guerrillas if the city
with its industry and other resources is necessary for the enemy's
war effort. Or if the enemy's policy is to attempt to befriend
the city's inhabitants. So, the advisability of conducting guerrilla operations in urban areas has to be decided by balancing
the advantages against the disadvantages.

The next characteristic of favorable terrain has to do with
transportation and communications. The transportation network has to be such that it facilitates the movements of guerrillas and hinders those of the conventional forces. A well
developed road and rail network will, as a rule, be an advantage to the conventional forces and detrimental to the guerrillas.

This network will make it possible for the conventional forces to move reserves speedily to any points where the guerrillas have struck or made an appearance. If, on the contrary, the communications network is not well developed, the guerrillas will be able to move across country and avoid pursuit by the enemy who will probably depend on wheeled vehicles for transport. In addition, the fact that the roads are limited, is in itself an added advantage to the guerrillas because any interruption of enemy traffic caused by their operations will have greater effect on the dispositions and resupply of the conventional forces.

The third characteristic of terrain has to do with the local food production. Subsistence can become a critical subject in guerrilla operations. It is very doubtful that a guerrilla force can assure its total resupply from outside friendly sources for prolonged periods of time. It will have to depend, therefore, on the local food production for subsistence. A desert, arid, unproductive land, such as the North African desert, can not sustain a large guerrilla force. However, with prudence, small bands may be able to operate for limited periods of time. In such territory, the conventional force with its well-functioning services of quartermaster and supply will have a decisive advantage over the guerrillas. The same holds true for a fairly productive territory which has been desolated by the war. One of the reasons why Sherman's Army on its March to the Sea was not bothered by Confederate guerrillas on its flanks and rear is that after Sherman passed through any part of the South, there was not much left that could be used by guerrillas. Sherman's troops had instructions to take from the Southern farms what was left of the ridable horses, destroy the crops, and drive along the beef herds.[2]

When the local inhabitants are reduced to a destitute state, they are not prone to support the guerrillas with food. This destitution can be the result of either low agricultural productivity of the land or the result of military operations. This is a point to remember when the commander of a retreating army decides to apply a scorched earth policy. This will prevent a guerrilla movement from developing, at least until after the next harvest. The retreating army should, therefore, destroy only those items which can be of no use to future guerrillas.

Such items would include industrial facilities, machinery, vehicles, roads, etc; but not crops, livestock, and related items which are in the custody of indigenous families. The retreating army should make a definite effort to leave and distribute to the civilians in a territory being evacuated, all surplus food, clothing, shoes, and medicines. If the civilians have any spirit of resistance, they will see that such supplies do not fall into the hands of the invading enemy and will share them later with guerrillas, if they appear on the scene.

Lastly we must discuss briefly the influence of weather and climate. Inclement weather is ideal for guerrilla operations. This holds true up to a certain point beyond which you begin to get diminishing returns. The natural tendency of conventional troops during a severe snowstorm or subzero temperatures is to "dig in" their quarters and wait it out. This period offers excellent opportunity for the guerrillas to attack or to move. If, though, the accumulation of snow becomes too great and the temperature drops to a point where the guerrillas can not expose themselves to the elements without suffering casualties from the weather, then we have reached the point where climatic conditions hinder the operations of both the conventional forces and the guerrillas.

Prevailing high temperatures and high humidity can be as adverse as snow and low temperatures for military operations.

If unfavorable weather conditions prevail during the most part of the year in a given territory, then maybe this territory is not suitable for guerrilla operations. The polar regions fall in this category and so do the African deserts, some of the Central Asian plateaus, certain regions of South Asia, and the interior of Australia.

A very important factor concerning climate is that guerrillas, if they are indigenous, will be better qualified to cope with the climate of the area in which they are operating than the troops of the enemy who, being foreigners, will not be used to the climate.

To recapitulate, the terrain best suited for guerrilla operations is something like this:

Fairly large land mass covered with mountains, forest or jungle, and maybe swamps.

There is in existence on this land mass a communications network including railroads, paved highways, airfields, and maybe canals and sea or river ports; but this network is not very dense nor fully developed.

There is sufficient agriculture and animal husbandry to support the local inhabitants and the anticipated number of guerrillas.

Weather conditions do not get severe to the point where existence outdoors becomes impossible.

3. Relationship with Psychological Warfare

Psychological warfare is a complex subject of its own and we do not propose to discuss it here except in reference to guerrilla warfare.

One of the objectives of psychological warfare is to influence the mental attitudes of the opposition. The means of accomplishing this objective are nonviolent. Therefore, psychological warfare may be waged in times of peace as well as in war.

Because of the complexity of the human mind, the direction of psychological warfare must be entrusted to experts. By experts we mean individuals who possess professional qualifications and who, in addition, have detailed knowledge of the enemy in matters such as History, national aspirations, politics, economics, minority groups, etc.

If psychological warfare is inexpertly waged, it is laughed at by the enemy. There are numerous such examples in World War II. In some cases, inexpertly waged psychological warfare has brought results exactly opposite to those desired. One such case was the following.

Early in 1945, the Allied Air Forces dropped leaflets among the Ostbataillone on the Western Front in which they urged the members of the Ostbataillone to cease resistance and surrender to the Anglo-Americans who could promise them speedy repatriation to their native USSR. The result was that the Ostbataillone fought fiercely to the end because the last thing in the world they wished for themselves was repatriation to the

USSR where they would, undoubtedly, be executed as deserters or traitors. The Allied officers responsible for this leaflet should have known that the Ostbataillone had been recruited among the former Soviet prisoners of war who were anti-Soviet in political outlook and, in addition, several belonged to ethnic minorities of the USSR marked for extermination by the then Soviet government. The individuals responsible for this imbecility are also responsible for the deaths of several hundreds of American and British soldiers who became casualties before the Ostbataillone could be subdued.

Influencing the attitudes of the enemy is one of the major objectives of psychological warfare. Equally important is the objective of influencing the minds of one's own troops and non-combatants, and the attitudes of allies and neutrals.

In guerrilla warfare, psychological warfare operations become extremely important because of the guerrillas' dependence on the good will of the civilians among whom they are operating. Consequently, a Guerrilla High Command is concerned with psychological operations aimed at three separate and distinct groups of individuals: The noncombatant civilians of the area where the guerrillas are operating, the members of the enemy armed forces, and the guerrillas themselves.

Psychological operations aimed at the non-combatants where the guerrillas are operating or plan to operate have a number of specific objectives.

The basic objective is to indoctrinate the civilians to the guerrilla cause. If the situation, for example, involves the domination of one ethnic group by an alien government, it is necessary to convince a large segment of the population that supporting the guerrillas is a necessary step towards obtaining national independence. In fact, if this attitude does not already prevail among the people, psychological operations must precede the launching of guerrilla warfare itself. If the situation involves operations in a land occupied by an enemy army, the civilians have to be persuaded to support the guerrillas in order to terminate foreign occupation. If the population is already on the side of the guerrillas, psychological operations are necessary in order to strengthen the people's will to resist the enemy, to improve their morale, and to convince them of the probability of final victory. This is important because no matter how undesirable the existing conditions may be, the civilians are not likely to actively support a guerrilla movement if they think that further resistance to the enemy is useless.

Simultaneously, a specific objective of psychological operations will have to be the discouraging of collaboration with the enemy and the neutralization of the enemy's propaganda. In dealing with this aspect of the problem one has to recognize the fact that the enemy has certain advantages because he probably controls the civil administration and the news media. These advantages of the enemy are offset by the fact that the enemy is normally required to restrict the civil liberties and activities of the people in order to facilitate his military operations. Again, the problem becomes considerably more difficult for the guerrillas if the enemy is taking a more-or-less tolerant attitude towards the civilians, he is utilizing a native civil administration and when collaboration is widespread.

Psychological operations which are aimed at the members of the enemy armed forces have the objective of reducing the enemy's will to oppose the guerrillas. This too constitutes a difficult task. But there will be situations where the enemy army will have morale and psychological weaknesses. This is particularly true in an age when conflicts tend to be identified with ideologies, such as democracy vs communism, etc. Those responsible for the conduct of psychological operations for the guerrillas must identify the psychological weaknesses among the enemy soldiers and exploit them. Particularly vulnerable are members of ethnic, racial, or religious minorities among the enemy. Other psychologically exploitable conditions are dissatisfaction with military life, homesickness, lack of promotions, effects of supply deficiencies, adverse news from other fronts, etc. In general, the desired results are to reduce the intensity of the enemy's animosity towards the guerrillas. Here it must be remembered that the best psychological efforts can be nullified by one incident of mistreatment of captured enemy personnel by guerrillas. However, exemplary punishment after trial of individuals who are known to have committed atrocities against guerrillas or noncombatants friendly to the guerrillas is psychologically effective in limiting such acts in the future.

The guerrillas themselves have to be subjected to psychological conditioning. Ideological indoctrination and devotion to a "cause" is extremely important in guerrilla warfare. Once this is achieved, then it becomes necessary to maintain among the guerrillas a strong attitude of militancy and to protect them from the enemy's psychological operations. After all, the guerrillas are no less human than their adversaries; therefore, they are susceptible to enemy psychological countermeasures. As a matter of fact, the emphasis which needs to be placed on psychological conditioning of guerrillas, is directly proportional to the broadness of the movement and the size of the guerrilla force. If the total guerrilla force consists of only a few dozen men (example: EOKA in Cyprus), the possibilities are that each one of them is fanatically devoted to the guerrilla objectives; therefore, one needs to spend a minimum of effort in psychological operations among them. However, if the guerrilla force consists of several thousand men (example: Soviet guerrillas in World War II), it is certain that among them will be individuals marginal in their loyalty, opportunists, etc. Much greater effort will be, therefore, required to keep these people in line.

The responsibility for taking the appropriate steps to maintain the desired psychological attitudes among the guerrillas is a command and responsibility. This means that each unit commander must conduct psychological operations within the members of his own unit. The problem, however, is that all good combat leaders do not necessarily excell in the field of psychological warfare.

The Soviet leadership recognized this problem in the days of the Russian Civil War and this is one of the reasons why they established the posts of military commissars with each unit. One other reason was the political unreliability of the ordinary unit commanders. The military commissars, therefore, in addition to their psychological tasks, shared command responsibility and authority with the corresponding unit commanders. This split responsibility and authority of command is highly undesirable. In addition, this system by no means guarantees loyalty to the political leadership. There are reasons to believe that in 1937 the Chief Soviet Military Commissar, Gamarnik, was behind the conspiracy for which Tuhhachevsky was blamed.[3] The Soviets, therefore, abolished the positions of military commissars in World War II and substituted the "political instructors" who had the mission of keeping the troops in line politically. The Soviet Army is not the only one which has utilized this solution. Others have followed suit from time to time; for example, the Chinese Nationalist Army.

Among guerrillas, the best solution is to furnish assistance for psychological operations to the commanders without relieving them from this responsibility. Overall direction of psychological operations should be assigned within the guerrilla High Command. The dissemination of psychological material should be made through selected individuals who are serving with the units and perform this task as an additional duty. The density of these individuals will depend on the availability of individuals with appropriate qualifications and the degree of effective control which the various Command echelons can exercise over their subordinate units. For instance, units with good communications with headquarters may require only one such individual per company, while remote bands of 10-15 men may need one each also. It is important that these individuals provide a two-way communication on psychological matters. They disseminate the information provided by the High Command and also report to the High Command on the attitudes, morale, and psychological status of the guerrillas. In this manner, the High Command has the opportunity to provide corrective action for any problems which may develop.

Psychological operations directed at the enemy and the non-combatant civilians should not be a direct responsibility of the guerrillas. The guerrilla organization is primarily a combat organization, therefore it should not be burdened with non-combat missions. It is best that this mission be given to the underground organization which will support the guerrillas. The guerrilla High Command must retain coordinative control of psychological operations, but the day-by-day conduct of psychological operations should be left to the underground.

What remains to be examined now is the media through which psychological operations can be conducted. There are three categories of media available to the guerrillas: Electronic, printed materials, and personal contacts. Each category has advantages and disadvantages.

Electronic media include radio and television. Their biggest advantage is that they can reach a large audience. Another significant advantage is that once the telecast or broadcast is made, there is no residual incriminating evidence left among the recipients, therefore they are highly desirable from the security point of view. Their disadvantages include the fact that the establishment of clandestine transmitting stations in territory controlled by the enemy is nearly impossible. This, therefore, requires that they be established in territory controlled by the guerrillas or in territory controlled by friendly forces or in neutral territory. In the latter cases, distance and range may be a problem. Another disadvantage is that operation and maintenance of transmitting facilities requires highly skilled personnel, who may or may not be available. A third disadvantage is their vulnerability to jamming and electronic countermeasures of the enemy. Finally, the audience may be limited by the availability of receiver sets.

Printed materials include leaflets, books, periodicals, newspapers, etc. They can also reach large numbers of individuals, particularly since they can be passed from one individual to another. Their disadvantages include the fact that they require the availability of printing presses and distribution operations which make them vulnerable to interception by the enemy. They have, therefore, a strong element of insecurity. The security of the recipients is also jeopardized if any of them are found with such materials in their possession. Another disadvantage is the fact that they are limited by the degree of literacy among the intended recipients. Illiteracy is a condition that still prevails in some parts of the globe.

Personal contacts include lectures in group meetings and informal discussions among two or more individuals one of whom is a psychological warfare agent. Their main advantage is that they are the most effective of all methods, particularly if the individuals used for this purpose have the necessary training and experience. Another advantage is that since the lecturer or agent has the opportunity to observe the reactions of his audience, this method provides a good opportunity to gauge the success or progress of the program. Among their disadvantages, the most serious one is their vulnerability to infiltration by enemy agents particularly since contacts have to be repetitive. Another disadvantage is that they require a relatively large number of individuals with proper training who can devote a lot of time to such contacts in order to reach a sufficient number of people.

The guerrilla High Command in coordination of its supporting underground organization will have to decide which media for the conduct of psychological operations can best be utilized. The possibilities are that a combination of at least two of the above will be utilized. The decision will depend on the prevailing local conditions and the resources available. The important points which need to be remembered about psychological warfare in relation to guerrilla warfare are the following.

1. Psychological operations are a necessity in guerrilla warfare.

2. The minimum number of guerrillas should be utilized in the conduct of psychological operations. Guerrillas should remain available for combat and the conduct of psychological operations has to be assigned to an underground organization. However, the guerrilla High Command should retain direction and overall control of psychological operations.

3. Psychological operations must be planned and conducted with extreme care by trained experienced personnel.

4. The success and progress of psychological operations has to be closely followed by the High Command.

4. Future Prospects

With the visibility obtained through this analysis of strategic considerations, it should be fairly easy to predict in generalities where guerrilla conflicts may take place in the future. If we were to do now or anytime in the future an analysis of recent and current international power politics we can foretell the specific areas of probable guerrilla warfare. In doing this, one

cannot ignore the fact that international relations and inter-
course among states during the last 50 years have been principally affected by one single factor. This factor is the "push"
for expansion by the communist states. Theirs has not been the
only expansionist effort during this period. However, the others
have either been unsuccessful (example: Axis efforts in the
30's and 40's), or are of only regional significance. Future conflicts, therefore, in which guerrilla warfare will be utilized are
determined in great part by the policies of the communist states.

Guerrilla movements which in the past have been under the
political and/or military control of the communists have followed three different patterns.

The first pattern was apparent in Russia during the Civil
War and World War II. In these cases, guerrilla movements
developed as auxiliary to the operations of the Red Army.

During World War II, a second pattern of guerrilla movements developed in European and Asian countries which were
temporarily under military occupation by the armies of the Axis
powers. The communists capitalized on the opportunities created by the war and occupation and organized guerrilla groups
which attempted, in some cases successfully, to take over the
governments of the countries in question after the withdrawal
of the Axis forces. As a sideline, the guerrillas engaged the occupation forces occasionally; however, their military objectives
against the Axis forces were very limited in relation to the
guerrillas' eventual capabilities. Primarily, the mission of these
guerrillas was to create a military force which could help the
communist party attain its political objectives after the elimination of the present enemy (occupation forces) by someone else.

The third pattern of communist guerrilla movements is the
one developing now in Asia, Africa, and Latin America. However, this pattern follows the basic methods developed by the
Red Chinese in the thirties. In most cases it involves people
who are, or have been until very recently, under colonial or
semicolonial domination. These guerrilla movements are developing as part of the nationalist revolutions taking place in
these countries. The ideas of communism and nationalism are
of course, incompatible. Marx considers national conscience as
a kind of anachronism and a hindrance to his concepts of inter-

national brotherhood among the world's workers. However, communism also accepts the necessity of compromise and the inevitability of political and military retreat.[4] Communism, therefore, has no inhibitions about making what appears to be a compromise of principles and espousing the cause of A or B nationalist group. As a matter of fact, the strong winds of nationalism sweeping the world since the end of World War II offer to the communists their golden opportunity. In contrast, the West has underestimated the potential force of nationalism.

The communists, therefore, associated themselves with the nationalist revolutions in Indochina, Indonesia, etc., for the purpose of dominating them. It is not surprising that the communist leadership in these cases takes its lessons from Mao Tse-Tung. Mao describes in his works how such revolutions should develop in three phases.[5] The first phase is the organizational phase during which the foundations for later action are established by developing an underground organization and by indoctrinating as large a segment of the population as possible on the necessity for revolt. During the second phase, military action begins by acts of sabotage and small scale attacks by the guerrillas. Mao expects this phase to be the longest and the most difficult for the insurgents. He expects, during this stage, the guerrillas to suffer casualties and the movement to have setbacks. The overall result of the activities of this phase, however, shall be that the guerrilla organization will gradually increase its strength, whereas the enemy will gradually weaken. When the enemy is sufficiently weakened, time has come for the third phase during which the guerrillas transition from guerrilla bands to a conventional revolutionary army, abandon guerrilla tactics, and meet the enemy army in conventional battle in order to annihilate it.

Mao developed the above ideas, of course, from the Chinese experiences between 1920 and 1948. The communist revolutionary movements in Southeast Asia and Cuba have copied Mao's operating methods with little variation even though conditions were not identical in these other places with the conditions that had prevailed in China prior to 1948. In view of the fact that the communists, so far, appear to be unimaginative rigid thinkers, very much dogmabound, we can expect the same pattern to develop in all places where potentialities for revolution exist.

In other words, one can expect that the communists will either instigate or attempt to control potential conflicts. On the other side of the coin, as the noncommunists become wiser and gain from recent experiences, they can be expected to apply those lessons learned from communist and other guerrilla movements to obtain their own objectives.

Therefore, unless radical changes of the prevailing world political and military conditions take place, guerrilla operations are likely to occur within the next ten or twenty years in one or more of the below listed places under the outlined conditions. For purposes of defining the long-range objectives of these potential guerrilla conflicts we chose to separate them as offensive and defensive.

Offensive guerrilla movements are those in which the guerrillas initiate hostilities and/or have the political offensive; i.e., they are attempting to bring about a political change, while their opponents are committed to the maintenance of the political status quo.

First of all we must list the Asian, African and other countries which are still under colonial or semicolonial domination. Unless such colonies are liquidated, insurrection is going to take place in every one of them. The initial stages of such insurrection will most likely take the form of guerrilla operations because of the obvious advantages which guerrilla operations offer to the insurgents. These insurrections may or may not be communist-controlled. It is certain, however, that the communists will make every effort to infiltrate such movements even though the movements may be strictly inspired by the ideals of national and political independence with no reference whatsoever to economic factors or the class struggle. Up till now, the communists have been successful in infiltrating nationalist revolutions to at least some extent. Exception to this was the case of Cyprus where EOKA, the organization which led the revolt for independence, had very strong anti-communist convictions because of the background of its leaders. Some of the countries which are likely to see nationalist insurrections of the above type are Angola and Mozambique, which are Portuguese possessions,

Rhodesia and the Union of South Africa where the large numbers of non-whites could be stirred up, Cyprus where the colonial establishment has not been completely liquidated, Turkey and Iraq both of which include concentrated minorities of Kurds, and Northern Ireland.

The next potential group is the independent, but underdeveloped countries where there is a wide separation between ruling class and the rest of the people. Most of the Central and South American countries fall in this group; so does Turkey, Portugal, Spain, Iran, Saudi Arabia, etc. Insurrections are likely to take place in the above countries in order to achieve, by violent means, economic and social changes. It is needless to point out that such insurrections can be forestalled if the ruling classes of the countries in question realize their social obligations and take a truly benevolent attitude towards their fellow citizens. Insurrections of this kind will also rely on guerrilla methods at their initial stages unless the armed forces of each country support the insurrection. No domestic revolutions can be successful without the support or toleration of the armed forces. The Russian Revolution of 1917 could not have succeeded if the Russian Army was not disintegrating in the face of military defeats and if what was left of it had taken a firm stand in support of the government. Similarly, the Nazi party in Germany in 1934 would not have had the opportunity to abolish the Weimar Republic had the German Army discharged its obligations towards the constitution which it had sworn to defend. But Hitler neutralized the opposition of the generals by promising to support the policy of rearmament. Therefore, the army tolerated the Nazi takeover. In June 1960, we witnessed the Turkish Army throw in its lot with the rebels in Ankara and overthrow the Menderes regime. It is more likely, however, that at the present time the armed forces of most of the underdeveloped countries which we previously mentioned, are loyal to the ruling classes or otherwise committed to the preservation of the status quo. The rebels therefore, must resort to guerrilla warfare in order to wear down the enemy and in order to build up their own military strength sufficiently to enable them to eventually challenge the enemy army in decisive battle.

This kind of revolt is more susceptible to communist infiltration than the purely national revolutions. Precisely, this is the reason why Cuba has today a communist government. Cuba has declared that promoting revolutions in Latin America constitutes a basic element of its foreign policy. The Cubans, pursuing this policy, have attempted to organize guerrillas in several Central and South American countries including Venezuela and Bolivia. In both of these cases they met with disaster and lost their outstanding proponent of guerrilla warfare, Ernesto "Che" Guevara. The reasons of their failure were different in each country. In Venezuela they lost out because of the enlightened social policy and strong counteraction of the Venezuelan Government and the support it received from the United States. In Bolivia they were unsuccessful because of gross errors committed by Guevara. The people whom Guevara was trying to incite to revolt were unmotivated by the issues he was trying to raise. The willingness of the people to support a revolt is a fundamental prerequisite in guerrilla warfare, as was pointed out earlier in this chapter.

Notwithstanding their failures, the Cubans will try again. In fact they have never given up, and nuclei of guerrillas or prospective guerrillas, sponsored by Castro, are in existence today in at least half a dozen countries. Some of them will eventually escalate into full-scale guerrilla war.

A third possible stage for offensive guerrilla operations could be any country where any kind of conditions for revolution exist and where a foreign power intervenes to support one of the dissident groups. Such was the case in Greece in 1946. Something similar could happen in the future between two Arab countries. For instance a revolt in Saudi Arabia, supported covertly by Egypt. This kind of revolution can also be exploited by the communists. In the case of Greece, which we mentioned above, the revolt was not only exploited by the communists, it was actually communist-instigated.

Among the newly independent African states the possibilities of revolts and guerrilla warfare are extremely strong. The principal reason is that most of these states include within their borders tribal minorities. The minorities are potential dissident groups and their dissents or dissatisfactions can be exploited by outsiders. Ethiopia, for instance, includes minorities of Somalis, Eritreans, and others. Somalia, which maintains claims on part of Ethiopia, actively promotes guerrilla warfare among the Somalis. So did Syria until its decisive defeat by the Israelis in 1967. Why would Syria, an underdeveloped country, expend resources to foster guerrilla warfare so far away from its borders is a question which defies logical answers.

Another example may be presented some day by Mali, which now has a far-left government. Mali includes the nomadic Tuareg, who are racially different from the rest of the Mali nationals. If the Mali Government some day attempts to tax or restrict the Tuareg, and the Tuareg can obtain assistance from outsiders who are interested in creating trouble for the Mali Government, we have an almost perfect setup for guerrilla warfare. Similar possibilities exist in Congo, Kenya, Uganda, and practically all African States. Canada may also be subjected to guerrilla warfare because of the upsurge of nationalism among the French-Canadians of Quebec.

We must not assume that the continental United States are immune from possible guerrilla operations in the future. Small bands of determined guerrillas, based on Mexican soil, with or without the connivance of the Mexican government, can easily infiltrate the U.S.-Mexican border and conduct raids and acts of sabotage which, although, they may not inflict great material damage, will have a tremendous psychological affect on the minds of the American people. It is foolish to consider such an event beyond the realm of possibility. Since the 30's, particularly since the conclusion of the Spanish Civil War, all kinds of communists, communist agents, and communist sympathizers, many of them fugitives from the Justice of other lands, have been assembling with impunity in Mexico. The attitude of the Mexican government towards these people is variable, but this has little bearing on their potential for trouble. The Northwestern States of Mexico have several areas ideal for the concealment of armed bands. As a matter of fact, numerous bands composed of ordinary criminals with no political affiliation are at large in these areas. Geographic conditions of the U.S. border are such that determined guerrillas can cross it on numerous points and escape detection from about 80 miles

East of El Paso, Texas to about 50 miles West of Yuma, Arizona. Anyone who is familiar with that part of the country knows that surveillance of over 1000 miles of border running through a desert is not the easiest task in the world. It is also known that no American military units have been utilized for border surveillance since 1920 and the job is entrusted to the very thinly manned U.S. Border Patrol Service which is primarily concerned in stopping illegal immigrant traffic and contraband.

Neither can we discount the possibility of guerrillas operating out of Canada and raiding the United States, including Alaska. After all, in the 19th century a similar situation existed in reverse with the Fenian raids into Canada. The Fenians raided Canada from bases in U.S. territory. Although the U.S. Army exerted a substantial effort to stop these raids, it was only partially successful. Actually, the U.S.-Canadian border is more vulnerable to infiltration than the U.S.-Mexican border because of the mountain ranges in Washington, Idaho, and Montana and because of the dense forests straddling the border in the area around the Great Lakes and West of the Dakota Plains. The Great Lakes do form a natural obstacle with the exception of the area around Sault Ste Marie. East of Lake Erie the densities of population and communications network are such that the country cannot be considered as being favorable to offensive guerrilla operations. The weather will also be a limiting factor to guerrilla operations at such latitude; the severity of the winters in the country adjacent to the US-Canadian border is such that only four to six months out of each year are suitable for military operations.

But the United States is also vulnerable to guerrilla activities from indigenous subversive groups. Particularly if such groups include a number of fanatics who consider the American society in general as their enemy, therefore, they are unconcerned about the casualties which they and the public may suffer.

Another potential area of future guerrilla action is the satellite countries of the communist bloc. Any revolutions against the communist governments of Yugoslavia, Albania, Czechoslovakia, Red China perhaps, etc. will use guerrilla methods during their early stages. Admittedly, the possibilities of revolutions in the above countries are very slim since the failure of West to come to the rescue of the Hungarians in 1956 and the Czechs in 1968. One of the strategic errors of the Hungarian rebels in 1956 was the fact that they concentrated their forces in Budapest and a few other cities where they were compelled to fight the Russian armor from almost static positions. Had they been able to extricate their forces from the cities and disperse through the rural areas, they could have lasted much longer. Of course, they could not hope to succeed finally without Western military or diplomatic intervention. But the Western powers were in no moral position to intervene since the Anglo-French opportunistic action in Suez was taking place almost simultaneously. In any case, guerrilla action against satellite governments should be pursued as a possibility by Western strategists. Such action would wrest the initiative from the communists and would place the West on the offensive for the first time since the conclusion of the Korean War. The most vulnerable of the satellites is Albania because of its ideological differences with Yugoslavia and Russia and because of the fact that a strong minority of ethnic Greeks inhabits the southern half of that country.

The Soviet Union itself could become a stage for guerrilla operations of the offensive type. Anti-Soviet guerrillas could take the field in conjunction with a major war and invasion of Soviet territory by a strong ground force of the Western Powers.[6] Even though all of the Soviet territory is potentially subject to guerrilla activities, the lands in the South and West are considerably more vulnerable. The reason is that the Soviet Union's ethnic minorities are concentrated in those regions. These ethnic minorities have a long tradition of revolts and guerrilla actions against their central governments, both Tsarist and communist. The expansionist policy of the Soviets since World War II has compounded their problem of ethnic minorities by the absorption of the Baltic States and other regions inhabited by millions of Poles, Karelians, Germans and Romanians. This, in combination with other factors, has resulted in the great Russians being only about 50% of the total population of the Soviet State. The Soviet government is acutely aware of this. It chronically suspects the minorities of disloyalty, and from time to time organizes mass migrations of its subjects as a remedy.

Guerrilla warfare could take place in Soviet territory unrelated to a major war with the West. Such guerrilla activity could be instigated by the Chinese along the 4000 miles of common frontier with the Soviet Union. An all-out war between Russia and China is a near impossibility in spite of their doctrinal and policy differences. No matter how strong these differences may be, neither of the two leading communist governments would wage total war against the other because the prospects are very real that the West would benefit from the outcome. There should be no doubt that they consider the West instead of each other as their ultimate enemy. But as long as their differences continue and intensify, it is conceivable that China may instigate guerrilla warfare aginst the Soviets in order to embarrass the Soviet Government, obtain a variety of limited objectives, or perhaps contribute to the collapse of the regime without a corresponding collapse of the communist system. To a lesser possibility one may expect the Soviet Government to instigate guerrilla operations against the Chinese in order to weaken the Chinese government and bring about a political change. Finally, it is conceivable that any Soviet bloc government may resort to guerrilla warfare against another Soviet bloc government in lieu of total war. In order for this to take place two conditions must preexist. First, the conflict between the two satellite governments has to be of sufficient intensity. Second, the authority of the principal communist government (Moscow or Peking) must be diminished sufficiently to allow such an event to take place. An example of this may be an Albanian guerrilla operation against the Yugoslavs in the Kosovo region. The Albanians would be aware that such an operation would create a multitude of ideological, political, and military problems for the Yugoslavs and yet they would be immune from conventional invasion by the Yugoslav Army because of the facade that Socialist governments do not wage war on each other.

Defensive guerrilla movements are those where the guerrillas are operating against an army which is invading their homeland or against an occupying army.

Under the above definition, any country is a potential stage for guerrilla operations in the future. The country's political orientation viz-a-viz the conflict between East and West is immaterial. For instance, we may see guerrilla activity of this category in Somaliland if the Somalis are invaded by the Ethiopians. Of course, we must allow for the existence (or nonexistence) of factors necessary for the development of a guerrilla movement any place, i.e. will to resist the invader by the people and favorable terrain.

Some kind of guerrilla activity will also continue in the Arab lands occupied by Israel. The desire of the Arab leadership to engage the Israelis in guerrilla warfare is extremely strong since they have failed in conventional warfare. However, geographic conditions in that part of the world do not favor prolonged operation of guerrilla bands in Israeli-held territory. The Arabs are also faced with the additional disadvantage of almost complete command of the air by the Israelis. At best, the Arabs can hope to launch guerrilla raids of limited duration with the raiders returning to sanctuary in Arab-held territory after each raid. The punitive counter-raids launched by the Israelis are not guerrilla in character.

Among the nations of what is known as the Western bloc, defensive guerrilla operations are particularly suitable in the Iberian Peninsula, the Balkans, Italy, and Norway. The rest of Western Europe is not too favorable to guerrilla operations because of the density of its communications network. India presents excellent conditions for guerrilla operations; probably, a substantial guerrilla movement would have developed in India had the Chinese attack continued beyond November 1962.

It is certain that if Western armies invade the Soviet Union, China, or any of the other countries of the communist bloc, they shall encounter vigorous resistance from guerrilla groups. The war plans of the above countries make detailed provisions for the utilization of guerrillas in such eventuality. At least, it is reasonable for us to assume this in view of what we know of prevailing contemporary Russian military thinking.[7]

Probably, defensive use of guerrillas in the United States will never take place. Guerrilla movements are not capable of bringing about final victory in a major conflict without outside help. If the United States is invaded by an enemy army, it probably means that the war is already lost and no help from outside sources is expected. Unless, of course, space technology advances to the point where we can establish solar bases from where we can launch weapons which can destroy the enemy in spite of the invasion or occupation of our Homeland.

In conclusion, it has to be recognized that the potential for future guerrilla operations of offensive or defensive nature exists in a great part of the world. It appears that the communist bloc will exploit every opportunity to infiltrate and control guerrilla movements which are related to national, tribal, or social conflicts. In addition, it can be expected that the communist bloc will initiate guerrilla uprisings, when conditions are favorable, in order to promote its expansionist policies. However, the communist bloc itself is vulnerable to guerrilla warfare, if and when the Western Nations decide to abandon the policy of containment and wrest the initiative from the communists.

VII

Tactical Applications
Planning and Conducting Tactical Operations

1. General

THE ULTIMATE success of a guerrilla movement depends on victorious combat against the guerrillas' adversary — the enemy conventional forces. Consequently, thorough understanding of tactics is an important requirement for all echelons of guerrilla leadership. However, because the guerrillas are usually inferior to their enemy in firepower, mobility, and logistic support, they cannot expect to achieve decisive victories against enemy conventional forces. In essence, the guerrillas' tactical objectives are to achieve temporary advantages over their enemy, inflict casualties, destroy materiel, and disengage from action as soon as possible. Guerrilla tactics, therefore, are modified conventional tactics. The extent of modification will depend on the conditions prevailing locally and will have to be developed by the guerrilla commanders in the field. In this chapter we will attempt to identify and analyze tactical principles which are basic in the application of guerrilla warfare.

Successful conduct of guerrilla operations requires compliance with the following tactical principles:

1. The initiative is maintained by the guerrillas. The guerrilla commander chooses the time and place of combat and also the duration of combat. When the enemy asserts the initiative and conducts anti-guerrilla operations, the guerrillas avoid battle.
2. The guerrilla force.always maintains organizational flexibility and operational fluidity.
3. Most important of all, the principle of concentration of force at the decisive point, is absolutely observed.

As stated previously, one of the reasons to engage in guerrilla warfare is that the ratio of forces is to the advantage of the enemy in great proportion. The important fact to remember in planning guerrilla operations, however, is the following: Regardless of how overwhelming the enemy strength is, it is absolutely impossible for the enemy force to be of such monolithic structure and deployment that it is simultaneously equally strong at all locations all the time. For instance, if the enemy is occupying a territory, he has to be dispersed in several garrisons of varied strength. He also has to maintain communications among his garrisons utilizing vehicular columns, railroads, etc, all of which may have to be provided with escorts for security. The nature of modern warfare itself is such that it creates situations where rear areas security is compromised. An advancing enemy armored column, in any theater, will lose contact with the slower-moving friendly infantry units for at least some time.

The guerrilla operational planners must, therefore, exploit the enemy's necessity for dispersal. Since the guerrillas have the choice of time and location of combat they must *strike the enemy at some point where the guerrillas can, temporarily at least, achieve superiority of force.* This is *the* fundamental requirement in conducting guerrilla operations. All other operational efforts are auxiliary to this principle and in the final analysis are intended to facilitate this objective.

To recapitulate, the guerrilla band, no matter how weak or how strong, always hits the enemy at a time and place of its own choosing and always engages an enemy unit of lesser strength. When the enemy asserts the initiative, the guerrilla band utilizes the several means at its disposal to avoid battle.

2. Planning Tactical Operations

All military operations include fundamentally two phases: the planning phase and the conduct of the operation itself. To plan an operation is one of the more serious responsibilities of command. The commander is assisted by his S-3 and other staff officers and subordinate commanders, but the responsibility for planning is still his. This is, of course, an elementary command concept known to any 4th classman at West Point and any freshman ROTC student. In this day of oversize staffs, however, some of us tend to forget this concept and rely on staff officers to assume command functions. No matter how able an operations' officer the commander has, he must inject his own ideas, his own personality, into the operations plan so that it is really his plan in concept. Then, the staff is allowed to work out the details; the commander then studies the details and he integrates his thinking to the details of the plan.

In guerrilla warfare, planning any tactical operation requires the following steps.

1. Establishment of the tactical objective. In some cases this may already have been established by a higher headquarters. The Supreme Guerrilla Command or a friendly conventional force Headquarters may have, for instance, decided that the guerrilla bands under its control must harass the enemy from withdrawing forces from this area and transferring them to an adjacent sector where it is reported that he plans to launch an all-out anti-guerrilla drive next month. The objective has, therefore, been established in general terms. The specific objective should be left to guerrilla headquarters under discussion; but this in actuality may be nothing more than a liberty to select the target. The tactical commander (the guerrilla commander in this case) has the opportunity to judge which one of the outposts can be attacked with good possibility of success and when; or how many of the outposts can be attacked. The decision on target selection will be dependent upon the relative strength of the enemy at the particular outpost, its proximity to other enemy units, its relative importance to the enemy, the psychological value of this to the enemy, to the guerrillas, to the noncombatant civilians in the area, and other possible

factors. In order to come to this decision, the commander utilizes all intelligence available. We shall discuss the intelligence aspect of guerrilla operations again.

2. Order of battle of guerrillas. The next step in planning a guerrilla operation is the determination of how many and what guerrilla units can be made available for this operation and what material resources can be allocated to it. This may not always be an easy decision because the availability of guerrilla units may be subject to a number of conditions. One item to be considered first is security. If the guerrilla bands include a substantial number of covert guerrillas, this could be a limiting factor in terms of available strength. Covert guerrillas are those who spend the daylight hours in their villages cultivating their fields or pursuing their normal civilian occupations and join the bands only at night or other specified times. If the villages are under surveillance by the enemy, the absence of large number of civilians will be noted and the security of the operation itself and the safety of the individual guerrillas and their families may be compromised. Another factor to be considered is the distance over which guerrilla units may have to travel in order to reach their assembly areas. The weather may be an impeding factor in the timely assembly of the guerrilla units. The surveillance or control of the routes by the enemy is another factor. Another one is the quality of personnel available. To establish superiority over the enemy, it is not simply necessary to engage two guerrillas for every enemy soldier. Allowances should be made for possible deficiencies in training and shortages in experience among the guerrillas.

The availability of materiel is another item requiring careful study. Guerrilla units usually suffer from various materiel shortages. It would not be wise to deplete ones ammunition supply in order to accomplish a secondary mission. In some cases it may be necessary to decide whether to commit ten riflemen with 50 rounds each or twenty riflemen with 25 rounds each. It is part of the planning mission to determine the optimum ratio of personnel and materiel to be used for each operation.

3. Assessment of Success Possibilities. Throughout the planning phase of the operation, the possibilities of success or failure

of the plan under study must be repeatedly reexamined. If success appears to be very much in doubt, the staff officer who is preparing the plan must not hesitate to advise his commander against the implementation and execution of that plan. Scrap it and start from scratch! Maybe an entirely different approach will offer more advantages. If that does not work either, maybe the operation should be abandoned. No guerrilla movement can accomplish its aims with tactical failures. We do not wish to advise timidity or lack of boldness here. Timidity can be as disastrous in guerrilla warfare as recklessness. But, it is necessary to emphasize the fact that careful and methodical planning can foretell, in most cases, the success or not of the operation.

4. Intelligence. A fundamental prerequisite for the success of guerrilla operations is to deny the enemy information about the guerrillas while the guerrillas obtain as much information as possible about the enemy. This is one of the few means which the guerrillas can utilize in order to upset the ratio of forces which is to the advantage of the enemy in great proportion. In planning tactical operations, therefore, the subject of intelligence becomes one of paramount importance for the guerrilla commander. In actuality, the term "intelligence" is a misnomer here because it does not cover the subject under discussion completely. We will venture to say that what we are discussing here may better be defined as "possession of pertinent information". In application, it includes the phases of counterintelligence, intelligence, reconnaissance, and surveillance.

Counterintelligence involves the interception of enemy intelligence operations in order to deny the enemy information about one's self. counterintelligence is related to security. Maintenance of security and effective counterintelligence are fundamental requirements in any guerrilla unit. If security has been compromised, it is best for the guerrilla commander to abandon the operation under study and move his unit to another locality.

Intelligence includes the collection and analysis of information about the enemy. The collection of intelligence is a continuous function for every guerrilla. In planning an operation, all available intelligence is studied by the commander and his staff. This means information from the guerrilla unit, other guerrilla units, the underground organization supporting the guerrillas, and the civilians in the area who are friendly to the guerrilla cause. Special caution must be exercised lest the civilian sources have been infiltrated by enemy agents. The intelligence officer in the staff analyzes the collected information and composes an intelligence estimate for the commander. The intelligence estimate is reviewed continuously and revised as necessary in order to maintain it current with the latest information received.

Reconnaissance is essential in order to complete the information necessary for planning a guerrilla operation. Whenever possible, the commander reconnoits the area near the projected target himself. He acquaints himself with the terrain in detail and notes the location of enemy outposts and all other physical characteristics of enemy dispositions. The assembly area is also reconnoited if not under guerrilla control; also the approach and escape routes.

To avoid being surprised by any changes which the enemy may make to his dispositions, deployment, or strength through reinforcements, it is necessary to keep the target and associated critical areas under continuous surveillance from the time of initial reconnaissance through the operation itself. This is best accomplished by utilizing civilians residing, traveling, or working near the projected target area. These civilians must be trustworthy and must be given proper instructions in order to ascertain that they report what they observe correctly. They should not have advance knowledge of the projected operation.

5. Detail Plan. The detail plan is worked out by the appropriate staff officer and then the commander makes whatever changes he deems necessary. The plan is revised as necessary to cope with any changes of the intelligence estimate or to incorporate any improvements which may become apparent through its rehearsal. In drawing a detail plan for a guerrilla operation special attention should be paid to the method of disengagement and withdrawal. Alternate courses of action must be provided for every eventuality whenever possible, and the principle of operational flexibility must be kept in mind without sacrificing the commander's retention of overall operational control. While working out the detailed plan, the guerrilla operations officer has to cope in detail with the problem of insuring that the

enemy's normal advantages are nullified. The advantages are superior firepower, mobility, and perhaps skill and experience. These advantages, however, can be offset in a number of ways. The most obvious way is by utilizing the element of surprise. If the enemy is surprised, it can be expected that his reaction will not be effective. Other ways include utilizing periods of poor visibility, such as the nighttime, adverse weather conditions, and unfavorable for the enemy terrain. Consideration should also be given to the relative morale of the enemy and the guerrillas. Indications of low morale among the enemy, regardless of the cause, should be exploited.

6. Rehearsal of Plan. After the commander is satisfied that he possesses the best possible plan, he explains it to his subordinate unit commanders. If conditions permit, the operation is rehearsed by all intended participants. Rehearsals have a twofold purpose. They give the guerrillas an opportunity to become familiar with their individual missions under the expected conditions of operation and they allow staff and commanders to detect and correct any flaws of the plan and any shortcomings of their troops. A critique should follow every rehearsal. Repeated rehearsals will give the guerrillas confidence and will increase their proficiency; these are the normal results of practice. Security should not be compromised by the rehearsals.

3.   Conducting Tactical Operations

In conducting tactical operations, the first consideration is given to the organization of the attacking force. The size of the attacking force must be commensurate to the selected target and the enemy strength. Regardless of its size, the attacking force is organized basically into two elements: the assault element and the security element.

Whenever possible the assault element should be placed under the direct command of the commander who is directing the overall operation. If circumstances do not permit this, it should be placed under the direction of the most experienced of the subordinate commanders. The assault element includes all personnel and materiel necessary to overcome enemy resistance. It also includes the special mission personnel. For example, if the operation has as objective the destruction of an enemy bridge or other installation, the demolition personnel are included in the assault element. Special mission personnel are organized as a separate group or groups under designated commanders within the assault element. Depending on the size of the participating force, the assault element may be subdivided into lesser units equivalent to squads, platoons, etc. These units are further subdivided into the maneuver and base of fire elements very much like conventional units. But these lesser units do not need to be composed in accordance with any rigid table of organization. They should vary in strength according to their specific mission. For instance, one platoon attacking a machine-gun emplacement may include thirty guerrillas with three automatic weapons while another platoon attacking a motor pool may include only fifteen guerrillas with one automatic weapon. If the operation is of such magnitude that the guerrilla force includes heavy mortars and artillery, special care should be exercised to the utilization of these weapons. Such weapons are most effective when controlled by a single fire control center. This is no absolute rule, however, and they may be allocated as sections or batteries to the support of the lesser units if enemy dispositions so require.

The security element has the following missions: It prevents the enemy from reenforcing the unit under attack; it prevents the enemy from escaping; it cover the withdrawal of the assault element; and where terrain conditions permit, it assists the assault element to overcome enemy resistance with its own supporting fire. The size of the security element depends on the terrain conditions and the enemy's ability to intervene to relieve the unit under attack.

The conduct of a guerrilla tactical operation includes, essentially, four phases. Those are: movement, attack, exploitation, and withdrawal and dispersal. They are explained below.

Movement
Movement includes the procession to the assembly areas and the advance on the target. It is desirable to delay movement to

the assembly areas as long as practicable in order to avoid detection by the enemy. In some cases this may not be possible, and then the guerrillas may have to remain at their assembly areas under cover for several hours or even a day or two. While at the assembly areas, all necessary steps must be taken to ensure security. We keep referring to assembly areas instead of an assembly area because from the security point this is more advantageous. This however, requires exact timing and coordination of the next phase of the movement which is the advance on the target itself.

It is important that the advance on the target is conducted in a manner which enables the guerrillas to approach the target undetected. It is preferred that the approach takes place over multiple routes. When the jump off positions have been reached, final coordination among the participating units takes place.

THE ATTACK

The attack commences on a signal by the commander or at a specified time. The enemy is engaged by the assault element while the security element maintains surveillance over the designated sites and assists the assault element with fire if conditions permit. The assault element's principal task is to place out of action as many of the enemy as possible in the shortest possible time. Every effort is exerted to prevent the enemy from rallying after the initial shock of the attack and offering organized resistance and, later, chase. For this reason, special attention is paid to the destruction of enemy vehicles, particularly armored. Enemy radio sets or other communications media are also destroyed in order to prevent the enemy from alerting neighboring units. In many cases the maneuver elements of the attacking units move into the target after initial resistance is overcome in order to complete destruction of the target or to accomplish special tasks; in some cases this can be accomplished from remote positions.

If the enemy appears to be offering stronger resistance than anticipated, the commander of the attacking guerrillas must make a quick decision as to whether he should press the attack until resistance is completely overcome or brake-off the engagement and withdraw. This decision will depend on his assessment of the enemy's remaining strength, the guerrilla losses, and the proximity to other enemy units. If the enemy appears to be demoralized and overwhelmed, the guerrilla commander must complete the destruction of the target before withdrawing.

EXPLOITATION

If the enemy appears to be beaten, abandoning his positions, and running away, the temptation will be great to enter the next phase of battle which is called exploitation. In battles between conventional forces, great opportunities have been lost because timid or overcautious commanders have failed to act with boldness during this phase. In guerrilla warfare, however, this phase will have to be omitted unless conditions are extremely favorable. Exceptions can be made if the enemy is retreating or withdrawing throughout the theater, which probably signifies a transition from guerrilla warfare to something else. Another exception can be made when the enemy unit under attack is geographically isolated or otherwise cut off from possible reenforcements. In this case, pursuit during the exploitation phase offers the opportunity to completely annihilate the enemy without taking an unnecessary risk. Extreme caution must be exercised lest this apparent retreat of the enemy is a ruse intended to dislocate the guerrilla band, draw it deeper into enemy positions, and destroy it. In all cases, parallel instead of frontal pursuit is preferred.

A more conservative approach would be the following:

If the enemy is abandoning his position, instead of pursuing him, make every effort to destroy as much materiel as possible. Priority should be given to vehicles of all kinds, particularly armored vehicles because their destruction will limit the enemy's capabilities of rallying and pursuing the guerrilla band. Next on the priority list should be any equipment which are known to be in short supply with the enemy; i.e. if it is known that the enemy has difficulty obtaining storage batteries for his radio sets, destroy any such items that may be found. Needless to state that the guerrillas will carry away for their own use any useful items that the enemy has abandoned. They should not attempt to carry items which will hinder the men during the withdrawal. They should take weapons and ammunition primarily; also boots and other clothing items and equipment useful to the band in general, not luxury items or items of personal comfort.

Prisoners will hinder the withdrawal. Unless a specific need exists to capture prisoners for interrogation, prisoners should not be taken except when they are officers of relatively high rank. Any captured enemy soldiers should be tied up and left on the battlefield. Do not shoot or otherwise mistreat enemy prisoners, as stated in the International Conventions.

It must be reiterated that the exploitation phase will be omitted unless conditions are very favorable and that the prudent thing to do after a successful strike is to break off the engagement and withdraw as planned.

WITHDRAWAL AND DISPERSAL

Regardless of the degree of success or failure of the raid, the guerrilla band must begin its withdrawal before the enemy has the opportunity to mount a counterattack or receive help from any adjacent units.

The withdrawal will commence either on command by the guerrilla commander or on a prearranged time.

The men of the maneuver element withdraw first; they move through the base of fire to the rear and continue to withdraw as swiftly as possible. They are covered by the men at the base of fire and by the security element. The base of fire element withdraws next, followed by the various sections of the security element.

The withdrawal route, or routes, should have been reconnoitred during the preparatory phase of the raid, so the men are moving over familiar ground. If the enemy is giving chase, it is mandatory that the band split up and withdraws through different routes. In fact, it may be prudent to disperse regardless of whether the enemy is giving chase or not. Reassembly should take place later at a predetermined rendezvous point.

It is important that during withdrawal the men are not burdened with excess equipment. This may mean that they may have to abandon some of their captured materiel. Every effort should be made though to evacuate wounded guerrillas.

If it has been decided to take enemy prisoners, they must be forced to move as fast as the guerrillas.

The security of the band must not be jeopardized for the benefit of any side missions during the withdrawal.

The withdrawal of the attacking force has as its sole objective the complete extrication of the unit from the enemy. After a guerrilla attack, in all probability the enemy can be expected to initiate a variety of countermeasures, such as a punitive expedition. It is necessary, therefore, that the withdrawal be followed up by a dispersal of the guerrilla unit. The guerrillas must literally disappear from the earth's face so that the punitive expedition of the enemy may find nothing on which to apply its retaliation. In this manner the guerrillas extract from the enemy an escalation of its effort which appears to be fruitless, therefore frustrating and irritating.

It is possible that the enemy, unable to locate any guerrillas, may retaliate on the civilians whom he suspects as being guerrilla collaborators. This is indeed the most difficult aspect of guerrilla warfare. The knowledge that they are exposing noncombatant civilians, many of whom may be their friends or relatives, is bound to affect adversely the psychology of the guerrillas. This is the reason why it has been stated that such considerations must be carefully examined by the commander prior to undertaking the operation.

It should also be noted that the guerrillas must resist the temptation to stay behind and defend the villages. This would defeat the purpose of withdrawal and dispersal which is to avoid engaging the enemy under conditions favorable to him. An exception to this rule can be made, of course, if the punitive enemy unit is of insufficient strength and its penetration into territory favorable to the guerrillas offers them an opportunity to ambush the enemy and cause him to suffer additional losses. In order to accomplish this, the guerrilla commander must possess exact information on the pursuing enemy's movements and strength and must also be in a position to affect timely reassembly and concentration of the elements of his unit which would be in the process of withdrawing and dispersing. Any such opportunities must be exploited. The success or failure of such an undertaking will be a demonstration of both the commander's correctness of judgement and the unit's effectivity.

With the successful dispersal of the guerrilla force, the cycle of guerrilla operations is completed. The guerrillas now should be ready for a repeat performance — the preparation and execution of a new raid.

4. Special Offensive Operations

The preceding discussion is general in nature, intended to point out certain fundamentals which we believe are universally applicable in guerrilla tactics.

We shall procede now to examine certain hypothetical, but possible and more or less typical situations where the above fundamentals can be applied. Again, however, it must be emphasized that in the field, book situations seldom duplicate themselves. The tactical commander, particularly the guerrilla commander, must therefore remember that in addition to whatever knowledge he may be able to obtain from studies such as this, his best asset is his own mind and his ability to judge situations correctly and make decisions accordingly.

Deployment for Attack on Weak Targets

The schematic of Figure 9 illustrates a typical, but by no means stereotyped, deployment for a strike by a guerrilla band of sixteen men who are moderately well equipped with weapons.

For optimum results, certain fundamentals must be adhered to in this kind of operation.

First of all, it is assumed that this operation has not been undertaken against a target of such strength that the attacking force has no possibility of negotiating successfully.

Secondly, it is assumed that the guerrillas have retained the element of surprise and are able to approach the target without being observed. Specifically, for this type of operation, they should be able to reach undetected the area where the base of fire element would be initially established. The distance between this area and the target should be less than the effective range of the weapons utilized by the base of fire element.

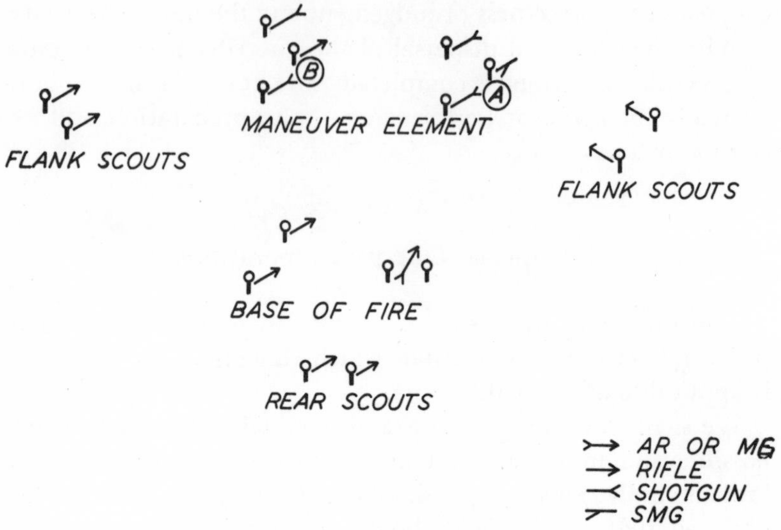

FLANK SCOUTS

MANEUVER ELEMENT

FLANK SCOUTS

BASE OF FIRE

REAR SCOUTS

>→ AR OR MG
→ RIFLE
—< SHOTGUN
⊤— SMG

Figure 9. Small unit deployment for attack.

To the base of fire element all fully automatic weapons, less the submachineguns, should be allocated. The schematic shows only one such weapon. If a second one was available, it should have also been positioned with this element. If additional automatic weapons were available, then those could be allocated to the flank scouts. Any mortars or rifle grenades available should also be positioned with the base of fire, except for any anti-tank rifle grenades which must be sent forward with the maneuver element.

During the attack phase of the engagement, the mission of the men assigned to the base of fire is to cover the men of the maneuver element with the largest possible volume of fire consonant with ammunition available. Remember that ammunition is always a limiting factor in guerrilla operations. Fire should be directed firstly against the visible enemy personnel that have recovered, or seem to be about to recover, from the surprise of the attack and about to get into action. Then, fire should be directed against points from where enemy fire appears to be coming, even though no enemy personnel are visible. If the enemy seems to be demoralized and unable to react, fire should be shifted to materiel targets such as vehicles, communications equipment, etc. If no targets are clearly visible or detectible from the location of the base of fire element, fire should be directed against estimated positions of the enemy, realizing that the effectiveness of such fire will be limited, but its volume may help to pin down or magnify the surprise of the enemy.

The flank scouts are necessary in order to detect any movement of reenforcements to directly assist the enemy at the point of attack or an attempt by the enemy to flank the attacking force. If such a movement is detected, the flank scouts will notify the commander through some prearranged means. The handiest means for such communications are portable radio transmitter-receivers; however, chances are that the guerrillas will not possess any (at least three are required for an operation of this kind); also there is a certain amount of risk involved in sending a radio message in such proximity to the enemy because the possibilities of interception are indeed good. The most practical method to send such a signal is by flare pistol. If such items are not available, tracer bullets could be substituted at night or improvised smoke signals in the daytime. The commander, upon receiving such a message, will have to decide whether to withdraw immediately or to continue pressing the attack. It is desirable to position the flank scouts, if possible, within range of the target. In this manner they can support the attack with their own fire and maybe also mislead the enemy into believing that the attack is taking place on a much broader front. This, however, should not interfere with the primary mission of the flank scouts, which is the timely detection of enemy movements.

The rear scouts do not actively participate in the attack phase of this operation. They are positioned in the best possible location to cover the withdrawal route. They are equipped with highpower rifles and smoke grenades, if available. In the event that the guerrilla band is mounted, they are also given the responsibility of caring for the animals or vehicles while the attack is going on.

The maneuver element should include the commander and the most experienced guerrillas of the unit. The maneuver element could be subdivided into two or more teams of at least three men each. The point man of each team could be equipped with a shotgun loaded with large diameter shot. If there is a shortage of rifles, shotguns loaded with shot or rifled slugs may be substituted for rifles among the members of the maneuver element. Submachineguns and other shortrange weapons are also best utilized here. If there are any portable anti-tank weapons available, they should be sent forward with the maneuver element because these weapons are most effective at close range. Knives and bayonets can also be used. Any special mission personnel will also be part of this element. For instance, if this is an attack against a unit guarding a bridge, the demolition team will be part of this element. During the attack, the men of the maneuver element use aimed fire only, even though they may be equipped with inherently inaccurate weapons such as submachineguns. Our purpose is to inflict casualties on the enemy, not to impress him with the amount of rounds we can fire or the noise we can make. Such impressions on the enemy are soon forgotten, but casualties are remembered for a long time. The men of the maneuver element must be able to fire with accuracy and move with precision and speed. The success or failure of the attack depends mostly on them.

The deployment illustrated by the schematic of figure 9 is in our opinion a basic deployment adaptable to larger or smaller guerrilla units for a variety of situations. It must not be construed though that this is the only recommended or the ultimate method of striking by guerrillas. Above all, guerrilla units must maintain their flexibility in operating methods. The success of a guerrilla commander depends to a great extent on his ability to devise new methods of operation in order to cope with new or changing situations.

ATTACKS ON VEHICULAR COLUMNS

The schematic of figure 10 illustrates a recommended deployment for attack against a column of vehicles.

In preparing such an attack the following must be considered.

The selection of the location for the attack is all important. A paved road is in itself dangerous to the guerrillas because through it enemy reenforcements could speedily arrive. Accidental arrival of other vehicles is also a possibility. The at-

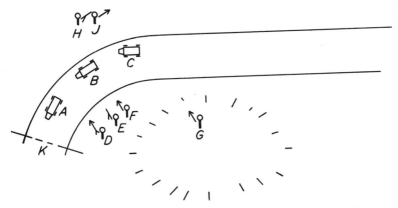

Figure 10. Attack on vehicular column.

tack should therefore take place in a section of the road where visibility from the road itself is limited. A road curve near a small hill is, therefore, the recommended location. The proximity of enemy blockhouses or outposts should be considered next. It is desirable that no enemy units are within ten minutes driving time from either direction of the road. This will give the attacking guerrillas sufficient time to execute the attack and extricate themselves.

Another factor to be considered is the rate of traffic on this particular road. Prior observation of several days is required in order to establish the frequency with which vehicles pass over the selected spot. The frequency varies at different times of the day. Night operations are generally preferred by guerrillas; however, it may be undesirable to perform this attack at night for many reasons, such as complete lack of enemy traffic at night or too dense traffic at night if the enemy avoids using the road during daylight in order to evade aerial surveillance, etc.

As always, the escape route or routes which the guerrillas will follow after the attack must be very carefully reconnoitred. In this case it is necessary that two entirely different escape routes are available so that the two men shown posted on the other side (North side in the schematic) of the road can leave the scene of the attack without crossing the road.

For an operation of this kind, it is necessary to have at least one automatic weapon. The remaining five men can be equipped with whatever is available, including pistols and shotguns. The man posted on the hill, however, must have a rifle because of the longer range involved. Mortars will not be useful in this operation since the fighting will take place at close quarters and shell fragments could hit guerrillas as well as enemy troops. One or two grenades could be thrown in the very early stage of the attack while the guerrillas are still under cover. Anti-tank rifle grenades or a light anti-tank weapon such as a rocket launcher are desirable and necessary if any one of the enemy vehicles are armored. Finally, a land mine is desirable so that it can be placed on the road to explode under the lead vehicle. If land mines are not available, some kind of an obstacle must be placed on the road near position K so that the column will be forced to stop or slow down. A barricade, or a fallen tree, or even rocks will do. Remember that the guerrillas must learn to improvise.

The execution of the attack should proceed as follows.

The guerrillas are deployed as shown in the schematic.

When the vehicles approach, G the lookout on the hill notifies the guerrilla commander F through some kind of a silent signal.

When the enemy vehicles have stopped, or slowed down, the commander F gives the order for the attack to commence. All the guerrillas engage immediately their predetermined targets. The man with the automatic weapon, D, fires at A, the lead vehicle, to insure that it completely stops and blocks the way for vehicles B and C. He then continues to fire at any personnel in or coming out of vehicle A.

Vehicle C is engaged by the men indicated at G, H, and J. It is imperative that this vehicle be prevented from making a u-turn to escape towards the same direction it came; a difficult maneuver anyway, unless the pavement is wide and the shoulders very solid. The men H and J, have the additional mission to prevent through their fire, any enemy personnel from escaping in that (North) direction or setting up a nucleus of resistance on that side of the road. Man G, after vehicle C is stopped, fires at targets of opportunity while he retains a sharp lookout for any vehicles approaching from either direction.

Vehicle B is engaged initially by guerrillas E and F. If possible, they should try to hit the driver first; then they engage any enemy personnel attempting to escape or rally on their side of the road.

This operation should last only four or five minutes. This is enough time to place out of action all the enemy personnel in the three vehicles. All enemy personnel who attempted to leave the vehicles should be easy targets. If the enemy has experience in this kind of ambushes, however, he may have trained his men to stay in the vehicles from where the survivors of the initial assault and vehicle destruction may try to set up resistance. Unless the number of the enemy remaining inside the vehicles is small and can be overcome within another one or two minutes, the guerrilla leader should not waste any time in an effort to completely subdue them. He must also be ready to withdraw if any time during the attack he receives a signal from G that additional enemy are approaching.

If, however, the attack has been a complete success and all the enemy are killed, wounded, or have surrendered, the guerrillas can take an extra few minutes to cautiously approach the vehicles and pick up enemy weapons or other materiel. They can also complete the destruction of the enemy vehicles; this can be accomplished by setting them on fire after pouring gasoline over them, or by exploding the fuel tanks through a long pyrotechnic cord, or by setting off a grenade under the hood, or by draining the crankcase from oil and letting the engines run, or even puncturing the radiators or tires.

Any enemy survivors should be tied up and left on the scene, but they should not be mistreated. If possible, enemy wounded should be treated on the spot. Enemy officers or other important personnel could be carried away as prisoners if they would not hinder the guerrillas' movements during withdrawal.

As said before, guerrillas H and J would withdraw through a separate route and rendezvous with the rest of the unit later, if for any reason the attack has to be broken off and joining the rest of the unit means that they must cross the road in view of the enemy.

If withdrawal has to be accomplished under enemy fire, of

the four guerrillas D, E, F, and G, the automatic rifleman D withdraws first, followed by E and F while G acts as both rear guard and flank scout. He is in best condition to act as such in view of his commanding position on top of the hill and because fire coming from that direction will probably deceive the enemy as to the direction of withdrawal.

The previously described plan to ambush a motorcade includes the customary risks of fighting at close quarters. The following plan minimizes these risks, but it cannot always be applied.

The next plan requires fairly rough terrain and substantially improved materiel means by the guerrillas.

The terrain has to be rough enough so that it is impossible for the enemy to chase the guerrillas with his vehicles. If terrain conditions are such that give the enemy this capability, the guerrillas would soon be overtaken. If the enemy though is roadbound, he can only give chase on foot, after dismounting; in this case the guerrillas should be in better condition to outdistance the enemy either on foot or with animals which may be available.

The second requirement is that of improved ordnance. Pistols, shotguns, and submachineguns are useless in this type of raid except as noise makers. Basically, rifles are required for this operation; rifles equipped with scopes are preferred. One or more automatic weapons are also required. An anti-tank weapon is very desirable; something like a 75mm recoilless rifle is preferred to the 3.5" rocket launcher because of the better accuracy and longer range of the former. Rifle grenades can also be used. Mortars could be used also, but it must be remembered that the duration of the attack probably will not be long enough for the gunners to zero-in on the target; therefore use of mortars may only mean waste of a few rounds of ammunition. Obviously, the number of men required for this raid will be greater than the number required for the previous raid since crew-served weapons have been included.

The same meticulous care should be exercised in reconnoitering the area, in order to select the proper location for the attack and the necessary withdrawal routes.

from the road, but within effective range of their weapons. This distance will probably be between 200 and 300 yds from the road itself. Maximum advantage should be taken of hills and other obstructions in order to effectively conceal the guerrillas and give them maximum protection from enemy fire. Simultaneously, care must be taken to insure that each position gives good visibility and wide field of fire. In order to insure maximum security, flank scouts and rear guards should be employed. There will be no maneuver element, since it has been established that there will be no attempt to move forward to engage the enemy at close quarters. It may be desirable, however, to place a few of the guerrillas on the opposite side of the road so that the enemy may get the impression that he has fallen in a trap and is being flanked on both sides.

In executing this operation, the guerrillas fire from cover against the enemy vehicles and the enemy personnel seen in them. The guerrilla riflemen must use aimed fire in order to increase their effectiveness. The duration of this phase of the operation should be between four to five minutes. Probably, the damage inflicted on the enemy column will be slight and the enemy will continue on its course in spite of its losses.

Then, the guerrillas will withdraw and try again some other day.

This type of raid is more in the category of harassment than offensive operations. The guerrillas are actually taking pot shots at the enemy. The damage done to the enemy will be slight, particularly if viewed in the light of materiel means utilized and ammunition expended. On the other side, the guerrilla losses will be correspondingly small. However, this type of raid, if repeated often enough, will have a disturbing effect on the enemy, will impede his movements on the road in question and force him to furnish heavier escort for his vehicular columns. The adverse psychological effect on enemy personnel is also important.

It is understood, of course, that if repeated raids of this kind are undertaken, they should not take place at the same location on the road, for obvious reasons.

The guerrillas must deploy themselves as far away as possible

ATTACKS ON RAILROADS

Interruption of enemy rail traffic should be placed high in the priority list of guerrilla objectives. Railroads constitute the easiest and cheapest means of moving cargo, therefore, chances are that the enemy is utilizing any existing railways to the utmost. In developing countries, the development of railways usually is more advanced than the development of highway systems; this constitutes an additional reason why the enemy would probably be depending more on the utilization of the railroads for his troop and equipment movements than on any other transportation media.

Railroads are usually vulnerable targets. The enemy cannot be expected to provide protection for every yard of track stretching over hundreds of miles length and for all the tech nical installations such as bridges, switching stations, repair fa cilities, etc. which are necessary for the railroad's operation. Ir addition, repairs on damaged sections of track and other facili ties are time consuming and require critical materials anc skilled labor.

Guerrilla attacks on railroads may be classified as attacks on moving trains, attacks on installations, and combinations ol both.

For the guerrillas, the easiest operation would be one having as objective the destruction of track. A small force of guerrillas, equipped with explosives could locate an unguarded stretch of track, destroy it and withdraw without encountering the enemy. However, unless a train is derailed over the interrupted track, this is a small damage which can be relatively easily repaired. Of course, such destructions, if they happen frequently enough, can be a source of major harassment to the enemy.

Much more effective in seriously impairing enemy rail traffic would be an attack on a critical installation such as a bridge or tunnel. It can be expected, though, that the enemy would be guarding such an installation with troops. The more critical the installation, the greater the strength of the enemy force to be expected. It would include heavy weapons, possibly emplaced in a system of earthworks, blockhouses, and barbed wire. A raid on such a place would, therefore, take the character of an assault against a fortified position, an operation which is difficult for guerrillas to execute successfully. If the overall military situation makes the destruction of such an installation extremely desirable, the operation can still be undertaken providing that:

1. The guerrillas can assemble a force which would be substantially superior to the enemy unit guarding the installation.

2. It can be reasonably assured that no enemy reinforcements can timely arrive to relieve the unit under attack.

Attacks on moving trains also require consideration of whether they are being protected by a security force mounted on the train or not. In an area of intensive guerrilla activity it can be expected that all such trains are provided with a security force. This force may be in one or more cars protected with light armor plate and will likely include several heavy automatic weapons, rocket launchers, and recoilless rifles. It is not unusual to see included in military trains several flat cars on which light antiaircraft cannon are mounted. Such cannon, if they can be depressed to an angle near or below the horizontal, can be very effective protection for the train against guerrillas. A moving train can be attacked from positions near the track with varied degrees of success, providing the guerrillas possess heavy weapons such as recoilless rifles and maybe pack artillery. However, it is much more effective to derail the train. Derailment will cause much greater damage to the train and higher casualties among the passengers. In addition, the subsequent necessity of clearing the wreckage off the track will cause an added burden on the enemy's repair facilities and will further interrupt his traffic.

Derailing of trains is best accomplished on a downgrade, curve, or bridge. This is likely to cause the locomotive and some of the cars to overturn. Immediately after the derailment, the guerrillas must attack with recoilless rifles whatever cars are remaining upright. Simultaneously, machinegun sections, automatic riflemen, and riflemen must fire at the exits of all cars in order to prevent the enemy from escaping. After resistance is overcome, the guerrillas should move forward to complete destruction of the train, track and cargo. This is accomplished by using explosives or setting the cars on fire. Special care should be exercised to ascertain that this particular train is not part of

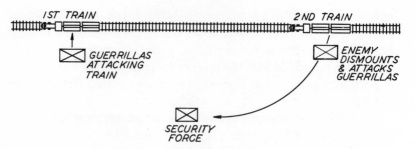

Figure 11. Attack against a train.

a trap and that it is not followed by a second train which carries an enemy force which will dismount and attempt to trap the guerrillas as shown in Figure 11. To prevent this, a strong security force must be utilized by the guerrillas.

The schematic of Figure 12 illustrates the deployment for an assault against a well-guarded railroad bridge. In this assumed operation, buildings A, C, D, and E are supposed to be blockhouses made of reinforced concrete. Building B is used as a barracks for the enemy garrison and also houses a telegraph station. Blockhouse D is so located that it commands view of both North and South directions of the gorge, therefore, the bridges' understructure is in full view from this location. Both the East and West approaches to the bridge are protected with barbed wire.

Guerrilla reconnaissance has established that the enemy garrison consists of one reinforced platoon. An automatic rifle with three or four men is normally located in each of the blockhouses C, D, and E. Blockhouse A has a heavy machinegun. It is believed that two light mortars and a rocket launcher are available inside barracks B. All enemy personnel not manning the blockhouses are usually inside the barracks. In addition to the aforementioned weapons, it is believed that five or six submachineguns are available; the rest of the men are equipped with rifles.

The objective of the guerrillas is to demolish the bridge. Since it is impossible for a demolition party to approach the bridge undetected, it is necessary to engage and overcome the enemy garrison before the demolition can be accomplished.

The next step which the guerrilla commander has to take is

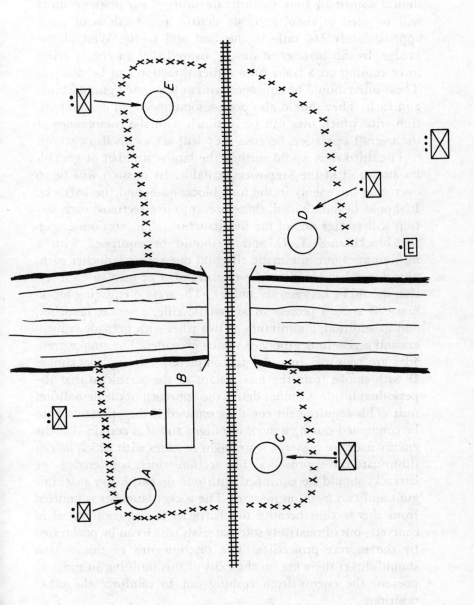

Figure 12. Operation against protected railroad bridge.

the assembly and organization of the attacking force. This force should consist of four subordinate units. Two of these units will be used to simultaneously destroy two sections of track approximately 1½ mile to the East and to the West of the bridge. In this manner, it can be assured that an enemy relief force coming on a train from either direction can be delayed. These units should be equipped with at least one light machine-gun each. They should also possess some means of communication with which they can be in touch with the commander of the overall operation because they will act as his flank scouts.

The third unit would include the largest number of guerrillas and most of the firepower available. Its mission will be to overcome the enemy in the four blockhouses and the barracks. It should be subdivided, therefore, into five sections; each section will engage one of the five structures. The sections engaging blockhouses A, C, and E should be equipped with a minimum of one automatic rifle and one rocket launcher each, plus a number of rifles. The total number of men in each section should be between six and ten. The section engaging blockhouse D should possess an automatic rifle, a rocket launcher, and in addition, a minimum of two rifles with grenade launchers and a generous supply of smoke grenades. The smoke grenades are required in order to completely envelop blockhouse D with smoke from the first instant of the assault so that the personnel inside it cannot detect the approach of the demolition unit. This requirement could be omitted if the operation is to be conducted during a moonless night and it is certain that the enemy does not possess a searchlight or flares with which he can illuminate the approaches. The section which is to engage the barracks should be equipped with one or two heavy machine-guns and two medium mortars. The rocket launcher is omitted from this section because the barracks is not constructed of concrete, but of relatively soft materials which can be penetrated by the mortar projectiles. The machineguns of this section should direct their fire on the exits of this building in order to prevent the enemy from rushing out to reinforce the other positions.

The next unit will be the demolition party. This group should approach from the North or the South and place its explosives on the bridge understructure. In order to save time, it should begin its movement to the bridge immediately upon the commencement of the attack. This of course would require that blockhouse D be neutralized immediately in the manner stated above. If this is not accomplished, the movement of the demolition party will have to be delayed until resistance from blockhouse D is overcome. The demolition party should be accompanied by at least one automatic rifle.

Finally, a reserve should be available for this operation, consisting of at least two squads with two automatic weapons. The reserve should move forward immediately behind the assaulting elements and should initially support the attack on a selected blockhouse with its own fire. It should be committed further, only on the decision of the commander of the overall operation. In view of the fact that movement from the East to the West approach of the bridge, or vice versa, during the engagement may be problematic, the commander should consider very carefully the optimum position of initially placing the reserve. He should avoid, however, splitting it into an East and West group because this will diminish its effectivity. During withdrawal the reserve could act as a rear guard.

Additional security elements such as rear scouts etc. may be required for this operation.

ATTACKS ON AIR BASES

One of the most useful types of raids that guerrillas can make are raids against air bases. When attacking an air base, the target of highest priority should be the aircraft maintenance shops. Such installations as those housing machine, electronic, armament, engine, and related shops and all the equipment in them should be destroyed as completely as possible. A secondary target should be the aircraft parked on the ramps, and all other facilities and installations fall under the category of targets of opportunity. Normally, an air base is still useful even without aircraft as long as aircraft replacements can be flown in. Likewise, an air base can still function despite the destruction of its mess hall, barracks, or headquarters building. But the complexity of aerial weapons today make air operations without extensive maintenance support impossible. With its maintenance facilities knocked out of commission, a base can be of practically no help to the tactical air unit it supports. The tactical air unit will, therefore, either suspend operations while the shops are being repaired and reequipped, or move to another base. Moving to another base means that the range of its tactical missions will probably lengthen and that the logistic support problems at the new location will increase.

One other factor in establishing target priorities when attacking air bases, are the prevailing local conditions, when known. For instance, if the guerrilla leader knows that a given air base which he is planning to attack has difficulties in resupplying itself with fuel, he should bypass other targets in order to set the fuel storage on fire. Or if he knows that snow drifts have been a particularly troublesome problem on the runways, he should try to get and destroy any snow-removal vehicles that may exist.

Security in air bases can become a very critical subject. Normally, the base commander need not worry much about it since bases are located well to the rear. For this reason security troops allocated to the air bases are few and relatively ineffective. When the base commander feels uncertain about security and considers attack by guerrillas a possibility, he can do one of two things. He can either take his airmen and use them on base peripheral defense, or he can request the area ground commander to furnish him with a defense force. In either case he has manpower wasted. If he is using his own troops he is probably wasting highly skilled manpower and his operational output will soon reflect this. A mechanic cannot work in the shop when he is packing a carbine and manning an outpost on the other side of the field. Also, if he is using a combat unit of ground forces to defend his air base, he is tying up this unit in a defensive mission that precludes its use at the front.

Engaging Enemy Armor

As a general rule, engagements with enemy armor must be avoided. The reason for this is that the guerrillas possess neither armor of their own nor sufficient anti-tank armament enabling them to engage the enemy with possibilities of success.

If, however, situations develop when combat with enemy armored units becomes necessary, a number of steps can be taken to minimize the effectivity of enemy armor.

The first of these steps is to ascertain that such combat will take place, if possible, on terrain unfavorable to armored vehicles. Rocky mountainous terrain, dense woods, and swampy ground will impede the mobility of the enemy armored vehicles. On the other hand, flat terrain, rolling hills, and areas with dense network of paved roads will favor the enemy. So, since the guerrillas are expected to maintain the initiative in conducting offensive operations, they must plan such operations in a manner which will preclude the possibility of any guerrilla unit being caught for any prolonged periods in the open on terrain favorable to the enemy.

The next step is to arrange that such engagements take place at night. Darkness will obstruct the enemy, no matter how well he is armed. Darkness, however, should not be a handicap to a well-trained guerrilla unit which is familiar with the terrain and has rehearsed the projected operation.

Another possibility would be to catch the enemy dismounted. This means that the enemy vehicles are not manned. Such a situation could arise when attacking a motor pool, for instance; or, if an enemy column has stopped for rest and refueling after a march; etc.

The availability of anti-tank weapons among the guerrillas is the paramount consideration for operations of this kind. A certain minimum number of light anti-tank weapons are necessary. To some extent the anti-tank armament of the guerrillas can be augmented through improvisation. Liberal use of land mines and molotov cocktails can increase the guerrillas' capability to face enemy armor successfully. Land mines can be improvised through the use of dynamite and other explosive materials. Old artillery ammunition can be converted to land mines also. This conversion requires some technical competence, but any sizeable guerrilla organization would include at least a few personnel with prior ordnance experience. All that molotov cocktails require are gasoline or other liquid flamable materials and glass or thin metal containers.

Thorough planning and detailed intelligence information about the enemy can overcome much of the enemy's superiority in resources, including armor.

5.   Defensive Operations

As stated previously, guerrillas are normally inferior to the enemy conventional army in both personnel and materiel. In order to overcome, therefore, this inferiority they must concentrate their forces and strike the enemy at one of his weaker points, thus reversing the ratio of forces during the particular engagement. When the enemy though assumes the initiative and conducts offensive operations, it can be expected that the enemy order of battle will surpass any force that the guerrillas may be able to concentrate. It becomes, therefore, necessary for the guerrillas to avoid defensive engagements. When the guerrilla commander is informed through his intelligence network that the enemy is preparing an offensive, his best course of action is to withdraw his units to another area, disperse, go underground, and avoid battle. This requires that the guerrillas possess very effective intelligence so that they can obtain this timely warning. For the guerrillas this should not be a too difficult task because a conventional army can hardly prepare an offensive without its preparations being detected by an alert underground organization which will be supporting the guerrillas and by the guerrilla intelligence itself.

The following specific events taking place among the enemy can give the guerrillas an indication about an impending enemy offensive.

1. Change of enemy commanders; especially if the new commander is one with previous experience in counter-guerrilla operations.

2. Arrival in the area of guerrilla activity of enemy formations which can be considered as units particularly suitable for counter-guerrilla operations. This type of units includes paratroopers, airmobile troops, commandos, mountain troops, and units of native collaborators.

3. Changes in the conventional battle situation which re-

lease additional troops for the area of guerrilla activity. Further indications of this would be increases in the strength of local garrisons and increased traffic of supplies over the road and rail networks.

4. Extension of enemy outposts, increased patrolling by the enemy ground forces, and intensified aerial reconnaissance.

The guerrilla commander must, as soon as he detects any of the above, increase his own intelligence effort and intensify his reconnaissance and surveillance of the enemy. If the information he subsequently receives confirms the suspicions that the enemy may be preparing an offensive, the guerrillas must make preparations for a timely withdrawal.

The withdrawal must leave no traces of the guerrillas. If time permits, all guerrilla equipment must be removed and relocated, including clandestine depots, bases, hospitals, and command posts. The equipment should be moved to the guerrillas' new location so that they may be available for use there. If removal of all equipment is impossible, it should be dispersed and hidden in safe locations or among the underground organization which will be cooperating with the guerrillas. If that is impossible too, it should be destroyed. By all means, sick and wounded guerrillas should be evacuated.

The withdrawal itself presents a problem. Specifically, where should the guerrillas withdraw to? The answer to this problem will depend to a large extent on geographic conditions and on the general operational situation. One possibility would be to withdraw to some location not included in the area of responsibility of the enemy headquarters which is preparing the suspected offensive, or to some area which the enemy considers as being free from guerrillas. Several operational and geographic conditions may limit the practicality of such movement. Another possibility would be the withdrawal to an area where terrain conditions are such that the enemy army can not follow the guerrillas or where it can not engage the guerrillas under favorable conditions. A third possibility would be to withdraw behind the lines of a friendly conventional army or to the territory of an ostensibly neutral country which, however, is willing to provide shelter or tolerate the guerrillas. The obvious difficulty here is the proximity from such a friendly army or neutral territory. Finally, we have the possibility of dispersing the guerrillas among the inhabitants of the territory in question so that they may appear as ordinary civilians to the enemy. This solution is accompanied by two substantial disadvantages. The first disadvantage is the fact that the guerrilla unit in this case becomes for all practical purposes disbanded and its reassembly for future action may be problematic. The second disadvantage is the fact that the so dispersed guerrillas become completely dependent on the local inhabitants for subsistence and are exposed to possible betrayals by local collaborators of the enemy. This solution, however, is most effective when the guerrilla unit is composed of natives of the region where the dispersal takes place.

In all cases, prior to any withdrawal and dispersal, the guerrilla commander must make detail plans for the maintenance of contact among the individual guerrillas who have gone underground and for the future reinfiltration of enemy territory and reassembly of the unit.

A more-or-less classic type of operation against guerrillas is that of encirclement. Encirclement involves the deployment of numerous enemy units which advance from all sides towards the center of the target area; i.e.; the area where the guerrillas are thought to be. As the enemy advances and the guerrillas fall back, the encircled area becomes progressively smaller. The operation ends with an assault from all sides by the enemy to annihilate the guerrillas.

For the guerrillas, the best defense from encirclement is to avoid it. If guerrilla intelligence has failed to obtain advance information on the projected enemy operation, guerrilla reconnaissance should be able to at least get a clear indication of the enemy intentions during the very early stages of encirclement when the enemy troops move to their starting positions. Appearance of enemy combat formations from two or more directions should alert the guerrilla commander to the fact that an encircling operation by the enemy may be in process and he should immediately execute his plan for escape and withdrawal. Such a plan, in general outline, should always be available in every guerrilla headquarters.

From the enemy's point of view, encircling operations present two formidable disadvantages. The first of these disadvantages is the fact that effective encirclement requires a high density of troops. The presence of an unusually large number of troops in the area will be observed by the guerrillas and give them advance warning of the impending operation. This disadvantage can be partially overcome by the employment of airborne or airmobile troops who can be assembled and embarked in airfields located in areas remote to the projected operations area, thus gaining an element of surprise over the guerrillas. The availability of airborne troops, however, is another matter dependent on the overall operational situation. The second disadvantage is the fact that no matter how well trained the enemy is, it is impossible for all of its units to maintain an equal rate of advance because of the terrain variations. This difference in the rate of advance will create gaps through which the guerrillas can escape.

If for any reason, escape from the encirclement is not accomplished immediately, the guerrillas must attempt to fight their way out of the encircled area. The guerrilla commander selects a point on the enemy line through which he will attempt to break through. This point should be a gap through the enemy line or the least dense point of the enemy line. The location of this point could be determined through the assistance of guerrilla reconnaissance and outposts. It is helpful in such case to locate several guerrilla observation posts on high ground so that the enemy advance can be better observed.

The breakthrough itself should be attempted at night or during periods of low visibility. Once the escape route has been determined, the guerrilla force is organized into three subordinate units. One of these units consists of the main force; to this are attached the supply train and any noncombatants moving with the guerrillas. The remaining two subordinate units constitute the advance guard and have the mission to seize and hold temporarily the flanks of the escape route on both sides of the point where the escape route crosses the enemy line (see Figure 13). The two units of the advance guard should be very strong and to them the guerrilla commander should allocate the more experienced guerrillas and the majority of available weapons. The advance guard holds the flanks of the

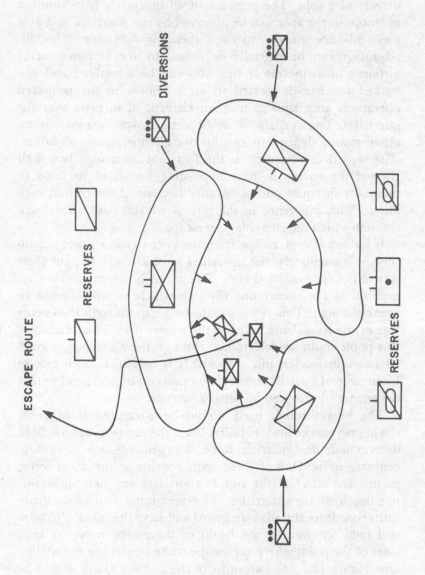

Figure 13. Breakthrough from enemy encirclement.

escape route until the main body passes through. Then they follow through the gap themselves, acting now as rear guard to the main unit.

If this phase of the operation is successful, the guerrillas must continue along the escape route with all deliberate speed, but with caution lest they encounter any enemy reserve unit which may be deployed behind the encircling perimeter for just such eventuality. The direction of escape must be altered to avoid engagement with such unit unless it is certain that the enemy unit is sufficiently weak and it can be speedily attacked and annihilated. Prolonged engagement with the enemy reserve can be disastrous for the guerrillas even when the reserve is fairly weak because the enemy, with its better communications, can alert units from the encircling perimeter and divert them to the flank and rear of the escaping force, thus catching the guerrillas into a trap. The guerrilla commander must always be ready to exploit any shortcomings of the enemy and attack a weaker enemy unit, but he must also always be alert to the possibility of a ruse.

If the breakthrough fails, or if the guerrilla commander decides that he does not possess the strength to fight his way out of the encirclement, then he has to disperse his force. He breaks up his unit into several small groups and instructs them to infiltrate through the enemy lines at several widely separated points or to hide within the encircled area if the terrain offers such opportunities. He also gives them instructions for later reassembly. In doing this it must be understood that some of the groups may not make it through. In addition, the morale of the unit may be adversely affected and the effectiveness of the unit is impaired, temporarily at least, because of the loss of centralized control. However, well-trained guerrillas should be able to infiltrate through the enemy lines even under very unfavorable conditions. It may be, therefore, a matter of whether the commander should chance to lose 10% of his unit through the infiltration attempt or suffer 30% casualties on an attempted breakthrough. The decision is one of the burdens of command.

During an encirclement operation, any guerrilla units which may be located outside the encircled area support the encircled guerrillas with harassing raids and diversionary attacks against the enemy rear. If the guerrillas outside the circle are of sufficient strength, and if communications and coordination between the guerrillas within and outside the encircled area are highly developed, the mission of securing the flanks along the escape route is given to the guerrillas on the outside. Again caution should be exercised lest the enemy is attempting to bait the guerrillas and trap an additional guerrilla unit into the encirclement.

A variation of the encirclement operation is the frontal sweep. In this case the enemy, instead of deploying his forces in a manner through which they can surround the guerrillas, deploys them frontally with the objective that as they advance forward, they will force the guerrillas against a substantial geographic obstacle or perhaps against another army. The geographic obstacle has to be one that the guerrillas can not overpass or infiltrate. This would mean a coastal area or the frontier of a neutral country.

Defensive measures against a frontal sweep which the guerrillas must take are identical with those recommended against encirclement.

The conventional army may resort to a number of different actions in order to coerce the guerrillas to fight defensive engagements. The guerrillas' willingness to accept such challenge by the enemy usually becomes proportional to the success of their movement.

The conventional army may "raid" a territory where the guerrillas have been active, hoping to upset the guerrillas' plans and force them to fight a pitched battle.

An attack on a guerrilla base may also be conducted in the hope that the guerrillas will defend their base instead of evacuating.

A punitive expedition may be sent as reprisal against the civilians of an area where the guerrillas have been active and the civilians are thought to be collaborating with the guerrillas, etc.

In World War II, the German occupation forces had virtually evacuated certain remote regions of Eastern and Southeastern Europe because of the relatively low military significance of those regions and the shortage of German forces. Guerrillas had correspondingly assumed control over those regions and even established clandestine civil government administrations. Subsequently, the Germans on several occasions conducted offensive operations against the guerrillas. Often the outcome of such engagements was favorable to the conventional forces, unless the offensive was undertaken with limited resources.

The tendency to defend geographic areas by the guerrillas could be defined as "positional" mentality and it is one of the worst qualities that a guerrilla commander could develop. It usually leads to disaster. Factors contributing to the development of this positional mentality are the all-too-human tendency to overestimate one's own capabilities, elation over previous successes, and prior conventional military indoctrination. The successful guerrilla commander must be on guard to detect any such tendencies in his plans and suppress them immediately.

The guerrillas must always avoid defensive battle unless they can be sure that they can assemble a superior force to meet the enemy. This is only common sense. Because no matter what sacrifices they may make in avoiding battle (such as loss of prestige, abandonment of equipment, reprisals on sympathetic civilians, etc.), no sacrifice can compare to a defeat in battle and destruction of the guerrilla band.

VIII

Comments on Special Tactical Problems

1. On the Tactical Use of Artillery by Guerrillas

ASSUMING THAT artillery is available, before committing his artillery to an operation the guerrilla commander must clarify in his own mind whether the anticipated use is for morale purposes alone, or whether he expects his artillery fire to materially contribute in obtaining fire superiority over the enemy. The operations plan for the artillery will differ considerably depending on which one of the above objectives has been decided on.

From the morale point of view, artillery fire can be expected to have an affect on both the enemy and the guerrillas. The enemy is bound to become demoralized to a degree when he realizes that the guerrillas possess and are using artillery. In view of the limited information that the conventional army usually possesses about the guerrilla order of battle and strength, in the enemy's mind such tangible demonstration of availability of material resources by the guerrillas is likely to affect the enemy's decisions. The surprise on the enemy will be by far greater the first time that the guerrillas use artillery. The psychological affect on the enemy will diminish with each subsequent time that artillery is used.

Simultaneously, friendly artillery fire will favorably affect the morale of the guerrillas.

In using his artillery for morale purposes only, the guerrilla commander must take the necessary steps to protect it from enemy countermeasures. This means that he must be prepared to withdraw the pieces before the enemy, through aerial reconnaissance or other means, is able to localize the position of the guns and engage in counterbattery. Provisions must also be made to avoid their interception by the enemy during the withdrawal. A substantial security force of riflemen must be allocated to protect the artillery in any such operation.

When the guerrilla artillery is to be used in a more or less conventional manner, i.e.: in helping overcome enemy resistance through fire superiority, the guerrilla commander is confronted with an entirely different situation. First of all, he must ascertain that there is a sufficient number of guerrillas trained as gun crews. It is very possible, if we judge from similar experiences of past guerrilla movements, that there may be a shortage of such crews. Training of artillerymen among guerrillas is problematic primarily because of the nonavailability of ranges — an essential commodity required for artillery training. In addition, there may be a shortage of qualified instructors. Both of the above difficulties must be overcome if proper utilization of the available pieces is to be made, or else the results will not be commensurate to the effort.

Ammunition always presents a problem for guerrillas; artillery ammunition is likely to be more of a problem because it is much more difficult to obtain. Local manufacture of artillery rounds by the guerrillas has to be discounted since the fabrication and assembly processes are relatively complex. The sources of supply will, therefore, be the enemy itself through raids and pilfering and external friendly sources.

In either case, the commander must ascertain the sufficiency of ammunition for the operation under study and must include in his plan details on how ammunition resupply will take place during the engagement. In establishing the number of rounds per piece required, we are confronted with another problem. The conventional method of counting units of fire is not applicable to guerrilla engagements, in our opinion. Instead, we propose the following: The number of rounds per piece should equal the estimated time duration of the artillery engagement times the rate of fire, plus 33%. Thus, if an engagement is planned to last twenty minutes and the rate of fire is two rounds per minute, the total number of rounds per gun should be 53. The 33% overage is recommended as a reserve to cover possible, but unforseen emergencies. Oversupply of ammunition is not recommended, however, because the unfired rounds will hinder the unit's movement during the withdrawal phase of the operation. During withdrawal it is best to utilize all excess transportation media such as motor vehicles, animals, carts, or porters to evacuate casualties.

During the attack phase of an operation, the guerrilla artillery should be moved forward immediately behind the maneuver element in order to support the attack with direct fire. In this manner the effectiveness of artillery fire is increased and ammunition expenditure lessened. In addition, this method of artillery employment requires less skill in fire direction and control, therefore it compensates to a degree for the fact that such skills may be short among the guerrillas.

Artillery should not be used by the guerrillas in defensive engagements. Use of artillery in defense implies a positional battle and this is something which the guerrillas must always avoid. The guerrilla artillery should be, therefore, withdrawn from the battle area when a defensive engagement appears to be a possibility. This subject is discussed in detail under the topic of defensive operations.

2. On the Use of Animals

From the very beginning of organized warfare through the early stages of World War II, horses and mules have constituted the basic means of transport for field armies. The technological progress of recent years, however, has changed all this and today all major armies depend heavily on various kinds of motor vehicles for both combat and logistic support.

From the guerrillas' point of view, the complete mechaniza-

tion of the enemy army constitutes an advantage. Assuming
that the area of guerrilla operations includes terrain favorable
to the guerrillas, as described in the previous chapter of "Strategic Considerations," the enemy conventional army will be de-
prived of much of its mobility because no motor vehicles
have been developed yet which are truly crosscountry vehicles.
Most heavy wheeled vehicles are completely road bound. Light
(one ton or less) vehicles can operate off pavements if the
ground is moderately flat and hard and if they are designed for
four-wheel drive. Tracted vehicles can do all of the above plus
negotiate moderate slopes. Relatively steep slopes, rocky terrain, dense forests, and swampy ground, however, are for all
practical purposes impassable to motor vehicles as we know
them today. On such terrain the conventional forces will have
to dismount and advance on foot. If the guerrillas, therefore,
are able to obtain and use animals they will have an advantage
on mobility over their enemy.

Animals can be used for the following different purposes in
guerrilla warfare:

1. To obtain mobility directly related to combat.
2. To furnish motive power in support of supply and transport operations.
3. For special missions such as sentry and messenger service.

Utilization of animals in combat may be resorted to in order
to improve one's ability to maneuver. An example of this could
be the withdrawal phase of any one of the raids described herein (see Chapter VII). This kind of operation resembles the calvary operations of earlier times, or more specifically, the
dragoons who maneuvered mounted, but fought on foot with
their carbines.

A horse usually can cover five miles in one hour at a walk over
fairly rough ground. For short periods of time it can be trotted
to more than twice that speed. Using horses, therefore, the
guerrillas can easily outdistance an enemy advancing or pursuing on foot because his rate of advance over the same terrain
will be about three miles per hour. These figures, of course,
are approximations. The speed of the horses will vary depending on their breed and condition. The speed of the foot soldiers
will also vary depending on their physical condition and their

loads. Specially-trained small units could probably match the speed of a walking horse, although not its endurance.

Mules are slower than horses, but more sure-footed on mountainous terrain and of better endurance. Other animals such as sled dogs and camels must also be considered, depending on the geographic and climatic conditions of the operations area. Draft animals pulling wheeled carts or other conveyances, however, cannot be included in movements directly related to combat. Wheeled conveyances require some kind of a road and the use of roads by the guerrillas will eliminate their advantage since the enemy motor vehicles can use the same road also and because of their much greater speed they will overtake the guerrilla column.

In a combat movement it becomes necessary to have a sufficient number of animals to mount all the personnel of the unit involved and carry all of its equipment. It is not practical to have part of a combat unit mounted and part of it on foot because then the rate of advance of the column has to be equated to the rate of its slowest moving element, i.e. the foot soldiers.

In supply operations, animals can be used instead of motor vehicles in order to avoid use of the roads which will be under the control of the enemy conventional forces. The same can be accomplished by using men as porters, of course, but the load which can be carried on a pack animal is far greater than the load which a man can carry. In addition, utilizing men as porters, whether they are guerrillas or friendly civilians, may produce a number of morale and psychological problems which any prudent guerrilla commander would just as soon avoid.

In supply columns, the minimum possible number of men should be utilized to lead and oversee the animals, thus releasing the maximum number of guerrillas available for security duties with the column.

Certain breeds of dogs can be trained to perform special duties for the guerrillas, such as sentry, messenger, and scout. Utilization of dogs for such duties has become more or less universal practice by conventional forces in recent years.

Utilization of animals, however, has certain disadvantages too. One of the disadvantages is the fact that aerial reconnaissance by the enemy becomes easier unless guerrilla movements take place at night or over territory which offers good cover (dense and high foliage). Another disadvantage is the fact that animals require a lot of care. Feeding may become problematic, particularly in winter when grazing becomes impossible. Unlike gasoline consumption of the vehicles, an animal has to be fed regardless of whether it is used or not. Additional training will also be required for the guerrillas in order to make effective use of the animals, plus the time devoted to training the animals themselves. Dogs, in particular, require a lot of training before they can be trusted to perform the tasks mentioned above. One of the most undesirable aspects of dog training is the fact that most well-trained dogs become responsive to only one handler. A problem exists, therefore, if the particular handler becomes a casualty and the animal cannot be retrained to a new handler; it may have to be destroyed. Finally, security could become a problem if the enemy was to detect the presence of an unusually large number of animals in an area.

To overcome some of the above disadvantages, the guerrillas can resort to borrowing suitable animals from the permanent inhabitants in the area of guerrilla activity. This practice shall require, primarily, that the population of the area in question is friendly to the guerrillas and willing to support them and their cause. Animals then can be borrowed for a specific operation or for a fixed period of time and then returned to their owners. Abuse of the animals by the guerrillas should be absolutely avoided; also, compensation should be given to the owners for any lost or injured animals. Requisitions of animals should not be resorted to because any such requisitions will turn the natives, especially if they are farmers or shepherds, against the guerrillas even if they were initially in sympathy with them ideologically.

3.   Joint Operations With Conventional Forces

Joint operations are those where the guerrillas and the friendly conventional army are operating in the same theater under complete coordination and, preferably, under single command.

Unity of command is a fundamental principle of war because it constitutes the only method establishing *one* individual responsible for the success or failure of the operation while it affords simultaneously to this individual authority to exercise control over all resources available. In joint operations with guerrillas, this principle may have to be compromised for political or other expediencies. Although this compromise should be avoided, it can, however, be tolerated. In such a case, special efforts should be made to establish effective liaison and communications between the two headquarters.

In our discussion, joint operations presuppose a number of conditions. The first of these conditions is that the guerrillas are operating in the rear areas of the enemy front and that the conventional force is engaging or about to actively engage the enemy on the same front. The next condition is that of geography. The distances separating the guerrilla targets from the axis of advance or defense line of the conventional force must not be too lengthy. To define more specifically this proximity is rather difficult in view of the varied terrain conditions and constant technological advances which continue to shrink, in reference to time, communications lines. However, a good standard which may be applied in this case is that the proximity of the guerrillas to the friendly conventional force should be such that the results of any specific guerrilla action can influence the course of events in this theater during the general operation which is being jointly conducted. This defines proximity in terms of functions rather than distance or time and is more applicable in a general discussion such as this one has to be. Guerrilla operations aimed at attrition of the enemy or other long-range results, even though they may be conducted at the request or guidance of the conventional headquarters, are not truly joint operations.

Joint operations can be either offensive or defensive. Offensive would be those conducted in conjunction with an offensive by the friendly force in the theater, or an amphibious landing, or an airborne operation. Defensive joint operations would be those conducted when the enemy is advancing and the guerrillas are employed at his rear in order to interrupt his advance, stop it, and perhaps facilitate the friendly conventional army to launch a counterattack. As defensive operations must be classified those where either force (conventional or guerrilla) conducts an offensive to relieve pressure on the other; such a case we would have, for instance, if a guerrilla unit is under attack and the conventional force sends a column in the direction of the guerrillas in order to divert the enemy or effect a junction with and rescue of the guerrillas.

When the joint operation is under the command of the conventional force commander, special consideration should be given to the missions alloted the guerrillas. Guerrilla units may not have the same capabilities as conventional units of similar size. Availability of weapons, munitions, mobility equipment, and status of training will influence the guerrilla capabilities. The conventional commander must, therefore, have detailed information on the guerrillas to ascertain that he does not overestimate their abilities. It is imperative, therefore, that close liaison be established between the conventional and guerrilla headquarters. This can best be affected by establishing an echelon of the conventional headquarters with the guerrillas. This liaison will serve a twofold purpose: It will furnish the conventional commander realistic information about battle conditions with the guerrillas and it will communicate to the guerrillas the orders and requests of the commander. The assignment of the senior liaison officer with the guerrillas is an extremely sensitive one. It should be entrusted to an officer who has the complete personal confidence of the commander and who, in addition, has the background, temperament, military acuity, and intellectual capacity to cope with the multitude of problems which may be encountered in such an assignment. Truly, finding an individual for such an assignment may be problematic unless the conventional army has had the prudence to forsee that such situations may develop and has prepared personnel for such assignments during the times of peace. The senior liaison officer must be supported by an adequate staff and must have at his disposal the necessary communications media enabling him to keep both headquarters in continuous contact.

The specific missions which may be allocated to the guerrillas during joint operations will depend, in addition to the guer-

rillas own capabilities, on the enemy situation and the degree
of stability of the front. Normally, during a static battle, disposition of enemy units is of high density and rear areas' security extremely tight. On the other hand, though, enemy tagets
are both easily definable and identified. Under these conditions,
guerrilla units may be used to isolate specific objectives, conduct diversionary attacks, and interrupt enemy communications. If, however, the battle front is fluid, such as the case may
be when the enemy is advancing with deep thrusts of armored
and other mobile columns, definition and identification of targets may be difficult, but flank and rear areas' security is necessarily compromised. In such a situation, it is best to let the guerrillas strike at targets of opportunity. Their contribution will,
therefore, depend on the degree of guerrilla initiative, boldness,
and luck.

4. Operations at the Rear of Advancing Enemy

In future warfare, situations will develop where one of the
two opposing conventional armies is rapidly advancing in
depth. This advance may be either over a broad front or the
result of a single thrust by a strong column. Such situations
offer good opportunities for the utilization of guerrillas by the
retreating army.

Situations such as the ones described above, are usually accompanied by the following conditions: Fuidity of the front,
dispersal of the advancing units, and communications problems
for both sides.

Under these conditions, if guerrillas are available, they have
good opportunities to inflict great damage to the advancing
enemy. In cooperation with their friendly conventional forces
they may be able to isolate enemy columns and affect their
destruction, or at least to cause him to suffer substantial casualties. They may be able to create the impression that strong
forces are active in the rear of the advancing enemy and induce
a change in the enemy's decisions, slow down or divert his advance, give an opportunity to the friendly conventional forces
to mount a counteroffensive or to withdraw to a secure position,
or even affect the enemy's withdrawal.

However, these opportunities are time-limited. Within a matter of days or weeks either the front solidifies, or the retreating army collapses. Consequently, there is no time to organize a guerrilla movement from scratch. In order to take advantage of the opportunities presented by these situations one must either have made preparations in advance to leave guerrilla units behind, or convert selected conventional units into guerrillas. Our Historical review has shown that both solutions have been tried in the past. The Russians in World War II utilized the first solution by the creation of the special "destruction batallions" which, however, were not too successful. The Finns in 1939 utilized the latter solution around Suomussalmi.

Even the conversion of selected conventional units requires some advance preparation because usually most conventional units are not suitable for this kind of employment. In the U.S. Army, at the present, suitable units can be considered the Special Forces Groups, Ranger Battalions, and some of the Airborne Infantry. Other types of units may also be considered, if they receive appropriate indoctrination and training.

The advancing enemy is most vulnerable to guerrilla activities at his rear if he is advancing over a broad front. In this type of situation the enemy units are most widely dispersed and have magnified security, communications, and logistics problems. The dispersal of enemy units is considerably less when the enemy is employing a single thrust or a pincers movement of two strong columns.

Guerrilla units operating under these conditions must be numerous and also widely dispersed. Otherwise the enemy will be able to localize them and bring about their destruction. Their size and strength will vary. They must be able to live off the land and operate with minimum or no support from the friendly conventional forces. Direction and control of the guerrillas by the friendly conventional headquarters will be problematic, therefore maximum freedom of action and initiative will have to be allowed to individual guerrilla commanders. Obviously, only exceptionally resourceful and energetic individuals should be given these assignments.

The guerrilla units, left on their own, will have as their major objective the creation of confusion amongst the enemy.

They will have to assume risks which are not normally acceptable in protracted guerrilla warfare. They must engage the enemy frequently and often under conditions unfavorable for the guerrillas. There will be occasions when even the complete destruction of a particular guerrilla unit is justified if by its loss the enemy can be prevented from reaching his objective.

We are discussing here a situation which, in spite of its inherent opportunities for success, constitutes one of the most difficult situations for guerrilla operations. One of the fundamental problems for the guerrillas is to locate a vulnerable enemy unit while they themselves remain undetected by the enemy until they launch their attack. If they have a choice of targets, they should attack them in the following order of priority: Regimental or higher headquarters, supply columns, bivouacked or resting troops, positioned or moving artillery, infantry, and armor. From the point of view of the psychological impact on the enemy, attacking an enemy headquarters is the most desirable. The higher the headquarters the better. Small and intermediate unit headquarters, such as battalion, are usually in close proximity to combat troops therefore the undertaking is too risky. But the advance headquarters of a division may be unprotected or weakly protected by headquarters service personnel. The loss of supply columns has both psychological and material impacts on the enemy. Since supply columns may be also inadequately protected, they make profitable targets. Bivouacked troops are easier to engage than troops which are ready for action. Artillery is extremely vulnerable to guerrillas unless in close proximity to the infantry. Infantry and armor are difficult targets, but as stated previously, there may be situations when they must be enegaged. Even in those situations, the guerrillas can improve their possibilities of success by making optimum use of terrain, surprise, periods of poor visibility or adverse weather, and the probable exhaustion of the advancing enemy troops.

Actually, the most opportune time to strike an advancing enemy mechanized column would be when and if the column has come to a temporary stop. Such an event may indicate that the enemy considers himself overextended; therefore, he is halting in order to allow his slower-moving units to catch up or close the gaps. It could also indicate that the enemy's fuel is exhausted and he is waiting for fuel supplies to come up. Finally, it is possible that a temporary halt may be the result of indecision on the part of the enemy commander or lack of specific orders from the next higher command echelon. If any of the above reasons are causing the enemy to halt, he is in a relatively vulnerable position. He is tired, perhaps completely immobilized, or worse yet, confused.[1] The guerrillas could capitalize on the enemy's condition and launch an attack then.

If the guerrillas can assemble a sufficiently strong force, they may be able to inflict serious losses on the enemy. If the guerrillas do not have a force strong enough to attack the enemy, they should try to raid some of the enemy's peripheral posts or make an operation of some kind at the enemy column's rear. At least, they should make their presence known to the enemy.

The presence and noted activity of the guerrillas will be reported to the enemy commander. No commander is going to feel at ease knowing that guerrillas are moving at will near his flanks and rear. His immediate plans, therefore, may be influenced by such guerrilla activity. Mopping-up operations may be undertaken by the enemy to the detriment of his prime objective. The enemy may go as far as withdrawing his most exposed units or halting his advance, temporarily at least, all along the front. All these alterations to the enemy's plans will be beneficial to the guerrillas or their friendly conventional forces. Delays of the enemy may give the friendly forces just enough time to organize a defense or launch a counterattack.

Eventually, the enemy's advance will come to a stop one way or the other. Then, the decision will have to be made whether the guerrillas should be infiltrated into friendly lines or left behind for protracted guerrilla activity.

From the point of view of the retreating conventional army commander, there is one task which has to be accomplished to the maximum possible point, in spite of the obvious difficulties. It is the task of maintaining effective communications with the guerrillas left behind. The difficulties of this are recognized. Yet, the most energetic guerrilla activity behind the enemy will be in part wasted unless the overall commander has the ability to direct the guerrillas and can obtain the benefits of their intelligence. If the commander can accomplish this task, the effectiveness of guerrilla operations behind the enemy will be maximized.

5. On Air Support for Guerrillas

If the guerrillas are cooperating with conventional friendly forces, it may be possible to provide them with air support. The following types of missions could be flown in direct support of guerrilla operations:

Resupply — aerial deliveries of all kinds

Evacuation — primarily medical

Reconnaissance and surveillance

Interdiction missions against targets which are significant to the guerrillas

Direct close fire support for the guerrillas

The subject of air support is associated with the problem of establishing air superiority over the area of guerrilla activity. This in turn, is related to the issue of which of the two parties in the conflict (the conventional enemy of the guerrillas or the conventional friendly forces) has overall air superiority. If the enemy has undisputed control of the skies over the area of guerrilla operations, he can prevent any effective support of the guerrillas by friendly air forces. At the same time, it has to be recognized that it is not prudent to conduct air operations in support of the guerrilla effort at the expense of other objectives which may be more critical. However, limited or temporary air support could be furnished.

The first step towards providing air support is to establish very close liaison between the guerrilla headquarters and the appropriate tactical air headquarters. The liaison is necessary for a number of reasons, two of which are fundamental. First, the tactical air headquarters must have realistic and up-to-date knowledge of the guerrillas situation in order to make the determination whether the operation is necessary or whether its resources should be directed towards other objectives. Second, the complexity of ground-air operations is such that nearly continuous contact between the two headquarters is necessary in its implementation.

It is probable that among the guerrillas there are no personnel with experience in maintaining ground-air contact. If this is the case, the deficiency must be corrected by the conventional forces who must infiltrate appropriate personnel to the guerrillas.

The next step has to be taken by the tactical air forces alone. They must establish temporary air supremacy over the area of guerrilla activity. If this cannot be accomplished absolutely and for the necessary duration, the operation need not be abandoned necessarily. Alternate approaches can be used with the understanding that the results will be correspondingly reduced. For example, the operation can still be undertaken during periods of adverse weather when enemy air opposition may be at its minimum. All this will have to consider the effort (including magnitude of casualties) against the anticipated benefits from the operation; not the benefits to the guerrillas, but to the overall war effort.

After the above have been accomplished, the actual support operations can be conducted. The cooperation and effort required from the guerrillas will vary depending on which ones of the missions previously identified are being conducted. For example, interdiction bombing may require from the guerrillas no more than target damage assessment reports. But resupply missions may require that the guerrillas capture and hold for a few hours a landing field so that transports can land.

An important constraint in operations of this kind will be the combat radius of the available aircraft and the distances from the air bases to the targets. This may become a problem for the United States in the future if withdrawal from overseas bases continues. Obviously operations in Central China, for instance, will be problematic without air bases in Japan, Formosa or SE Asia. Improved aerial refueling capabilities and the availability of aircraft carriers may provide a solution to this problem, however.

Looking into the future, one may naturally wonder about the necessity of developing new aircraft for this specific purpose.

It is obvious that two different types of aircraft will be required. Transports with STOL capability and light assault aircraft. Both should have capability for electronic and infrared suppression countermeasures. Development of new aircraft is a very expensive undertaking. The decision, therefore, on whether to develop new aircraft or not must be weighed against all other factors bearing on national defense policy. As an alternate, one could utilize, after appropriate modification, existing aircraft types. Most suitable would be the C-130's, OV-10's and A-1E's.

6. Guerrilla Base

Guerrilla base is a location which is relatively free from enemy interference and which is suitable for the establishment of equipment storage facilities, training facilities, and medical facilities for the guerrillas.

The guerrilla base is, therefore, a permanent or semi-permanent installation by necessity. This requirement is in conflict with the mobility and fluidity requirements of guerrilla operations; therefore the establishment of a guerrilla base on territory firmly controlled by the enemy becomes problematic. Deception must be utilized then, in order to establish a base under cover among ordinary civilian facilities. This, of course, involves substantial risks in the event that the base is discovered by the enemy with the subsequent loss of materiel and capture of guerrillas and guerrilla collaborators. This kind of arrangement requires a very efficient underground organization.

In the event, however, where the enemy is not in firm control of the territory in question, a base can be established and be reasonably well secure in remote areas.

Another approach may be the establishment of the base on neutral or friendly territory if geographic conditions are favorable and if such territory can be made available within reasonable proximity to the area of guerrilla operations.

In reviewing recent guerrilla movements, we find that all three solutions have been tried. In Cyprus, for instance, EOKA successfully utilized the method of maintaining covert guerrilla bases within the Island, in many cases literally under the eyes of the British security forces. The success of this arrangement is predicated on the magnitude of support that the local population is able to furnish the guerrilla movement.

During World War II, control of the occupied territories by the Germans was spotty. The size of the territories under occupation and the manpower demands of the active fronts made it impossible for the Germans to maintain absolute control of the occupied areas in their entirety. Control was limited to industrial areas and communications lines only, while the rest of the occupied territories were left to policing by relatively weak units or native collaborationist police, in many cases unfriendly to the occupying forces. It was relatively easy, therefore, for the guerrillas to establish bases on the mountain villages in the Balkans and in the forests and marshes of Eastern Europe. Under the above conditions destruction of the guerrilla bases by the Germans required not only their discovery first, but offensive operations over difficult terrain which gave the guerrillas the opportunity to either assemble sufficient forces for defense of the base or timely warning for evacuation of the base and relocation elsewhere.

The guerrillas in Indochina were supplied by bases located in Red China. The Viet Cong guerrillas today are utilizing bases in North Viet Nam, Laos and Cambodia. The communist guerrillas in Greece in 1946 to 1949 had their bases in Albania, Yugoslavia, and Bulgaria. The Algerian rebels used the border areas of Tunisia and Morocco to establish their bases, etc. This is the most advantageous arrangement for the guerrillas; but it requires, of course, that a country which is actively supporting, or at least sympathetic to the guerrillas has a common border with the country where the guerrilla activity takes place. Less advantageous, but still effective would be the location of the base in a country not bordering the guerrilla territory, but still in close proximity to it and with access through unobstructed sea and air routes. Such a case we may see in Venezuela, for instance, where guerrilla activity may commence in the future, with the guerrilla bases having been established in Cuba.

Several military leaders with experience in counterguerrilla warfare have asserted that the success or failure of a guerrilla movement is dependent on the availability and suitability of guerrilla bases. A few have claimed the establishment of a guerrilla base is a prerequisite to launching guerrilla warfare. These opinions are probably correct as long as one is not confused by semantics. The experiences in Viet Nam have influenced some of us to think of guerrilla bases and guerrilla sanctuaries interchangably. Sanctuary in neutral territory, where guerrillas can escape when hard-pressed, may or may not be a guerrilla base. Conversely, a guerrilla base may or may not be established in a sanctuary. There is very little doubt that the availability of sanctuaries makes counterguerrilla operations very difficult. But the two terms must not be confused. And we have the example of EOKA in Cyprus where no bases were established until after guerrilla operations were well underway. Confusion may also exist with the term guerrilla base itself. One cannot expect the guerrilla base to be a large staging area with elaborate facilities and to have such a base available in the early stages of guerrilla movement. But it is reasonable to assume that as the guerrilla movement develops and the enemy in part relinquishes control of outlying areas, guerrilla bases have to be established otherwise the guerrillas will be seriously handicapped.

In strictly indigenous guerrilla movements, with no outside support, the problem of establishing guerrilla bases remains a serious one. The solution can be found in establishing clandestine guerrilla bases which are concealed among civilian facilities. Again it must be emphasized that this solution requires an efficient underground organization to support the guerrillas and a favorable attitude towards the guerrilla cause among the civilian population.

IX

Preparing for Future Guerrilla Warfare
Selection of Personnel
Selection of Leaders
Training

1. Personnel

THE MOST important factor in a guerrilla force is the individual guerrilla soldier. George Patton in "War as I Knew It" makes a similar statement about the relationship of Army and soldier. Although Patton had only conventional armies in mind, the same holds true for guerrillas since they are a specialized kind of military unit.

The resultant capability of any military unit, or any group of humans assembled for a specific action, is the sum total of the combined capabilities of its members; leaders and rank and file. Any qualitative improvement in any one of its members adds that much to the unit sum total; likewise, any deficiency by any one member subtracts that much from the unit total.

Effective use of guerrilla forces requires, therefore, careful selection and proper subsequent treatment of each individual guerrilla.

In many cases, in the past, the only factor for selecting a man to join a guerrilla band was his availability without any consideration given to the man's abilities, motivation, and background. This method is not the most desirable.

The most important quality that the individual guerrilla should possess is the proper conviction in the righteousness of the cause he is called to fight for and determination to exert every possible effort towards the successful conclusion of this struggle. Without a doubt, this conviction will frequently overlap the realm of politics, but after all, war is a continuation of politics in the international scene. By proper conviction we do not mean that he should be a fanatic of a sort. Fanatics are usually people with sallow minds, without depth of thought, and quite often emotionally unstable. The sallow and unstable individual is not likely to react rationally at times of mental stress, physical fatigue, and tactical adversity. He is the one, also, who will most likely abuse his power when he finds himself in a position of power. Ideally, the individual guerrilla should be a man of intellect and philosophic inclination. How many such individuals can be spared for use as guerrillas in a society used to stereotype thinking and preoccupied with material things is a difficult question to answer. On the other hand, refugees and defectors from some of the Captive Countries, including Russians, could provide the nucleus for such force in the future if our High Command ever decides to wage offensive guerrilla warfare in the future.

Guerrillas fall into two general categories of origin. We have indigenous guerrillas and extrinsics. Indigenous guerrillas are those who are natives or residents of the country or territory where the guerrilla activities take place. Most guerrilla forces in the past have been composed of indigenous guerrillas. Extrinsic guerrillas are the members of the military forces of a belligerent who are infiltrated in the country or territory controlled by the enemy for the purpose of conducting guerrilla operations. An example of extrinsic guerrillas were the Long Range Penetration Groups in Burma during World War II. The extrinsic guerrillas may be used either to conduct operations per se (example: Burma) or to organize, advise and control indigenous guerrillas (example: occupied Europe).

The organization of the Special Forces and Air Commando

units within the U.S. Armed Forces in recent years provides a satisfactory nucleus of extrinsic type guerrillas who, in the future, may be called upon to operate in countries under the control of an enemy. Other nations are also organizing similar units, but of a much lesser scope.

The primary consideration in selecting guerrillas for operation in a specific country is the knowledge of the language or one of the languages spoken by the natives of the country in question. This is particularly critical if the outsiders will be required to operate with the indigenous guerrillas or mix with the native population. Obtaining a sufficient number of individuals who qualify in all other respects and who have proficient knowledge of the native language, could be an acute problem if the language of the country in question is relatively unknown to the outside world. In the United States, because of the large number of immigrants from diverse sources and because of the relatively high academic development, a more-or-less adequate pool of individuals fluent in European languages exists. Unfortunately, however, the most likely areas of guerrilla conflicts in the near future are in Africa and Asia. The number of people with knowledge of some of those languages (for instance: Lao or Thai) is very limited.

It may become necessary, therefore, that only a fraction of the infiltrated guerrillas will possess this most important qualification. In such cases, guerrilla operations by the infiltrators will be correspondingly reduced in scope.

There are other qualities requiring consideration in selecting guerrillas of this type. They are both specific and general.

The specific qualities correspond to specific conditions prevailing in the area of prospective operations and to specific mission requirements. For example: In World War I, the British infiltrated into the Arab Peninsula teams of machine-gunners from the Indian Army. Those teams operated with Lawrence's Arab guerrillas. The specific requirement here was to have individuals with a particular military skill (machinegun crews). In addition, the prevailing climate conditions required that these individuals had been acclimated to the desert. For similar reasons, the Long Range Penetration Group in World War II was composed of individuals who had received jungle training and had served in the Canal Zone.

Among the general qualities which are desired in selecting extrinsic guerrillas, the following three are absolutely essential.

The individuals must be dedicated soldiers and absolutely convinced on the righteousness of the war objectives. If not, they will react unfavorably to possible tactical adversity and to enemy psychological warfare.

Secondly, they must be highly proficient in their particular military skills; in fact, each ought to possess more than one military skill. For instance, one man could be a demolitions expert and a weapons maintenance man. Or, first aid man and radio operator, etc. In this manner, quality can be substituted for quantity, thus reducing the size of their units.

Finally, they have to be of good physical condition. War is no picnic. Guerrilla operations, in particular, severely tax any man's strength. Obviously, sick and overage men have no place in guerrilla units. It is wrong though to believe that one needs professional athletes for this kind of work.

In preparing for future guerrilla warfare, a High Command should have a program of preselection of prospective guerrillas of the extrinsic type. These people should be organized into units of special composition. If the areas of prospective infiltration and guerrilla activity can be identified in advance, the units should be earmarked for operation in particular area or areas. Provisions should also be made to augment these units, if necessary, with reservists, replacements, and the possible creation of additional units after the beginning of hostilities. Absolute secrecy must be maintained about the missions and strength of such units.

The selection and organization of indigenous guerrillas confronts us with an entirely different set of problems.

The easiest and most expeditious method of fielding indigenous guerrillas is to preselect units of the conventional military establishment and to instruct these units to allow themselves to be bypassed by the enemy if he is advancing into one's own territory. Subsequently, these units can conduct operations at the enemy's rear. Some of the Soviet guerrillas of World War II constitute an example of this method. In following this method, one has to ascertain that the individuals assigned to these units are ideologically reliable and possess the necessary military skills for operations of this kind.

However, operational situation can not always favor this type of solution. For example, this solution is not practical if the High Command feels that guerrilla operations must not commence immediately after the enemy advance. In such a case, the preselected units will have to maintain themselves underground for months or, maybe, years and this will probably be impossible. Another type of unfavorable situation will exist if the preselected units are not successful in evading the enemy and they are captured or destroyed.

Lastly, this solution is not possible in situations where guerrilla operations need to be used as an initial stage of revolution, or where conventional military forces are not available.

When any of the above situations prevail, the High Command, or whoever is responsible for organizing guerrilla warfare, must recruit guerrillas from scratch, train them, and organize them into cohesive formations. Accomplishment of this task requires the existence of an efficient underground organization.

When one is faced with one of these situations, he must, of course, consider first whether all other prerequisites for guerrilla warfare exist. Those prerequisites include favorable terrain conditions and the availability of materiel. The next consideration, which should precede the recruiting of guerrillas, has to do with the type of tactical operations projected. In this respect there are two classifications of the indigenous guerrillas. Essentially, we have part-time guerrillas and full-time guerrillas.

Part-time guerrillas are almost always covert guerrillas. They remain in their usual places of residence and pursue their normal day-to-day activities. They assemble for specific operations near the area of their residence and after the conclusion of each operation they return to their homes and resume their normal activities. Part-time guerrillas have a number of advantages. Subsistence is simplified for them; since they are familiar with local conditions, escape and concealment are easier for them. However, they also have disadvantages. The principal disadvantage is their restricted mobility, because they are not available for operations away from their home area or operations of long duration. The reason is, of course, that prolonged absences from their home areas will be detected by enemy agents and their safety and the safety of their families will be jeopardized. Another disadvantage is that their proficiency can be expected to be lesser than that of full-time guerrillas.

Full-time guerrillas are usually overt guerrillas. They have severed all ties with civilian life. They are not localized in the sense that they operate near their homes only, but they are available for operations of general nature. In addition to this advantage which is related to mobility, full-time guerrillas can be expected to reach a higher level of military proficiency, simply because they have more time available to practice. The disadvantages of full-time guerrillas include the fact that they require an auxiliary underground organization to furnish them logistic support and that they require relatively secure areas where they can hide between operations.

In future conflicts, it can be anticipated that a combination of both kinds of indigenous guerrillas will be used. The part-time guerrillas will probably predominate during the early stages of development of the guerrilla movement.

After the problem of projected tactical operations has been fully considered, one has to proceed with the recruiting of individual guerrillas. All along, it has been assumed that the psychological conditioning of the population base from which the indigenous guerrillas will be selected has already taken place. The next question, therefore, will be the following: What types of individuals or groups should be recruited?

The first choice is easy. One should try to recruit former members of the armed forces because such people possess, at least in part, the necessary training. Individuals with previous military experience, including officers, enlisted men, policemen, career people or reservists, etc., if available, should be recruited as guerrillas. These people are particularly suited for operations requiring full-time guerrillas.

However, a problem exists if such people are not available, or not available in sufficient numbers. This can be expected in countries which have not had national armies of their own, such as colonial or dominated countries. It can also be expected in a country where the members of the armed forces are prisoners following a military defeat, or in any occupied country where all individuals with military experience are controlled by the occupation authorities. The problem then becomes considerably more acute, not because of difficulties in recruiting, but because of the expected difficulties in training totally inexperienced personnel.

Next to individuals with previous military experience, students in their late teens and early twenties make the best prospective guerrillas. This is because they are idealistic, usually of good physical condition, and have no obligations to earn a living and support a family. Engineers and industrial laborers are good prospective guerrillas because their technical skills are usually needed in the guerrilla units. Farmers and livestock men are also very desirable because of their familiarity with outdoor conditions. They are almost indispensable if part-time guerrillas are required in the overall guerrilla master plan.

Shopkeepers, teachers, and members of what is commonly called the "intelligentsia" usually do not make good guerrillas. They seem to lack the ability to adapt to situations which are not under the control of the individual. Consequently, they respond unsatisfactorily under strenuous conditions and particularly under situations of tactical crises. A notable exception was Colonel Adam I. Kocable, Commander of the Polish Underground in World War I. He originally intended to be a teacher of literature. Thus, no individual should be excluded from the guerrillas strictly on the basis of his occupation. There are no two human beings that are exactly alike. You could therefore, find a musician who can make an excellent guerrilla, while an officer with long conventional military experience could make a poor one. The recruiters will have to be able to judge human character correctly and make the best possible selections. They must also be alert for possible enemy agents who may try to infiltrate the organization. In addition, it can be taken for granted that endeavors of this kind will attract some opportunists and people motivated by desire for purely personal gains. All these have to be identified and weeded out because they will be a source of future trouble and a liability to the organization.

How about women in the guerrillas? Women can make ex-

cellent underground agents. For example, Maria Vladislavovna
Zahharchenko was the most effective White Russian agent and
became a thorn in the side of Soviet authorities between 1925
and 1935. Women have served with guerrillas in the recent
past. The Soviet guerrillas in World War II had several women
with the guerrilla staffs and the Greek communist guerrillas
used women extensively in 1949 when their manpower was being depleted. But in general, the presence of females in the
operating echelon of guerrilla units creates problems which
can get out of control. Mixing male and female guerrillas is
bound to create emotional attachments between some of them.
These may result in pregnancies which are definitely undesirable in a military environment. In addition, since the males
will probably outnumber the females, psychological problems
will be created among the male guerrillas who do not establish
a successful liaison with guerrillas of the opposite sex. The
whole thing already begins to sound ridiculous. In reality, all
these problems create diversions among the guerrillas and the
end result will undoubtedly be a general reduction of the unit's
efficiency and operational capability. The answer to the question, therefore, will have to be that women are undesirable
among the guerrillas, but capable and dedicated women can be
successfully utilized with the guerrillas auxiliary and underground organizations.

2. Leaders

The subject of military leadership is of such magnitude that its
thorough discussion is definitely beyond the scope of this work.
Even definitions of what is leadership vary in the various text-
books. There is one definition though, that we find fitting at
least in relation to guerrilla leadership, and wish to repeat:

>Military leadership is the leader's ability to employ
>in a superior manner the personnel and materiel as-
>signed.[1]

One other aspect of leadership appears to us as obvious: That
military leadership in its application is not a science, but an

art. Scientific knowledge of human behavior will be an asset to the leader, but this knowledge by itself will not insure effective leadership. This is indeed unfortunate because it complicates the task of choosing and training leaders.

We must also differentiate here between leadership and command, although as we shall see below this difference in guerrillas is a narrow one.

In a conventional military establishment all officers and noncommissioned officers are leaders by definition. However all leaders are not commanders. Command is the ultimate position of leadership associated with a unit. The commander is assisted in his task by other leaders of his unit, but he alone commands.

The lowest echelon of command in the Infantry is normally the company. The company is authorized, in addition to its commander, as many as five lieutenants and maybe 25 noncommissioned officers. In the Air Force, the lowest echelon of command is the squadron. A fighter squadron may have as many as 35 officers and 50 or more noncommissioned officers assigned. All these leaders in the company and the squadron function as assistants to the commander — either as staff members or as troop leaders. The reason for this distinction between leadership and command is that although a leader is required for every few men or groups of men in order that they may be effectively led, command is related to the tactical function of each unit, overall organizational structure of the army, and communications media.

The leader of guerrillas is a military leader. As such he should possess all qualifications required for an officer of his rank and all the specific qualifications listed previously for the individual guerrilla.

Unlike politics, business, and other human activities, the military have established clearly defined leadership qualities. Thus, in theory at least, the military establishment protects itself from having to put up with leaders or commanders who are appointed because of demagogic appeal, servility to the boss, loyalty to a clique, and other subjective reasons not necessarily revelant to the man's real ability in relation to the job.

By definition, each man holding any rank in the military is a leader per se. However, it is unrealistic to assume that al military leaders possess all qualities of leadership to the same degree. The one quality of leadership that the guerrilla leader must have very highly developed is the ability to plan and act independently; i.e. the quality commonly referred to as initiative. The reason for this is that the nature of guerrilla operations is such that even the smallest unit leader will be in many cases compelled to decide and act without the benefit of consultation or direction from higher headquarters. In other words, every leader will probably have to make command decisions. This is the reason why we stated above that in guerrillas the difference between an ordinary leader and a commander is narrow.

Higher headquarters should, therefore, give the guerrilla leader sufficient and clear instructions covering the widest possible range of conditions. Thus, the leader will know, generally, what headquarters' policies and wishes are, but he will be empowered to act according to his own judgement within the frame of the instructions given him.

Among the instructions given, there should be sufficient guidance in regards to questions of politics. Political problems are very distractive in military operations; yet they are often encountered, particularly in guerrilla warfare. Once they have been encountered it is prudent to ignore them as long as they do not affect military operations; but when there is a chance that politics may have an affect on operations, then it is best that the commander be prepared to cope with them or else he may cause both political and military blunders.

One typical case of political ineptitude in a politico-military situation was the case of Brigadier E. C. W. Meyer in World War II. He was appointed by British Headquarters, Middle East, in 1943 to head a military liaison mission with the guerrillas operating in Greece. In effect, The Chief Liaison Officer was in command of the guerrilla operations because the British Headquarters expected him to plan and direct certain military operations. Meyer was a professional soldier from the Engineer Branch. He was militarily well qualified for the task. Once he landed in Greece, he found that the local communists were interfering with his mission. Being politically naive, he allowed the communists to influence his decisions and for the price of their limited participation in some operations he persuaded

Headquarters Middle East to furnish them substantial materiel which they stashed away to use later in their bid to overthrow the constitutional government of Greece.[2] Details of these events are dealt with elsewhere in this study.[3] Unfortunately too, this was not the only case of political ineptitude displayed by the Allies in World War II. The events in Yugoslavia and our abandonment of Mihailovich in favor of Tito followed the same general pattern. In the future, such errors must be avoided and this will depend largely on the accuity of the leader on the spot.

Politics are among the potential problems of guerrilla leadership, but by no means the only one. Among the potential problems of leadership one must also include:

Shortcomings of the guerrilla organization

Insufficient training among the guerrillas

Lack of experience in this type of operation

Shortages of materiel

Inability to provide for satisfaction of the men's basic needs

Inability to provide for the safety of the men's families

Indifference or hostility of the local inhabitants

Conflict of war aims (particularly when operating in an allied country)

Enemy propaganda

Antagonism of rival guerrilla groups (an offshoot of political problems)

Difficulty in enforcing discipline.

Some of the above problems are so interrelated that the existence of one will necessarily mean the simultaneous existence of another one. There are no fast rules of thumb that will automatically provide a solution to any one of these problems. Their solution will depend on the abilities of the leader. The leader who can direct his subordinates toward accomplishing their assigned mission in spite of any or all the above problems, has indeed passed the ultimate test in leadership and his superiors should recognize this fact.

Among the above listed problems, there is one that requires further discusion. That is the problem of enforcing discipline.

Discipline can be defined as *the willingness to accept with conviction and without reservation the necessity for a common law that directs and coordinates the effort of a unit.*[4] When a unit is composed of individuals who understand the necessity of such discipline in the military, this willingness to accept is already present and a discipline problem will not likely develop in such a unit. This is the reason why we stressed previously the necessity of highly discriminatory selection of potential guerrillas.

Yet, all human virtues are a matter of degree. Combinations of problems and the magnitude of problems, such as those listed above, could cause a breakdown of discipline even in the best units. History is full of such examples, for instance, the retreat of Napoleon's Army from Moscow. On the other hand, examples of units which suffered no breakdown of discipline in spite of the extreme adversity of the situation are also plentiful. A recent example is the conduct of the 6th German Army in Stalingrad.

One other situation could also cause a serious problem of discipline. This is the case where the leader is not accepted by his subordinates. The nonacceptance of the leader would be, most likely, covert or even subconscious. In extreme cases it could become overt and would result in the leader's authority being questioned and his orders not carried out. The most common cause for a subordinate not accepting his leader is the belief on the part of the subordinate that the leader is not professionally qualified.[5] A platoon of veteran regulars will receive with reservations the assignments of a young Second Lieutenant fresh out of OCS. If, subsequently, this Second Lieutenant successfully leads the platoon in combat or maneuvers, the reservations are withdrawn and the men accept him mentally as their leader. If, however, the Lieutenant makes one or two errors or demonstrates ignorance of any sort, then his men are not likely to have any confidence in him. They will begin to question the correctness of his judgment and, mentally, will debate the propriety of his orders. As a result his orders, even when carried out, will not be executed expeditiously and efficiently. This leader will have to revert to driving his men instead of leading them in order to accomplish the unit's mission. Driving, in lieu of leading, is never effective in the long run.

With this method there will be an eventual breakdown of leadership. The above example of the platoon leader applies to other echelons of command also.

It is imperative, therefore, to assign leaders to the guerrilla units who are proficient in every aspect and capable of obtaining their subordinates' confidence.

The above have general application in all situations of guerrilla warfare. However, there are additional considerations which depend on the origin of the guerrilla units. Extrinsic guerrillas and indigenous guerrillas who have been converted from a conventional military establishment do not have the same problems of leadership and command assignments as the indigenous guerrillas who have been organized from scratch.

The former already have an established hierarchy. They need only to ascertain that their leaders possess or acquire two additional qualifications. First, that their unit commanders have received the specialized training required for guerrilla operations under their particular conditions of deployment. Second, that the High Command has full understanding of guerrilla warfare.

The problem for the indigenous guerrillas who have to be organized from the bottom up it that they need to *find* leaders. The magnitude of their problem is inversely proportional with the number of individuals with prior military experience they can recruit. If they can obtain even a relatively small number of former officers and NCO's, the problem is minimized because they can use them as a nucleus to staff their units initially and to train additional leaders.

Fundamentally, indigenous guerrillas need small unit commanders (squad and platoon), intermediate unit commanders (company or battalion), and leaders to staff their general headquarters. A small-size guerrilla movement (example: Cyprus) may not even need commanders for the intermediate echelon. Conversely, a very large-size movement (example: Soviet guerrillas in World War II) will need commanders corresponding to practically all conventional echelons up to brigade and division. Obviously, a large-scale indigenous guerrilla movement cannot be developed without adequate availability of leaders even if rank and file are plentiful.

What is to be done, then, in the cases where one needs to organize an indigenous guerrilla movement without having available individuals with previous military experience who can be assigned commands in the guerrilla units?

One solution to the problem is to "borrow" extrinsic guerrillas as leaders from allied or friendly sources. The difficulties associated with this solution have already been discussed. Mainly, they are the difficulties of language, infiltration into the area, and acceptance by the indigenous rank and file.

The other possible solution is to develop leaders from among the indigenous guerrillas available. The difficulties associated with the solution are primarily related to the time element. First echelon commanders can be developed within six to twelve months. The exact time lapse depends on the state of their experience before their training commences. However, to develop second echelon commanders requires considerably longer time. Company-size units have to be commanded by individuals who have had experience in commanding lesser units, otherwise their performance will be unsatisfactory. If, therefore, second echelon commanders have to be developed from scratch, one year will not be enough.

In this kind of situation, the magnitude of the guerrilla movement will have to be escalated gradually. Few small-size units will be fielded at. first. As the personnel of these units gain experience, they will be used as cadres to form new units of progressively larger size. Thus, experienced squad leaders could be assigned to command platoon-size or company-size units. After a lapse of about 30 months, or so, leaders should become available to assume commands of battalions and regiments. Obviously, this solution can be utilized only in situations of protracted guerrilla warfare where the overall war plan is not time-limited.

The remaining question under the topic of leadership is how to recognize potential leaders among the indigenous guerrillas. The answer is not an easy one. But first, let us state this: Leaders should not be selected on any basis other than their military potential. Individuals should not be selected on the basis of political reliability, personal friendships, or other irrelevant considerations. This may sound somewhat controversial in view of what was discussed previously about political complications inherent in guerrilla warfare. In reality, though, it is not because what needs to be done is to select good military leaders and then instruct them how to handle political problems, instead of taking politically reliable individuals and then train them how to be effective commanders.

The most effective method of recognizing leadership qualities among the guerrillas is through close personal observation. The following can provide guidance for recognition of each individual's potential as a leader among the guerrillas.

1. Ascertain that the man is accepted by his comrades.

2. Ask the man for advice on specific matters on which he has expertise. Then, assess the quality of his advice. This will give an indication on the soundness of his judgement.

3. Observe the completeness and timeliness with which he performs assigned tasks. This provides an indication of his reliability and his inclination to pay attention to detail.

4. Assign him tasks slightly beyond the scope of his normal duties. Observe his ability to use initiative and improvisation.

5. Get indications of his attitude and concern about the welfare of his comrades and maintenance of equipment in his unit. Guerrilla Commanders should be preoccupied with both of these subjects.

6. Observe his stability and clearmindedness in combat or under adverse situations. This is the guerrilla commander's ultimate test.

It has to be acknowledged that the suitability of any regular army man to command guerrillas has been questioned in some quarters. They claim that regular army men, indoctrinated with conventional theories, are too inflexible in their thinking to understand and apply unorthodox methods such as those required by guerrilla warfare. This position is not valid because it is implying that the regular military men are incapable of developing new ideas of warfare. If that was so, then who brought about the changes of the last thirty years? One other issue is that if we exclude the regular army men from positions of guerrilla leadership, then we must seek them elsewhere. But where? Is a non-prior-service lawyer or school teacher potentially more capable of becoming a guerrilla leader than a graduate of one of the Service Academies? It is true that in the past, individuals who have had no formal military schooling rose to command guerrilla units successfully. Mao-Tse-Tung is without a doubt the outstanding one among them. But this has not always been the case. Guerrilla movements sponsored by the communists have had a great number of commanders who were appointed to military command positions because of their political reliability rather than military qualifications. This was prompted by necessity though. Trotsky recognized this as a shortcoming and in 1918 coerced a large number of officers of the old regime to serve with the Red Army. He established the institution of Military commissars to oversee the politically unreliable professionals.

It is possible that few gifted individuals may have a deep understanding of military affairs without having had prior military experience. But this is the exception and not the rule.

We must conclude, therefore, that since guerrilla warfare is in essence a military subject, we must look for potential guerrilla leaders in the military establishment. Without excluding individuals from other sources, we must search for relatively junior officers and noncommissioned officers, career men or reservists, who have not become attached or committed to a particular theory or dogma, as our best source for future guerrilla commanders. Then, we must take these men and train them to be leaders of guerrilla units just like we train men for all kinds of specialization in the Service.

3.   Training Guerrillas

The subject of training guerrillas has the following similarity to the subject of guerrilla leadership: The problems associated with it are related to the origin of guerrillas.

We will again differentiate between two types of guerrillas by origin. Those with previous military experience and those without. Guerrillas with previous military experience are usually extrinsic guerrillas or indigenous guerrillas who have been converted from conventional units. Guerrillas without previous military experience are usually indigenous guerrillas who have been organized clandestinely in a "grass roots" effort to develop a guerrilla movement.

The problems of training are fundamentally different between the two groups.

In the first group, one should begin with selected individuals who already have some military proficiency. This means that more-or-less experienced soldiers are selected and assigned to the designated units which will undertake guerrilla missions. As a minimum, these individuals should have received basic training or its equivalent. After selection, they should be given specialized guerrilla training. The problems in conducting specialized guerrilla training in this case involve the probable difficulties in simulating the conditions which prevail in the area of projected employment. This is an important requirement if the training is going to be realistic.

This problem will be more acute in the case of extrinsic guerrillas. For example, Sweden will have extreme difficulties if it decided to train guerrillas to operate in Libya, because Sweden does not have any kind of a training area which resembles the topography and climatic conditions of Libya. This, of course, is an extreme example, but it illustrates the point. Neither are topography and climate the only conditions which need to be simulated. Demographic conditions and enemy forces should also be included in the simulation.

Indigenous guerrillas who will be converted from conventional units have a simpler problem, providing their training is not a last minute improvisation. Ordinarily, they should have no difficulties in training right on the area of projected employment.

There are two phases in the training of future guerrillas. The first is individual skill and proficiency training and the second is unit training. The objective of both is to develop the maximum operational capabilities for the guerrilla force. Individual training should precede unit training. After the individual learns certain basic skills he should be introduced to unit training, but his individual training should also continue. This is the only way that individuals can maintain and improve their military proficiencies and develop confidence and self-reliance.

The next topic requiring discussion is the subjects which

need to be taught to future guerrillas. Because of the wide variety of operational missions which may be assigned to guerrillas, it is not possible to suggest a complete training subject outline which can cover all possible requirements. We will list, instead, a number of subjects which will be applicable in many situations.

1. Concealment, evasion, and escape. This is a subject of major importance. Therefore it should be taught in depth to all guerrillas. It applies to both phases of training, individual and unit. The reason is that the methods of concealment, evasion, and escape are likely to differ between situations where one or a few men are involved and situations where guerrilla units are involved. Survival in a hostile environment is a topic under this subject, and should be included in this training. This subject could become wasted effort if it is taught under conditions lacking realism. It is, therefore, very important to conduct training in this subject under conditions which resemble the conditions in the area of projected operations as close as possible.

2. Weapons training. This is also a very important subject. Every guerrilla must acquire the highest expertise with the basic small arms. The reason is that all guerrillas, including those assigned to staff or logistics support positions, should be able to effectively participate directly in combat. In this manner the guerrilla units optimum firepower can be achieved with minimum personnel overhead. Weapons training should also include training in demolitions and explosives. It should also include thorough familiarization with the weapons of the enemy because it can be expected that ·captured or pilfered enemy weapons will be used by the guerrillas. Maintenance of proficiency in small arms requires continuous practice. Therefore, if ammunition is plentiful, marksmanship should take place at frequently scheduled intervals. The results of this will be that in combat the guerrillas will be able to inflict more casualties with lesser ammunition expenditure. It probably will not be practical to train all guerrillas in the crew-served weapons. However, the crew-served weapons of each guerrilla unit should have a ratio of crews-to-weapons which is greater than 1/1. For example, for each mortar there should be more than one mortar team trained. The reason is to ease the replace-

ment and training problems which will develop after the guerrillas are committed to active operations.

3. Special equipment training. It can be expected that guerrillas would be using various kinds of special equipment. Signal equipment fall in this category. It is neither necessary nor practical to train all guerrillas to be expert operators of such equipment. But provisions should be made to train a sufficient number of guerrillas in their operation and maintenance.

4. Maintenance training. Guerrilla units can be expected to have problems with equipment resupply. Consequently, it is necessary that they get maximum serviceability from their equipment on hand. This can be accomplished through good equipment maintenance. Each guerrilla, therefore, should be thoroughly indoctrinated about the necessity of equipment maintenance and be taught the necessary skills of maintenance. It should cover all equipment including weapons, personal equipment such as clothing, etc. and unit equipment. Again, familiarity should be obtained on the maintenance of certain types of enemy equipment (example: radios and vehicles) because it can be expected that acquisition of such equipment from the enemy through capture or pilfering may be easier than resupply from friendly sources.

5. Training in the use and care of animals. The nature of guerrilla warfare is such that the guerrilla force can often be expected to operate on terrain unsuitable to use by wheeled vehicles. When this is the case, animals are the only means of transport besides the men themselves. If the guerrillas have an urban background, it is probable that they lack the necessary skill. The individual guerrilla's training, therefore, may need to include instruction in the use and proper care of animals. The animals may be dogs, mules, horses, camels, etc., depending on the country of projected operations.

6. Physical conditioning. A program of physical conditioning should be instituted as a companion to all other training. This program should be designed to prepare the individual for specific physical tasks. For example, crosscountry marching. Infiltration into new areas and other tactical problems usually generate requirements for the guerrillas to move on foot over relatively long distances and over unfavorable terrain. The

physical conditioning of prospective guerrillas, therefore, should include frequent marches with appropriate loads of weapons and ammunition over terrain similar to that which will be encountered in the operations area. Since exercises of this kind can become very time-consuming, it is necessary to eliminate from physical conditioning all those elements which are not relevant to guerrilla operations. For instance, fancy calisthenics or perhaps, judo. Acquisition of proficiency in judo requires more time than that which would normally be available to guerrillas. Giving them only limited instruction in judo, therefore, could amount to so much wasted effort. The key idea in physical conditioning of guerrillas is that like all other aspects of guerrilla training it should be tailored to prepare the guerrillas for specific tasks.

7. Unit operations training. After the guerrillas have achieved a predetermined proficiency level in their individual skills, they should spend most of the available training time in unit tactical exercises. This type of training is beneficial to commanders, staffs, and rank and file. In order to conduct this type of training it is necessary to organize the guerrillas into formations similar to those in the field and to plan tactical problems similar to those projected in actual operations. The tactical problems should cover both the routine and unusual. They should include operations such as surveillance of enemy units, assaults on anticipated targets, withdrawals, dispersals, reassemblies, etc. If possible they should not be limited to operations of small units only. Assuming that space is available and that such operations are anticipated and possible, they should in clude maneuvers involving several guerrilla regiments. If space is not available to conduct exercises of such magnitude, the exercises should be rehearsed on a realistic sand map. When rehearsals on sand maps are conducted, attendance and participation should not be limited to major unit commanders and staffs. As many individuals as possible should attend them, even if they have to be split up in groups. After each unit operations exercise it is imperative to hold an objective review and critique. The critique should be conducted by the commander or senior instructor and should be attended by all participants of the exercise. For exercises involving large numbers, simul-

taneous attendance by all would be impractical. Therefore, the critique should be conducted in two parts. The first part would be attended by the senior and intermediate commanders. Then they, in turn, would conduct the second part of the critique for personel of their own units. Critiques of this kind provide a two-way communication between instructors and trainees (or commanders and troops). They point out mistakes and methods of correction to the trainee and they also furnish to the instructor visibility on the effectiveness of training and identify areas which need improvement. In the case of extrinsic guerrillas and indigenous guerrillas who may be converted from conventional formations, operational exercises can be very much improved through the participation of conventional units which can simulate the enemy.

For the indigenous guerrillas the fundamental training problem is the following: Where can training be conducted, in view of the probability that the country is controlled by enemy forces. By enemy forces it is meant either an enemy occupation army or indigenous security forces.

The easiest solution to this problem is to infiltrate indigenous prospective guerrillas out of the area of projected operations into territory controlled by friendly forces or neutrals. There, training of guerrillas can be conducted without fear of intervention by the enemy. After training is completed the guerrillas can be reinfiltrated into the projected operations area.

This solution has been applied consistently since World War II. Some of the examples are the cases of Greece, Algeria, Indochina and South Viet Nam, etc. However, there are both military and political risks associated with this solution. The purely military risks are those involving the possibilities of interception by the enemy during the processes of infiltration and reinfiltration when the guerrillas are, as a rule, very vulnerable. The political risks have to do with the possibilities of change in conditions in the friendly or neutral country. Such changes may be brought about through international pressure or through a change of attitude caused by political changes in the host country. Then, the guerrillas-in-training may find themselves stranded in hostile or semihostile environment or they may be interned. Examples of this have occurred with the

Malaysian guerrillas in Indonesia and the Palestinian Arab guerrillas in Jordan.

If establishing a training base in a friendly or ostensibly neutral country is found to be impractical or unfavorable, then training must be conducted in-country. Relatively secure areas can be found even if the country is controlled by enemy forces. Some kinds of training can take place in restricted space. For example, weapons training can be given to small groups in basements of private buildings, but of course, with no live firing. More extensive training can be conducted in woods, swamps, and rural areas located at some distance from enemy garrisons and under infrequent surveillance by enemy patrols.

In general, the subjects to be taught should be the same as those listed for the extrinsic guerrillas. Exceptions would be made as necessitated by the restrictions of space and security requirements. After the maximum possible training has been given under the above restricted conditions, then the guerrillas are sent to the field to continue their training by undertaking missions of limited scope. These missions must be carefully selected and planned to preclude the possibility of disastrous defeats in such an early stage of the guerrilla movement.

The disadvantages in the application of this solution are the risks involved by engaging the enemy with guerrillas whose training is insufficient and those resulting from the enemy's reactions. For instance, once the guerrillas presence becomes known through an operation by them, it can be expected that the enemy will intensify his surveillance and consequently the availability of training areas will become even more restricted.

The problem of training indigenous guerrillas is simplified if among them are included ex-servicemen in sufficient proportion. In fact, it is imperative to have some ex-servicemen or people with extensive military background to use as cadre, otherwise training cannot be conducted. If such people are not available from indigenous sources, then they must be made available by infiltrating a cadre from external friendly sources. If neither can be made available, the success of an indigenous guerrilla movement is very much in doubt.

It is extremely difficult to establish a minimum ratio of ex-servicemen to guerrilla trainees without knowing other details of the situation. This ratio will depend on the abilities of the trainers, the aptitudes of the trainees, the time available, possible language problems if the trainers are not indigenous, and numerous other factors.

It can be expected that other lesser problems will need to be overcome in training indigenous guerrillas. Availability of materiel for training, for instance, can be such a problem. Others may be related to the projected tactical operations. For example, infiltration of urban areas and attacks on major industrial targets could create special problems or compound existing ones. If requirements for use of artillery exist, both the problems of training area and availability of instructors are magnified, because training artillery crews requires the availability of large impact area and expert instruction.

One cannot ignore the obvious fact that military operations cannot be conducted successfully with untrained or inappropriately trained troops. Providing the necessary training and solving the related problems will constitute, therefore, one of the basic tests of ability for the guerrilla High Command.

X

Preparing for Future Guerrilla Warfare — Materiel — Organization of Guerrilla Units — Relationship with Supporting Underground Organization

1. Materiel Considerations

MATERIEL ACQUISITION and, its companion, logistic support must be included as an essential element of overall planning in guerrilla warfare. Lack of, or inadequate planning in this area can result in serious setbacks for the guerrillas. This is why Mao Tse-Tung has written that victory cannot be achieved by going beyond limits imposed by material conditions.[1] One of the problems confronting any guerrilla High Command is the one of identifying these limits.

All evidence available shows that in most past guerrilla conflicts this subject has been only superficially covered by initial planning. More often than not, this consideration was an afterthought by the planners. This tendency is caused, perhaps, by the prevailing belief that guerrilla operations can be launched with limited material resources. This is true as far as it goes. But one has to balance the objectives against the available means.

In order to accomplish the above balancing of resources and objectives, the following planning tasks need to be done.

1. The possible sources of materiel have to be established and what can be obtained from each source identified. The possible sources of materiel for guerrillas are discussed in Chapter VI.

2. The desired materiel for the projected guerrilla operations need to be analyzed. Generally, one can expect differences in materiel requirements to exist in different types of operations. For example, protracted harassing operations against the enemy's communications can be accomplished with small arms, whereas operations with the objective of complete destruction of industrial targets will require equipment of higher complexity and sophistication.

3. Criteria need to be established for the materiel which can be obtained from the possible sources against qualitative requirements resulting from the tactical requirements of paragraph 2 above. These criteria would take under consideration all factors bearing on the operations including terrain, climate, enemy forces, guerrilla adaptability, etc.

4. Quantitative criteria have to be established in relation to the objectives.

5. After all of the above have been considered, one has to establish the trade-offs and reach a decision.

The qualitative criteria of the above paragraph 3, as far as guerrilla weapons are concerned, would include the following:

> weapon accuracy
> destructiveness or lethality
> reliability
> maintainability
> weight (minimum)
> rate of fire
> effective range
> ammunition complexity and weight
> flexibility for multiple uses

The reasoning behind the establishment of the above qualitative criteria is not too complex. Regardless of whether one is considering a rifle or a rocket, the accuracy requirements are important; otherwise one wastes ammunition and prolongs the engagement which can be disastrous for the guerrillas.

Destructiveness is important in relative terms because one does expect to destroy the targets, not to make noise only.

Reliability and maintainability are extremely important in guerrilla warfare. Guerrillas cannot afford unreliable weapons nor weapons requiring excessive maintenance.

The requirement for minimizing the weight results from the constraints of transport which are common among guerrillas.

Either high-rate or low-rate of fire may be desired. High-rate is usually associated with ammunition waste and relative inaccuracy. However, high-rate of fire could be necessary if the guerrillas are planning engagements of short duration when they have to bring the maximum number of rounds on the target in the shortest possible time.

Maximum effective range would be a critical factor if the guerrillas are planning to engage the enemy only at long range.

Ammunition complexity and weight could eliminate an otherwise desirable weapon.

Flexibility and adaptability to multiple uses, such as anti-vehicle and anti-personnel capabilities, utilization of varied ammunition, etc., add to the desirability of many weapons.

More difficult is the task of establishing an order of magnitude for the above qualities. For example, how important is it to have a weapon weighing 90 lbs vs one of 100 lbs? Such quantitative values for the qualitative requirements can only be established after considering the specifics of the projected operations. Maybe a point system can be utilized in order to facilitate the analysis. For example, if one is considering ten different rifles, he can compute their average weight and establish that as point zero; each pound of weight under the average could be given a point above zero on some valuation scale and each pound heavier a negative point.

Equally difficult is the task of establishing an order of magnitude among the qualitative requirements. It has to be recognized that optimizing all qualitative criteria is not possible because of the contrasts which exist among them. This part of the analysis is the one which culminates in the establishments of trade-offs and reaching decisions.

Tables I through V list comparatively the principal technical characteristics of certain small arms, support weapons, and light artillery. The listed weapons have specific suitability for guerrilla operations and have been produced in large quantities. However, their availability differs from one part of the globe to the next. It is not practical to include all pertinent characteristics of each weapon in these tables. Certain necessary characteristics, such as reliability and maintainability, can not be reduced to simple values suitable to tabular listing. It is, therefore, interesting to discuss further at least some of these weapons.

Most important in guerrilla warfare are the rifles and carbines. They are the basic weapons of the infantry, and guerrillas are primarily a type of infantry. Rifles are the most effective among the relatively easily obtainable weapons; the others are pistols and shotguns which have limited utility in guerrilla warfare.

Among the rifles, bolt-action rifles have some distinct advantages for guerrilla use. They are generally lighter than other types and their lower rate of fire contributes to reduced ammunition expenditure. Some experienced infantrymen also claim that bolt-action rifles contribute to compelling the individual rifleman to fire more aimed shots instead of spraying the target. This contributes to a higher percentage of hits per rounds fired. However, riflemen firing automatic or semi-automatic weapons can do the same, if properly trained to practice fire discipline. The disadvantages of bolt-action rifles are two. They are of little help in situations where it is necessary to fire a lot of rounds on a target in the shortest possible time, and most of them are by now old and relatively wornout since they are not being produced any longer for conventional military establishments.

Among bolt-action rifles the Mauser Kar 98, along with its many variations, is definitely one of the very best. It has been manufactured in Germany, Austria, Belgium, China, and Czechoslovakia. Millions of them are available throughout the world. The Springfield M 1903 also has a basically Mauser action with many refinements. It is an excellent weapon for guerrilla use. The Austrian-made Mannlicher-Schoenauer has been proven a very effective weapon, particularly in mountainous terrain where light weight is a strong consideration. Most of these weapons have been made in 6.5 mm caliber; this projectile is very accurate at long ranges because its velocity curve is fairly flat, but it is too light to be lethal at the longer ranges. The British SMLE, the Italian, Japanese, and Soviet bolt-action rifles listed in Table I we consider inferior weapons for guerrilla use and only the factor of a possible easy availability should induce guerrillas to use them in the future.

Among semi-automatic and selective (capable of selective fire: semi-automatic or automatic) rifles, the US M1 is the best for guerrilla use. It is lighter and more troublefree than any of the others. Next to it ranks the FN 7.62 mm. The US M14E2 is too heavy for guerrilla use. But it has to be recognized that having a rifle such as the M14 eliminates the need for a separate fully automatic weapon at the squad echelon. It means that at the company echelon one can have only two instead of three types of rifles; i.e. a combination rifle such as the M14 and a machinegun, instead of rifle, automatic rifle, and machinegun. The guerrilla High Command will have the task of establishing the trade-offs for these considerations.

The Soviet SKS and its Chicom copy are exceptionally good weapons in situations where long-range firing is not common. We believe them to be superior to the US M16. The reason is their much better reliability and maintainability. The M16 requires too much care in the field to be recommended for guerrilla use. The Soviet AK 47, which has the capability of firing fully automatically, is an improved version of the SKS and equally reliable.

In reviewing rifles, consideration should be given to each rifle's suitability for mounting telescopic sights and use of rifle grenades.

The fully automatic weapons listed in Table II can be divided into three groups: Light machineguns and automatic rifles which can be fired from a bipod or from the hip; medium machineguns which require a tripod; and heavy machineguns which require a tripod and have a cartridge of .50 inch or over.

Whether guerrillas need all three kinds or not depends again on the types of projected operations. Light machineguns or automatic rifles are necessary in all attack situations. Medium machineguns are useful for increasing the firepower of the base of fire element in an attack, but one has to pay a corresponding weight penalty for them. Heavy machineguns are of doubtful utility. Their projectiles are unnecessarily heavy for anti-personnel use and not heavy enough for use against armor. They could be utilized, however, in certain situations such as long range attacks on parked aircraft, light structures, or against low-flying aircraft.

One of the best machineguns is the German MG 34. It has operational flexibility because it can be fired from either a bipod or a tripod in addition to having selective fire capability. The Bren gun is also a good weapon for guerrilla use, prefer-able to the US M1919A6 and the Browning automatic rifle be-cause of its selective capability. The US M1919A4 is a satisfactory medium machinegun. The Czech M26 is a little too unstable and the Vickers too heavy for guerrilla use. The Soviet machineguns are also too heavy for guerrilla use.

Mortars can provide a very considerable increase in the fire-power of a guerrilla unit. Most mortars can fire a variety of ammunition, including smoke, incendiary, and high explosive. Consequently. they can be used effectively against all kinds of targets with the exception of heavy armor and structures of reenforced concrete. The heavier mortars, those of 107mm and over, provide a substitute for artillery to some extent. Heavy mortars are lighter than artillery, therefore more maneu-verable. However, they are not as accurate as artillery. As far as guerrillas are concerned, the big drawback of mortars is the complexity of training crews in their effective use. The next drawback is that of ammunition weight, a factor which limits the number of rounds that can be brought forward for any operation.

Availability of mortars with a range of over 2500 meters will be a requirement in most future guerrilla conflicts. This re-quirement is more important in situations where the guerrillas are considerably inferior to their adversaries in firepower and personnel proficiency. The mortars do give the guerrillas the capability of engaging targets beyond the range of enemy rifle and machineguns. A small guerrilla unit, therefore, with two mortars can set itself during the night at appropriate distance from the enemy outposts, fire a few rounds at the target, and then withdraw before the enemy can engage in effective counterbattery and before the enemy infantry can come within small arms range of the mortar location. This type of operation avoids close contact with the enemy, it causes confusion and frustration among enemy personnel, and is bound to create among the enemy leaders a preoccupation with security.

Among the mortars being listed, those of up to 60mm caliber are of limited use to guerrillas. Their range is too short and their missions in most guerrilla operational situations can be undertaken by rifle grenades. However, again one has to consider the matter of availability. If they are readily available, they probably will be used in preference to something else. The fact is that in certain areas of probable future guerrilla activity they are available in large quantities. Mention must also be made of the fact that models similar to those listed here have been produced by a number of other countries. For example, variations of the French Stokes-Brandt 60mm have been manufactured in about half a dozen countries including the United States and Red China.

The US 81mm mortar is also an improvement of a French model. It is a most useful weapon for guerrilla application. Variations of the original French 81mm mortar have also been manufactured in Germany, Italy, and elsewhere. The Soviet 82mm mortar is at least as good as its American counterpart. An identical version of this weapon is being manufactured in Red China. The British 3 inch mortar is inferior to the other models discussed in this paragraph because of its shorter range, lesser muzzle velocity, and generally inferior ballistics.

The mortars discussed so far, are either individual weapons or weapons transportable on backpacks by two men — one carrying the base plate and the other the tube and attachments. Of course, ammunition bearers have to be added to the mortar team. However, mortars of higher calibers do present a mobility problem because of the corresponding increase in weight. Towed mortars, as a rule, will not be suitable for guerrilla operations. It is desirable, therefore, that the mortars of higher calibers be disassembleable into loads of appropriate weight for transport by animals or men. It appears that the Soviet bloc countries have paid more attention to this subject than others.

Both' the US and the Soviet 107mm mortars can be disassembled into two pack loads each for animal transport. However, the Soviet mortar is superior in range, muzzle velocity, and rate of fire. This weapon too is being manufactured by the Red Chinese.

Outside the Soviet orbit, the only mortar of caliber above 107mm is the French M1951. This heavy mortar of 120mm caliber is not suitable for guerrilla operations. Its traveling weight is almost equal to that of a mountain howitzer, but it does not have a howitzer's range nor accuracy. In addition, it has the disadvantage that it must be fired from its wheeled carriage.

The best of the 120mm mortars is the one manufactured by the Czechs. This weapon has superior ballistics than the others and it is light enough to be easily transportable on five pack animals. A version of this mortar may be manufactured by the Finns.

The Yugoslav mortar of the same caliber is heavier and of slightly shorter range. The Yugoslavs have exported significant quantities of this weapon to Asian and African countries. The Soviet 120mm mortar is considerably lighter than the other two and has a shorter range. It is a weapon of older design, therefore not current in the state of the art.

Anti-tank weapons will be extremely important in future guerrilla operations. The need for anti-tank weapons among guerrillas originates from the fact that armor constitutes the primary striking element of all contemporary conventional establishments. All indications are that the trend to armor and mechanize all arms of the ground forces, which originated before World War II, will continue. In future large-scale conflicts one can expect to see all advance elements of the attacker to be mostly armored. This means that in addition to tank formations per se, most of the infantry will be carried in armored personnel carriers and the artillery will be self-propelled on tank chassis. Therefore, guerrillas will encounter fewer opportunities to engage "soft" targets. Consequently, it becomes important that the guerrillas possess effective anti-tank weapons. If such weapons are not available, the guerrillas will have to restrict their operations accordingly. This will probably mean that offensive guerrilla actions could be taken only against second line enemy troops, garrisons, etc., or revert to utilizing semi-passive anti-tank weapons such as mines and traps. With these restrictions the effectiveness of the guerrilla movement will be correspondingly reduced.

Among the anti-tank weapons listed in Table IV, we find essentially two categories. One category includes individual weapons with an effective range of less than 200 meters. The other category includes crew-served weapons fired from mounts and with much longer range.

The former category is not particularly useful to guerrillas. The reason is their extremely short range which compels the users to come to very close contact with the enemy. Only in situations where the guerrillas may encounter a few isolated armored vehicles can such weapons be used effectively. In situations where the guerrillas may encounter a substantial armored force (battalion for instance) with only light anti-tank weapons, they will be risking probable annihilation. Therefore, only the US 75mm and 106mm recoilless rifles and the Soviet B-10 and B-11 are recommended weapons for guerrilla use.

Light artillery constitutes one of the most effective weapons which guerrillas can use. But one must consider that the availability of artillery pieces is but one of the many problems associated with the use of artillery by guerrillas. Among the other problems are those of training artillery crews, ammunition availability and resupply, mobility, concealment, and other. The review of past guerrilla conflicts has revealed that when artillery was available to guerrillas its tactical use by them was less than satisfactory. There have been, however, notable exceptions to this which indicate that artillery can be effectively used by guerrillas. One of the exceptions has been in Viet Minh in Indochina.

In considering artillery pieces for guerrilla use, one has to limit them to the pack or mountain type only. The obvious reason is that towed or self-propelled pieces are restricted to movement through roads which the guerrillas are not likely to control. Table V, therefore, lists only pack or mountain artillery, with the exception of one light anti-aircraft gun. Some of the pieces listed are old and obsolete as far as conventional forces are concerned. But this obsolescence does not apply to guerrilla warfare. The age of a weapon is indifferent to guerrillas as long as weapon and ammunition are available and the weapon meets operational requirements.

Among the weapons listed in Table V, the most modern and most effective in terms of range and destructiveness is the Italian M 1956 mountain howitzer. Other countries have adapted this weapon as their standard airborne and field artillery piece. This weapon fires the standard US 105mm ammunition with the exception of zone 7 propellant increment.

The Yugoslav M 1948 in 76.2mm caliber has only slightly shorter range than the Italian gun, but it is much lighter, therefore more mobile. This weapon is an improved version of the Skoda M 1928 and it is reported that the Yugoslavs have exported quantities of it to Asian and African countries.

Of the pack pieces of around 75mm, the US pack howitzer M1A1 is perhaps the best, with the possible exception of the above Yugoslav gun. The US howitzer is light, but the savings in weight have not affected adversely the weapon's stability. It has some drawbacks. The most serious one is the lack of a split trail, which limits its traverse; this, however, is not too much of a disadvantage in such a light weapon. Another drawback is the lack of protective shield. Large quantities of this weapon are available throughout the world, including in communist countries which obtained them through the Red Chinese who captured them from Chiang Kai-Shek's armies in 1948.

Another noteworthy gun is the German LeIG37. This piece can be disassembled into ten loads for backpacking by as many men. This characteristic is important to guerrillas. On the negative side, this gun has low muzzle velocity and very short range.

The Schneider and Skoda guns of both 75 and 105mm and the Swedish L/20 are satisfactory weapons. Although old in design and manufacture, they are available in fairly large quantities in some parts of the world. Schneiders will be found in SE Europe, N. Africa, and the Middle East. Skodas are being used by some of the Soviet satellite armies and elsewhere. The

Swedish L/20 has been exported to several countries including SE Asia.

There are two very light weapons that should be considered by guerrillas. They are the French M906 and the Chicom 70mm howitzers. The importance of these weapons is in their light weight which makes them very mobile in guerrilla applications. But otherwise, they are only slightly better than mortars of around 81mm caliber. The French gun has not been manufactured since before World War II, but it is available in quantity in certain areas. The Chicom howitzer is a copy of an earlier Japanese weapon and both versions have been produced in quantity and are available in the Far East.

Some of the less desirable weapons are the Soviet 76.2mm mountain howitzer which is too heavy for guerrilla use, the British 3.7 inch mountain howitzer which is too heavy and ballistically unsatisfactory, and the Japanese type 94 which is not stable enough in firing.

Anti-aircraft artillery are primarily defensive weapons to protect static positions. Therefore, the need for anti-aircraft artillery is doubtful. However, in some situations anti-aircraft guns can be used offensively. For example, guerrillas may be able to infiltrate near an air base and engage aircraft during their final approach for landing when they are most vulnerable. Of course, it is necessary that the guerrillas will be able to withdraw quickly before the enemy's countermeasures take effect. But such operations are extremely useful because of the impact they create on the enemy, as the US forces in Viet Nam have experienced. This is why the German M38 is listed in Table V. This weapon can be disassembled for animal transport. It is considerably more effective than heavy machineguns and has been used by several armies throughout the world.

In addition to the weapons which have been listed and discussed, there is a multitude of other types of weapons which can be made available to guerrillas. Among them, the most easily obtainable are pistols, revolvers, and shotguns. Pistols and revolvers are practical only as secondary weapons to be issued to officers, auxiliary troops, and members of crew-served weapons. Shotguns are weapons of last resort, when one can not obtain enough rifles, etc. In addition, their legality according to the International Conventions is in doubt.

Submachineguns constitute another category of weapons which the guerrillas can use. In World War II they became very popular among guerrillas. However, they are prestige weapons mostly, not very practical in situations where close contact is not desired.

Resourcefulness, imagination, and technical expertise can find substitutes for several conventional weapons. Explosive devices, mines, traps, crude anti-tank weapons, etc. can be literally home-made or fabricated in elementary shops. Obtaining raw materials for these is some times difficult, but by no means impossible. This is particularly true in countries of advanced industrial development and in mining areas. There is no practical way that security forces can control the supply or traffic of basic materials from which such weapons can be fabricated. But it is doubtful that serious guerrilla warfare can be waged depending entirely, or to a great extent, on the availability of such devices.

In considering weapons which can be used practically by guerrillas one should not exclude some of the later, more sophisticated weapons. These would include anti-tank rockets fired without tubes such as the French SS series and the German Cobra. They can be adapted to guerrilla use. Rockets such as the Soviet 122mm have also been used by guerrillas effectively. The conventional parent weapon of this rocket is a 16-tube assembly with a very heavy mount. Guerrillas in South Viet Nam have utilized single tubes, thus bypassing the weight problem. This type of weapon is no substitute for artillery because it lacks the accuracy and range of artillery. But it does fire a very lethal projectile with high dispersion on burst; therefore its effectiveness when used against massed materiel is great.

After reviewing the information presented above, one must conclude that a variety of weapons exists which are technically suitable for guerrilla application. This is particularly true in the area of basic weapons such as rifles and machineguns. There are however, some deficiencies in anti-tank weapons, mortars and/or light artillery.

Keeping this in mind, the next conclusion has to be that equipping a guerrilla force with appropriate weapons would not present a problem if the guerrillas have the overt or covert support of any conventional military establishment. Guerrillas without this kind of support will have to overcome the problem of weapons availability, but they too can obtain or make primitive weapons and explosive devices which will have at least nuisance value.

A country with the necessary resources, such as the United States, should consider the advisability of developing new weapons specifically suited for guerrilla operations. Again the point must be stressed that a balanced effort has to be made in developing new weapons. If the thesis is accepted that a future major war will be primarily a nuclear or conventional conflict in which guerrilla warfare will play a supporting role, a determination needs to be made as to how much of the available resources should be utilized towards the development of weapons for guerrilla applications in relation to the overall effort. Under no circumstances should resources be allocated to guerrilla development at the expense or neglect of conventional and nuclear defenses.

However, once this determination is made, the resources which may be allocated to the guerrilla effort should be utilized to close the gaps which we identified above as existing in certain areas of armaments. Consequently, the effort should be exerted in the following specific areas.

Anti-tank weapons. We have seen that the guerrillas' operational capabilities are restricted by the availability of armor among the enemy. The guerrillas need, therefore, a weapon which will enable them to effectively engage at least lesser armored units. Such a weapon should be able to destroy targets beyond the effective range of enemy small arms. This means that the guerrilla anti-tank weapon should have an effective range of around 1500 meters. At this range, the armor penetration should be about 100mm (approximately 4 inches) which appears to be the practical armor thickness of present and future medium tanks. In addition, the weapon should be light and uncomplicated from the operator's point of view. Probably, the above objectives can best be achieved by a rocket-type anti-tank weapon with a very simple launcher. Developing such weapon is not easy, but by no means impossible. The biggest problem will be the one of guidance system because line-of-sight aiming is not desirable in situations that the guerrillas encounter. Figure 14 shows a possible method of how this kind of weapon could work. The rocket is launched in the general direction of the target from the simple launcher and is propelled by some kind of solid propellant. At near the peak of its trajectory, the guidance system is energized and directs the projectile to the target. The guidance system could operate on an infra-red seeking, magnetic, or radiowave principle. This kind of guidance system must be very sensitive, therefore, very costly to develop. But this system would have many advantages. It would give the guerrillas the ability to engage armor from favorable distances and can be effective against moving targets. It presupposes the absence of friendly armor units in the vicinity. Each rocket with guidance and warhead could weigh as low as 25 lbs. If the launcher is maintained simple enough, its weight could be around 10 lbs. Since the system would not provide a separate ground target acquisition and control device, the above weights are practical for effective utilization by guerrillas.

Mortar. What is desired for guerrilla operations, is improvement in the 81mm mortar so that its effective range can increase to around 5000 meters and its weight reduced to 75 lbs. In addition, the mortar should be disassembable into three approximately equal lands so that it can be carried by the normal crew of three men. The stability problems created by the weight reduction can be overcome with the incorporation of a muzzle brake or similar device. Corresponding effort would be made to reduce the weight of each round to about 5 lbs. This will be somewhat difficult in view of the increased range requirements, but not impossible in view of the continuous advances in the state of the art.

Artillery. It is desirable to develop a pack howitzer of about 600 lbs weight. This piece should be disassembable into three loads of 200 lbs each. In this manner it can be packed on three animals, or three dog sleds, or if necessary it can be ported on three litters with a team of two or four men carrying each litter. If motor transport is available, this piece could be loaded on the vehicle instead of being towed, thus eliminating the requirement and weight of carriage and wheels. The design should be such that, when firing, three of the crew members can sit on it so that the weight of the men will help stabilize the piece. The desirable range is 9000 meters. The caliber should not be less than 75mm with provisions for firing supercaliber projectiles at reduced range. Ammunition weight should be minimized and serious consideration should be given to developing a consummable cartridge.

Night vision devices. A definite requirement will exist to develop devices which give the guerrillas improved night vision. Such devices should be light enough to be mounted on rifles and other small arms and have a range equal to the effective range of each weapon. When such devices become available, the ability of the guerrillas to engage the enemy when he is vulnerable is increased drastically. This is a relatively new technological field, but significant advances can be expected within the next few years.

So far we have discussed only ordnance materiel. However, military operations require many other kinds of equipment. Generally speaking the other kinds of equipment fall into three broad categories: communications (signal) equipment, quartermaster supplies, and medical equipment.

In any future conflict signal equipment will be nearly as important as the weapons themselves. In guerrilla warfare signal equipment are required for communication among the various guerrilla units and between the guerrillas and extrinsic points; i.e. friendly groups located outside the area of guerrilla activity. In guerrilla warfare communications are particularly critical just prior to and during combat.

Of the signal equipment available in conventional military establishments, the most suitable ones for guerrilla operations are portable AM radios such as the AN/PRC-10 set. Future improvements in this type of equipment should be oriented towards weight and cubage reduction, increased range, and improved reliability and maintainability. The disadvantages of radio equipment include vulnerability to interception, jamming, and localization of the transmitters by the enemy. These disadvantages are not easily overcome. Interception can be off-set by encoding the messages. However, encoding requires de-coding by the receiver and this is time consuming. The effects of jamming can be neutralized technically if one is willing to pay the necessary penalties in weight increases and equipment complexity. Localization of the guerrilla transmitters by the enemy is something that has to be taken for granted in view of the enemy's probable superiority in technical resources. Local-ization will result in ground or air attacks of the transmitter area. To minimize this danger, the guerrillas must limit the duration of transmission and frequently change transmission sites.

Wire communications can not be utilized by guerrillas unless they control the area over which the wire runs. This situation does not prevail in guerrilla operations. Limited use of field telephones, however, can be expected. There will be situations where the guerrillas can establish temporary control over a small area. For example, an area between an observation post and a heavy weapons element, providing that they are both located at an appropriate distance from the targets and forward guerrilla elements.

When there is a shortage of available radios and telephones, communications can be accomplished through the use of pyro-technics (such as flair pistols) and messengers. These media, however, restrict the scope of communications and are time-consuming. Another alternative is to infiltrate existing com-mercial facilities such as the public telephone network. This probably can be successfully done for routine communications, but it is doubtful that it can be helpful in actual combat. Mes-sage drops by aircraft can be utilized if the guerrillas are being supported by friendly conventional forces. This type of com-munications is particularly useful for communications btween the guerrillas and the extrinsic points.

Among the Quartermaster equipment, clothing and footwear are most important to the guerrillas. There will be situations, however, when the problem of availability of clothing may be overshadowed by the necessity of using civilian clothing iden-tical with what the natives of the area wear. This is the case in

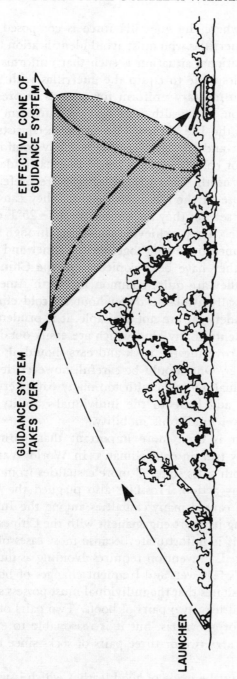

Figure 14. Artist's conception of anti-tank weapon.

situations where the guerrilla force is composed of covert or part time guerrillas who must avoid identification by the enemy. If the operational situation is such that uniforms can be used, then it is desirable to equip the guerrillas with some kind of a utilitarian military uniform for reasons of prestige, morale, identification, and health. The best such uniform is the fatigue uniform of the U.S. Army. This uniform consists, basically of cotton shirt and trousers. It can be fairly comfortable in hot weather. For cold weather, a set of thermal underwear can be worn underneath. Thermal underwear are preferable to overcoats because of their lighter weight. They can weigh about 1½ lbs per set, yet they are protective at $-25°F$ or even lower temperature. They achieve insulation through multiple air pockets formed by sewing together the inner and outer fabrics. Probably, they have been copied from the Chinese uniforms. Although they are quite common in North America, they are not universally available throughout all cold climates. Where thermal underwear are not available, it is prudent to use wool outer garments of any kind which are easily obtainable. Gloves and hoods covering the neck and ears should also be issued in cold weather. One should be careful, however, lest he burdens the individual guerrilla with too many paraphernalia of clothing which add little to the individual's ability to resist the elements, yet hinder his mobility.

Footwear is even more important than garments. This is particularly true in cold climates. In World War II, many armies on both sides suffered more casualties from frostbite than from enemy action. Frostbite also plagued the U.S. Army in Korea and caused many casualties among the Indian Army in 1962 during its short engagement with the Chinese in the Himalayas. This is unfortunate because most cases of frostbite can be prevented. Prevention requires avoiding as much as possible to get one's feet wet, and frequent changes of boots and socks. This necessitates that the individual must possess several pairs of socks and at least two pairs of boots. Two pairs of boots may be a luxury for guerrillas, but it is reasonable to expect them to have and carry two or three pairs of socks since their weight is negligible.

Boots must be made of good leather which is water repellant.

Figure 15. Artist's conception of light artillery piece and crew.

They must be high enough to provide support for the ankles and have soles with deep treads. Socks should be thick and made of either cotton or wool.

Among the medical equipment predominant place have the litters for the evacuation of casualties. Fortunately, they can be easily made locally, using readily obtainable materials. Next come surgical equipment and medicines which also should be obtainable from indigenous sources unless the area in which operations are projected is very underdeveloped.

2. Logistic Support

Besides the acquisition of materiel, the guerrilla staff planners should be concerned with all other aspects of logistics support.

Logistics operations include all phases of the cycle of getting war materiel to the user (guerrillas) from the source of supply. Between the source and the user a multitude of functions have to take place. In conventional operations this process is very complex. In guerrilla operations this process must remain relatively simple, but it is still a requirement which cannot be ignored. In other words, simple acquisition of the weapons and other material is not enough. The weapons and other material have to be delivered to the user and the delivery must be made in a timely and safe manner. The logistics cycle, therefore, includes in addition to acquisition, the processes of transport, storage, and issue to the user.

For ammunition, food rations, fuel, fodder, and other consumables the end of the cycle occurs with the issue to the user. For non-consumable items the cycle continues. A retrograde movement becomes necessary to locations where repair or refurbishing of the non-consumable items can take place.

In planning guerrilla operations all this has to be considered in detail. The logistics of guerrilla warfare are very much simplified if most consumable items can be obtained from indigenous sources. This shortens the logistics pipeline, but it creates other problems. For example, let us consider food rations. If they are to be obtained from indigenous sources, the plan has to analyze the quantities of food available to the local population, their attitude towards the guerrillas, the extent of enemy control over the population, and whether acquisition will be made through requisitioning in the form of taxation or purchase. In any case, it should not impose unnecessary hardship on the local population, otherwise they will turn against the guerrilla movement even if they were initially sympathetic towards it. This is a good example of how the logistics of guerrilla warfare can affect psychological operations and ideological attitudes.

Among consumable items, ammunition of all kinds are very critical. Ammunition has usually been in chronic shortage in past guerrilla conflicts. Conversely, oversupply of ammunition creates other problems among guerrillas. Guerrilla units should not carry more ammunition than that required for a given operation plus a predetermined extra amount for emergencies. Attempting to carry the surplus ammunition will result in serious impediment of the unit's mobility. Surplus ammunition, therefore, requires storage, which is another of the multiple aspects of logistics planning and support. One partial solution to the problem of ammunition shortage is to reclaim used cartridges

TABLE I
RIFLES AND CARBINES

WEAPON	CALIBER	OPERATION*	WT LOADED (lbs)	EFFECTIVE RANGE (Met)	RATE OF FIRE (rpm) (Man or Semi-Auto)	RATE OF FIRE (rpm) (Auto)	MUZZLE VELOCITY w/STD AMMO (fps)
US M16	5.56mm	Gas Selective	7.6	460	45-65	150-200	3150
Jap Mod 38	6.5mm	Bolt	9.25	400	15		2400
Mannlicher-Schönauer	6.5mm	Bolt	7.5	500	15		2400
Italian Carcano	6.5mm	Bolt	7.5	400	15		2200
US M1903	30	Bolt	8.75	500	15		2700
US M1	30	Gas Semi-Auto	9.6	500	40		2700
UK SMLE No. 4	303	Bolt	8.9	500	15		2440
FN (NATO)	7.62mm (NATO)	Gas Selective	10	500	40	100	2800
UK L1A1	7.62mm (NATO)	Gas Semi-Auto	10.5	500	40		2800
French M1949	7.5mm	Gas Semi-Auto	10.4	500	30		2700
Soviet M1891/30	7.62mm rimmed	Bolt	10.2	500	10		2660
Soviet SKS	7.62mm rimless	Gas Semi-Auto	8.8	400	35		2411
Soviet AK47	7.62mm rimless	Gas Selective	10.6	400 Semi 300 Auto	40	90	2329
US M14E2	7.62mm (NATO)	Gas Selective	14.5	460-700²	15-40¹	20-60¹	2800
US M1 Carbine	30	Gas Semi-Auto	6	300	40		800
Mauser K98	7.92mm	Bolt	9	600	15		2564
German G-3	7.62mm (NATO)	Blowback Selective	10.25	500	45	120	2800
French M1892	8mm	Bolt	6.8	400	10		2080

* Selective means Semi-Automatic or Automatic.
1 Max rate during first 2 minutes of operation; progressively diminishing afterwards.
2 700m in Semi-Auto Mode with bipod; 460m in Auto with bipod; considerably less without bipod.

TABLE II

AUTOMATIC RIFLES AND MACHINE GUNS

WEAPON	CALIBER	OPERATION	FEED	WT LOAD. (lbs)	WT MNT. (lbs)	EFFECTIVE RANGE (Meters)	RATE OF FIRE (Semi) (rpm)	RATE OF FIRE (Auto) (rpm)	MUZZLE VELOCITY (fps)
US Browning AR	30	Gas Auto only	Magazine	21.5		800		100	2680
US M1919 A6	30	Recoil Auto only	Belt	32.5	14	800		150–200	2680
US M1919 A4	30	Recoil Auto only	Belt	31	14	1000		150–200	2800
US M60	7.62 NATO	Gas Auto only	Belt	23.6	51	1000		125–550	2800
Soviet SGM	7.62mm	Gas Auto only	Belt	29.8		1000		250	2756
Soviet RP-46	7.62mm	Gas Auto only	Belt	28.7		800		230–250	2756
UK Bren	303	Gas Selective	Magazine	24.9		800	25–60	110	2440
UK Vickers	303	Gas, Water cooled Auto only	Belt	41	50	1000		200–300	2440
German MG34	7.92mm	Recoil & Gas Selective	Belt	26.4		800	45	100–120*	2564
Czech M26	7.92mm	Gas Selective	Magazine	21.3		800	40	180–200	2564
US M2	50	Recoil Auto only	Belt	84	44	1000		120	2660

* Practical rate; it can exceed 1000 rpm in a/a configuration.

TABLE III
MORTARS

WEAPON	CALIBER (mm)	WEIGHT (lbs)	NO. OF LOADS*	STD MUZZLE VELOCITY (met/sec)	MAXIMUM RANGE (meters)	RATE OF FIRE (rpm)
UK 2 inch1	50	20		80	490	8
US 60 mm M2	60	42		158	1820	20-35
Stokes-Brandt M1935	60	39		158	1530	20-35
UK 3 inch	76	133		192	2560	10
US 81mm M1	81	132		235	3018	18-30
Soviet 82mm M1937	82	123		210	3040	25
US 4.2 inch M2	107	330	2	256	4020	20
Soviet 107 M1938	107	375	2	302	6300	15
Soviet 120mm M19432	120	606	3	272	5700	15
French M19513	120	705		290	6700	10
Yugoslav UB M52	120	853	5	300	6300	25
Czech 120	120	732	5		6600	10

* No. of pack loads for animal transport
1 This Weapon is trigger-fired.
2 Its traveling weight is 1100 lbs.
3 Its traveling weight is 1168 lbs.

TABLE IV
ANTI-TANK WEAPONS

WEAPON	CALIBER (mm)	WT W/O MOUNT (lbs)	WEIGHT OF MOUNT (lbs)	STD MUZZLE VEL (met/sec)	EFFECTIVE RANGE (met)	RATE OF FIRE (rpm)	ARMOR PENETRATION
Chicom A/T Grenade Launcher	40	6.3		84	100	4–6	6" @ 0°
Czech A/T Grenade Launcher	Tube 45 Grenade 120	14		140	100	4	6" @ 0°
US RR M18A1	57	40		365	4500*	15	3.4" @ 0°
US RR M20	75	11.5	55.5	428	6565*	10	3.6 @ 0°
Soviet RR B10	82	20	148	320	4470	6	7.8 @ 0°
US Rocket Launcher 3.5" M20	87	13		147	183	10	10.75" @ 0°
US RR	106						
Soviet RR B11	107	172	500	400	6650	5	15" @ 0°

*Maximum range

TABLE V
ARTILLERY

WEAPON	CALIBER (mm)	WEIGHT (lbs)	NO. OF LOADS	ELEVATION	TRAVERSE	STD MUZZLE VELOCITY (met/sec)	MAX HORIZ RANGE (met)	ARMOR PENETRATION	RATE OF FIRE (rpm)
German M38	20	1630	6	+90° / -20°	360°	900	48001	2.5" @ 0°	200
French M1906	65	520	3	+70° / -10°	5°	200	2750	3" @ 0°	9
Chicom Howitzer	70	468	3	+70° / -11°	45°	200	2800	3" @ 0°	4–6
US Pack Howitzer	75	1270	8–92	+45° / -5°	6°	380	8790	3" @ 0°	16
French 75/19	75	1500	8	+45° / -5°	6°	350	8000		12
Skoda M28	75	1400	8	+45° / -5°	5°	350	8000		15
Swedish L/20	75	1753	8	+50° / -10°	5°	400	9200		12
Jap Type 94	75	1182	6	+45° / -10°	40°	386	8230	2.8" @ 0°	10–12
Rhinemetal LE 1G37	75	880	6–103		45°	275	4000	2.75m	8–12
Yugoslav M1948	76.2	1543	8	+50° / -15°	50°	420	9000	4" @ 0°	20
Soviet Mtn Howitzer	76.2	17314	10	+37°	54°	600	8500	3" @ 0°	15
British Mtn Howitzer 3.7"	94	1856	6	+45° / -5°	5°	300	5400		8–10
Skoda 105	105	2250	12	+45° / -5°	5°	275	9000		2–3
French 105/19	105	2450	12	+45° / -5°	6°	280	9300		2–3
Italian M1956	105	2888	11	+65° / -5°	56°	420	10200	4.6" @ 0°	3

1 Effective A/A range is 2200 meters.
2 Pack loads: 8; Airdrop loads: 9
3 Animal loads: 6; Backpack loads: 10
4 Its traveling weight is 3108 lbs.

and reload them in clandestine shops. This is a fairly simple operation for small arms ammunition, but considerably more complex for the ammunition of heavier weapons. Reloading ammunition will require setting up clandestine shops and a retrograde movement of the used cartridges to the shops. The prevailing conditions may force a decision against this kind of solution because of the disadvantages of retrograde movements.

Even though it is unrealistic to expect complete elimination of retrograde movements of supplies, it can be safely stated that keeping the number of items requiring retrograde movement to the minimum will be highly desirable. Cost effectiveness, in this case, is not a consideration. In fact, in guerrilla logistics, cost effectiveness is considered after the subjects of availability and security. To illustrate this point let us consider the supply of storage batteries for radios in a situation represented in the sketch of Figure 16.

In this sketch A represents the source, which can be either in-country or at some extrinsic location; B represents the user, in this case a guerrilla unit; and C represents some location between A and B where facilities can be established to recharge the batteries. It may be desirable to eliminate the movement from B to C altogether and furnish, instead, a new battery each time, which will be transported from A to B. This decision would eliminate:

The shops at C

the need to have discharged batteries move from B to C

the need to have recharged batteries move from C to B.

But it will necessitate:

movements of empty conveyances from B to A

additional movements of loaded conveyances from A to B.

The factors influencing the tradeoffs are the availability of new batteries from A, the frequency of necessary movements between locations, the availability of conveyances, the extent of enemy control over routes A B and B C, etc. The decision cannot really be spelled out here. It is more important to point out that problems such as this have to be considered in detail as part of the overall planning for guerrilla warfare.

Other elements of logistics support are those of transportation and storage. Transportation may involve two basic legs.

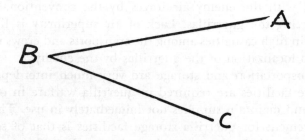

Figure 16. Problems with retrograde movements of supplies.

One leg from some extrinsic source to an initial point in-country and a second leg from that point to the user. Problems usually associated with transportation in guerrilla warfare include the availability of conveyances and the maintenance of security during the in-country movement. The optimum solution to the transportation problem is to infiltrate the existing transportation network and use it to serve the guerrillas' purpose. This in many situations will not be possible either because of the extent of the enemy's control of transportation facilities or because of limitations on the network's capacity. In such a case, the guerrillas will have to organize their own transportation system and expend resources for this objective. The ever-present problem in such cases is that the enemy in all probability controls or maintains effective surveillance over all public roads. This fact restricts the guerrillas' ability to use motor vehicles. Then, transportation has to be organized over cross-country routes using pack animals or human porters. Solving the problem of transportation, thus ensuring relatively unrestricted flow of supplies and replacements, will constitute a big step towards the success of a guerrilla movement. Examples of this have been presented by the Viet Minh and the Viet Cong.

If the guerrillas are being supported by conventional forces, the problems of supply transportation can be drastically reduced through the use of aerial deliveries. Such deliveries can be made very close to the user, thus bypassing intermediate points. Aerial delivery techniques have improved substantially since World War II. However, effective utilization of this method for bringing supplies to the guerrillas requires air superiority, or at least parity, with the enemy air forces by the conventional forces supporting the guerrillas. Lack of air superiority is likely to result in high casualties among the transports and crews in addition to localization of the guerrillas by the enemy.

Transportation and storage are very much interdependent. Storage facilities are required in guerrilla warfare in order to store and maintain supplies not immediately in use. The basic requirement for guerrilla storage facilities is that of security. However, it is by no means the only one. In addition, storage facilities must be within reasonable proximity to the user, accessible to the transportation media available to guerrillas, and reasonably weatherproof.

If the guerrillas have managed to establish an in-country guerrilla base; i.e. they have a remote part of the country under their control, they will be prone to establish storage facilities within that base. Thus, the requirement for security appears to have been taken care of. This is not necessarily so. Guerrilla bases are subject to air strikes by the enemy and also to occasional assaults by enemy ground troops. When an enemy ground operation against the guerrilla base takes place, the guerrillas must not fight statically, but withdraw, otherwise they accept the risk of probable defeat in detail by a superior enemy. In withdrawing, the guerrillas will probably be unable to evacuate their storage facilities and their supplies will be lost. Since we can assume that as a rule the guerrillas are not oversupplied with materiel, such a loss of concentrated supplies could be catastrophic for a guerrilla force, or at least negate its ability for offensive action for several months.

It is far better for the guerrillas to disperse their supplies by establishing underground storage facilities among their collaborators and sympathizers. The risk here is that some of them will be discovered by the enemy security forces, the supplies will be lost, and the custodians will be compromised and subjected to reprisals by the enemy. The decision to accept this risk, or not is another responsibility of the guerrilla commanders. If this risk is not taken, then the only other solution is to utilize unused or little-used buildings. Abandoned buildings of all kinds, including barns, specially constructed cabins in forests, and natural or artificial caves are suitable for this purpose.

Once the decision of location has been made, the methods of preservation and retrieval of supplies can be worked out.

What we hope to have accomplished with this discussion is to show that logistics planning should be an integral part of the overall guerrilla plan.

3. Organization of Guerrilla Units

Military organization and order of battle are not novel ideas, but have been in existence since prehistoric times. The earliest combatants, no doubt, just fought each other in packs like animals without leaders and without organization. Before long, however, the human animal, with its superior intelligence, understood that when two or more members of the species get together for the purpose of conducting a joint venture (in this case combat), one of them must be acknowledged as the leader of the others in order to direct and coordinate their efforts. The strongest of the members was the leader at first. As time went by, intelligence and experience replaced physical strength as requirements for leadership. The leader was identified as chief, prince, king, or other linguistic equivalent with the same meaning.

As the size of the pack increased, particularly, when two or more packs (or hunting parties, families, tribes, etc.) allied themselves against a common enemy, one or more subchiefs, or chiefs of lesser rank were chosen or appointed in order to assist the big chief in controlling the group. At first the subchiefs were merely assisting the chief. Later, the subchiefs actually directed the activities of a segment of the group. When this took place we had, in essence, the beginning of military organization. Homer tells us in the Illiad that when the Greeks assembled for the Trojan War, each Greek tribe had its own King whom it obeyed in battle. The individual kings were subordinate to Agamemnon, the big king, who was chosen "strategos", i.e. general or commander-in-chief because he was the king of the most numerous and prosperous of the Greek tribes.

The Illiad, however, is not a Historical document. The earliest record of military organization that we are aware of appears in Xenophon's account of the insurrection of the Persian prince Cyrus against his brother King Artaxerxes. Cyrus employed Greek mercenaries and Xenophon describes how the Greeks were organized into ἴλας and τάξεις. These formations appear to correspond roughly to troops of cavalry (ἴλη) and battalions of infantry (τάξις).

Since Xenophon's days, military organizational developments appear to tie-in with the general commercial, industrial, and intellectual development of societies. Thus, primitive African, Australian, Asiatic, and until a couple of generations ago, American Indian tribes have not advanced beyond the state of chiefs and subchiefs. Among the Europeans, however, military organization has evolved through various stages into the complexity of present-day formations.

It appears that the following three factors have influenced military organization: mission, geography, and material means available. This is why the Romans developed the organization of the legion, a self-sustained unit of combined arms (infantry and cavalry) capable of fighting independently at the far-off frontiers of their empire. In the Middle Ages, the feudal setup of society promoted the creation of territorial units recruited among the peasants of each region. This influence is still quite predominant among the World's armies today.[2] In the last two centuries the technological advances are influencing the development of military organizations more than the other two factors.

The above discussion is, perhaps, of only casual interest to one who is concerned with the organizational structure and composition of guerrilla units. We believe, however, that it is useful because it points out the fact that the purpose of military organization is to facilitate the optimum effectiveness of the military units in combat. This is, therefore, the thought that one must maintain when he attempts to establish the equivalent of a table of organization for guerrilla units. It is obvious then, that the organization of a conventional unit is not necessarily applicable to a similar guerrilla unit. If we analyze the three factors influencing the composition of military formations — mission, geography, and resources, we will conclude that substantial differences exist between the affects of these factors on the two types of units (conventional and guerrilla) .

Let us consider the mission first. The mission of conventional formations is, in general, to overcome the enemy with superior firepower and mobility in conventional engagements. The mission of guerrilla formations should be to strike the enemy when least expected and then disengage and disperse. There is a certain similarity in both missions in the idea that the immediate objective is to overcome the engaged enemy unit; but here the similarity ends. Whereas the conventional formation is expected to follow through his anticipated victory with pursuit of the enemy and possession of the battlefield, the guerrilla unit is not likely to pursue the enemy and is definitely not going to remain on the battlefield. When not engaged in active combat, the conventional unit is not hiding from the enemy, although it may be concealing its exact position and movements. But the guerrilla unit, when not engaging the enemy is literally trying to give the impression that it does not really exist. These differences necessitate that, above all, the guerrilla unit's organization is such that it assures flexibility. Flexibility to engage different kinds of targets, to facilitate its assembly and movement, and to insure its security through withdrawal and dispersal. In other words, flexibility to cope with all those characteristics of guerrilla tactics which we have discussed in previous chapters.

Geography and climatic conditions are influencing the composition of conventional formations to a lesser degree than the other two factors. A few of the world's major armies today include large units (division and above) which are specifically intended for deployment in one kind of terrain only.[3] It appears that most armies today are sacrificing this geographic specialization for the benefit of standardization. The argument in favor of this approach is based on the fact that a unit specialized for warfare on one kind of terrain only loses a great amount of its effectiveness if employed on terrain of a different kind. The general staffs of these armies have, therefore, found it more practical not to indulge in this kind of specialization.[4] The guerrillas, however, are not confronted with this problem of employment on different types of terrain. Indigenous guerrilla units organized in Yugoslavia are not likely to be required 'to operate in the African desert or the jungles of Malay. Specialization according to geographic conditions is therefore a prudent decision in organizing guerrilla units.

The last factor is the one of material means available. In this area the widest differences exist between conventional and guerrilla formations. Conventional armies have at their disposal all the material resources of their respective governments. Guerrillas, however, have only limited material means. It becomes imperative, therefore, for the guerrillas to organize in a manner which insures the maximum utilization of whatever materiel is available. This is perhaps the most important single factor that one must consider when organizing a guerrilla unit.

The conclusion of the above discussion has to be that in order to achieve the optimum effectiveness of guerrillas the conventional organization must be disregarded and the guerrilla units must have an entirely different organizational structure. This may become a difficult undertaking if we assume that the individuals who may be charged with such responsibility are products of a conventional military establishment and, therefore, conditioned to think in terms of squads, platoons, companies, battalions, etc. Yet, it is imperative for those individuals to extricate themselves from this type of thinking. Guerrilla organization can then proceed, retaining in perspective the following principles which have been developed by the analysis of the factors of mission, geography, and material available:

1. The guerrilla units must be organized in a manner that assures tactical flexibility.

2. The guerrilla units must have special composition which takes advantage of the prevailing geographic and climatic conditions.

3. The organization of the guerrilla units must facilitate the maximum utilization of available materiel.

In the following paragraphs we will describe a purely hypothetical guerrilla organization for the purpose of demonstrating how the above-discussed principles could be applied. The reader must remember, however, that this organization is hypothetical; it could be applied partially or in its entirety under some conditions in a real guerrilla situation, but it is not recommended as the optimum guerrilla organization by any means. Different situations will require different solutions to the problem of guerrilla organization. Remember that one of the principles of organizing guerrilla units is flexibility.

We will start from the lowest units and proceed to the higher. This is because guerrilla bands are usually developed in this manner, from the roots up so to speak.

The elementary unit in conventional armies is the squad. This unit is also applicable in guerrilla formations although, as we shall see, its composition will differ from similar conventional units. In order to depart further from the conventional mentality we may choose a different term for the squad; we may decide to call this unit a "team". Changing the labeling of units by itself, however, will not accomplish the purpose of establishing a purely guerrilla organization. We could, therefore, continue to use identical terms with the conventional armies in order to identify similar units as long as we do not confuse the composition, functions, and capabilities of each.

In guerrilla applications there should be basically three types of squads. Rifle squads, support weapons squads, and support services squads.

A rifle squad should be composed of four to ten men. The exact number will depend on the number of guerrillas qualified as NCO's, the size to the next higher units, the equipment available, and numerous other factors. If squads are normally expected to be employed separately, in general, the number of guerrillas should be closer to ten. If squads are normally expected to act as subordinate elements to higher units, the number of guerrillas in the squad can be closer to the lower limit, thus giving the commander of the higher unit greater flexibility in his deployment and control of his unit. The number of guerrillas in the squad may vary from time to time in order to adjust to changing situations. All members of the rifle squad should be armed with rifles of the same caliber. If there is a shortage of rifles, shotguns may be substituted, but their number should remain as low as possible unless the terrain favors the use of shotguns (jungle). If available, one automatic rifle should be included with each squad. Since effective use of automatic rifles may require two men for each — one automatic rifleman and an assistant to carry the extra ammunition, rifle squads equipped with automatic rifles should be composed of a minimum of five men. If the number of automatic rifles available is insufficient to equip all rifle squads, such weapons should be allocated one each to every other, or every third squad, or whatever the ratio may be.

Support weapons squads should be organized around a specific support weapon. Thus, we would have machinegun squads, mortar squads, anti-tank squads, demolition squads, etc. The number of guerrillas in each of these squads would be equal to the number of men necessary to crew each weapon, plus one squad leader. This would normally mean from four to eight guerrillas. In the case of light mortars and light anti-tank weapons (bazookas), two such weapons instead of one should be included in the composition of the squad. The number of rifles allocated to the support weapons squads should be limited to one or two per squad. In this manner, the available rifles are conserved and utilized for the formation of extra rifle squads. This is prudent because members of crew-served weapons teams need personal weapons only as secondary armament for security purposes and very special situations. If available, therefore, the members of the weapons squads should be issued pistols, revolvers, and submachineguns. The submachineguns should be issued to the squad leaders, preferably.

The support services squads include those organized to operate signal devices, transportation media, supply, etc. They should be composed of one squad leader and ten to fifteen specialists. Their equipment will vary with their missions. Signal squads will include radio transmitter-receiver sets; transport squads may include five to ten vehicles or ten to twenty animals; medical evacuation squads may include six to ten stretchers. Except for the medical squads, the others should be allocated some weapons for security. If these service units are not given any weapons for self-protection, the burden of their protection will fall on the rifle squads and during combat a number of them will have to be assigned this mission, thus taken away from the effort against the main objective. The service squads should, therefore, be issued a number of small arms; the amount and kind will depend on what is available.

The next higher echelon to the squad should be the company. Between six and twelve squads should be included in each company. Of these $\frac{1}{3}$ to $\frac{1}{4}$ should be support weapons squads and the remaining rifle squads. In addition, a small company headquarters should be established which should include the company commander and a minimum of personnel to assist him in the administration and command of the company.

It is obvious here that the platoon echelon, which exists in conventional formations, is being omitted. This is done in order to insure flexibility. In the company headquarters can be attached two or three lieutenants. The lieutenants can lead in combat a varied number of squads depending on the company's missions. Thus, if the company is assaulting, for instance, two adjacent targets of unequal strength, three squads under one lieutenant can be used against the weaker target while the remaining seven (if the company includes ten squads altogether) under the company commander can assault the prime target. By not having platoons of standard composition, the company commander would be free to establish the size and strength of its subordinate task teams without any restrictions imposed by the existence of standard-sized platoons. When not engaged in actual combat the lieutenants, since they are assigned to company headquarters, could be assisting in the company administration. In this manner, the company commander will be given the opportunity to establish a more direct and personal command relationship between himself and the troops and the junior officers will be given the opportunity to serve an apprenticeship and gather experience under the direct supervision of a more senior officer.

In addition to the above-described companies, which are in essence rifle companies, other types of companies could be formed which would be support weapons companies, artillery batteries perhaps, and support services companies. The exact composition of these units will depend on the materiel available and the prevailing terrain conditions. More will be said about the composition of these special units under the discussion of the composition of the higher-echelon units.

The guerrilla companies should be grouped into regiments. Here again we omit the battalion echelon which exists in con-

ventional armies. A regiment should include not more than
twelve companies, two or three of which would be heavy
weapons companies. A regimental headquarters would also be
established to perform the necessary functions of supply, signal,
medical, veterinary, etc.

Two or more companies could be grouped into a battalion
when the tactical need for such a unit exists. Command of the
battalion would be assumed by the senior of the company commanders or by an officer from regimental headquarters who
would be so designated. When the tactical need no longer
exists, the battalion ceases to function as such and the companies will revert to the direct control of the regimental commander. The only exception to this would be made if the territory over which the regiment is active is extended and the
communications media limited so that the regimental commander cannot maintain continuous effective control over all
his companies. In such a case one or even two battalions could
be established on a permanent basis. However, the regimental
commander must keep a number of companies under his direct
control and with these companies he can reinforce his remote
battalions when necessary. This approach is not recommended
for the company echelon; i.e. the permanent establishment of
platoons. The reason is that the company, being a smaller unit,
is not likely to be found in a terrain situation where the company commander is unable to have reasonably good contact
with his subordinate squads.

It may be argued that the span of control for the regimental
and company commanders is entirely too wide. Among some
individuals the idea of one man directly supervising the activities of ten or twelve subordinates is not acceptable. A theory
has been advanced which supports this point of view and asserts that the maximum number of subordinates that one individual can effectively supervise or command is seven. We
fail to see how this magic number seven has been derived. We
believe that the span of control depends to a great extent on
the capabilities of the individual commander. Guerrilla officers
who assume the command of companies and regiments should
be very capable leaders or else they should not be charged with
such responsibility. In any case, the existence of subordinate

officers in the company and regimental headquarters, as has been recommended above, offers a solution to this problem because these officers can act as the commander's deputies and relieve him from the routine functions of command.

If the guerrilla army includes a number of regiments, it is not necessary to have each one of them include the same number of companies. In this manner the flexibility of the guerrilla organization can be further extended. Regiments engaging in frequent activities against the enemy should be reinforced, while regiments not so active could have a reduced number of companies. It would be preferable to have a standard composition among the companies of the various regiments. This concession to standardization at the expense of flexibility could be made, in our opinion, in order to facilitate the logistics of the guerrilla operation. By having standard-size companies, a baseline can be established to facilitate base of issue and estimates of supplies and ammunition consumption.

Two or more guerrilla regiments should be grouped under a guerrilla district headquarters. Although geographic factors should be considered in the assignment of regiments to the guerrilla district, the primary consideration should be the anticipated intensity of guerrilla activity in each district. Regiments should be assigned and withdrawn freely from district to district as the operational situation may necessitate. At the discretion of the district commander, when the number of regiments assigned to the district exceeds four or five and if the tactical situation warrants it, two or more regiments can be grouped into a provisional brigade for the purpose of conducting a specific operation.

In addition to the regiments, the guerrilla district should include, if available, a number of heavy mortar companies and artillery batteries. Whenever such units are available, an artillery headquarters should be established under the district headquarters for the purpose of insuring optimum utilization of these weapons. Heavy mortars (4.2 inch and greater) are not truly artillery pieces, but infantry support weapons. However, in guerrilla units they are more effectively utilized if placed under the control of the artillery headquarters. Besides, they are a more or less satisfactory substitute for short-range artillery and if a shortage of artillery exists among the guerrillas, the heavy mortars can take its place. A heavy mortar company should include four to six mortars. An artillery battery should include four pieces. In addition to the firing pieces, the above units should include a fire direction and observation section and an ammunition resupply section plus the necessary vehicles or animals.

Medium and light mortars, machineguns, and anti-tank weapons should be assigned to the lowest echelon possible consistent with their overall availability in order to insure timely maximum support to the riflemen. These light support weapons could be grouped into separate companies and assigned to the district only if they are in extremely short supply and their allocation to the regiments and companies becomes impractical.

Unlike the guerrilla regiments and companies, the guerrilla district headquarters should have a defined territory of responsibility. This headquarters must be responsible for all guerrilla activity in this territory. The size of the territory will depend on a number of factors such as geographic frontiers (rivers, mountain ranges), normal political subdivisions, population density, road network, enemy dispositions, etc. However, as a rule of thumb we may establish 5000 square miles as a maximum territory which can be effectively controlled by one headquarters. If we assume that to this district there are assigned four guerrilla regiments of about ,800 guerrillas each, plus the artillery and the headquarters personnel we have a total of about 3500 guerrillas. This is a substantial guerrilla force and, if they are moderately active, they should be able to keep two enemy divisions occupied.

The guerrilla district headquarters should be adequately staffed. Again a difference exists here between this headquarters and the headquarters of guerrilla companies and regiments where we recommend that only a minimum of administrative and other noncombat personnel be assigned. The reason is that whereas the lower headquarters are primarily concerned with tactical missions, the district headquarters should be responsible for a multitude of other activities. Among these activities, intelligence and espionage are very important ones. The district headquarters should organize a well-functioning intelligence network independent from the other guerrilla units. The district headquarters should also be charged with the responsibility of maintaining continuous liaison with the underground organization which will be cooperating with the guerrillas. Any military missions from friendly conventional armies should be located at the district headquarters. Finally, all functions of guerrilla supply, recruiting, etc. should be coordinated by the district headquarters.

The next higher echelon in the guerrilla organization should be the area headquarters. This echelon is necessary only when the territory over which the guerrilla activities take place is so great that the number of guerrilla districts is over five or six. The area headquarters is then established to control the activities of two or more districts headquarters. Ordinarily, all tactical units are assigned to the district commands and the area commander does not retain any guerrilla regiments as area reserve. The reason for this is that with the limited mobility equipment available to the guerrillas, it is not possible for such a reserve to react speedily in response to any emergency situation. It is best, therefore, to have all tactical units assigned to the districts and when the need to reinforce a particular district arises, such reinforcements can be obtained by reallocating tactical units from the adjacent districts to the one where reinforcements are required. When this takes place, tactical control of the reallocated units is assumed by the district headquarters in whose territory the tactical units have moved.

The area headquarters should also be adequately staffed and its functions in the nonpurely tactical matters should be similar to the functions of the districts, only in a larger scale.

Finally, the top echelon in the guerrilla organization would be the guerrilla general headquarters. The commander in this headquarters would be responsible for the overall conduct of the guerrilla warfare and would report either to a political authority, if this happens to be a purely indigenous guerrilla movement, or to an allied theater commander.

A guerrilla general headquarters should be established regardless of the numerical strength of the guerrilla movement or the number of subordinate echelons existing in the guerrilla organization. In other words, it is necessary to establish a general headquarters regardless of whether the guerrilla organization includes several thousand men and engulfs an area as large as Ukraine (as was one of the cases in World War II), or includes less than 100 guerrillas in an area of a few thousand square miles (as the case was in Cyprus in the 1950's).

The guerrilla headquarters may or may not be located within the area of guerrilla activity. The Algerian guerrillas, for example, maintained their headquarters in Tunis or Morocco during the greater part of the Algerian War. Locating the headquarters outside the guerrilla territory has the advantage that it ensures its security and facilitates the contacts of the guerrillas with the outside world. On the other hand, locating this headquarters within the guerrilla territory enables the commander to exercise more direct control of guerrilla operations. This decision will depend on the particular conditions and problems facing the guerrilla movement.

The above description of a guerrilla organization must be concluded by reiterating the fact that this is not recommended as a stereotyped guerrilla organization. To recommend such a thing would be as serious a mistake as recommending that a conventional organization should be adopted by the guerrillas. Any organization for future guerrilla operations must be developed to suit the prevailing conditions and not copied out of any particular book.

4. Relations with the Underground Organization

Before we proceed with the discussion of this topic we must define what is an underground organization. A dictionary definition of underground organization would be: "an organization whose activities are not in accordance with the law". Hence, the need for concealment from which the term "underground" comes. In order to narrow down this definition and relate it to the subject of guerrilla warfare, we may say that an underground organization consists of civilians who are in sympathy with the guerrilla objectives and who are organized secretly for the purpose of assisting the guerrillas and/or pursuing the

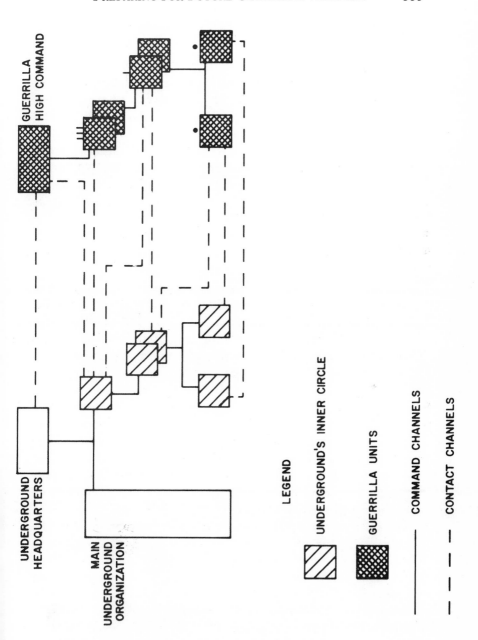

Figure 17. Relationships between guerrillas and supporting underground
organizations.

same strategic or political objectives as the guerrillas by non-military means.

The above statements require amplification and clarification.

The guerrilla organization and the underground organization have a commonality of ultimate objectives. The objectives would be the defeat of the enemy army which occupies the fatherland, or the overthrow of an undesirable domestic regime, etc. Another characteristic which the two organizations share is the fact that they are both operating outside the law. No underground organization can be envisioned within the legal framework; if such is the case, it is not an underground organization, but an overt political group.

The fundamental difference between the two organizations, however, lies in the means by which they are pursuing their common objectives. The guerrillas are attempting to accomplish their objectives through military operations. Any other activities with which the guerrillas may get involved should be incidental to their military operations. The underground organization's activities are nonmilitary. This does not imply that they are necessarily nonviolent. Among the activities of the underground one must include psychological warfare, civil disobedience, intelligence and espionage, sabotage, etc. Obviously, some of these activities may require resorting to violence. And obviously, a certain amount of overlapping will exist between the activities of the guerrillas and the activities of the underground. For instance, both organizations will be preoccupied with the collection of intelligence. Acts of sabotage against the enemy may be carried out by either organization, depending on the circumstances.

In spite of the similarity of the two organizations and the commonality of objectives, it is necessary that they remain two separate organizations and not be integrated. The reason for this is the probability that any attempt to merge the two organizations will result in an overall reduction in military effectiveness. The guerrilla organization will be burdened by numerous nonmilitary personnel, will be distracted by non-military projects, and may find individuals ignorant of military matters occupying positions of responsibility within the hierarchical chain. The two organizations must, therefore, remain separate, but with parallel lines of communications which insure contacts and mutual support at the various echelons. To illustrate this point we can say that the two organizations may operate separately and have their own command channels but in each village or political subdivision there are individuals of the underground who can be contacted by the guerrillas and through them the guerrillas can obtain from the underground information about the enemy, food, lodging, etc. More will be said about the details of such contacts later.

In general, what can the guerrilla organization expect from the underground?

Well, the principal contribution of the underground to the guerrillas and to their common objectives goes beyond the scope of furnishing intelligence and a few supplies. The important thing about the underground is that it provides the psychological link between the guerrillas and the population — the noncombatant inhabitants of the area in which the guerrillas are operating. The importance of this link cannot be overemphasized because, as stated previously, no guerrilla movement can be successful without the active support or, at least, toleration of the local inhabitants. Herein lies the importance of the underground. In fact, underground activities must precede guerrilla activities in any area. The underground organization will conduct a propaganda campaign among the civilians, long before the appearance of any guerrilla bands, for the purpose of establishing a psychological and ideological basis for the development of the guerrilla movement. This effort of mentally conditioning the population by the underground continues after the commencing of guerrilla activities. It should be intensified in any area where the guerrillas have suffered reverses.

In addition to the all-important function of providing a psychological link between the guerrillas and the population, the underground organization can be expected to provide for the guerrillas the following.

Supplies. In particular rations and clothing. Men have to eat in order to live. Where the food will come from can be an acute problem for the guerrillas. In fact it can become an acute problem for any army. Scarcity of food will compel the guerrillas to forage through the countryside or oblige the guerrilla command to resort to requisitioning food from the civilians in the area. Such activities present two quite serious dangers for the guerrillas. One is the fact that security is compromised when foraging or requisitioning parties appear in the countryside. The guerrillas should not disclose their whereabouts, if possible, except in direct connection with a military operation. The second danger to the guerrillas comes from the fact that foraging and requisitioning of food constitutes a sure method to turn the civilians against the guerrillas even if they were at first in sympathy with the guerrilla cause. This will be particularly true if the civilians are improverished farmers, as is the case in most underdeveloped countries of Asia, Africa, and South America. If the guerrillas, therefore, have to subsist off the land, the task of obtaining food should be left to the underground. It is best that the underground obtains food through purchases and then transfers it to the guerrillas. If requisitioning must be resorted to, again it is best that such requisitioning is done through the underground so that the guerrillas do not come in direct contact with the civilians during the requisitioning.

Besides food, clothing, medical supplies, transport, and other such items can be obtained through the underground. In some cases weapons and ammunition can be included in the list, although the guerrillas themselves should be in better position than the underground to obtain these items.

Another function of the underground would be to recruit for the guerrillas. Men of military age and preferably with military experience, would be tapped by the underground for joining the guerrilla units. Possibly, all guerrillas might have been members of the underground organization before joining the military units. In this manner they can be screened for proper ideological orientation, reliability, and ability to withstand the severity of guerrilla life.

The underground organization should be a substantial addition to the guerrilla intelligence network. Since the underground is located in the population centers (towns and villages) whereas the guerrillas would be operating in relatively remote areas, the underground is in better position to observe the enemy. In fact, members of the underground should be in a position to establish contacts with the enemy and infiltrate the enemy organization. This can be done by members of the underground who may find jobs as laborers, servants, or technicians in the enemy installations. Underground members could also establish social contacts with individuals of the enemy army and obtain some information through them. Of particular value are underground members who could establish themselves as waiters, waitresses, or bartenders in places frequented by enemy personnel and who understand the enemy's language. They can pick up a lot of information indirectly by listening to the enemy's conversations. All intelligence collected by the underground should be transmitted to the guerrillas immediately.

Finally, the underground could provide for the guerrillas numerous other auxiliary services such as couriers from one guerrilla unit to another, medical attention for sick or wounded guerrillas, hiding places for guerrillas or their equipment, etc. The conditions prevailing locally will determine the extent of these services and the method of their dissemination.

The structure of the underground organization is of some concern to the guerrillas. Since the underground has the mission of psychologically conditioning the civilians in the area, it will include, by necessity, a relatively large number of members. This necessity stems from the fact that the communications media at the disposal of the organization may be limited. The enemy in all probability controls the press and the radio, the two most expedient media of mass communication. To counter this, the underground may have a radio transmitter located in friendly or neutral territory, but reception would be subject to jamming by the enemy. Locating a radio transmitter secretly within the territory controlled by the enemy is very difficult under present-day conditions because of the numerous means available for localizing such transmitters. The underground's most effective means of communication may be the printed material which can be distributed by members of the underground and local propagandists[5] who circulate among the civilians and spread the ideas of the underground through lectures, discussions, etc. in secret or semi-secret meetings. This kind of operation requires a lot of participating members. For this and certain other reasons, the degree of success in an underground movement is sometimes gauged by the number of members initiated in the underground organization.

It is obvious that the safety of the guerrilla units can be placed in jeopardy if all members of the underground are free to come in contact with the guerrillas during the course of their daily activities. It is necessary, therefore, to separate the underground organization into two branches. One branch should be given the mission of maintaining psychological contacts with the civilians; this is by far the more numerous of the two. The second branch of the underground constitutes an inner circle of members who are highly reliable and experienced in conspiratorial work. These members should be organized separately for the purpose of conducting sensitive operations such as intelligence and espionage, acts of sabotage if needed, and maintaining contact with the guerrillas. The guerrillas need to be concerned only with this inner circle of the underground. (see Figure 17).

The elemenary unit of this select group of the underground organization should be a team of three to six members. These teams should be allocated on a geographic basis; i.e.: one such team in each town, rural region, and certain individual villages. Ordinarily, there is no need to have more than one team operate in the same location. Exceptions to this rule can be made in certain critical areas where the complexity and multitude of underground activities require more manpower than one team can provide. In such a case, multiple teams could be provided and organized along mission specialties. For instance, one team of three members could be active in special intelligence missions, while another team of five members could operate a courier service for the guerrillas, and another team could have the mission of assembling supplies. In most cases, however, as we said previously, all of the above activities plus several others can be handled by the members of one team only.

Secrecy is a prime consideration in the functions of these underground teams. Their membership, therefore, should not be known to the other members of the underground. Their membership should only be known to an individual who will be in charge of a number (five or six perhaps) of these units. In turn this individual need not be known to every team member either, but only to the team leader and one other member only. In this manner the chain is not broken if the leader is removed from the picture. Actually, these elements of the underground organization would be operating in semi-isolation because their only contacts with the rest of the organization should be through the regional commander and the guerrilla commanders or their representatives whenever the guerrillas are operating within the area of the team's responsibility. The teams must have no contacts with the rest of the underground in their area, nor with any similar units in other areas.

The initiative of contacts between the guerrillas and the local underground must be left to the guerrillas. Whenever a guerrilla commander decides to contact the underground, he should arrange a meeting with one of the team members through a predescribed method which insures positive identification of both parties. If satisfaction of the guerrilla requests is not possible within the team's own resources, the team leader would contact the regional commander and enlist his assistance. The only time when the initiative of contacts with the guerrillas is taken by the underground would be when the underground is in possession of significant intelligence such as change of dispositions of enemy troops, etc., in which case this intelligence must be dispatched to the guerrillas with all deliberate speed.

A guerrilla commander must not be limited to contacting this lowest element of the underground. He could contact the individual responsible for the operation of the underground teams in the region, or any echelon of the underground organization or the underground headquarters itself. Direct contacts should also be made between the guerrilla High Command and the underground headquarters.

The above discussion indicates that the methods of maintaining expeditious and safe contacts between the guerrillas and the underground organizations are of paramount importance. The exact details of these methods are difficult to describe because they depend on many variables which may prevail in each case.

XI

Counterguerrilla Warfare — Nonmilitary and Military Opposition To Guerrillas

1. General Considerations

IN VIEW of what has been learned about guerrilla warfare, it can be stated with certainty that this method of warfare will be utilized with increased frequency in the future. It can be expected that future guerrillas will be better organized and advised or led by more experienced personnel. If they are communist-inspired or controlled, they will also have relative affluence of material resources. Hence, the problem of guerrilla warfare must not be underestimated. All military establishments, therefore, in coordination with the civilian branch of their governments, must make plans to cope with the possibility of future guerrilla warfare in defense of their own national interests. Such plans must be suited to each country's particular situations.

Basically, there are two kinds of guerrilla situations which require advance planning of countermeasures.

One situation has to do with guerrilla operations conducted in direct coordination with conventional operations. Generally, any army operating within or near its homeland, or operating in an allied friendly country will be reasonably free of guerrilla diversions. There will be some exceptions to this, of course, as in the cases where severe dissension exists among the population in regards to the objectives of the waged war. Conversely, an army operating in an enemy country will be confronted with the probability that eventually it will have to cope with guerrilla activity. The exception to this will be when the enemy population is completely demoralized or has accepted defeat as final, as was the case with Germany after World War II.

The other situation is the one wherein guerrilla warfare is being utilized as a method of insurrection in order to overthrow an existing regime or for some other related objective.

The countermeasures required in both situations are different in some respects, but in many more they are identical.

The first and most effective step in countering guerrilla warfare is its prevention, whenever that is possible. In the situation where conventional warfare is involved, the best way to prevent guerrilla warfare from developing is to insure a decisive defeat of the enemy and termination of hostilities. A prolonged conflict and occupation of enemy territory, however, is not conducive to this solution.

In the other situation, prevention requires principally nonmilitary solutions. It requires the elimination of the "cause" for guerrilla warfare. The objectives of potential guerrillas must be analyzed and acceptable alternatives offered. This may mean taking such steps as granting political independence, autonomy, more civil liberties, economic or social reforms, etc. Several of the insurrections which involved guerrilla warfare since World War II could have been avoided if such solutions had been sought. In many cases involving colonial insurrections, the degree of independence obtained by the insurgents after the termination of hostilities is greater than what they would have had accepted as a concession from the colonial power before the insurrection commenced.

However, situations will exist where diffusion or deflection of the objectives of potential guerrillas is not possible. Such will be the case where conciliation of the guerrilla objectives with those of the State is impossible. Situations of this nature will exist when the guerrillas are part of a militant minority determinded to launch guerrilla warfare as a means to impose their will on the majority, or when the guerrillas are acting under the direction of an enemy state.

If nonmilitary methods of countering the guerrillas can not be applied, or if they have been applied and they do not prove effective, then a military solution must be sought and pursued energetically. In seeking a military solution the maximum available resources must be utilized immediately. Experience has shown that most guerrilla movements go through a period of growth after their initial appearance. Keeping this in mind, it is a mistake to expect to eliminate the guerrillas through the use of minimum force. This policy was followed in SE Asia between 1964 and 1968 and it has not been successful.

The problem of how much is needed to suppress a guerrilla movement can be a very critical one for a High Command which is already engaged in conventional warfare or may be considering the commencing of conventional hostilities as a probability. The problem then becomes one of establishing priorities. What would be the impact of guerrilla success and what would be the impact of success by the conventional enemy army? These are problems that need to be analyzed in detail before solutions can be applied. If the threat from the conventional enemy is far greater than the one from the guerrillas, then the obvious solution is to abandon the territory and population in question to the guerrillas. If the territory is vital for the conduct of conventional operations, then it must be defended through a holding action. This will probably mean relinquishing control of most of the territory to the guerrillas, but securing certain vital areas. Precisely, this is what the German Army attempted to do in the occupied Soviet lands in World War II.

But if there is no immediate threat from a conventional force, the objective must be the complete annihilation of the guerrillas as soon as possible.

While seeking a military solution, the nonmilitary countermeasures must be continued and in certain instances intensified. The objective of these countermeasures is to reduce the support which the guerrillas receive from the population in the general area of operations. This again can be accomplished through administrative and psychological activities which will make the guerrilla "cause" appear less attractive to the civilians.

Certain aspects of psychological operations have been discussed in a previous chapter.[1] It was explained then that the scope of this study does not include a detail analysis of psychological operations which is a very complex subject of its own. But it is necessary to repeat here certain important points of it.

One of them is the fact that psychological warfare must be expertly waged, otherwise it brings negative results. Another important point is that, in counterguerrilla operations, it is necessary to obtain and hold the loyalty of at least a segment of the population. This is because the conventional forces opposing the guerrillas need civilian support almost as much as the guerrillas themselves. They do not need supplies and shelter from the civilians, like the guerrillas do, but they do need information. The success of military operations against guerrillas depends to a great extent on intelligence that can be developed. Developing this kind of intelligence is extremely difficult without the cooperation of at least a few of the local civilians.

Unless psychological and other nonmilitary efforts are completely ineptly applied, this should not be a too difficult task. In every society there are dissident groups, including ethnic or religious minorities, social dissidents, political opposition, etc. They can be exploited to form the basis of counterguerrilla support. This basis of civilian support must be provided with reasonable security from guerrilla reprisals. If there is unanimous support of the guerrillas among the population, the mission of their suppression is very nearly impossible. This needs to be recognized and appropriate changes of policy made or else consideration should be given to abandoning this objective as being unattainable.

Another point that needs to be raised is the probability that in some instances there will be a conflict between the required nonmilitary countermeasures and the military ones. These conflicts can be resolved only if overall responsibility for military and nonmilitary activities against the guerrillas is assigned to a single individual. This individual should be a military commander, preferably, but not necessarily. A civilian official could have this responsibility providing he has a thorough understanding of military necessities. Similarly, if a militaⅰy man is chosen, he should have deep insight of the nonmilitary problems of guerrilla and counterguerrilla warfare.

2. Basic Military Counteraction

As stated above, once the decision is made to oppose the guerrillas militarily, the maximum effort must be exerted immediately in order to destroy the guerrilla movement before it is fully developed. The sooner the military countermeasures are applied, the more effective they will be.

We have seen that in order to wage guerrilla warfare successfully, one has to have personnel, equipment, and favorable terrain. There is little that can be done about the terrain. But in order to prevent a guerrilla movement from developing fully, consideration should be given to what can be done about denying the guerrillas personnel and materiel.

In order to accomplish this it is necessary first to identify the potential guerrillas and, most important, the potential guerrilla leaders. This identification can be made through the application of police and intelligence operations. The guerrilla and associated underground organizations need to be infiltrated so that this information can be obtained. If such infiltration is successful, the guerrilla movement will have very little probability of developing. However, this operation is usually time-consuming. It requires an extensive network of informers and agents to be established long before the danger signs appear. The fact is that most free societies have constitutional and statutory constraints which make the surveillance of citizens by police or the armed forces difficult. It can be expected, therefore, that this method will only be a partial success.

In some situations, such as the occupation of enemy territory, denying personnel to the guerrillas can be accomplished through the confinement or surveillance of individuals who could be expected to lead guerrillas by qualification of past experience. This would mean all officers, career NCO's, and people with extensive military experience in general. Before the decision to apply this method is made, its advantages and disadvantages have to be carefully weighed. First of all, it should be ascertained that such roundup can really be effective. If only a portion of such individuals can be rounded up, it is certain that the remaining ones will head for the hills and join the guerrillas. Then, it has to be established whether or how many of such individuals are indeed in sympathy with the guerrillas. It would be a big mistake to treat in this manner individuals who may be potential recruits for a counterguerrilla force.

In situations where the guerrillas are not indigenous, but extrinsic, consideration should be given to sealing off the borders of the country or territory in question. This step will also prevent indigenous guerrilla recruits from going outside the country to be trained and reinfiltration back in. The success of this step will depend on the terrain of the border areas and the amount of forces that can be made available for guarding the borders.

Another potential source of guerrillas are the members of conventional forces who have been cut off or bypassed by fast moving enemy columns during conventional operations. Such units already possess the required materiel and organization. If their leaders have been instructed in guerrilla techniques, they will present a formidable threat to an advancing enemy when left unattended. The problem then for the conventional advancing force is simply this: How can such units be rounded-up without impeding the advance? The problem can be solved easily if there is not a shortage of slower-moving units which are following the thrusting columns and can perform thorough mopping-up operations. If such units are not available in sufficient numbers, then this risk has to be carefully assessed by the commander and appropriate changes made, if necessary, to his operations plan. The relative results of a situation like this can be illustrated by comparing the operations of the Germans in France in 1940 and in the East between 1941 and 1943. In both fronts the Germans employed deep thrusts by their strong panzer groups.[2] In both fronts the panzer groups were followed by slower moving standard (for the period) infantry divisions, most of which utilized horse-drawn transport. The difference was that in France the employed standard infantry divisions were adequate to effectively cover and mop-up the encircled French. But in the East, the German forces were inadequate in relation to the numbers of their opponents and the size of the area involved. Their situation deteriorated progressively. Thus, early in the campaign they were able to effectively round-up all of the 600,000 Russians encircled in the Kiev pocket. But as their own casualties mounted and the length of their lines increased, they simply did not have the manpower to effectively capture and confine all of their enemy. Many Russians, therefore, were able to infiltrate through the lines and join the other side of the front or remained behind to be recruited in the Soviet guerrilla formations. This is one of the reasons why the Germans were confronted with a guerrilla problem in the East, but not in France.

Restricting the flow of manpower to the guerrillas will remain a problem for the conventional forces throughout the life cycle of any guerrilla movement. Characteristically, it can be said that the magnitude of the military effort required to stem this flow will be inversely proportional to the effectiveness of the nonmilitary countermeasures. If the nonmilitary countermeasures are ineffective, strong security forces will be required to control the population and prevent recruiting by the guerrillas. The size of the security forces required for this mission will depend on a number of factors including population, population density and distribution, proximity of transportation media to the area of guerrilla operations, proximity to the guerrilla training base, etc. The conventional force commander must analyze the situation very carefully when he is allocating forces for missions such as this. If there is a guerrilla force already in the field, the problem again becomes one of establishing priorities and balancing the objectives. Which will be more important — finding and engaging the active guerrilla force or controlling the population? For example, it would be an error to allocate a battalion for garrisoning an area from which the guerrillas may recruit a dozen individuals. This battalion could be better utilized in offensive missions against the guerrillas. Conversely, if the same area is very vital to the guerrillas for obtaining replacements and other resources, then the control of the population in the area justifies the allocation of any size conventional security force.

In the situations where the guerrillas are receiving replacements from extrinsic sources, the control of the population is not as important as the interdiction of the infiltration routes. Interdiction may require permanent occupation of the routes by conventional forces. This will depend largely on the terrain. In some types of terrain, such as desert country with very low population density, interdiction can be accomplished through aerial action. In most types of terrain, however, (example: most of SE Asia) aerial action alone cannot accomplish this mission. Then, the routes have to be held by ground forces and this again may require a very sizable force.

It is problems such as these that make counterguerrilla warfare the extremely complex venture that it is.

In addition to personnel, guerrilla movements require materiel. We have seen[3] that in even moderately industrialized societies weapons and other materiel suitable for guerrilla use can be easily obtained. However, the conventional forces must take steps to make the obtaining of weapons difficult. Such steps should include the following:

Confiscation of weapons already in the hands of civilians. The advantages and disadvantages of this must be carefully weighed. Special attention should be paid to the probability that weapons may be taken from those elements of the population who may oppose the guerrillas.

Prevention of pilfering of weapons and other materiel from the conventional force's own stores.

Collection of all weapons abandoned by a retreating enemy army or in the hands of captured troops. This should extend to small arms and ammunition. Usually the emphasis is placed in the collection of sophisticated weapons such as tanks, artillery, rockets, etc., while the small arms are overlooked. Yet, the small arms are precisely the backbone of guerrilla weapons requirements.

Interdiction of infiltration routes through which

weapons and other supplies can be brought in from extrinsic sources. The method of accomplishing this is identical with the method of interdicting routes through which personnel can be infiltrated.

It is doubtful that both of the above discussed countermeasures, i.e.: denying the guerrillas personnel and materiel, can be applied with complete success in future situations. But the extent of success of these countermeasures will directly influence the overall solution of the counterguerrilla warfare problem.

We have seen that these countermeasures, although primarily military, include serious nonmilitary considerations. If, in spite of these, the guerrilla problem persists, the nonmilitary considerations will exert progressively lesser influence on the decisions and the purely military considerations will prevail.

The most radical and most effective of the purely military solutions to a guerrilla problem would be the following: Conduct a major conventional operation to destroy the guerrilla base. This may require the violation of neutral or ostensibly neutral territory which provides a sanctuary for the guerrillas.

The complexities of this solution are many. They include the following:

First, the location of the guerrilla base or bases needs to be established. If the guerrillas are strictly indigenous, such locations will be covert. Their positive identification, therefore, may be impossible.

Next, the operation needs to be a very thorough one to ascertain that the bases are captured prior to their evacuation and that their destruction is such that they cannot be reestablished within a relatively short period of time.

If the bases are located in neutral or ostensibly neutral territory, the problem is compounded by the possible reactions of the government controlling that territory, the international reactions to such a step, and the possibility that one may encounter a conventional enemy force or forces allied to the enemy.

In spite of all these drawbacks, this solution merits serious consideration and it is the recommended solution when one possesses superiority of conventional forces in relation to those which may be encountered.

When any of the above considerations preclude the use of conventional forces to invade the territory where the guerrilla bases are located, then there is still one more possibility: Organize friendly guerrillas and send them into the enemy area. This solution has not been tried in recent years, yet it offers a number of substantial advantages.

First of all, it bypasses the problems created by adverse international reaction to a conventional military invasion. Secondly, it minimizes the risks to be taken by the conventional force which remains free for utilization elsewhere. Finally, it creates a diversion with which the enemy has to cope. In order to cope with the diversion, the enemy will be compelled to abandon or diminish his effort in support of his own guerrillas. Consequently, a compromise could be reached with the enemy on the basis of "you stop your own guerrillas and we will also stop ours".

It has to be admitted that this decision appears bold and not likely to be adopted by conventional staffs. Yet, it is the most effective one that can be applied and in the long run the one which will require the least investment in resources. But it does require the presence of conditions favorable for guerrilla operations, including the availability of determined and proficient personnel.[4]

It should be by now obvious to the reader, that several options of counterguerrilla measures are available. These options are being discussed here in an order which is reverse to their complexity and difficulty of application. It is, therefore, apparent that as we eliminate the relatively easier options, the remaining ones are progressively least desirable and more difficult in their application.

So far we have examined nonmilitary countermeasures which, if successful, will eliminate the need for military counteraction altogether. We have also examined some countermeasures which are in essence a combination of military and political-psychological action. Finally, we have seen that offensive military action against the guerrilla bases and sanctuaries can solve the problem. At this point, we feel, that all the relatively easy solutions have been exhausted. The remaining possible solutions are the most difficult ones because they require meeting the guerrillas in the field under conditions of the guerrillas' own choice, therefore, most favorable to the guerrillas.

Yet, the conventional forces can still defeat the guerrillas if they can maximize their inherent advantages and bring the weight of such advantages to bear in combat against the guerrillas.

The advantages of the conventional forces are usually the following:

Superior firepower.

Superior mobility over some terrain conditions.

Superior technological resources available in general.

Personnel more proficient in conventional warfare techniques.

However, the mere existence of these advantages does not necessarily bring about their proper utilization. The problem, therefore, for the conventional force is how to make maximum use of these advantages in combat with the guerrillas.

The advantages of the conventional force will result in decisive defeat for the guerrillas if the guerrillas ever engage the conventional force in a major pitched battle. Of course, it has been explained that prudent guerrilla commanders should never take the initiative to challenge the conventional force in this manner, but should stick to guerrilla tactics. Yet, it is quite possible that such an event could occur. The probable reasons for guerrillas fighting a conventional battle are the following:

When the engagement is not of the guerrillas choice; i.e., they have inadvertently encountered a conventional force under conditions precluding the application of guerrilla tactics.

If the guerrilla High Command has decided to change from guerrilla to conventional tactics because of some miscalculation or incorrect assessment of their adversaries' situation.

If the guerrilla High Command has been pressured

or compelled to do so by nonmilitary considerations, or by request from a cooperating friendly military headquarters.

In such a situation the guerrillas are risking defeat in detail. But they can still reduce the magnitude of their defeat by withdrawing successfully. It is precisely this situation that the counterguerrilla forces must be ready to exploit at all times.

The need for readiness to exploit this opportunity by the conventional force is something that must be emphasized. In counterguerrilla operations the most difficult task is the one of locating the guerrillas. This task is bypassed if the guerrillas on their own make their whereabouts known through a conventional operation. When and if that does happen, the conventional force commander must bring the maximum of his available forces to the battle area with all possible speed, with the objective to fight the guerrillas in place and to pursue them if they try to disengage. Pursuit must be immediate and relentless.

It is appropriate at this point to compare two situations in which the guerrillas found themselves fighting their opponents in major conventional battles and the subsequent results. One is the battle of Grammos-Vitsi near the NW frontier of Greece in 1949, and the other is the Tet Offensive of 1968.

In Grammos-Vitsi the guerrillas were fighting a defensive positional battle of their own choosing. In the Tet Offensive the guerrillas had the offensive initiative, in fact they achieved a complete strategic surprise.

In both cases the guerrillas were defeated decisively and retreated into their sanctuaries. In neither case were they persued extensively. In Grammos-Vitsi the reason for not pursuing them was the proximity of the Albanian frontier. In fact, the whole Grammos-Vitsi position was anchored on the frontier. The conventional army in this case was not allowed to pursue. In the Tet Offensive the pursuit was minimal. The reason here was the relative exhaustion of usable reserves. All available reserves had been committed to defeat the guerrillas positionally.

After the Grammos-Vitsi operation the guerrillas gave up. After the Tet Offensive they continued.

Why? The reasons are many. The principal reason, in our opinion, is the relative condition of the conventional forces after the battle. After Grammos-Vitsi the conventional forces were and felt victorious. The political climate was also unfavorable to the guerrillas. After the Tet Offensive the conventional army was not in position to exploit the success and the political climate was unfavorable towards them.

It is tempting to speculate what could have happened in both cases if the guerrillas had been pursued. One of the possibilities is that after the Grammos-Vitsi battle, pursuit of the guerrillas into Albania could have brought about the collapse of the Albanian communist regime. After the Tet Offensive, pursuit of the guerrillas into Laos, Cambodia, and North Viet Nam could have destroyed their capability to stage a substantial new effort for a very long time.

3.   Search and Combat

In guerrilla operations, the basic problem for the conventional forces remain the one of locating the guerrillas. Once the guerrillas are located, the task of engaging and destroying them in combat should not be too difficult if the conventional forces make effective use of their superiority in firepower and mobility. Those are the two significant advantages that the conventional forces normally have over the guerrilla enemy.

But how can the guerrillas be found?

The following methods are available to the conventional force:

> Aerial reconnaissance.
> Ground search.
> Application of intelligence.
> Or any combination of the above.

Aerial reconnaissance is useful, but it has many limitations. The limitations are caused by the effects of adverse weather and topography. Bad weather over the takeoff sites or over the area of guerrilla activity imposes a constraint on aerial reconnaissance. If the guerrillas have rudimental knowledge of guerrilla tactics they will take advantage of inclement weather to conduct their operations and aerial reconnaissance will be unavailable when needed most. The same holds true for night operations. Topography restricts the effectivity of aerial reconnaissance if the guerrillas are operating in areas which offer good cover. Forests, jungle, swamps, etc., which make observation from the air ineffective. This is usually true even in low-altitude, low-speed flying which can be provided by helicopters.

Advances in technology, such as the developments of particular sensors, could in the future eliminate these limitations. In the meantime, aerial reconnaissance can be utilized primarily for its deterrent effect. The presence of aerial reconnaissance will restrict the guerrillas to operations in favorable areas and during periods of low visibility only.

Ground search, or reconnaissance by ground forces, when properly conducted brings positive results. The difference in effectivity between aerial reconnaissance and ground search can be illustrated by the appropriate statements of their reports. The aerial observer should report: "I saw nothing". But the man who searched on the ground should be able to say: "There is nothing". However, there are serious disadvantages to ground search also. They include those caused by the terrain difficulties and the fact that effective search of large areas requires large numbers of specially trained troops.

The most effective method of locating guerrillas is, of course, the possession of accurate intelligence. This requires infiltration of the guerrilla organization and its auxiliaries. Therefore, every effort should be exerted by the leaders of the conventional force to maximize their intelligence capability.

It is obvious that the limitations and disadvantages of each of the above methods necessitates that no complete reliance be placed on any one of them. It is required, therefore, that all of them be used in the hope that they complement each other and that their combined utilization brings the desired results. It is, however, necessary to realize that in most situations primary emphasis will have to be placed on ground search. In some situations where topography is particularly favorable to the conventional forces, ground search could be subordinated to aerial reconnaissance. In a few other situations, when the confidence in the intelligence capability is exceptionally high, reliance could be placed on this method.

Ground search techniques will have to be developed to suit the particular situation within each theater. Admittedly this will be a tedious process and planning should allow for initial mistakes. The establishment of effective search techniques will be based on trial and error. However, there are some basic rules which are useful and ought to be followed.

The first rule requires that the area to be searched is as small as possible. But arbitrarily limiting the area to be searched is not effective because it is easy for the guerrillas to slip outside the area. The long range objective must be to restrict the overall area within which the guerrillas can operate comfortably. This can be accomplished progressively by establishing strong points or strong garrisons in vital areas. Within the garrisoned areas there should be absolute security from guerrillas. Within a reasonable radius from the garrisons there should be relative security. The garrisons should be strong enough to be able to withstand a guerrilla attack of intermediate intensity without assistance from reserves. This will probably require that each garrison consists of a force of approximately battalion strength. In order to overcome a statically deployed force of one battalion in prepared positions, with appropriate firepower, the guerrillas will need two or three battalions. Such a force the guerrillas should not be able to assemble without detection. Therefore, relative superiority is ascertained. As the number of such strong points and garrisons is increased, the area available to the guerrillas is diminished; consequently the areas to be searched are also reduced in size. Within the garrisons, elements of the indigenous population who are opposing the guerrillas should be concentrated for safety. They should provide at least part of the garrison force and some of the supporting activities.

The next rule has to do with the use of indigenous individuals in the search parties. If the conventional force is entirely indigenous, this should be no factor. But if the conventional force is extrinsic, a sufficient number of natives must be recruited and trained to be used as scouts. The reasons are obvious. Natives are not only familiar with the topographic con-

ditions of the area, but also with the people of the area. They
should be, therefore, best qualified to provide guidance to the
conventional forces and detect conditions signifying the proximity and activity of guerrillas. Of all the factors influencing
search operations, this is the most important one. There have
to be indigenous people working with the conventional forces,
otherwise the effort will not bring the expected results.

The next rule is the one of surprise. Search operations must
be conducted in such a manner that the guerrilla intelligence
is not aware of them in advance. The guerrillas must not be
given forewarning to go underground or leave the area. In
order to achieve this it is necessary that the whereabouts of the
search units be kept absolutely secret until they reach their
initial jump-off points. There are difficulties in accomplishing
this, but such difficulties must be overcome. One method of
accomplishing this is to airlift the search forces from staging
areas remote from the area to be searched. This, however, will
have certain drawbacks which will be discussed later.

In conducting a search, even under favorable conditions, and
in observance of the above rules, one has to realize that in
essence he is playing a game of probabilities. To illustrate in
a gross manner what this means, let us look at the following
figure.

The sketch represents an area on which the guerrillas may
be operating. The area is divided into 16 blocks, each one of
which represents the area which can be effectively searched
by a ground patrol during a day's patrolling. Let us assume
that today the guerrilla unit is located in block #6.

If we had one patrol available for searching, we can expect
that the patrol will have 1/16 or 6.25% probability of locating
the guerrilla unit on this one day. If we used the patrol for 16
consecutive days and if each day it searched a different numbered block, we can expect that the guerrilla unit would be
located.

It follows that if we had two patrols searching different
blocks on the first day, we would have a 1/8 or 12.5% probability to locate the guerrillas. It would take 8 days patrolling
by the two patrols to give us the necessary 100%.

We can also say that if we had 16 patrols searching simultane-

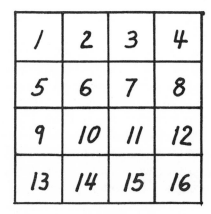

Figure 18. Dividing area to be searched.

ously, we could locate the guerrilla unit during the very first day.

Or would we?

Yes, we would, if we could control the scenario and eliminated all other factors which may influence the outcome. For instance, we must get all of our patrols to enter the area simultaneously without going through each other's subdivision. This would require that blocks #6, 7, 10 and 11 be reached without going through one of the others. Is this possible in actual practice? Probably not. In addition, there are many other practical problems. Assembling and deploying 16 patrols to search the whole area may expose the whole operation to detection by the enemy. What would stop the guerrillas then from slipping outside the area before the operation begins?

The only lesson that can be learned from the above is that search operations, in order to be effective, should utilize the maximum number of separate patrols commensurate with retention of security. If patrolling is continuous, it will bring favorable results because the mathematical probabilities favor the searcher. But remember that this rule does not apply if the guerrillas have advance notice about the location or intentions of the patrolling units.

There are a few additional problems associated with the effort to locate the guerrilla units. One of them is the risk of ambush. This is a risk that has to be accepted. A conventional

unit searching for guerrillas could very well suffer 100% casualties in an ambush. But if the searching unit can notify headquarters about the location of the ambush the mission of
locating the guerrillas has been accomplished. Then, it is up
to the conventional force reserves to react and engage the guerrillas. However, one must also be alert to the fact that if too
many of the conventional patrols are being ambushed, there is
something wrong with the employed search technique.

Attention should be paid to avoid superficiality in searching.
This is quite important when one is operating among strange
peoples. Assistance from the intelligence organization should
be obtained so that concealment and underground methods
employed by the guerrillas can be detected.

The geographic conditions and their impact must be studied
in detail. This will lead to decisions on the size of the patrols
and whether to utilize infantry patrolling exclusively or obtain
assistance through the use of vehicles, boats, or animals. In
some types of terrain only foot patrols can really be effective.
Most types of jungles are included in this. Flat or gently rolling
country with tall grasses could be suitable for motor vehicles,
particularly tracked vehicles. The high grasses conceal the
silhouettes of the vehicles for considerable distances. Mountains and forests of thick trees, however, preclude the use of
vehicles. In such situations serious consideration should be
given to utilizing horse patrols. The big advantage of horses is
not so much their pace which is slightly speedier than the man's
(5 vs 3 mph), but their much greater endurance which allows
the mounted unit to stay in the field longer and cover a much
greater area. If not mounting the men, one should consider the
possibility of making pack animals available to carry the heavy
loads such as radios, extra ammunition, etc. In some types of
terrain shallow draft boats may also be used.

There is no sure-fire method of locating the guerrillas. All
of the above discussion serves to highlight the many difficulties
involved in this phase of counterguerrilla operations. But the
guerrillas must be found if they are to be fought and defeated.
Search missions constitute, therefore, the deep core of military
counteraction against guerrillas. Consequently, the conventional
forces must accept the challenge and search for their enemy

methodically and persistently. Continuous searching for guerrillas is a tedious and frustrating task. But if done properly, the results will be commensurate to the effort. Not only occasional contact with the guerrillas will be made, but it will force them to stay on the move, separate them from their sources of support, exhaust them, and deny them opportunities to conduct operations of their own initiative.

Once a guerrilla unit has been located, it is essential that contact with it be maintained. This task should be the responsibility of the patrolling force which located the guerrillas, with the assistance of surveillance aircraft and reinforcements of highly mobile forces. These forces must be able to react immediately. In order to do this they have to be deployed in advance in suitable secure areas and they must be able to reach the area of contact within a very short time. Air mobile units are desired for this purpose. If air mobile units are not available, paratroops, mechanized infantry, or armored calvary should be used as a substitute. Paratroops will be less effective than air mobile units because their reaction time is longer and because terrain difficulties could restrict the drops. Mechanized and armored units have the great disadvantage of surface movement which is substantially slower, in addition to the fact that it exposes these units to roadblocks, ambushes, and terrain obstacles which will impede their reaction.

Simultaneously with the dispatch of forces to assist in the maintenance of contact, reserves from the main battle force must be dispatched to the battle area. These reserves must be strong enough to overwhelm the guerrillas with their firepower. In general, a ratio of 7 or 8 to 1 in firepower over the guerrillas must be established. They must also have sufficient mobility to reach the battle area within a reasonably short time, but they need not have the extremely high mobility of the units which will be dispatched for the purpose of ascertaining the maintenance of contact. It is more important that the reserves reach the area equipped for sustained battle.

At this point, the guerrilla unit should be trying to break-off contact and escape. The conventional force commander must do everything possible to prevent their escape. If the guerrillas do not appear to be trying very hard to escape, the conventional force commander must be alerted to the probability that the guerrillas may be up to something new. They may be trying some kind of a deception or coverup for some other operation.

It is important that the reactions of the conventional forces are not spontaneous and haphazard. Detailed tactical planning and rehearsals to the extent possible will be required in order to ascertain successes in operations of this kind. Appropriate planning will require thorough knowledge of geographic conditions and an analysis of the guerrilla tactics in the particular area to the extent that they are known. The intelligence contribution to such plans will be substantial.

The preoccupation of the conventional commanders and staffs in these plans will be with the problem of sustaining combat. If combat is sustained the guerrillas will come off second best because, by definition, they do not have available the firepower and other resources of the conventional forces. In order to sustain combat the guerrillas must be prevented from escaping. Consideration, therefore, should be given to the possibilities of completely encircling the guerrilla unit, or cutting off its retreat through the occupation of escape routes, or frontally attacking in combination with flanking maneuvers.

Each one of the three approaches has advantages and disadvantages.

Full encirclement, if properly conducted, has the advantage that it can be the most effective method of destroying a located guerrilla unit. The disadvantage of this method is the relatively large number of conventional troops it requires. This disadvantage will be compounded by the existence of any adverse terrain conditions such as swamps, thickly wooded areas, and mountainous terrain.[5]

If there are sufficient forces available to utilize encirclement, the operation must proceed as follows: The encircling units are deployed frontally along the perimeter. Reserves are deployed behind them in second and some in the third echelon. The forces on the perimeter advance frontally, gradually constricting the area within the perimeter. A minor variation of this may be the driving of a wedge into the area while the perimeter remains fixed. The reserves follow the advance and are ready to engage any concentration of guerrillas and any attempted breakthrough along the perimeter. If the guerrillas are attempting a breakthrough against a particular point on the perimeter, they should be engaged by the reserves only and not by adjacent forces from the perimeter itself. In this manner the creation of gaps through which other guerrillas can escape is avoided. Mopping-up operations must follow the main encirclement immediately.

Attempting to cut off the retreat of guerrillas by occupying the escape routes constitutes a modification of the encirclement method. The difference is that instead of occupying a continuous perimeter line, the conventional forces occupy only identified possible escape routes; simultaneously, a strong conventional force attacks the guerrilla unit frontally attempting to drive it against the occupied positions. This method requires fewer forces than the full encirclement. However, its disadvantage is the fact that it can not be successful unless all possible escape routes are positively known to the conventional forces in advance. The risk of having guerrillas escape is increased through this method. In essence, its application is limited by geographic factors.

The third method requires fewer troops than the other two. However, in order to be successful, this method requires that the employed forces be sufficiently mobile, with very high firepower so that in their attack they can overrun the retreating guerrillas.

If such forces are available, and if the search units of the conventional force are able to maintain strong contact with the guerrilla unit immediately after they have located it, there are no reasons to say that this method is not the one preferred. But it has to be emphasized here that successful use of this method is predicated on the availability of the right kind of forces.

After the guerrilla unit has been encircled, overrun, or otherwise destroyed, the operation is not over yet.

The first concern of the battle area commander should be the continuation of mopping-up in order to capture all escapees and stragglers.

The next concern should be that of the treatment of captured guerrillas, sympathizers, collaborators, their relatives, and the noncombatants or inhabitants of the battle area and immediate environs.

All captured guerrillas and known guerrilla collaborators should be turned over immediately to the intelligence specialists for very thorough interrogation. After the interrogation, they should be confined for the duration of hostilities. Releasing captured guerrillas under amnesty or parole is not recommended. Exceptions could be made in cases where individuals were involuntarily conscripted into the guerrilla units, providing that they can be released for residence in secure areas and effective police surveillance can be maintained over them. Once these people have been coerced by the guerrillas they remain susceptible to guerrilla pressures as long as the guerrilla movement remains active.

Finally, noncombatant civilians who have not collaborated with the guerrillas, even if suspected of being sympathetic to the guerrilla objectives, should not be molested in any way, but helped to continue their routine pursuits as soon as the battle is over. Show of concern for their welfare by the conventional force will be a strong psychological weapon to turn them against the guerrillas or to strengthen their opposition to them.

4.   Organization of Counterguerrilla Forces

Conventional military forces have organizational structures which are optimized for operations against other conventional forces. Counterguerrilla operations, however, differ characteristically from conventional operations. Therefore, it is reasonable to conclude that when any conventional force is given a counterguerrilla mission, its standard conventional organizational structure is probably not the optimum one for its new mission.

Hence, a conventional High Command which is confronted with the possibility of using conventional forces in protracted counterguerrilla operations, has to consider the problem of training and organizing a segment of its forces specifically for this kind of operations. This should be done as far in advance as possible in order to avoid mistakes caused by last-minute improvisations. Again, this point needs to be stressed: The resources allocated to the counterguerrilla effort should be within balance of the overall strategic necessities. The counterguerrilla forces should not be developed out of proportion with the other forces which will be required in order to protect a State from probable conventional threats.

In counterguerrilla operations the conventional forces usually have the apparent problem of manpower insufficiency. This is caused by such factors as those of the initiative, which initially belongs to the guerrillas, the need to secure numerous vital areas, the requirement for continuous search missions, the need to maintain a substantial reserve as battle force, etc. The manpower problem is further compounded by the necessities to provide logistic support for complex equipment and, perhaps, the maintenance of long pipelines. The conventional forces, in order to take advantage of their materiel superiority, have to pay a corresponding price in personnel overhead. The maintenance of complex mechanical and electronic equipment in the theater of guerrilla operations requires the availability of skilled technical, supply, and other support personnel who normally do not contribute directly to the delivery of fire to the enemy.

This particular aspect of the manpower problem became outstandingly acute during the recent U.S. involvement in SE Asia. It has been said that the ratio of support troops to those capable of delivering fire to the enemy has ranged from 12:1 to 19:1 among the U.S. forces. This is, without doubt, unsatisfactory. It means that out of 500,000 men only 25,000 fall in the category of being able to deliver fire. It further means that 500,000 conventional troops can successfully cope with only a very small number of guerrillas.

In the future, therefore, appropriate changes must be made to the organizational structure of counterguerrilla forces in order to enable them to operate effectively in the particular geographic environment and to maximize their combat capability. This does not infer that logistic support needs to be neglected. It means that optimum balance must be provided between combat and support forces. We believe that the solution of this problem will be found in specialization. It is unrealistic to expect a division of infantry or armor to transition overnight into a force of efficient counterguerrilla troops. It is infinitely more productive to take the same number of men, organize them appropriately, and train them to the necessary special skills.

If our previous analysis of counterguerrilla operations is valid, it indicátes that the counterguerrilla force should be composed of three broad specialties of troops. Those are: Static defense forces, quick reaction forces, and a reserve or main battle force.

Static Defense Forces. These are the forces with the mission to provide defense of vital or significant areas, including urban centers, lines of communications, industrial complexes, depot area, etc. This mission requires the least amount of specialization in counterguerrilla warfare. In fact, in many situations troops with very limited military experience (such as recruits with three or four months training) can provide the bulk of these forces. However, in most situations, these forces will have to be the most numerous of the total counterguerrilla force. The ratio of the static defense forces out of all others may be as high as 60% or 90%. This is why it is important that these forces consist of indigenous troops. In some situations the total counterguerrilla force will be indigenous. But in the situations where the counterguerrilla force is extrinsic or mixed, these missions should be given to native forces primarily. If the reliability of these forces is ascertained, they will provide reasonably effective protection in their areas of responsibility. If, on the contrary, these missions have to be given to extrinsic troops, two extremely adverse situations will develop. First, the counterguerrilla force will be wasting manpower in defensive missions and its offensive capability will correspondingly suffer. Secondly, the impression of foreign occupation wi be created among the civilians of the area, and this always results in adverse psychological reactions.

The conventional infantry battalion with some modifications and reinforcements should provide the basis of organization and composition of the static defense forces. For instance, the rifle companies could number four, instead of three. Support weapons companies could be two, instead of one. In some cases an artillery battery may also be added. The allocation of small arms and support weapons to this type of unit should take in consideration the prevailing conditions of the particular theater. For example, since the guerrillas probably will not possess any armored vehicles, the anti-tank weapons can be drastically reduced. However, the number of high-rate-of-fire medium machineguns (example: the Browning M1917) and area anti-personnel weapons (example: any 81mm mortar) should be increased. The reason is that these weapons are particularly effective in positional defense against infantry assaults like those that can be expected from guerrillas. The number of motor vehicles in these units can be drastically reduced, since there are no requirements for mobility. But communication equipment such as radio sets should be made available in sufficient quantity.

Each of these battalion-size units should be given an area of responsibility which can be defended truly statically. In practice this will mean that the total area should be small enough so that the battalion's companies can be deployed within distances covered by the effective range of their weapons. But the battalions do not need to be within supporting distance of each other, providing that ground communications among them can be maintained. This may require relatively strong escorts which may need to include light amored vehicles; therefore, provisions for such units need to be made. Ordinarily, the battalions should be grouped under area headquarters. There is no point in arbitrarily fixing the number of battalions that can be effectively controlled by one area headquarters. It could be two and it could be ten, plus the armored escort units. The number of battalions will be determined by proximity among the units, natural boundaries, political administrative subdivisions, and other factors. Two or more area headquarters could be grouped into region headquarters which, in turn, should be directly subordinate to the theater headquarters or to the headquarters which has overall responsibility for the counterguerrilla warfare. If the area is large enough that the echelon of region headquarters is used, then it should be made certain that within the region are stationed units of the battle force, or maybe even assigned to it. This type of force will be discussed later.

Quick Reaction Forces. The mission of these forces is to search for the enemy and when the enemy is found to maintain contact until the enemy can be engaged by the main battle force. The term "Quick Reaction" is not exactly descriptive of the mission of these forces because they are not intended to react to someone else's initiative, but they are intended to provide the initiative for the counterguerrilla force. The term is more descriptive of the high mobility which is a requirement for these forces. These will probably be the least numerous, but certainly the most specialized and most proficient of the counterguerrilla troops.

In order to accomplish the search missions the quick reaction forces should include company-sized units which have good mobility on the prevailing terrain and sufficient firepower to reduce their vulnerability to ambushes. Basically, therefore, such units should be special infantry companies (example: mountain or jungle rangers), armored cavalry troops, or even horse cavalry troops. If the counterguerrilla force is not indigenous, native soldiers should be attached to these units as guides or scouts and one or two intelligence specialists should be organic to each company or troop headquarters.

In order to accomplish the mission of maintaining contact once the enemy is found, there should be available battalion-size units of extremely high mobility. The most mobile formations for this kind of operations are formations similar to the present U.S. Army air mobile units. This type of unit is freed from surface movement, therefore, it becomes the most effective. Air mobile units are not recommended for the search missions because their ability to conduct effective search is reduced by many factors including those of noise and sighting over the horizon. If air mobile units cannot be made available, then mechanized cavalry and armored infantry are suitable substitutes in some, but not all, terrain conditions.

The search companies should be grouped under regimental headquarters for administrative support. The other units should be under brigade or division headquarters. Both types of units should be under the direct control of the headquarters having overall responsibility for the conduct of the counter-guerrilla warfare. It is not recommended to make them organic to area or region headquarters because in this manner they lose some of their mobility advantages.

Main Battle Force. The mission of the main battle force is to annihilate the guerrillas whenever the guerrillas' whereabouts are disclosed. In order to accomplish this mission, the main battle force needs to have unequivocal superiority in firepower over the guerrillas, numerical adequacy, and reasonable mobility in the particular terrain conditions. It is probable that conventional units of brigade size or higher, can meet the above requirements by altering their organization very little and obtaining the necessary training.

It is necessary to stress the importance of obtaining a balance between firepower and mobility in these units. As long as quick reaction forces are available, the need for mobility in the main battle force is not too prominent. Contact with the located guerrillas will be maintained by the quick reaction forces for a while. The main battle force must be able to sustain combat; otherwise the guerrillas will give it the slip.

For this reason, certain types of conventional forces are preferable to others. The prevailing terrain conditions, however, influence the choice of units considerably. In most situations, standard infantry divisions with organic armor and substantial artillery are well suited. Armored divisions are also suitable if reinforced in infantry. Without infantry augmentation they will be unable to effectively prevent infiltration of the guerrillas through their lines. Air mobile divisions are not recommended unless the prevailing terrain conditions are extremely difficult and surface movement is nearly impossible. The reason that air mobile divisions are not desirable are, primarily, their limited capability for sustained ground combat, sensitivity to weather and visibility conditions, and their increased requirements for logistic support.

If the theater of guerrilla operations is not too large, the reserve or main battle force should be directly subordinate to the theater commander. However, if the theater is large and the incidents of guerrilla activity widely dispersed, it is better to allocate part of the main battle force to regional headquarters. In this manner quicker reaction timing is ascertained and operations of local initiative can be undertaken.

It has been explained previously that intelligence is a very important function in counterguerrilla operations. Therefore, the intelligence capability of the counterguerrilla army needs to be improved. Basically, this is accomplished through broadened intelligence sources. Contacts with residents in the area of guerrilla activity need to be increased. Existing police files could provide an initial source of intelligence. But primarily, the organization of a substantial network of collaborators, informers, and agents is required. A determined effort to penetrate the guerrilla inner circle should be made.

Intelligence specialists may have to be assigned to tactical units down to company level. Experienced intelligence specialists are not normally available in such quantities among conventional forces. Therefore, a training program will have to be established to develop such specialists.

Every effort should be made to make full use of probable technological advantages possessed by the conventional force. For instance, monitoring of electronic transmissions, aerial surveillance of areas of suspected enemy concentrations, etc.

In addition, in order to obtain maximum benefits from the intelligence effort, a method will need to be devised to insure continuous flow and crossflow of intelligence products among the field units and headquarters.

Earlier, in the discussion of this topic it was pointed out that the conventional forces are usually confronted with the problem of manpower insufficiency. In order to improve its posture in this respect, the conventional anti-guerrilla force in the future must rid itself of superfluous services and personnel that would be considered necessary under other conditions. The retention in the theater of operations of dependents of military personnel, exchange and commissary services, and other functional elements of indifferent tactical value should be examined very critically. A realistic assessment of the contribution of each of these usually will conclude that their contribution in terms of improved morale, etc., is more than offset by the added requirements to provide security and increased logistics overhead for them.

However, a drastic improvement of the personnel posture cannot be achieved without elimination of those principal causes which result in the big increases in personnel overhead. In modern warfare such causes are those of equipment performance in terms of availability, reliability, and maintainability.

It may be worth the time to examine the significance of those terms in counterguerrilla warfare.

Availability as a term by itself can have a very general meaning. However, the only relevant definition of availability is the one which specifies availability as "operational availability". Operational availability (A_0) for any equipment is best defined by the following equation:

$$A_0 = \frac{MTBM}{MTBM + MDT}$$

Where: MTBM = Mean time between all (scheduled and unscheduled) maintenance actions.

MDT = Mean down time; i.e., all time during which the equipment is not operationally ready or performing a mission.

Reliability should be narrowed to "mission reliability". It should be expressed as a percentage of probability that the equipment will not fail during a mission, unless the failure is caused by enemy action.

Maintainability, within the U.S. forces is defined as ". . . . . . a built-in characteristic of design which is expressed as the probability that an item will conform to specified conditions within a given period of time when maintenance action is performed in accordance with prescribed procedures and resources."[6] The trouble with this definition is that the prescribed maintenance procedures and resources could be very elaborate and expensive. In counterguerrilla warfare maintainability is a comparative term. We would define maintainability as the design quality of an item that allows the operating unit to maintain it in service with the expenditure of minimum maintenance man-hours and the utilization of minimum special tools and spare parts. Since this definition does not establish a reference, it can only be applied when comparing two like items. For instance, two rifles like the SKS and the M16.

It is obvious that equipment with high operational availability rates, high mission reliability, and maintainability characteristics like those defined here, should be easy to service and maintain. Therefore, such equipment will require relatively small numbers of personnel for their service and maintenance. However, the realities are considerably different. Materiel developments since World War II have been spectacular in terms of operational performance. But the qualities of maintainability, reliability, and availability of these equipment are not correspondingly advanced. The more complex the new materiel become, the heavier the logistic load is. So far, we have not detected any signs of reversing this trend, among Western armed forces anyway. It becomes necessary, therefore, for the conventional forces to pay this high logistics overhead price, if they are to take advantage of their technological supremacy over the guerrillas.

What, then, can be done to effect a reduced ratio of support personnel? Several answers can be found to this question. Basically, however, the answers evolve from two considerations.

First is the consideration of personnel skills. If highly skilled support personnel are available, their overall number can be reduced. The extent to which this substitution of quality for quantity can be made, however, is hard to assess.

The other consideration has to do with the materiel itself. If a choice is available, equipment should be selected with the aforementioned factors of maintainability, reliability, and availability weighing heavy on the decision. This will mean that reduced operational performance may be expected in order to improve logistics posture. The establishment of trade-offs will not be an easy problem to solve.

Generally, the conventional commander should avoid using equipment which are traditionally or inherently poor logistic risks. At least, he should try to reduce their quantities. Such equipment include most of the newer electronic equipment, which are not too important in counterguerrilla warfare. But they also include aviation items, particularly helicopters, which are highly desirable. The solution to this problem will be found by obtaining a balance and establishing appropriate trade-offs. If available, some helicopter units must be used in certain combat missions. But, saturating the theater with helicopters to do menial tasks that could be accomplished by simple ground vehicles is not prudent.

The obvious lesson here is that a conventional force should be able to maintain substantial technological superiority over its guerrilla enemy without absorbing disproportionate quantities of the available materiel and human resources. If the technological superiority cannot be maintained under these terms, then the counterguerrilla effort is in serious jeopardy.

It is this problem, and other similar ones discussed throughout this volume, that make counterguerrilla operations quite frustrating for the conventional forces. It is clear that if guerrilla warfare has been launched after careful consideration of all relevant conditions and if it has reached the stage of frequent field operations, the probabilities of success are on the side of the guerrillas.

Chapter Notes

Chapter I

[1]Mao Tse-Tung: Selected Works, p. 198.
[2]Liddell Hart: Strategy.

Chapter II

[1]E. Foord: Napoleon's Russian Campaign, p. 250.
[2]Murat, Napoleon's brother-in-law, was commander during the campaign of the "cavalry reserve" which consisted of eleven divisions in four corps.
[3]John Scott: Partisan Life with Colonel John S. Mosby.
[4]John Scott: Partisan Life with Colonel John S. Mosby, p. 76.
[5]John Scott: Partisan Life with Colonel John S. Mosby, p. 430.
[6]The best, in our opinion, was J. E. B. Stuart.
[7]See Chapter IX ibid.
[8]C. W. Breihan: Quantrill and His Civil War Guerrillas, p. 166.
[9]Harrison Trow: Charles W. Quantrell, p. 39.
[10]Britton Davis: The Truth About Geronimo, p. 74.
[11]Britton Davis: The Truth About Geronimo, p. 32.
[12]Britton Davis reports that Nachite was fond of the ladies, dancing, liquor, etc.
[13]Mickey Free, of Irish-Mexican parentage, had been captured and raised by Apaches as a young boy. He was later an official interpreter of the Army.
[14]Jason Betzinez: I Fought With Geronimo.
[15]Jason Betzinez: I Fought With Geronimo, p. 57.
[16]Britton Davis: The Truth About Geronimo, p. 41.
[17]Betzinez claims that about ten Apaches did not surrender with Geronimo, and that they and their descendents have been living ever since in parts of Mexico as outlaws.
[18]John Reed: Insurgent Mexico.
[19]This is an extremely contradictory statement since Mexican sovereignty had been violated already.
[20]Churchill had taken the job as correspondent after failing in his first bid for election in the Parliament.
[21]T. E. Lawrence: Seven Pillars of Wisdom, p. 55.

379

[22]T. E. Lawrence: Seven Pillars of Wisdom, p. 166.
[23]The words are Greek. They mean science, glory, and understanding. Lawrence is using them as metaphors. We find his conclusions incompatible with pragmatic reasoning. If one takes Lawrence's thesis on the value of the commander's intuition literally, we can cancel all advance military schooling and search for individuals endowed by the Divine Providence with those qualities necessary for military leadership.

Chapter III

[1]The exact amount of military aid received by Chiang in World War II is not known. Stilwell had a plan to reequip 60 Chinese divisions. Later, after Stilwell was replaced by General Wedemeyer, 39 Chinese divisions were partially or totally equipped with U.S. materiel. The Chinese High Command has acknowledged receipt of 422 75 mm pack pieces. The American sponsored Field Artillery Training Center has reported that it trained and equipped 12 battalions of truck-drawn 105 mm howitzers in addition to the pack artillery. This is enough artillery for 16 divisions of three battalions (36 pieces) each. All this equipment eventually fell to the communists. See C. F. Romanus: Time Runs Out in CBI.
[2]C. F. Romanus: Stilwell's Command Problems.
[3]C. F. Romanus: Stilwell's Command Problems, p. 31. On one occasion Mme Chiang withheld a letter from President Roosevelt to Chiang Kai-Shek.
[4]C. F. Romanus: Stilwell's Command Problems, p. 306.
[5]An acquaintance of ours, the pilot of a B-29 based in India, had to bail out over communist-held territory after a mission over Japan. He and other members of his crew were guided back to Allied lines by the Chinese communists. In doing so, he had to cross Japanese held territory. He reported that he saw communist guerrilla bands behind the Japanese lines.
[6]A number of Chinese provincial commanders, particularly in East China, were plotting to overthrow Chiang. They tried to enlist support from the Allies and the Japanese. See C. F. Romanus: Time Runs Out in CBI.
[7]In 1939, Soviet divisions were grouped into armies. The corps echelon did not exist except in the cavalry and armored forces. Sometimes cavalry divisions or tank brigades were grouped under corps headquarters.
[8]This unit had been formed in 1915 by the Germans. See 1966 issue of Deutches Soldaten Jalrbuch.
[9]IMRO is a Macedonian underground organization established around 1900. IMRO and Ustasha had for a time cooperated against their common enemy, the Yugoslav State. IMRO's last known leader, Ivan Mihailov found asylum in Zagreb in 1943 after he was chased out of Sofia, but he disappeared after the Axis collapse.
[10]Leigh White: The Long Balkan Night.
[11]David Martin: Ally Betrayed, p. 66.
[12]Leigh White: Balkan Caesar.
[13]One of the causes of the failure of the Whites during the Russian Civil War was their attempt to return to the prewar status quo in regard to land reform. See R. L. Gartoff: Soviet Military Doctrine, p. 51.
[14]David Martin: Ally Betrayed, p. 183.
[15]Here is what Leigh White says about this policy in the "Balkan Caesar"; " . . . . . , Surely the lives of Serbs were as precious as the lives of British and Americans — or were they? Let us face it: they were not. We fought the war according to a double standard of human values."
[16]The Bulgarians were by then having doubts about the ultimate victory of the Axis. They probably felt that a communist regime in Yugoslavia would be more friendly to them than the Nationalist Yugoslavs who had an old score to settle with the Bulgarians.
[17]See 1966 issue of Deutsches Soldaten Jahrbuch.
[18]MacLean has since been elected a Conservative member of the Parliament.

Has attracted some attention with his opposition to granting independence to the colonies. Randolph Churchill occasionally made the headlines because of his bouts with the police.

[19]Kluggman's communist background goes back to the 20's when he was an undergraduate contemporary of Kim Philby and Ray Burgess. It appears that the British had allowed all kinds of communists, homosexuals, and other misfits to infiltrate all echelons of government, but this is another story.

[20]Mao Tse-Tung: Selected Works, p. 202.

[21]David Martin: Ally Betrayed, p. 122.

[22]Dixon & Heilbrunn: Communist Guerrilla Warfare.

[23]Such as the emigré governments of Yugoslavia and Greece, to a lesser degree, the governments of France and the Philippines.

[24]Units in German service composed of Soviet citizens.

[25]J. A. Armstrong: Soviet Partisans in World War II.

[26]Commissars (военком—voyencom) were usually found in company and higher headquarters. Political instructors (политрук—politruk) were assigned to smaller units, sometimes down to the squad echelon.

[27]G. Reitlinger: A House Built on Sand, p. 244.

[28]The 8th SS was commanded by Herman Fegelein, an ex-circus rider with little military background, who was married to Eva Braun's sister. As such, he became eventually Hitler's brother-in-law. Hitler had him shot a few days before he himself committed suicide.

[29]R. Garthoff: Soviet Military Doctrine. Also November 1960 issue of "Military Review".

[30]M. H. Cannon: The Return to the Philippines.

[31]C. F. Romanus: Stilwell's Command Problems, p. 34.

[32]C. F. Romanus: Stilwell's Command Problems, p. 240.

[33]This was a Texas National Guard unit. Consisted of three squadrons, plus machinegun and heavy weapons troops. Although it was shipped dismounted, when it arrived in Burma it obtained enough animals to pack all its heavy weapons and mount part of the troopers.

Chapter IV

[1]The Southern part of Albania includes large numbers of ethnic Greeks.

[2]W. L. Shirer: Berlin Diary, p. 547.

[3]But it is necessary to mention that the success on Crete proved to be a pyrrhic victory as far as the German airborne forces were concerned. All combat units engaged (7th Parachute Division, 5th Mountain Division, and 1st Assault Regiment) suffered very heavy casualties. This affected subsequent decisions of the German High Command and airborne operations were not conducted later in spite of more-or-less successful uses of paratroops by the Japanese and Allies.

[4]The initials of the Greek words National Liberation Front, which is a more-or-less stereotyped title for such movements when sponsored by communists.

[5]He was an old communist who probably had fought in Spain.

[6]He had succeeded his Brother, King George II, who died in April 1947.

[7]It appears that part of the French forces attempted to cut their way through to the North and join the Ally forces there. See C. F. Romanus: Time Runs Out in CBI.

[8]Several American air crews participated in the runs over Diem Bien Phu on contract basis.

[9]G. K. Tanham: Communist Revolutionary Warfare, p. 105.

[10]In the pre-World War II days, the French Ecole Superiere De Guerre was very highly thought of. Therefore, several European and American military establishments sent their outstanding officers to that school in order to complete their studies.

[11]G. Grivas: Memoirs, p. 23.

[12]G. Grivas: Memoirs, Annex.

[13]G. Grivas: Memoirs, Annex.

[14]G. Grivas: Memoirs, p. 75 to 77.

[15]Kemal had renounced all Turkish expansionist ambitions and admonished his successors to follow the same policy as a matter of political wisdom. Dallin deals extensively on this subject and how it affected Turkish attitude during the German advance on Caucasus. See Dallin: German Rule in Russia, p. 226 and ff.

[16]January 1970.

[17]Overthrows of communist governments through subversion or coups have taken place, but these did not employ guerrilla methods.

[18]An example of who is a "collaborator" by the communist definition is the following. In a small city near Saigon, a Vietnamese widow with two small children was employed as a cleaning woman in an apartment rented by three American civilians. Her husband had been killed in the South Vietnamese Army. In the eyes of the local communists she is a collaborator, not because of any ideological affiliation with the Americans, but because she was employed as a cleaning woman. Another incident that many people forget is the photo of a South Vietnamese 2nd Lieutenant carrying his dead child out of his home in a suburb of Saigon. This photo appeared in some American newspapers on 2 February 1968, the same day that the now famous photo of General Ngo Loan shooting a captured guerrilla appeared. Most papers did not publish the first photo although they all published the photo of the General with hypocritically indignant comments. Yet, it is possible that the execution of the captured guerrilla may have been in accordance with the rules of war. See discussion on this subject under Chapter V.

[19]The Kozak guerrillas, angered by the loss of property which their stanitsas (villages) had sustained in the hands of the commissars, were doing their best to replace their lost property by taking it back from the "inogorodni" (foreigners), i.e. non kozaks, regardless of who the foreigners or what their political sympathies were. This is an old kozak custom, but its results were disastrous because to the peasants it appeared that there was no difference between raiding White kozak bands and marauding commissars. See Vrangel's Memoirs.

[20]The apparent lack of spectacular success does not infer a complete lack of success in the field by the insurgents, by any means. One reliable traveler from the U.S. has reported that in 1963 all areas around Aght amar seemed to be under the control of insurgent Kurds. Travel on secondary roads was also difficult without escort from the Turkish Army. The traveler was provided such an escort for part of his journey. However, the escort commander felt that his force was not strong enough. So, the solution was to pay a substantial sum of money to the Kurd agents so he could proceed unmolested.

Chapter V

[1]See C. A. Dixon and Otto Heilburn. "Communist Guerrilla Warfare"

[2]A fact recognized by the War Crimes Trials. See decisions on the cases of Field Marshal List, Field Marshal Leeb, and others.

[3]See C. A. Dixon & Otto Heilbrum "Communist Guerrilla Warfare". The leaflet reads as follows:

    1. "Always preserve your authority towards subordinates!

    Avoid superciliousness. The Russian is very critical of false and only 'superficial' authority. The so-called 'master attitude' is usually advertised by those who are lacking in it. Real authority grows from greater efficiency and exemplary conduct.

    2. "Be just!

    Every subordinate can be treated strictly, but must be treated justly. In Russia the German has always had a high reputation for unerring justice. The Russian hates nothing as much as injustice. The Russian is a particularly good worker. If he is decently treated, he works eagerly and hard. He is intelligent and learns easily. If he is shown something new, he is at first full of suspicion. If however he sees that this thing is good, he gladly adapts himself to the new method of working.

The Russian is used to being directed by somebody standing over him. Instructions and orders must be given in such a manner as to make them understandable to the person addressed. It is inadvisable to give long orders and to leave the execution of the individual stages of the work to the initiative of the Russians. The work must be supervised as far as possible. An admonishment is certainly called for, should the order be badly executed.

3. "Praise the Russian if he works well!

If he is not praised he loses his eagerness to work. Small presents and special rewards if they are justified and if the reason for these is given, often work wonders.

4. "Avoid beating Russians.

The Russian values his honour. If he is beaten he never forgets it. Thrashing is regarded as uncultivated in Russia. The Tsarist system was and still is so terribly hated because the knout and punishment by hanging were daily occurrences. The Bolshevists realizing this clearly, have strictly forbidden public thrashings and death by strangulation. In a propaganda lasting for years hanging and thrashing were described as the highest measures of uncivilization. Today Soviet propaganda even makes use of the hanging of bandits in order to put the Germans on the same level as the Tsarist regime.

5. "Avoid any expression about the Russians implying that the Germans are a superior race to the Russians!

The Russians, in particular the White-Russians, Ukrainians, and the Great-Russians in the north belong to the racial family of Aryans. They often have Viking blood in their veins, of which they are proud. The Russian knows that in many respects he has not yet reached the cultural level of Western Europe. He has endeavoured to reach it for centuries and not without success. He is greatly offended if he is looked upon as a second-class human being, or regarded as a member of a 'Colonial People'. The propaganda of the bandits also makes use of the argument that Germany wished to enslave all Russians and turn them into a 'Colonial People'.

Do not despise the Russians as a whole or individually because owing to the climate he is dressed uniformly and inconspicuously and because he frequently looks poor and ragged due to the Soviet era and the exigencies of war.

6. "Respect Russian women and girls the same as German women and girls on principle.

In relations with the Russian population one must never forget that Germany is regarded and wishes to be regarded as a leading cultural state. Avoid rudeness, any indecent behaviour, insults, and insolence towards women and girls.

7. "Desist from independent procurement and arbitrary requisitioning of food and chattels.

All such arbitrary actions are forbidden. They give rise to a feeling of having no rights and bitterness against the Germans by the Russians. Furthermore, they cause the Russian to put the German on the same level as Bolshevist exploitation.

8. "In conversation with Russians always make a differentiation between Russians and Bolshevists!

As convinced Bolshevists only make up a small part of the population of the Soviet Union, the Russians lay great store on being regarded as apart from the Bolshevists. If anything is to be criticised it must be charged to the Bolshevists. The Russians are to be criticised strictly but with justice and dignity.

9. "Be reserved in conversation with Russians on religion!

The Russian is to be granted absolute freedom of faith. We are not to use any pressure in any direction. Any encroachment on religious life is considered a disturbance and irreverence, and a damage to German reputation.

10. "Treat the Russian decently and serenely, you get on better with him like this than if you shout or scream!

No Russian can stand shouting and screaming. Admonishment is only

384   Guerrilla Warfare

called for if he knows that he has done something wrong. The Russian often understands little German. By shouting and screaming at him the German language does not become more comprehensible to the Russian but only more confusing. It is silly to believe that by shouting one can make one's own language understandable and convey one's wishes and orders to the inhabitants of a foreign country."

[4]See Guderian "Panzer Leader" p. 379
[5]See Leigh White: "Balkan Caesar" p. 52
[6]See U.S. War Crimes Trial against Field Marshal List, case no. 7
    U.S. War Crimes Trial against Field Marshal Leeb
    U.S. War Crimes Trial against Ohlendorf et al; Eisatzgruppen case no. 9

Chapter VI

[1]Best example of this is von Lettow-Vorbeck's operation in East Africa in World War I.
[2]See W. T. Sherman: Memoirs.
[3]See the "Conspirators" by Goffrey Bailey. Also a small booklet on Tuhhachevsky published (in Russian) in 1965 by the Military Publishers of the Defense Ministry of the USSR. It comprises of a collection of articles by many authors. It rehabilitates the Marshal and several of his associates, but Gamarnik is excluded.
[4]Mao Tse-Tung: "Selected Works" p. 202.
[5]Griffith's translation of Mao's works on guerrilla warfare, p. 20
[6]Notwithstanding what communist propaganda may claim on this subject, the fact still remains that twice within one generation thousands of Russians took arms voluntarily against the Soviet Government. During the Russian Civil War there were four major armies operating against the Moscow government: Udenich in the Northwest; the Ukrainian separatists in Ukraine; the Volunteer Army in the South, successively commanded by Generals Kornilov, Denikin, and Wrangel; and the Siberian forces under Admiral Kolchak in the East. These armies came within a few miles of Moscow and could have been successful in overthrowing the Soviet government had they been better led. Fortunately for the communists, of the three outstanding generals in the White Camp, one, Grand Duke Nicholas, was never utilized in the Civil War; another, Kornilov, was killed in action early in the struggle; and the third, Vrangel, assumed command only after the issue had already been militarily decided. In World War II, the total number of ex-Soviet citizens who fought on the German side was over 1,000,000. There were 665,000 still in German uniforms on the day of capitulation. (see Dallin p. 658n). The above indicate that in a future conflict the West could have the Russian people on their side, or at least a substantial part of the Russian people. In such eventuality, the subject of the Soviet Union's ethnic minorities should be very carefully approached because it has indeed been a thorny problem in the past. The anti-communist Soviet citizens and ex-citizens are divided into two distinct groups. One group includes the so-called Russian Solidarists, composed of great Russians and Russified Little Russians or non-Russians. This group wishes the overthrow of the present Soviet government, but actively opposes any idea of disintegration to the Russian state. This group has included Kolchadk, Denikin, and the ex-Soviet general Vlassov. In the Civil War, Denikin's slogan "Russia, one and Indivisible" caused a lot of friction between him and the ardent anticommunist Kozaks and people of Caucasia. Denikin claimed to be a republican; his successor, Baron Vrangel was an avowed monarchist, but was more moderate on the subject of nationalities. The second group includes the ethnic minorities i.e.; those who advocate the carving of independent states from the present Soviet Union, such as Ukraine, Georgia, Armenia, etc. In this group are included some of the Kozaks, although the existence of Kozak "nations" is doubted by most historians.
[7]See Ely "The Red Army Today" and Garthoff "Soviet Military Doctrine"

Chapter VIII

[1]A classic example of such situation was the condition of the German 56 Panzer Corps on 27 June 1941. The Corps found itself at Dvinsk after four days rapid advance, with its fuel depleted, 60 and 100 miles from the nearest friendly units of its left and right respectively. See Manstein "Lost Victories" p. 185.

Chapter IX

[1]See pamphlet "Leadership in the Air Force" Squadron Officer Course, the Air University.
[2]And also to attack their benefactors, the British, in Athens in December 1944.
[3]E. C. W. Meyer in 1961, published a book in which he attempts to justify his actions in the Greek mountains in 1943-44. Although his good intentions are not in doubt, looking at Balkan events in retrospect, one has to conclude that he was duped into committing some fundamental errors of judgement.
[4]See pamphlet "Leadership in the Air Force", the Air University.
[5]By no means the only one though. Any personality conflict may cause such un-acceptance; it will be isolated to a few subordinates though and not universal in the unit.

Chapter X

[1]Mao Tse-Tung: "Selected Works" p. 188.
[2]The National Guard in the Country is organized on a territorial basis.
[3]The Swiss, Indian, and Russian armies possess "mountain" divisions; these units are suitable for employment on rough terrain, but would become virtually static units anywhere else. Other armies do not make such distinctions between standard and special formations, but in actual practice all their units are oriented towards a specific kind of terrain.
[4]The U.S. is included in the group. The only units in the U.S. Army organized for specific geographic deployment are the Eskimo Scouts of the Alaska National Guard. Other units for mountain, arctic, desert, or tropical warfare have been formed on experimental basis only.
[5]"instructors" as they are called among communist underground movements.

Chapter XI

[1]See Chapter VI ibid.
[2]A panzer group consisted of two or more panzer corps. In essence it was a panzer army although not designated as such early in the war. There were four panzer groups through 1941.
[3]See Chapter VI ibid.
[4]See Chapter VI ibid.
[5]Bernard Fall, in "Street Without Joy" suggests that for operations of this kind in swamps each battalion should not hold ground wider than 1500 yards. He cites an example in July 1953 when one Vietminh regiment managed to escape an encirclement by a French force consisting of ten infantry, three armored cavalry, and two artillery regiments. Another example is the German operation near Briansk between 21 and 30 May 1943. The Germans annihilated 3,000 guerrillas, but had to commit the following units: 5th Panzer Division, 6th Infantry Division, 707th Security Division, 747 Infantry Regiment, and 455th Ost (Russian defectors) Regiment.
[6]See AMCP 706-134 and MIL-STD-721B

General Bibliography

1. BOOK TITLES (In English)

Armstrong, John A.: *Ukranian Nationalism 1939-1945;* Columbia University Press; New York 1955. *Soviet Partisans in World War II;* University of Wisconsin Press. Armstrong editor; other contributors: Gerhard L. Weinberg, Alexander Dallin, Kurt DeWitt, Wilhelm Moll, Ralph Mavrogordato.

Aten, Marion and Orrmont, Arthur: *Last Train Over Rostov Bridge;* Julian Messner Inc.; New York 1961.

Bailey, Geoffrey: *The Conspirators;* Harper & Bros.

Baker, Nina Brown: *Garibaldi;* The Vanguard Press; New York 1944.

Barmin, Alexander: *One Who Survived;* G. P. Putnam's Sons, New York.

Bassechens, Nikolaus: *The Unknown Army;* The Viking Press; New York 1943; Translated by Marion Saerchinger.

Becvar, Gustav: *The Lost Legion;* Stanley Paul & Co., Ltd; London 1939.

Behr, Edward: *The Algerian Problem;* W. W. Norton, Inc.; New York 1962.

DeBelot, Raymond: *The Struggle for the Mediterranian;* Princeton University Press 1951.

von Dach Bern, Major H.: Total Resistance; Paladin Press; Boulder, Colorado.

Betzinez, Jason with Strutevant, Nye: *I Fought With Geronimo*; The Stockpole Co., Harrisburg, Pa.

Blanch, Lesley: *The Sabres of Paradise;* the Viking Press; New York.

Bor-Komorowski, Tadeus: *The Secret Army;* MacMillan Co.; New York 1951.

Brihan, Carl W.: *Quantrill and His Civil War Guerrillas;* Sage Books; Denver.

Byrnes, Robert F.: *Yugoslavia;* Frederick A. Praeger; New York. Mid European Studies Center of Free Europe Committee, Inc.

Cannon, M. Hamlin: *The Return to the Philippines;* Office of the Chief of Military History, U.S. Department of the Army, Washington, D.C.

Carley, Kenneth: *The Sioux Uprising* of 1862; Minnesota Historical Society; St. Paul, Minnesota 1961.

Churchill, Winston: *The World War II;* Volume 5.

Clark, Alan: *The Fall of Crete;* William Morrow & Co.; New York 1962.

Coggins, Jack: *Arms & Equipment of the Civil War;* Doubleday & Co., Inc.; Garden City, New York 1962.

Craig, Gordon: *Politics of the Prussian Army, 1640-1945;* Princeton University 1956.

Crisp, Robert: *The Gods Were Neutral;* Frederick Muller Ltd; London.

388   GUERRILLA WARFARE

Dallin, Alexander: *German Rule in Russia 1941-1945;* MacMillan & Co., Ltd; New York 1957.
Dardy, H. C.: *A Short History of Yugoslavia;* Cambridge University Press 1966.
Davis, Britten: *The Truth About Geronimo;* The Yale University Press 1929.
Davitt, Michael: *The Boer Fight for Freedom;* Funk & Wagnalls Co.; New York & London 1902.
Dedijer, Vladimir: *Tito;* Simon & Schuster; New York 1953.
Dedijer, Vladimir: *The Road to Sarajevo;* Simon & Schuster; New York.
Dellin, D. A. D.: *Bulgaria;* F. A. Praeger, New York. Published for the Mid European Studies Center of Free Europe Committee.
Denikin, Anton Ivanovich: *The White Army;* Jonathan Cape; 30 Bedford Sq, London. Translated by Catherine Evegintzov.
Dixon, C. Aubrey and Heilbrunn, Otto: *Communist Guerrilla Warfare;* Frederick A. Praeger; New York.
Djilas, Milovan: *Conversations with Stalin;* Harcourt, Brace and World; New York.
Duke, Basil W.: *History of Morgan's Cavalry;* Indiana University Press.
Dunn, J. F.: *Massacres of the Mountains.*
Ely, Colonel Luis B., USA: *The Red Army Today;* The Military Service Publishing Co.; Harrisburg, Pa.
Fall, Bernard B.: *Street Without Joy;* The Stockpole Co.; Harrisburg, Pa.
Fall, Bernard B.: *Hell Is a Very Small Place;* J. B. Lippincott Co. 1967.
Fischer, George: *Soviet Opposition to Stalin;* Harvard University Press 1952.
Fuller, J. F. C.: *Military History of Western World;* 1954.
Foord, Edwars: *Napoleon's Russian Campaign;* Little, Brown & Co.; Boston 1915.
Footman, David: *Civil War in Russia;* Frederick Praeger; New York 1961.
Galvin, John R.: *Air Assault;* Hawthorn Book Inc.; New York.
Garthoff, Raymond L.: *Soviet Military Doctrine;* Free Press; Glencoe, Illinois 1953.
de Gaulle, Charles: *War Memoirs;* American Book — Stratford Press, New York.
Green, Thomas, & Roots: *The U.S. Army in World War II — The Ordnance Department;* Office of the Chief of Military History, U.S. Department of the Army, Washington, D.C. 1957.
Greenfield, Palmer, & Wileg: *The U.S. Army in World War II — The Organization of Ground Combat Troops;* Office of the Chief of Military History, U.S. Department of the Army, Washington, D.C. 1957.
Guderian, Heinz: *Erinnerungen Eines Soldaten* (English translation title: Panzer Leader); English edition: Dutton & Co., New York 1952.
Guevara, Ernesto (Che): *Guerrilla Warfare;* Monthly Review Press; New York 1961.
Haines, Francis: *The Nes Perce's;* University of Oklahoma Press.
Hannula, LTC J. O.: *Finland's War of Independence;* Faber & Faber Ltd; London.
Heckstall-Smith, Anthone and Baillie-Grahman, Vice Admiral H. T.: *Greek Tragedy 1941;* Anthony Bond; London.
Hillegas, Howard C.: *The Boers in War;* D. Appleton & Co.; New York 1900.
Howard, Michael: *The Franco-Prussian War;* MacMillan Co.; New York 1962.
Hunter, Charles Newton: *Galahad;* Naylor Co.; San Antonio, Texas.
Huxley-Blythe, Peter J.: *The East Came West;* The Caxton Press; Caldwell, Idaho 1964.
Hyde, George E.: *A Sioux Chronicle;* University of Oklahoma Press.
James, Danier: *Red Designs for the Americas;* The John Day Co.; New York 1954.
Johnston, G. H. L.: *Famous Indian Chiefs;* L. C. Page & Co. 1909.
Keats, John: *They Fought Alone;* J. D. Lippincott Co.; Philadelphia and New York 1960.
von Klausewitz, Karl: *On War;* Infantry Journal Press; Washington, D.C.
Kruger, Rayne: *Good-Bye Dolly Grey;* J. P. Lippincott Co.; Philadelphia and New York 1960.
LaFarge, Oliver: *The Book of the American Indian;* Crown Publishers; New York.

Lawrence, T. E.: *Seven Pillars of Wisdom;* Doubleday & Co.; Garden City, New York 1936.
Lee, Asher: *The Soviet Air and Rocket Forces;* Frederick A. Praeger; New York 1959
Lettow-Vorbeck, Paul Emil Von: *East African Campaigns;* Robert Speller & Sons; New York 1957.
Liddel-Hart, B. H.: *Strategy;* Frederick A. Praeger; New York 1955.
Liddel-Hart, B. H.: *The Red Army;* Harcourt, Brace, & Co.; New York.
Liu, F. F.: *A Military History of Modern China;* Princeton University Press.
Luckett, Richard: *The White Generals;* The Viking Press; New York.
McKenzie, Compton: *Wind of Freedom.*
von Manstein, Erich: *Lost Victories;* Henry Regency Co.; Chicago, Illinois 1958.
Martin, David: *Ally Betrayed;* Prentice-Hall; New York 1946.
von Mannerheim, Baron Gustaf Emil: *Memoirs;* Cassell & Co., Ltd; London 1953.
Mao, Tse-Tung: *Selected Works;* International Publishers; New York and London 1954.
Mao, Tse-Tung: *On Guerrilla Warfare;* Frederick A. Praeger; New York 1961.
Matthews, Tanya: *War in Algeria;* Fordham University Press; New York 1961.
von Mellentine, F. W.: *Panzer Battles;* University of Oklahoma Press 1955.
Miller, David Humphreys: *Custer's Fall;* Duell, Sloan, & Peare; New York.
Millis, Walter: *Arms & Men;* G. P. Putnam's & Sons; New York 1956.
Moorehead, Alan: *The Russian Revolution;* Harper & Bros.; New York.
Moorehead, Alan: *The White Nile;* Harper & Bros.; New York.
Moraes, Frank: *The Revolt in Tibet;* MacMillan Co.; New York 1960.
Myers, E. C. W.: *Greek Entanglement;* Rupert Hart Davis; London 1955.
Orlov, Alexander: *Handbook of Intelligence & Guerrilla Warfare.*
Osanka, Franklin Mark: *Modern Guerrilla Warfare;* The Free Press; Glencoe Illinois.
O'Balance, Edgar: *The Greek Civil War;* Frederick A. Praeger; New York — Washington.
Palmer, Frederick: *John J. Pershing;* The Military Service Publishing Co.; Harrisburg, Pa.
Patton, G. S.: *War As I Knew It;* The Riverside Press; Cambridge, Mass.
Pinchon, Edgcumb: *Viva Villa;* Grosset & Dunlap; New York.
Priestly, H. I.: *The Mexican Nation, A History;* MacMillan Co.; New York 1926.
Quirk, Robert: *The Mexican Revolution;* Indiana University Press.
Reed, John: *Insurgent Mexico;* D. Appleton & Co.; New York & London 1914.
Reitlinger, Gerald: *The House Built on Sand;* The Viking Press; New York 1960.
Romanus, Charles F. & Sunderland, Riley: *Stillwell's Command Problems;* Office of the Chief of Military History, U.S. Department of the Army; Washington, D.C. 1956.
Romanus, Charles F. & Sunderland, Riley: *Time Runs Out in CBI;* Office of Chief of Military History, U.S. Department of the Army; Washington, D.C. 1959.
DeSegur, Count Philippe-Paul: *Napoleon's Russian Campaign;* The Riverside Press; Cambridge, Mass. 1958.
Scott, John: *Partisan Life with Colonel John S. Mosby;* Harper & Bros.; New York 1967.
Sherman, William T.: *Memoirs;* The Indiana University Press.
Shirer, William B.: *The Rise and Fall of the Third Reich;* Simon & Schuster; New York 1960.
Shirer, William B.: *Berlin Diary.*
Skendi, Stavro: *Albania;* F. A. Praeger; New York; published for the Mid European Studies Center of the Free Europe Committee.
Smith, W. H. B.: *Small Arms of the World;* The Stackpole Co.; Harrisburg, Pa.
Standing, Percy Cross: *Guerrilla Leaders of the World;* Houghton Mifflin Co.; Boston, Mass. 1913.
Steward, George: *The White Armies of Russia;* The MacMillan Co.; New York 1933.
Stowe, Leland: *No Other Road to Freedom;* Alfred A. Knopf; New York 1941.

Strausz-Hupe, Robert: *Protracted Conflict;* Harper & Row; New York and Evanston.
T'ang, Leang-Li: *Suppressing Communist Banditry In China;* China United Press; Shanghai 1934.
Tanham, George K.: *Communist Revolutionary Warfare — The Vietminh in* Indochina; Frederick A. Praeger; New York 1961.
Taylor, Telford: *Sword and Swastika — Generals and Nazis in the Third Reich;* Simon & Schuster; New York 1952.
Taylor, Telford: *The March of Conquest;* Simon & Schuster; New York 1958.
Thomas, Hugh: *The Spanish Civil War;* Harper & Bros.; New York.
Trow, Harrison & Burc, John P.: *Charles W. Quantrell;* 1923.
Vignerus, Marcel: *Rearming the French;* Office of the Chief of Military History; U.S. Department of the Army; Washington, D.C.
DeVomecourt, Philippe: *An Army of Amateurs;* Doubleday & Co.; Garden City, New York 1961.
Vrangel, Piotr Nicholayevich: *Memoirs;* Williams & Norgate Ltd; London 1929. Also published in the U.S. under the title *"Always With Honour"* by Robert Speller & Sons; New York 1957.
West Point, U.S. Military Academy: *Atlas of American Wars.*
White, Leigh: *The Long Balkan Night;* Charles Scribner's Son; New York 1944.
White, Leigh: *Balkan Caesar;* Charles Scribner's Son; New York 1951.
Woodhouse, C. M.: *Apple of Discord;* Hutchison & Co., Ltd.
Woodhouse, C. M.: *The Greek War of Independence — Its Historical Setting;* Hutchison House; London 1952.
Woodhouse, C. M.: *British Foreign Policy Since the Second World War;* Hutchison & Co.; London 1961.
Wyeth, John Allan: *Life of Nathan Bedford Forrest;* Harper & Bros; New York and London 1899.

2. BOOK TITLES (not available in English translation)

Военное издательство министерства обороны СССР: маршал Тухачевский (Military Publishers Of Defense Ministry of the USSR): (Marshall Tuhhashevsky); Mockba 1965.

Γ. Γρίβα: 'Απομνημονεύματα 'Αγῶνος ΕΟΚΑ 1955-1959
G. Grivas: Memoirs of the EOKA Struggle 1955-1959.

Γενικοῦ 'Επιτελείου Στρατοῦ: 'Ο Δεύτεροσ Παγκόσμιος Πόλεμος
Army General Staff (Greek): The Second World War. In five volumes. Another volume on the Bandit War is unpublished yet.

Γενικοῦ 'Επιτελείου Στρατοῦ: 'Εκστρατεία εἰς Μεσημβρινήν Ρωσσίαν
Army General Staff (Greek): Campaign in South Russia.

Ζαφειροπούλου, Δ. Γ.: 'Ο 'Αντισυμμοριακός 'Αγών
Zafiropoulos, D.: The Antibandit War.

Παπάγου, 'Αλεξάνδρου: 'Ο Πόλεμος τῆς 'Ελλάδος 1940-1941
Papagos, Alexander: The War of Greece. 1940-1941

Schild Verlag: *Deutsches Soldatenjahrbuch 1966;* Munchen-Lochhausen. German Soldiers Yearbook 1966.

3. ARTICLES IN PERIODICALS.

Aviation Week — 10 December 1962: *Urgent COIN Aircraft Program Planned;* by Lary Booda.

Military Review — November 1960: *Guerrilla Warfare in the Ukraine;* by Enrique Condo.

Military Review — May 1969: *Horsepower for Viet Nam;* by Major James L. McCoskey.

Infantry Journal — Nov/Dec 1969: *Pack Transport;* by Major Michael F. Parrino.

Ordnance — Sep/Oct 1962: *Weapons for the Irregular War;* By Jac Weller.

Selected Bibliography

For the convenience of those who may wish to study in depth any of the conflicts described in Chapters II, III, and IV we cross-reference the published sources below.

Chapter II

1. Guerrillas During the Napoleonic Wars.

Foord, Edward: *"Napoleon's Russian Campaign"*.

Von Klausewitz, Karl: *"On War"*. In this classic book on warfare, Klausewitz makes several references to specific events of Napoleon's invasion of Russia.

DeSegur, Philippe-Paul: *"Napoleon's Russian Campaign"*.

2. American Experiences in Guerrilla Warfare through the Civil War.

Breihan, Carl W.: *"Quantrill and His Civil War Guerrillas"*.

Carley, Kenneth: *"The Sioux Uprising of 1862"*.

Duke, Basil W.: *"History of Morgan's Cavalry"*.

Scott, John: *"Partisan Life with Colonel John Mosby"*. The author served under Mosby and gives a personal account of events.

Sherman, William T.: *"Memoirs"*.

Trow, Harrison & Burc, J. P.: *"Charles W. Quantrell"*. An account of Quantrell's activities by a participant.

Wyeth, John Allan: *"Life of Nathan Bedford Forrest"*.

3. Campaigns Against the Western Indians.

Betzinez, Jason: *"I Fought with Geronimo".* An Apache who was a member of Geronimo's family and later accepted the White American culture, gives a first-hand account of Geronimo's activities.

Davis, Britten: *"The Truth About Geronimo".* Mr. Davis as a Lieutenant was in charge of the Reservation in which Geronimo and his Band were confined. He obtained, in part, Geronimo's trust. He gives an objective account of events; some of which he knows first-hand.

Dunn, J. P.: *"Massacres of the Mountains".*

Haines, Francis: *"The Nes Perce's".*

Hyde, George: *"A Sioux Chronicle".*

LaFarge, Oliver: *"The Book of the American Indian".* An excellent book; profusely illustrated. The emphasis is on Indian culture, but contains valuable historical information and information related to the Indians' methods of combat.

Miller, David H.: *"Custer's Fall".*

4. Guerrilla Activities in Mexico.

McCann, I. G.: *"With the National Guard on the Border".*

Pinchon, Edgcumb: *"Viva Villa".*

Priestly, Herbert Ingram: *"The Mexican Nation, A History".*

Palmer, Frederick: *"John J. Pershing".*

Quirk, Robert: *"The Mexican Revolution".*

Reed, John: *"Insurgent Mexico".* A rather romanticized account of events in Mexico around the turn of the Century.

5. The Boers.

Davitt, Michael: *"The Boer Fight for Freedom".*

Hillegas, Howard C.: *"The Boers in War".*

Kruger, Rayne: *"Good-Bye Dolly Grey".*

Lettow-Vorbeck: *"East African Campaigns".* Good account of German activities in WW I and very useful general information.

6. Lawrence and the Arab Revolt.

Lawrence, T. E.: *"The Seven Pillars of Wisdom".* This book has to be regarded as a classic. Lawrence gives an account of events in which he was the protagonist. In addition, he analyzes the nonmilitary factors of insurgency and guerrilla warfare.

West Point: *"Atlas of American Wars".* Includes information on the operations in Mesopotania, Palestine, and Syria.

There is a lack of information from German and Turkish sources on this subject.

Chapter III

1. The Chinese Communists.

Liu, F. F.: *"A Military History of Modern China"*.

Mao Tse-Tung: *"Selected Works"*, and *"On Guerrilla Warfare"*. Both of these works are valuable for their treatment of the theory of insurgency and guerrilla warfare. They do not include much detail on military operations in China, however.

Romanus, Charles P. and Sunderland, Riley: *"Stillwell's Command Problems"* and *"Time Runs Out in CBI"*. These two volumes on World War II are published by the Office of Military History, Dept. of the Army. They contain some information related to the activities of Chinese Commuist guerrillas and the problems facing the Western Allies and the Chinese Nationalists between 1937 and 1945. Most works on China tend to be biased either pro- or anti-Chiang. These two volumes, however, include considerable amount of related information objectively stated.

T'and, Leang-Li: *"Suppressing Communist Banditry in China"*.

2. The Battle of Suomussalmi.

Hannula, J. O.: *"Finland's War of Independence"*.

Luckett, Richard: *"The White Generals"*.

Mannerheim, Gustof: *"Memoirs"*.

West Point: *"Atlas of American Wars"*. Includes maps and related information about the 1940 Winter War and the Battle of Suomussalmi in particular.

3. The Guerrillas in Yugoslavia.

Byrnes, Robert F.: *"Yugoslavia"*.

Dedijer, Vladimir: *"Tito"* and *"The Road to Sarajevo"*. Dedijer has been one of Tito's old personal friends. Although now reputed to be out of favor, he has had access to Yugoslavia's official archives and both books include considerable factual information. His works are somewhat less biased than what is usual to expect from official communist sources.

Djilas, Milovan: *"Conversations with Stalin"*.

Dardy, H. C. et al: *"A Short History of Yugoslavia"*.

"Deutsches Soldatenjahrbuch, 1966" in German. Includes an article on anti-guerrilla operations in Yugoslavia, conducted by the XV Kozak Cavalry Corps.

Martin, David: *"Ally Betrayed"*.

White, Leigh: *"The Long Balkan Night"* and *"Balkan Caesar"*. Mr. White was war correspondent in Yugoslavia early in World War II. He also fought in Spain on the Republican side. His analysis of events in Yugoslavia during World War II is objective and in-depth.

4. Eastern Front.

Armstrong, John A.: *"Soviet Partisans in World War II"* and *"Ukranian Nationalism 1939-1945"*. The first of the two volumes is edited by Mr. Armstrong with several other authors contributing. It provides the most detailed account of guerrilla activities on the Eastern Front. Of all publications available on the subject, it is the one which provides the greatest quantity of information.

Dallin, Alexander: *"German Rule in Russia 1941-1945"*.

Dixon, C. A. and Heilbrunn, Otto: *"Communist Guerrilla Warfare"*.

Fischer, J. F. C.: *"Soviet Opposition to Stalin"*.

Galvin, John R.: *"Air Assault"*. This book is concerned with airborne operations. It describes in detail some little-known operations by which the Soviet Army attempted to relieve pressure on its front through the combined efforts of guerrillas and paratroops who landed behind enemy lines.

Guderian, Heinz: *"Erinnerungen Eines Soldaten"*.

Huxley-Blythe, P. J.: *"The East Came West"*.

Von Manstein, Erich: *"Lost Victories"*.

Von Mellentine, F. W.: *"Panzer Battles"*.

Reitlinger, Gerald: *"The House Built on Sand"*.

Taylor, Telford: *"The March of Conquest"*.

"Military Review" Nov. 1960: *"Guerrilla Warfare in the Ukraine"*. Article by E. Condo.

5. Guerrillas in the Philippines.

Cannon, M. H.: *"The Return to the Philippines"*. Another publication from the Office of the Chief of Military History, Dept. of the Army. Like all publications from this source, it contains a lot of detail and excellent documentation.

6. The Long Range Penetration Groups.

Hunter, Charles N.: *"Galahad"*. Colonel Hunter was a senior officer with the Long Range Penetration Groups. He furnishes an account of the field operations and other related information.

Romanus, C. F. and Sunderland, R.: *"Stillwell's Command Problems"* and *"Time Runs Out in*

CBI". Publications of the Office of the Chief of Military History, Dept. of the Army. Contain the usual detail and documentation.

Chapter IV

1. The Bandit War in Greece.

Clark, Alan: "*The Fall of Crete*".

Myers, E. C. W.: "*Greek Entanglement*". Brigadier Myers was head of the British Mission in Greece in 1942 and 1943. In this book he provides an apology for his actions and decisions and attempts to explain why he favored the communist guerrillas.

O'Balance, Edgar: "*The Greek Civil War*".

Woodhouse, C. M.: "*Apple of Discord*".

Papagos, Alexander: "*The War of Greece*" IN GREEK.

Zafiropoulos D.: "*Anti-Guerrilla War*" IN GREEK. Details of anti-guerrilla operations in Greece between 1946-1949. Many details, but some inaccuracies, probably caused by the fact that it was written too soon after the conclusion of operations.

Historical Service of Greek General Staff: "*The 2d World War*". IN GREEK. Seven volumes covering operations in 1940 and 1941. Excellent documentation and detail. An eighth volume covering the anti-guerrilla operations is unpublished yet.

2. Indochina.

Fall, Bernard B.: "*Street Without Joy*", and "*Hell is a Very Small Place*". In these two books Bernard Fall gives the French point of view of operations in Indochina. He does not provide a satisfactory answer to why the French failed. Both books, however, are a must reading for anyone interested in this area.

Tanham, George K.: "*Communist Revolutionary Warfare — The Vietminh in Indochina*".

3. The Algerian War.

Behr, Edward: "*The Algerian Problem*".

Matthews, Tanya: "*War in Algeria*".

4. EOKA and the Revolt of the Cypriots.

Grivas, George: "*Memoirs*" IN GREEK. Grivas led the Greek Cypriot insurgents against the British. In this book he gives an objective account of events. However, he provides better coverage of underground and behind-the-scenes activities than field operations.

Woodhouse, C. M.: "*British Foreign Policy Since the Second World War*".

5. On the War in Viet Nam.

There are no references for this topic. Its nature is such that no references are necessary.

6. Other Conflicts and General Conclusions.

Aton, Marion and Orrmont, Arthur: *"Last Train Over Rostov Bridge"*.

Baker, Nina Brown: *"Garibaldi"*.

Basseches, Nikolaus: *"The Unknown Army"*.

Becvar, Gustav: *"The Lost Legion"*.

Blanch, Lesley: *"The Sabres of Paradise"*.

Bor-Komorowski, Tadeusz: *"The Secret Army"*.

Footman, David: *"Civil War in Russia"*.

Guevara, Ernesto: *"Guerrilla Warfare"*.

Luckett, Richard: *"The White Generals"*.

Moraes, Frank: *"The Revolt in Tibet"*.

Stewart, George: *"The White Armies of Russia"*.

Thomas, Hugh: *"The Spanish Civil War"*.

DeVomecourt: *"An Army of Amatuers"*.

Vrangel, P. N.: *"Always with Honour"*.

Historical Service, Greek General Staff: *"Campaign in South Russia"* IN GREEK.

Index